# Foundations of
# Library and
# Information
# Science

## Richard E. Rubin

D0103995

Neal-Schuman Publishers, Inc.
New York                                    London

Published by Neal-Schuman Publishers, Inc.
100 Varick Street
New York, NY 10013

Printed and bound in the United States of America.

**Library of Congress Cataloging-in-Publication Data**

Rubin, Richard, 1949–
    Foundations of library and information science / Richard E. Rubin.
    —Updated version
        p.   cm.
    Includes bibliographical references and index.
    ISBN 1–55570–402–6 (alk. paper)
    1. Library science—United States.    I. Title.
    Z665.2.U6R83   2000
    020—dc21                                    00–057879

# Table of Contents

# Foreword

The forces that are shaping the information environment, the challenges facing librarians and the perspective needed to understand problems faced in the future are the subject of *Foundations of Library and Information Science*. Richard E. Rubin has focused on organizations whose purpose is to collect, organize, and disseminate recorded knowledge or information where emphasis is on promoting the accessibility and utility of that knowledge to meet human information needs. He has done this through examination of institutions where information or knowledge is organized and disseminated based on user-initiated inquiries.

Dr. Rubin has completed his work at a critical period in the evolution of libraries. Those of us teaching in programs that have been responsible for education of libraries are faced with some pressure to redefine the central tenets of our philosophy and purpose. The word, "library," laden as it is with historical and cultural resonance has been questioned as to its relevance in a society where so much value is being placed on the importance of "information."

This volume examines major issues with attention to the larger political, societal, and economic environment in which libraries and information centers function. It examines the historic mission, intellectual organization, ethical aspects, and organizational structures of libraries. Rich supplementary appendices provide primary sources of exploration of critical topics.

Dr. Rubin's book provides the profession with a new resource for introductory classes. His holistic approach encompasses some aspects of traditional foundation texts but essentially expands the arena of concern with a more emphatic discussion of points of convergence of information policy and delivery.

This volume respects the past, analyzes the present and delineates complex topics that will affect the future. It is a substantive introduction to our discipline that demonstrates the promise of a future wherein librarians will play a vital role—in collaboration with information scientists—in designing and using information systems.

Dr. Rubin's final observation on the future of the profession is to ask the question whether social values of librarianship should form the context for the use of new technologies or whether these technologies should create a new social context? This book will provide the basis to forge that answer.

—Kathleen de la Peña McCook, Director
School of Library and Information Science
University of South Florida
Tampa

# Preface

These are not quiet times for anyone involved with library and information services. Librarians and other information professionals are experiencing both excitement and trepidation as sweeping societal changes impact our users and our institutions—and indeed transform our discipline. We need to respond with adaptability, creativity, flexibility and resolve. Not long ago a basic library and information textbook would simply have been about libraries and librarians. A discussion of the history of libraries, a review of the basic services provided by them, some observations on organizational structure, and a review of library classification systems would have sufficed. This is no longer a possibility. The library is now imbedded in a complex and dynamic society, a society that has placed considerable emphasis on information: its creation, organization, and access.

## PURPOSE

The primary purpose of *Foundations of Library and Information Science* is to explain the current information environment to students of library and information science and practitioners who are grappling with these issues, so that further study and practice will be informed by a realistic picture of the still developing information society. Without such a context, it is impossible to grasp the challenges that the profession faces.

There is ongoing debate as to whether library science and information science are separate disciplines. There is also argument about what constitutes the domain of each. *Foundations of Library and Information Science* is focused on the complementary nature of these two disciplines using Boyd Rayward's 1983 description of the relationship between library and information science as "a disciplinary continuum . . . with no easily identifiable boundary separating them, though the difference between the extreme ends of the continuum are clear and even dramatic" (p. 344). This book assumes that library and information science can be discussed jointly in a manner that is fruitful to those entering the profession: it emphasizes the points of convergence and the interrelationships.

Bearing this emphasis in mind, *Foundations of Library and Information Science* was written to accomplish the following six objectives:

1.  To provide an introduction to the field for individuals intending to work in libraries or "library-like" institutions. Reference will also be made to other institutions in the information field that share the mission of libraries or information centers.
2.  To identify and discuss major topics and issues in library and information science that are current in the United States.
3.  To provide librarians and information professionals with an opportunity to refresh their knowledge through a systematic review of major issues and topics. Library and information science is changing rapidly, and this book provides a summary of some of the issues that are likely to have the greatest impact.
4.  To introduce the profession to interested individuals or those undecided about entering the library and information science field. There is ample evidence that many individuals will be needed to create, organize, and disseminate information—not only librarians, but also many individuals who will not be called "librarians," but who perform similar functions.
5.  To place librarianship in a larger social, economic, and political context. It is too easy to view the work of librarians purely within the institutional setting, noting only those topics that deal directly in the day-to-day affairs of librarianship. Increasingly librarianship must interact with a variety of political, economic, technological and social forces.
6.  To invite the interested reader to further explore topics raised here, such as the history of library science; reference, cataloging, and computer science; and the many facets of library and information science that continue to have an impact on librarianship and on our society.

## ORGANIZATION

*Foundations of Library and Information Science* discusses the field's broader, contextual issues first; the focus then narrows in on libraries and librarianship.

Chapter 1 presents a context for library and information science by placing libraries and librarians within the broader perspective of the information infrastructure. To grasp the role of libraries today, it is necessary to examine the vast array of societal information components and channels and to understand how these information channels are used.

Chapter 2 concentrates on information science, calling special attention to those aspects of the discipline that inform the work of librarians and information center personnel.

Chapter 3 deals with the growth of information technologies, especially those that have affected the organization and delivery of information in libraries. Information technologies have changed the way information providers in all types of organizations interact with their users. Issues arising out of these changes are addressed.

Chapters 4 and 5 define and examine information policy. Government, business and industry, public institutions, librarians, and citizens all are stakeholders trying to shape how information will be disseminated and who will disseminate it. Chapter 4 discusses the more general aspects of information policy; in Chapter 5, the focus shifts to libraries in particular, including those information policies (e.g., intellectual freedom and equitable access to information) that govern library use.

Chapter 6 discusses one of the truly remarkable aspects of libraries and other information providers—their organization of information. In spite of the vast amounts of disparate knowledge stored in them, refined use of classification systems, subject headings, thesauri, databases, and powerful catalogs enable libraries to offer information retrieval on demand.

Chapter 7 reviews the historic mission of libraries and reveals the underlying values that help define the role of libraries today. Many of the field's contemporary values have their roots in the ideals of the past. This discussion also provides a foundation for Chapter 8, which deals with the ethical aspects of library and information science. The relationship between information provider and information seeker must be one of trust and honesty and the provider must have a strong sense of professional obligation. This chapter discusses areas of ethical concern to information providers, especially the competing interests that are involved in making ethical judgments.

Chapter 9 examines the various types of libraries, their internal functions, and the major organizational issues that they face. An understanding of this institutional infrastructure is necessary for all information professionals.

Chapter 10 reviews the evolution and development of the library profession. The contemporary American librarian is a product of more than a hundred years of professional evolution. Understanding the development of librarianship will help contemporary librarians place the current professional tensions and demands in perspective.

To allow an examination of the same topic from different vantage points, *Foundations of Library and Information Science* tackles most topics solely in one chapter, but others are raised anew in a different context in a different chapter. For example, censorship and intellectual freedom issues are found in chapters on information policy (Chapters 4 and 5) and on library organization (Chapter 9). The Internet, because it will undergird most information transmission in the future, is, of course, covered in many chapters.

A list of highly selective readings follows Chapter 10. These readings not only provide sources of further information, but should also stimulate thought on the basic issues raised in this text. Of course readers must understand that continuous consultation with the most recently published material is essential if one is to stay current.

Appendices are included to provide supporting information. They include a selective listing of library and information science periodicals, indexes, dictionaries, and encyclopedias that may be helpful to those interested in the profession; a listing of accredited graduate programs of library and information studies; a discussion from the *Occupational Outlook Handbook* on librarianship as a career; and a variety of supporting documents to further explore the issues raised in the text.

In the final analysis, no librarian can function unless he or she understands the importance of information, how libraries are organized intellectually and administratively, the effects of information policies and the values and ethics of libraries and the profession. The world in which the modern library operates is in flux and the issues and the concerns of library and information science reflect this turmoil. The library is a special place, librarianship a special profession. The roles of the former and latter, as well as the broader forces that shape those roles, constitute the major focus of this work.

## REFERENCE

Rayward, Boyd. "Library and Information Sciences," in *The Study of Information: Interdisciplinary Messages*. Edited by Fritz Machlup and Una Mansfield. New York: Wiley, 1983, 343–363.

# Acknowledgments

This book would not have been possible without the considerable help and support of many individuals. Thanks go to Allyson Carlyle, Carolyn Brodie, Lois Buttlar, Greg Byerly, William Caynon, Tschera Connell, Thomas Froehlich, Linda Smith, Connie Van Fleet, Danny Wallace and Marcia Zeng for carefully reviewing and commenting on drafts of various chapters. Thanks also to my graduate assistants Matthew Lynn, Andrea Rostek, Scott Vine, and Elaine Womack, who provided invaluable assistance locating and verifying information. Thanks must also go to my two anonymous readers of the manuscript, whose many valuable criticisms improved the work substantially. Special thanks to my wife, Marcia; daughter, Rachel; and father, Milton. For them, the two years of book preparation must have seemed like ten.

# 1

# The Information Infrastructure: Libraries in Context

As the amount of information grows, so does the challenge of providing information to those who need it. No group is more aware of this than librarians, who have been trying to collect, organize, and disseminate recorded knowledge for centuries. Information once obtained primarily through books, periodicals, and other print materials is now available in additional formats such as videocassettes, audiocassettes, microfilm, laser discs, CD-ROMs, and the Internet. Librarians, as well as the public, often feel uneasy with the tremendous growth of information. This uneasiness is evidenced by the way we talk about the growth of information. Consider some of the expressions that are used to describes it:[1]

Information *explosion*: This common expression reflects many of our concerns. An explosion is dangerous, terrifying, and unanticipated; it suggests a world out of control. To come near it is to risk being destroyed; to ignore it does not mean it does not exist or that its effects can be avoided.

The *flood* of information: The flood is another symbol of catastrophe. It conveys an image of being overwhelmed and of victims helplessly swept away. As with an explosion, there is lack of control over the raging tide of information. In its wake are left ruins.

*Bombarded* by information: Yet another image of destruction, this time by repetitive bursts; information crashing in on the heads of its

1

victims and destroying them. It is descriptive of warfare with an enemy that produces a firestorm of chaos.

Information *overload*: This image is an electronic one conveying the sense that the amount of information is so great that it short circuits our brains, causing us to malfunction and break down. It conveys the discomforting notion that we need information to live, just as a machine needs electricity to function, but too much information coming in at an unregulated pace is destructive.

All of these images suggest fear and trepidation. One seldom hears an optimistic phrase like "cornucopia of information," reflecting pleasure at its abundance, although "wealth of information" is sometimes heard. Are we in an age of information anxiety? If so, it is the librarian who can help reduce this anxiety. Few professions have been so devoted to helping people find their way among the bewildering variety of information sources.

If the librarian is to continue to collect, organize, and disseminate information on demand, it is vital that the way information flows in our society be understood. Only then can libraries exploit the ever-expanding information resources and channels and serve the information needs of library users. Today, such an understanding comes, in part, from the realization that the library is part of a much larger structure: the "information infrastructure." An infrastructure is both a foundation and a framework, much the same as the infrastructure of a house includes its foundation and frame. Without such a structure the house would collapse. Societies have a variety of infrastructures. For example, the United States has a transportation infrastructure that is necessary for efficient travel. This includes highways, train tracks, air routes, and waterways. It also includes the governmental agencies that regulate transportation. An information infrastructure is in many ways like a transportation infrastructure, except that the "traffic" is information rather than modes of transportation. An information infrastructure makes it possible for information to be created and disseminated. Information infrastructures vary greatly in their sophistication: some are very primitive and inefficient; others are highly advanced and efficient. As might be expected, the U.S. information infrastructure is advanced and complex, and libraries are but one part of it. This is not to diminish the role of libraries. On the contrary, as we will see in subsequent chapters, the values and traditions of libraries make them a vital part of that infrastructure. But if libraries are to thrive within it, they must become increasingly aware of how they fit in.

How can we understand the components of the information infrastructure and the place of the library? One way is to consider this structure in terms of the process that begins with the creation of information and ends with its use. This is sometimes referred to as the information cycle and one such characterization is provided in Figure 1.1.

From the perspective of the information cycle, the information infrastructure consists of institutions and individuals involved in the dynamic process by which information is created, disseminated, and used in the society. At the foundation of such a cycle are the creators of information, and here, information should be seen very broadly as any message to be conveyed. So writers, researchers, artists, musicians, and database producers can be seen as creators of information. Generally, creators of information embody their ideas in a product or physical form—traditionally a book, article, painting, sheet music, more recently a multimedia presentation or a database. In general, the products are made available by someone other than the creator, a distributor, such as a publisher or vendor (who make the products of many creators available). Databases are often distributed by database vendors such as Knight-Ridder. In turn, there are many agencies that perform the function of disseminator. This is a function similar to wholesalers in that they acquire significant volumes of materials from distributors and disseminate the materials to individual users. In the information world, many

---

**Figure 1.1**
**Information Infrastructure Viewed as**
**Part of the Information Cycle**

| Creators | Products | Distributors | Disseminators | Users |
|---|---|---|---|---|
| Authors | Books | Publishers | Schools | Individuals |
| Artists/Musicians | Magazines | Vendors | Libraries | Researchers |
| Database | CD-ROMs | Internet | Universities | Students |
| producers | Databases | providers | Museums | Employers |
| | Web pages | | Businesses | Employees |
| | | | Governmental | |
| | | | agencies | |

---

Source: Adapted from Science Applications International Corporation (SAIC). *Information Warfare: Legal, Regulatory, Policy and Organizational Considerations for Assurance.* Washington, D.C.: Joint Staff, 1995.

of these entities are part of the public as well as the private sector and include schools, universities, governmental agencies, book stores, and libraries. Finally, there are the users, those who consume and use the information. The user may be the average citizen or business person who visits the local book store or library, a student visiting the school library, or a researcher using a special research collection at a governmental research center or academic institution.

Overall, the library can be viewed as an institution involved in the dissemination of information—it is an intermediary between the user and the information that has been created. There is a describable pattern to the dynamic process of information creation and use, and librarians are engaged in each aspect of this cycle. The character of their collections are affected by the creators of information, they must organize the various products provided, they must negotiate with vendors, and they deal with library users.

Another way to look at the infrastructure is to examine the various networks that serve as major channels for the transmission of information, such as telephones and telephone lines, online services, cable television, and the Internet (Figure 1.2).

Viewing the infrastructure from this perspective reveals the extent to which the library is part of a much larger system or network that makes broad dissemination of information possible. Libraries are deeply interested in information networks because of the large amounts of information that can be accessed by many of them. The promise for librar-

---

**Figure 1.2**
**Typical Information Infrastructure Networks and Services**

| | |
|---|---|
| Internet | Direct Broadcast Satellite |
| Public Switched Telephone Network | Online Services |
| Public Data Networks | Publishing Services |
| Cellular Networks | Entertainment Services |
| Commercial Satellite Networks | Financial Networks and |
| Broadcast Radio Networks | Services |
| Broadcast TV Networks | Power Networks |
| Cable TV Networks | Transportation Networks |
| | Public Safety Networks |

Source: Adapted from Science Applications International Corporation (SAIC). *Information Warfare: Legal, Regulatory, Policy and Organizational Considerations for Assurance*. Washington, D.C.: Joint Staff, 1995.

ies is greatest with the Internet because of its capacity to connect many information networks on a national and international scale. Such networks are, however, a double-edged sword. On the one hand, they provide access to vast amounts of information; on the other hand, as more and more information is created and transmitted in electronic form, there may be greater and greater reliance on the electronic components of this infrastructure and less reliance on traditional disseminators of information such as libraries.

Librarians also interact with the information infrastructure in other ways. For example, they must be familiar with the numerous media that make effective information transmission possible (Figure 1.3).

One is struck by the variety of media and equipment and the multitude of information channels implied by the variety. The dominance of electronic and computer technologies is obvious. If librarians are to continue to make substantial contributions as information disseminators, they will have to understand and exploit these resources. The increasingly sophisticated electronic information technologies have great promise for increasing the dissemination of information, but they also provoke concern over the cost of purchasing and maintaining such equipment. Again, there is concern over the effect of electronic transmission of information on the use of traditional materials such as books and periodicals.

---

### Figure 1.3
### Typical Information Infrastructure Components

| | |
|---|---|
| Scanners | Cable |
| Keyboards | Wire |
| Telephones | Satellite |
| Fax machines | Optical fiber |
| Computers | Microwave |
| Switches | Televisions |
| Compact disks | Monitors |
| Video- and audiotape | Printers |
| Facilities | Cameras |
| Radios | |

---

Source: Adapted from Science Applications International Corporation (SAIC). *Information Warfare: Legal, Regulatory, Policy and Organizational Considerations for Assurance.* Washington, D.C.: Joint Staff, 1995.

## USES OF THE INFORMATION INFRASTRUCTURE IN THE U.S.

Understanding the composition of the information infrastructure gives the librarian a good idea of what it is, but it does not tell us about the extent and nature of its use. Because libraries serve primarily as disseminators, it is useful also to examine more closely which media people use and what trends have developed concerning their use (Figures 1.4 and 1.5).

As can be seen from Figure 1.4, surprisingly, the total number of hours that people spend using the various media has changed only slightly since 1990 (3,263 hours in 1990 compared to 3,402 hours in 1997). Yet, a variety of patterns emerge concerning changes in which media are being selected. Below is a more specific analysis of different sources of information.

### *The Print Industry*

Print materials have been around since the invention of written languages and paper. After the printing press was developed in Germany in the mid-1400s, the influence of print materials vastly increased. (Martin Luther used the printing press quite effectively in stimulating what was to become the Protestant Reformation). Despite predictions that print materials will disappear in the onslaught of electronic access, the numbers do not suggest this. Book sales, for example, have grown from 12 billion in sales in 1987 to more than 23 billion in 1998 with growth rates of about 6 percent per year. U.S. publishers printed more than 65,000 titles (Bowker 1999). There are more than 28,000 bookstores marketing more than 3 million titles in print. The time spent reading books has remained stable: ninety-five hours per person per year in 1990 and ninety-four hours in 1999 (Veronis and Suhler 1999).

Magazines are also a healthy part of the information marketplace. About one million magazine articles in a vast range of subject areas are published every year in the United States. The magazine marketplace is widely diversified with more than 80,000 regular scientific journals alone. There are more than 9,600 periodical titles available at newsstands with hundreds of new periodicals launched each year. Of interest, however, is that in terms of number of hours spent reading consumer magazines, the trend is gently downward from ninety hours per person in 1990 to eighty-one hours in 1999 (Veronis and Suhler 1999).

Historically the newspaper has been a popular source of print infor-

**Table 1.4**
**U.S. Media Usage**
**Hours per person/per year**

| Year | Network-Affiliated Stations* | Independent Stations* | Total Broadcast Television | Basic Networks† | Premium Channels | Total Subscription Video Services | Total TV | Radio | Recorded Music | Daily Newspapers | Consumer Books | Consumer Magazines | Home Video‡ | Movies in Theaters | Video Games | Internet | Total |
|---|---|---|---|---|---|---|---|---|---|---|---|---|---|---|---|---|---|
| 1990 | 780 | 340 | 1,120 | 260 | 90 | 350 | 1,470 | 1,135 | 235 | 175 | 95 | 90 | 38 | 12 | 12 | 1 | 3,263 |
| 1991 | 838 | 227 | 1,065 | 340 | 90 | 430 | 1,495 | 1,115 | 219 | 169 | 98 | 88 | 40 | 11 | 18 | 1 | 3,254 |
| 1992 | 914 | 159 | 1,073 | 359 | 78 | 437 | 1,510 | 1,150 | 233 | 172 | 100 | 85 | 42 | 11 | 19 | 2 | 3,324 |
| 1993 | 920 | 162 | 1,082 | 375 | 78 | 453 | 1,535 | 1,082 | 248 | 170 | 99 | 85 | 43 | 12 | 19 | 2 | 3,295 |
| 1994 | 919 | 172 | 1,091 | 383 | 81 | 469 | 1,560 | 1,102 | 294 | 169 | 102 | 84 | 45 | 12 | 22 | 3 | 3,393 |
| 1995 | 836 | 183 | 1,019 | 463 | 88 | 556 | 1,575 | 1,091 | 289 | 165 | 99 | 84 | 45 | 12 | 24 | 7 | 3,391 |
| 1996 | 803 | 177 | 980 | 498 | 89 | 587 | 1,567 | 1,091 | 289 | 161 | 99 | 83 | 49 | 12 | 26 | 16 | 3,393 |
| 1997 | 748 | 178 | 926 | 537 | 98 | 635 | 1,561 | 1,082 | 265 | 159 | 95 | 82 | 50 | 13 | 36 | 28 | 3,371 |
| 1998 | 708 | 176 | 884 | 582 | 107 | 689 | 1,573 | 1,050 | 284 | 156 | 95 | 82 | 56 | 13 | 43 | 74 | 3,426 |
| 1999 | 660 | 180 | 840 | 632 | 107 | 739 | 1,579 | 1,037 | 288 | 154 | 94 | 81 | 57 | 13 | 48 | 97 | 3,448 |
| 2000 | 627 | 178 | 805 | 675 | 111 | 786 | 1,591 | 1,024 | 294 | 152 | 95 | 80 | 60 | 14 | 59 | 122 | 3,491 |
| 2001 | 596 | 177 | 773 | 712 | 110 | 822 | 1,595 | 1,014 | 300 | 151 | 97 | 79 | 62 | 14 | 65 | 146 | 3,523 |
| 2002 | 570 | 181 | 751 | 738 | 116 | 854 | 1,605 | 1,003 | 308 | 150 | 98 | 79 | 64 | 14 | 66 | 168 | 3,555 |
| 2003 | 548 | 181 | 729 | 762 | 119 | 881 | 1,610 | 992 | 319 | 149 | 99 | 78 | 66 | 15 | 67 | 192 | 3,587 |

Sources: Veronis, Suhler & Associates, Wilkofsky Guen Associates, Nielson Media Research, Simons Market Research, Interactive Digital Software Association, Paul Kagan Associates, Motion Picture Association of America, Recording Industry Association of America, Newspaper Association of America, Book Industry Study Group, Magazine Publishers of America, Software Publishers Association

* Affiliates of the Fox network are counted as network affiliates for part of 1991 and all of 1992 but as independent stations in earlier years. Includes UPN and WB affiliates, 1995–2003.

† Includes TBS beginning in 1992

‡ Playback of prerecorded tapes only

Note: Estimates of time spent were derived using rating data for television and radio, survey research and consumer purchase data for recorded music, newspapers, magazines, books, home video, admission for movies, and Internet usage. Adults 18 and older were the basis for estimates except for recorded music, movies in theaters, and video games, where estimates included persons 12 and older.

Veronis, Suhler and Associates, New York, NY: Comunications Industry Forecast

**Table 1.5**
**U.S. Use of Selected Media by Households**
**(1980–1995)**

| Media | Unit | 1980 | 1990 | 1991 | 1992 | 1993 | 1994 | 1995 | 1996 | 1997 |
|---|---|---|---|---|---|---|---|---|---|---|
| Telephone Service | Percent | 93.0 | 93.3 | 93.6 | 93.9 | 94.2 | 93.9 | 93.9 | 93.8 | 93.9 |
| Radio | Percent | 99.0 | 99.0 | 99.0 | 99.0 | 99.0 | 99.0 | 99.0 | 99.0 | 99.0 |
| Television | Percent | 97.9 | 98.2 | 98.2 | 98.3 | 98.3 | 98.3 | 98.3 | 98.3 | 98.4 |
| Cable Television | Percent | 19.9 | 56.4 | 58.9 | 60.2 | 61.4 | 62.4 | 63.4 | 65.3 | 66.5 |
| VCRs | Percent | 1.1 | 68.6 | 71.9 | 75.0 | 77.1 | 79.0 | 81.0 | 82.2 | 84.2 |
| Television Stations | Number | 1,011 | 1,442 | 1,459 | 1,481 | 1,506 | 1,512 | 1,532 | 1,533 | 1,574 |
| Cable Systems | Number | 4,225 | 9,575 | 10,704 | 11,075 | 11,217 | 11,214 | 11,218 | 11,119 | 10,950 |
| Cable Subscribers | Millions | 17.7 | 54.9 | 55.8 | 56.4 | 57.2 | 60.5 | 63.0 | 64.6 | 65.9 |
| Daily Newspapers | Millions | 62 | 62 | 61 | 60 | 60 | 59 | 58 | 57 | 57 |

Source: U.S. Bureau of the Census. *Statistical Abstract of the United States: 1999.* (119th edition) Washington, D.C., 1997

mation. Therefore, it is interesting that newspapers are one of the few media that have not experienced an increase in use. Daily newspaper circulation has remained flat or declined slightly when compared to 1990 data. In addition, the average person reads the daily newspaper about 161 hours per year compared to 175 in 1990. Reasons for this might be that other sources of information, such as TV, are more interesting, more timely, and more appealing to a visually oriented culture. The combination of well-edited pictures and sound are strong competitors to the more sedate quality of the written word. Nonetheless, the endless sounds of printers producing reams and reams of paper products is testimony to the enduring character of the printed word. This, of course, does not mean that everything will remain the same for print materials. There are already information products that are produced only in their electronic formats (e.g., electronic journals) and the numbers of such products will, no doubt, grow. This may signal less the demise of print products than the addition of new and novel uses of electronic ones.

*Telephones*

The importance of the telephone cannot be underestimated in the history of communications and in the contemporary world. Nearly 94 percent of all households in the United States have telephones. The amount of information transmitted from one individual to another is undoubtedly great, and the growth of conference calls merely increases this volume of information. In addition, what makes telephone access even more important today is that the telephone lines are now used for telecommunication with computers and databases. Over these lines are transmitted e-mail, computer data, and interactions with computer databases for search purposes. The telephone and its infrastructure represent crucial underpinnings for the computer information revolution.

*Radio*

More than 98 million people in the United States have radios, accounting for 99 percent of American households. The average household has more than five radios. Today, there is not only the traditional news broadcast on commercial and educational radio stations, there is the ever-present radio talk show spanning the political spectrum, sometimes stimulating us and sometimes infuriating us. There are also distinct radio programs that educate us about issues in the community and the nation. The ubiquitous radio not only sits on our bedsides and coffee tables at home, it is plugged into our ears when we walk, run, and drive. It is broadcast in restaurants and other public places, copyright violations notwithstanding. The number of radio stations has also increased, especially FM stations. The number of FM stations has increased from about 3,200 in 1980 to 5,542 in 1997, an increase of 69 percent (U.S Bureau of the Census 1997). In terms of actual use, an average individual listens to the radio more than 1,000 hours per year, which is second only to TV in hours of use.

*Television*

One cannot avoid the omnipresent television. The number of households owning televisions is only slightly fewer than those with radios. Ninety-seven million households have 229 million television sets, which accounts for more than 98 percent of all households. The average home owns two.

Television, like radio, provides information in many different formats including traditional news programs, special informational programming, and talk shows. One might debate the quality of content in many of these sources, but one cannot ignore that Americans draw much information from the television. For example, in 1996–1997, the average U.S. household has the TV on more than seven hours a day, nearly 50 hours a week. One should not assume that it is the kids watching the TV. In 1997, men over eighteen were the heaviest users of TV. The group who watches the most actually fluctuates between men and women; teens and children consistently watch the TV less than adults. This is not to trivialize young people's exposure to TV; they watch approximately three hours a day, but their viewing habits mirror those of adults (Television and Video Almanac 1999).

In addition, the television marketplace is growing in diversity when it comes to delivery. For example, in the 1960s the concept of cable television stations was new and not well received. By 1980, only 15 million households (20 percent) had cable television, but in the last decade this has changed dramatically. By 1997, 66 million households had cable television, accounting for 67 percent of all households in the U.S. Each cable user was expected to watch approximately 450 hours of cable TV in 1995. Similarly, the number of television stations is expected to increase, especially commercial stations which have risen from 734 in 1980 to 1,177 in

1997. This is a 60 percent increase. The number of cable systems also is increasing steadily. In 1980, there were 4,225 such systems serving 62 million subscribers. By 1997, there were nearly 11,000 such systems serving more than 66 million subscribers. Overall, while viewing of network TV stations has dropped, consumption of basic cable has increased substantially (U.S. Bureau of the Census 1999).

Perhaps even more fascinating is how U.S. citizens are turning their homes into satellite reception areas. Those umbrella shaped antennae once thought to be the domain of radio astronomers at observatories or at universities now adorn the roofs and yards of many American homes. There were no home satellite stations in 1980, but by 1997, there were more than seven million satellite subscribers (*International Television and Video Almanac* 1987, 1999).

The development of the videocassette for home use has also meant that the TV is being used in a new way for information (as well as entertainment). In 1980, only one million households owned a VCR (videocassette recorder). By 1997, 82 million households had them, accounting for more than 84 percent of all households (U.S. Bureau of the Census 1997). In 1980, approximately 805,000 videocassette recorders were sold in the U.S. In 1993, more than 12 million recorders were sold. The use of home video has grown as well (Table 1.4). In 1990, the average person watched home video thirty-eight hours per year; in 1998 that figure is projected to grow to fifty-four hours per year, an increase of 42 percent.

The sources for videocassettes have also expanded. They are found in libraries, video specialty shops, grocery stores, discount and convenience stores, record and book stores. By 1992, there were more than 70,000 such stores retailing videocassettes (*International Television and Video Almanac* 1987, 1994). This tremendous expansion probably helps explain the unchanging character of movie theater attendance (Veronis and Suhler 1997).

*The Database Industry*

Over the last decade, access to electronically stored information in computers has been increasing regularly. The revenues accrued are a clear demonstration of this growth rising from $40 million in 1978 to $1.5 billion in 1998. The highest revenues are earned by Lexis/Nexis, West, and DIALOG (Williams, National Online Meeting 1999). An excellent summary of the character and growth of the database industry is provided by Williams (1999) in the *Gale Directory of Databases*. Unless otherwise noted, the following data in this section have been taken from this source.

The number of searches grew from 750,000 in 1974 to 90.3 million in 1998, increasing more than 120 times (Figure 1.6). Most of the databases are online (44 percent), while about 37 percent are CD-ROM. Far fewer are on diskette or magnetic tape, 9 percent and 6 percent respectively. This is not to diminish the importance of the CD-ROM market. Today there are more than 16,200 CD-ROM products available, including games, available from 4,200 companies (*CD-ROMs in Print* 1999). Some of these titles are subscription-based, that is, the individual or organization subscribes at an annual fee; many others are one-time releases. Many are now oriented to children and their reasonable pricing (often under $100) is bound to secure a permanent and growing market (Hogan and Shelton 1995).

Williams (1999) reports that the number of computer databases has grown more than thirty-nine times since 1975. The growth in the number of producers has also grown substantially, although this growth began to slow down and actually declined in 1992. The decline may be due to the economic effects of mergers and competition in the highly competitive database production market. The number of vendors has increased more than twenty-three times since 1975 and continues to rise slowly. Although the number of vendors continues to grow, 93 percent of the use is concentrated among four vendors: Lexis/Nexis, Westlaw, OCLC's FirstSearch, and DIALOG (Williams, National Online Meeting 1997).

### Table 1.6
### Growth of the Database Industry

|  | 1975 | 1991 | 1993 | 1995 | 1997 | 1998 | 1999 |
|---|---|---|---|---|---|---|---|
| Databases | 301 | 7637 | 8261 | 9207 | 10,338 | 11,339 | 11,681 |
| Producers | 200 | 2372 | 2744 | 2860 | 3,216 | 3,686 | 3,674 |
| Vendors | 105 | 933 | 1629 | 1810 | 2,115 | 2,459 | 2,454 |
| Records (in millions) | 52 | 4060 | 5572 | 8160 | 11,270 | 12,050 | 12,860 |

Compiled from data provided in Williams, Martha. "The State of Databases Today: 1999." *Gale Directory of Databases*. Detroit: Gale, 1999.

Predictably, as the amount of information increases, and the number of vendors and producers remains high, the number of electronically stored records has increased greatly. Williams's (1999) data reveal that since 1975 the number of records has increased more than 247 times, with more than 12.8 billion records now being stored. Most of the databases are business oriented (25 percent); followed by science, technology, and engineering (17 percent); general (15 percent); law (11 percent); life sciences (12 percent); social sciences (6 percent); humanities (6 percent); news (4 percent); and multidisciplinary (5 percent). More than four-fifths of the producers (81 percent) are from business and industry, while about 9 percent are governmental. Approximately 8 percent are produced by not-for-profit enterprises. These data reflect a trend since the 1970s of declining government participation in database production. Nearly 64 percent (6,962) of all databases produced are from the United States.

In terms of the types of databases available, Williams reports that most (70 percent) are word-oriented databases (bibliographic or full text), far fewer are number-oriented (12 percent), and even fewer are image- or audio-oriented (12 percent and 3 percent respectively). The trend is toward full-text databases, that is, those in which the entire text is available for viewing, not just the abstract or bibliographic citation. In 1999 there were 10,056 word-oriented databases, 54 percent of which were full text, compared to only 28 percent in 1985. Bibliographic databases, on the other hand, have dropped from 57 percent in 1985 to 23 percent in 1999. This shift suggests that computer databases as information channels are improving substantially in the extensiveness of the information available. It is expected that with continuing developments in technology and the desirability of viewing photographs and graphs as well as text, that image databases will take a prominent place in the market.

With the rapid expansion of personal computers, access to this information has become commonplace. There can be little doubt that, at least for millions of Americans, access to vast amounts of information will increase. However, access to great amounts of information does not necessarily mean that Americans will get the right information. In fact, one can easily foresee that most citizens, awash in information, will drown in it, or at the least lose their bearings. Perhaps that is why the term "navigation" has become so popular in attempting to assist people along the information highway. Nonetheless, one cannot consider the information context in which libraries are placed without recognizing the importance of computerized access to electronic data. It is not unreasonable to presume that librarians will become expert navigators for future information seekers.

The growth of electronic databases has also spawned a burgeoning market of electronic publishing. There are many reasons why the electronic production of information is increasing. In the academic sphere it may be the result of the ever increasing production costs for print journals, especially scientific and technical publications. Increasing costs and the inevitable delays in the refereeing and publication process make electronic production and dissemination of information increasingly attractive. The result is that the number of refereed electronic journals increased in one year from 74 to 142 in 1994. Today, there are thousands of electronic journals, newsletters, and discussion lists that have created an entirely new means of publication. There is no doubt that these publications are increasing at a rapid rate. With increasing interest in the creation of digital libraries and the digitizing of current and back issues of periodicals, increased use of electronically published resources is inevitable.

One cannot leave the subject of electronic databases and electronic publishing without mentioning the Internet and the World Wide Web. (See Chapter 3 for a more detailed discussion.) The Internet and World Wide Web has created a rich environment for the creation, organization, and dissemination of information. The Web provides a special electronic environment that permits the user to move from one electronic document to another using electronic links imbedded in the text. There are millions of such Web sites now available serving commercial, research, educational, and recreational purposes. Use of the Internet has grown from one hour per person per year to a projected ninety-seven hours for 1999 (Veronis and Suhler 1999). As the Web grows, it is becoming a critical component in the information infrastructure.

*Libraries*

The information infrastructure is a complex and dynamic environment. The role of libraries within this context is also dynamic. Traditionally libraries were part of this infrastructure long before electronic information technologies were even conceived. They have been a constant source of knowledge since the settlement of America, although the number and sophistication of these libraries were quite limited until the nineteenth century. Today, there are more than 122,000 libraries in the United States; 9,837 are public libraries, 4,723 are academic, 10,808 are special, and 98,000 are school or media center libraries (*American Library Directory* 1999; *Digest of Education Statistics* 1995). Their many and varied purposes will be discussed later. Suffice it to say here that libraries have played a role in the infrastructure largely by providing institutional support to individuals or small groups through the provision of services and materials for educational, informational, and recreational purposes. Historically, libraries have been an especially important channel of exposure to books, promotion of reading, literacy, and self-development within the population.

In addition, the contemporary library integrates many other information channels in its continuing mission to meet the needs of its users. Most libraries are actively engaged in developing electronic information links and introducing electronic information technologies to their users. In this sense, they are evolving, becoming part of the larger national information infrastructure.

The complex interrelationships among the various components of the information infrastructure present many challenges that libraries must meet if they are to prosper. Some have predicted that libraries may be coming to an end, that their electronic competitors will render them obsolete. It is an intriguing prediction, but do the data support it? Figure 1.7 shows a retrospective look at the number of libraries as reported by the *American Library Directory* since 1980.

From this perspective, the prediction seems unconvincing. The number of libraries, if anything, is increasing, not decreasing! One might predict that with the development of electronic access, they will become even more popular as information seekers look to libraries and librarians as important sources of expertise and assistance in an ever more complex information environment.

## SUMMARY

Library and information science is a discipline oriented to providing access to vast amounts of accumulated knowledge and information. In many ways the growth of information technologies and the expansion of knowledge is an exciting prospect, but it also raises many crucial questions. Certainly, the library and the librarian must address these questions if they are to survive and prosper, and by addressing these questions, they must also re-examine their own values and mission.

Information providers must realize that developments in electronic

**Table 1.7**
**Number of Public, Academic, Government and Special Libraries**
**1980–1997 (Excludes Branches and Junior Colleges)**

| Year | Public | Academic | Government | Special | Total |
|------|--------|----------|------------|---------|-------|
| 1980 | 8,717 | 4,618 | 1,260 | 8,609 | 28,665 |
| 1981 | 8,782 | 4,796 | 1,615 | 8,571 | 29,278 |
| 1982 | 8,768 | 4,924 | 1,565 | 8,453 | 28,949 |
| 1983 | 8,822 | 4,900 | 1,591 | 8,387 | 29,044 |
| 1984 | 8,796 | 4,989 | 1,551 | 8,574 | 29,465 |
| 1985 | 8,849 | 5,034 | 1,574 | 8,955 | 29,843 |
| 1986 | 8,865 | 5,592 | 1,237 | 9,704 | 32,995 |
| 1987–88 | 9,170 | 4,824 | 1,760 | 9,147 | 31,524 |
| 1989–90 | 9,068 | 4,607 | 1,676 | 8,990 | 30,751 |
| 1990–91 | 9,060 | 4,593 | 1,735 | 9,051 | 30,761 |
| 1991–92 | 9,075 | 4,613 | 1,773 | 9,348 | 31,127 |
| 1992–93 | 9,076 | 4,620 | 1,776 | 9,811 | 31,850 |
| 1993–94 | 9,097 | 4,619 | 1,871 | 10,149 | 32,414 |
| 1994–95 | 9,101 | 4,684 | 1,864 | 11,280 | 32,441 |
| 1995–96 | 9,165 | 4,730 | 1,875 | 11,340 | 32,666 |
| 1997–1998 | 9,767 | 4,707 | 1,837 | 11,044 | 33,004 |
| 1999–2000 | 9,837 | 4,723 | 1,874 | 10,808 | 32,852 |

Source: *American Library Directory.* New Providence, N.J.: R.R. Bowker, 1978–1999.

information technologies have led to the emergence of many powerful stakeholders in the development of the information infrastructure. Business and industry, the communications industry (cable and telephone companies), electronic database producers, the federal government, the military, libraries, researchers, academic institutions, and citizens all are eager to influence developments related to the infrastructure. Among the many issues that must be addressed are open access to information; copyright protection and, at the same time, protection of citizens' right to access copyrighted information; appropriate security for information; individual privacy; and the cost of information access. Given these important and often competing interests, it becomes increasingly important that libraries, as institutions that often reflect the public interest rather than personal gain, play critical roles in influencing the policies that affect information dissemination. It is a tremendous responsibility, and it becomes increasingly ponderous as the world of information and the social and technological environment grow in complexity.

Among the questions that librarians must address are

> *What are the role and mission of the library and librarian in our society?*
> *Where do libraries fit in the developing information infrastructure?*
> *What are our citizens' rights to information and how do we protect those rights?*
> *What are the barriers citizens face in getting information?*
> *What ethical responsibilities and dilemmas do information providers face in providing information?*
> *How can we assure that our libraries survive and prosper?*
> *How does the growth of information in electronic formats change the way information providers develop adequate collections and services for their patrons?*
> *What kinds of library and information professionals do we need for the future?*

There is no one right answer to these questions. It is hoped that the remainder of this book will improve the reader's understanding of the issues.

## ENDNOTE

1.  I wish to acknowledge Dr. Brett Sutton, who first proposed the use of such metaphors to understand how the growth of information is understood. This is not to say that he would necessarily interpret the significance of these metaphors in the same way.

## REFERENCES

*American Library Directory 1996–97*, 49th ed. New York: R.R. Bowker, 1997.
*American Library Directory*. New York: R. R. Bowker, various editions.
*The Bowker Annual: Library and Book Trade Almanac*. 42nd ed. New Providence, N.J.: R.R. Bowker, 1997.

*CD-ROMS in Print*. New York: Gale, 1999.

*Digest of Education Statistics 1995*. Washington D.C.: U.S. DOfE, 1995.

Hogan, Kathleen M. and James H. Shelton, eds. *CD-ROM Finder*. Medford, N.J.: Learned Information, 1995, ix.

*International Television and Video Almanac*. Edited by Barry Monush. New York: Quigley, 1987, 1994, 1999.

King, Lisabeth A. and Diane Kovacs Kovacs, et al. In *Directory of Electronic Journals, Newsletters and Academic Discussion Lists*. Edited by Ann Okerson. Washington, D.C.: ARL, 1995, i–ii.

Nielsen Media Research. "Television Usage: Hours of TV Usage Per Person Per Day . . . " Cited in *International Television and Video Almanac 1994*. Edited by Barry Monush. New York: Quigley, 1995.

U.S. Bureau of the Census. *Statistical Abstract of the United States 1999*. Washington, D.C.: GPO, 1999.

Veronis, Suhler & Associates. Communications Industry Forecast Report. New York: Veronis, Suhler and Associates, 1999.

Williams, Martha E. "Highlights of the Online Database Industry and the Internet 1997." In *National Online Meeting Proceedings—1997: Proceedings of the 18th National Online Meeting*. Medford, N.J.: Information Today, 1997, 1–6.

———. "The State of Databases Today: 1999." In *Gale Directory of Databases*. Detroit: Gale, 1997, xvii–xxix.

# 2

# Information Science:
# A Service Perspective

Familiarity with the issues to which the field of information science is devoted provides an enriched understanding for the work of librarians and other information professionals. Definitions of information science abound, but the first definition was proposed in the early 1960s and will suffice for the general discussion that ensues.

Information Science:

> the science that investigates the properties and behavior of information, the forces governing the flow of information, and the means of processing information for optimum accessibility and usability. The processes include the origination, dissemination, collection, organization, storage, retrieval, interpretation, and use of information. The field is derived from or related to mathematics, logic, linguistics, psychology, computer technology, operations research, the graphic arts, communications, library science, management, and some other fields. (Taylor 1966, p. 19)

Several features of this definition stand out: (1) The focus of information science is on the phenomenon of information. Information science deals with information regardless of the package, e.g., a book or a database. Sometimes libraries are not seen within this more general focus because they are viewed as "document-based." (2) Information science deals with the entire information cycle, from creation to use. (3) The field is clearly interdisciplinary, drawing from scientific, social scientific, and psychological fields. (4) Although the definition is not institution-based, that is, it does not mention libraries or information organizations per se, it does emphasize a central purpose of libraries—accessibility and usability of information. This notion has usually been preserved in subsequent definitions and is an edifying aspect for the librarian for it demonstrates a substantial similarity in objectives.

To the librarian, the importance of information science lies not so much in **what** is done as in **why** it is done. The goal of information science is the resolution of human problems. Information science's emphasis on usability and accessibility comports very closely with one of the major objectives of librarians and reveals the substantial instrumental value of the field of librarianship. It is no wonder that information science has sometimes been characterized as deinstitutionalized library science; it is the library without walls, the entire world of information is the "collection," and the librarian or information scientist is the agent who acquires, organizes, and disseminates that information. The librarian or information scientist facilitates the transmission of information to people to meet their needs. This could be seen as the defining character of library and information science if one wants to see it as a single discipline: it focuses on the transmission of information to meet human needs, be they practical, theoretical, religious, or aesthetic. As Brittain (1980) has observed: "it may be that information science is a different way of looking at many of the problems and tasks that have confronted librarians for many decades" (p. 37).

If one accepts that information is a critical aspect of our lives and our society as a whole, then librarians and other information specialists must develop information systems that can acquire, organize, maintain, and disseminate information with minimum effort and cost to users. In information science there are countless areas that have direct and indirect application to the work of libraries and librarians. Clearly if librarians are to respond to the changing information environment and provide the best service, they must integrate information science into their professional outlook.

The growth of information technologies and studies of the information-seeking behavior and information needs of the population suggest that the traditional perspectives of the librarian may require a substantial shift, if not in values, then in librarians' expectations of user needs and what is required of them. Our current concept of information provision has been historically conditioned by a traditional preoccupation with the collection rather than people. It may well be that the conceptualization of library collections and services is woefully inadequate to meet the information needs of the citizenry, and as information becomes increasingly available from other sources, the library will need to decide what role it will play and how it will synthesize these new sources. If librarianship is to focus on truly serving its users, it must understand how and why they use information.

From a historical perspective, the definition of information science provided above suggests that information science in some form has been around for a very long time, although it may not have been called by that name. Libraries, librarianship, and bibliography, for example, are part of the foundation of information science. The history of libraries and librarianship is primarily one of collecting, organizing, and disseminating materials, largely of the print variety. One could go back to the organization of library materials beginning nearly 5,000 years ago in Sumeria and find early attempts to organize information, at that time impressed in clay tablets. Similarly, over the centuries there have been many attempts to organize the available literature through the compilation of bibliographies, and there have been systematic attempts to organize published knowledge through the development of classification systems such as the Dewey Decimal System. Each of these attempts to organize information and to make it available and usable is part of the important foundation on which the field of information science is constructed (Shera and Cleveland 1977).

Capturing the contemporary spirit of information science, however, requires us also to look to more recent antecedents, especially those in the first half of the twentieth century. These developments represent additional layers in the foundation. Among these developments was a shift in emphasis, *away from the book to information itself*. For years the book played the central role in the transmission of information, and certainly was central to librarianship. With the significant proliferation of scientific and technical information in the twentieth century, considerable interest had grown in the theoretical and practical aspects of how to organize it and improve access. This information was often stored in media other than books: in periodicals, documents, research reports, and microfilm. It was clear that the package in which the information was contained was far less important than locating specific information stored within these media. This was substantially different from the way libraries had traditionally satisfied information needs—by providing a physical item (usually a book)—and presented significantly different, although still related, challenges. As it became clear that scientific and technical information was distributed in a variety of formats, and that it was the information not the format that was of special interest, a new field developed outside the traditional discipline of librarianship. This emerging field was systematically developed first in Europe and was known originally as "Documentalism." The focus of documentalism was on the creation, organization, and dissemination of information in all formats. Important organizations were developed to promote these techniques, most notably the Federation Internationale de Documentation (FID) and its U.S. counterpart, the American Documentation Institute, which continues today as the American Society of Information Science (ASIS). It might be said, then, that two of the changes central to the way information was accessed in the twentieth century was a shift in emphasis away from the item that held the information to an emphasis on accessing the content of the information. Taken together, documentalism and librarianship, including bibliography, constitute the critical foundation of information science.

The foundation of information science has at least one additional and critical component on which it rests: the development of computers. One can immediately see how, with the strong interest in organizing and retrieving scientific and technical information, that computer technologies would have a magnetic attraction. Early articles on the information potential of computers following World War II predicted great things. Vannevar Bush's (1945) article "As We May Think" in which he projected "Memex," a machine for the storage and retrieval of documents, was certainly a prominent exemplar of the hopes raised by computerized information technologies and is recognized as a seminal work in the field. It was only five years after Bush's article that the phrase "information retrieval" was first used in this context (Wellisch 1972, p. 161). Computers, of course, significantly increase the capacity to store information without the need for a physical document. Therefore it was logical to exploit the computer for information retrieval. Interestingly, despite the importance of the computer to information science, definitions of the field seldom mention computers directly. However, these electronic information technologies have given information science much greater prominence and have provided for much of the subsequent research and development in the field to the present day. With the integration of the computer, information science took on its current cast, which emphasizes electronic information: its creation, storage, retrieval, and use.

## THE FEATURES OF INFORMATION SCIENCE

Although the debate about the nature and definition of information science will not be resolved here, it is useful to identify briefly some of the areas of activity in the field of information science that directly contribute to our understanding of how information can be created, organized, and disseminated to meet human information needs. The breadth and variety of fields explored by information science can be seen at a glance by looking at the categories of information science as identified by *Information Science Abstracts* (see Figure 2.1).

Librarianship is only one of the seven major categories, which also include information generation, promulgation, recognition, description, process and control. Obviously, electronic information technologies are very important to information science, but there are also other issues that the field addresses, including socioeconomic, educational, psychological, international, national, and legal aspects. Below is a more detailed summary of some of the major issues addressed by information science that directly affect libraries. Information technology and information policy are discussed in Chapters 3 and 4 respectively.

*Area 1: Examination of Information Needs, Information Seeking, Information Use, and Information Users*

One major area of study is how users of information systems solve information problems. Allen (1996) observes that user-centered approaches are especially useful in the information professions which are intended, in large part, to resolve the information problems of their clients. Such approaches focus "on the ways that information systems meet the information needs of users" (Allen 1996, p. 14). Allen suggests that understanding the nature of information needs and their resolution is extremely complex and requires clarity on a variety of levels. For example, one must distinguish information **devices**, which include individual things such as books and electronic databases, from **information systems**, which are composed of information devices that are linked or otherwise related for the purpose of informing the user. Sometimes, there are collections of information systems designed to help users resolve their information problems; these are referred to as **information services**, e.g., a reference department. Information services may be grouped to serve a particular clientele or variety of client groups to form **information institutions**, such as libraries (Allen). In a user-centered ap-

## Figure 2.1
## Information Science Abstracts Classification Scheme

**Abstract Classification and Contents**

INFORMATION SCIENCE AND DOCUMENTATION

1.0    General aspects
1.1    Primary and secondary sources
1.2    Education for information work
1.3    Professional and organizational aspects
1.4    Socioeconomic aspects
1.5    International aspects
1.6    National and local aspects
1.7    Legal aspects

RESEARCH METHODS

2.0    General aspects
2.1    Definitions, Theoretical considerations
2.2    Historical aspects
2.3    Bibliometrics
2.4    User and usage studies
2.5    Vision and brain functions
2.6    Psychological aspects, Cognition
2.7    Social studies, Demographics
2.8    Mathematics, Logic

INFORMATION GENERATION AND PROMULGATION

3.0    General aspects
3.1    Writing and recording
3.2    Editing
3.3    Publicity
3.4    Meetings, Personal interchange
3.5    Instruction
3.6    Technology transfer
3.7    Publishing
3.8    Copying, Printing
3.10   Optical and laser techniques
3.11   Communications and telecommunications systems
3.12   Radio, Television, Video
3.13   Office communications and automation

INFORMATION RECOGNITION AND DESCRIPTION

4.0    General aspects
4.2    Computer languages
4.3    Artificial intelligence, Cybernetics
4.4    Abstracting and reviewing

4.5     Translation and dictionaries
4.7     Classification, Indexing, and Thesauri
4.8     Coding, Compacting
4.9     Pattern and character recognition

## INFORMATION PROCESSING AND CONTROL

5.0     General aspects
5.1     File design, Building, and Updating
5.2     Computer systems (General)
5.3     Supercomputers
5.4     Advanced computing, Parallel processing
5.6     Software and programming
5.7     Storage
5.8     Graphics and display
5.9     System interfacing
5.10    Security considerations
5.11    Searching and retrieval

## INFORMATION SYSTEMS AND APPLICATIONS

6.0     General aspects
6.1     Networks, Regional systems, Consortia
6.2     Bibliographic search services, Databases
6.3     Abstracting, Indexing, and Review services
6.4     Audio-visual and non-print media
6.5     Physical sciences and biomedicine
6.6     Life sciences and engineering
6.7     Social sciences and humanities
6.8     Business, Commerce, and Industry
6.9     Management information systems and Decision systems
6.10    Law
6.11    Government

## LIBRARIES AND INFORMATION SERVICES

7.0     General aspects
7.1     Planning, Administration
7.2     Automation
7.3     Collection development and preparation
7.4     Collection management and preservation
7.5     Circulation control
7.6     Interlibrary lending and resource sharing
7.7     User services, Assistance, and Orientation
7.8     Academic and general research libraries
7.10    Public libraries
7.11    Archives and museums

Reprinted with permission by Documentation Abstracts. Information Science Abstracts. Plenum Publishing Corporation, New York.

proach, a significant part of designing and evaluating how user needs are met requires an understanding of user characteristics and needs on all levels.

The approaches to studying information needs vary considerably. Some focus on individuals, others on institutions, often libraries; others focus specifically on the information needs of various disciplines such as executives, scientists, nurses, and engineers. Information systems cannot be well designed without a clear understanding of what the intended users want or need to know, how they seek information, and how they evaluate the information that they receive.

The concept of an information need can be understood very generally; it is when an uncertainty arises in the individual that the subject believes can be satisfied by information (Krikelas 1983). But the concept can also be separated into information wants (or desires) and information needs. An information want is a *desire* for information to satisfy an uncertainty; an information need is the condition, whether recognized by the individual or not in which information is required to resolve a problem. Such a distinction is especially important for librarians if they intend to satisfy both their patrons' wants and needs. Merely answering a patron's question may not be enough. The person may want a particular piece of information, only to discover that something else is needed after all. If librarians are to perform their jobs well, they must find out what is wanted and needed.

Seeking and gathering information is a highly complex process that requires much explanation and refinement. How someone seeks information may vary by age, level of education, intelligence, and discipline. Many models for how people seek information have been advanced. Scientists, for example, rely heavily on informal communications with their colleagues, information gleaned at conferences, journal references and articles, and electronic sources of information, while humanities scholars rely more heavily on references in books, the library's subject catalog, and printed indexes and bibliographies (Broadbent 1986; Van Styvendaele 1977; Meadows 1974). Scientists may have a greater need for currency than humanities scholars, while humanities researchers may have a greater need to browse information. These differences have been confirmed in the online environment. Humanities scholars' search strategies when conducting online searches are significantly different from those used by scientists. Humanities scholars use more named individuals, geographical terms, chronological terms, and discipline terms (Bates, Wilde and Siegfried 1993). As Durrance (1989) has observed: "What people *do* drives their need for information" (p. 161).

Effectively assessing individuals' information wants and needs requires knowledge of how patrons search for information and how they learn, as well as how to interview effectively, how to evaluate the patron's need, and how to evaluate the degree to which the information has satisfied the need. It also requires that the librarian possess thorough and current knowledge of the available electronic, print, and human resources and know how to access these sources. This approach places a very serious responsibility on the librarian, one beyond that of merely getting pieces of information requested by the patron.

Interestingly, despite the unique character of some groups' information needs, there is also great commonality when one considers the general population. Chen and Hernon (1982), for example, found that among the general population, the primary reason for seeking information was personal. That is, more than half the subjects they studied (52 percent) sought information to solve day-to-day problems and nearly three-quarters (73 percent) described their information need as personal. Among the information of greatest interest were the following: (1) Job related issues relating to performing specific tasks or establishing businesses; or issues related to getting or changing jobs, career advancement, or obtaining promotions; (2) Consumer issues relating to the quality or availability of a product or obtaining product information; (3) Housing and household maintenance issues relating to dealings with landlords, obtaining loans and mortgages; performing do-it-yourself repairs on the car or home; (4) Education and schooling issues relating to information on adult education, parenting, and obtaining support for education. Certainly, these findings are of great value to libraries, especially public ones in building their library collections.

There are many other studies concerning information seeking that provide a useful context for librarians and other information professionals. The following is a highly selective summary of findings from these studies that can be useful in understanding and designing information services:

THERE IS A DIFFERENCE BETWEEN INFORMATION SEEKING AND INFORMATION GATHERING.

The notion of information seeking is a broad one. Krikelas (1983) has suggested that there may be two different basic activities: information seeking and information gathering. Information *seeking* is "an attempt to satisfy an immediate need by searching for relevant information."

Information *gathering* is "an attempt to satisfy a deferred need by searching for relevant information" (p. 8). In information gathering there is no immediate need for the information, but the search is expected to yield useful information for future use.

For libraries, these differences may have a profound effect on how a library is used. An information seeker may be looking for a specific item, ask the reference librarian a specific query, or have a specific time requirement. An information gatherer may browse a collection in a specific area without need for specific information or time requirement. Newspaper and magazine collections may be best suited, although not exclusively, for information gatherers, while reference materials may be best suited for information seekers.

PEOPLE USUALLY SEARCH FOR INFORMATION IN SOME TYPE OF CONTEXT.

People seldom seek information as an end in itself; they usually seek it within a particular context—what Durrance (1989) refers to as a "problem environment" (p. 162). The individual is usually trying to solve a particular problem or make a particular decision. A scientist may be trying to locate information on a procedure, an English teacher trying to locate an essay, a neighbor trying to repair a refrigerator, or a minister seeking quotations for a sermon.

The fact is that people ask questions for a purpose, and this has considerable implication for the librarian. Traditionally, reference librarians have been taught not to probe "why" a particular question is asked, for fear that this would violate the patron's privacy. There is a fear that such a query could deter an information seeker from using the library. But this is not consistent with what we know about information seeking. The seeker enters the library with a problem that needs to be solved, and it seems logical that the objective of the librarian is to help solve the problem. This harkens back to distinguishing between information wants and information needs. As Durrance has observed, the issue is not only "What do you want to know?" but "How and why is the information needed? How is it likely to help? What does the user know already? What is expected? What are the parameters of the problem?" (p. 163). This is not to suggest that the librarian is to probe into the personal lives of patrons, but it does suggest that merely answering the questions asked without understanding the real issues can be problematic. As noted above, this is hardly a universally accepted doctrine—in fact restrictiveness in questioning tends to be preferred. Wilson (1986) suggests a middle ground which he calls the "face value rule," which emphasizes question clarification rather than inquiry into the purposes of the questions (p. 469). Nonetheless, information-seeking research suggests that we should not be too restrictive if we are actually to deal with why individuals come to ask their questions, the traditional prohibitions of the library profession notwithstanding.

PEOPLE PREFER PERSONAL RATHER THAN INSTITUTIONAL SOURCES TO SATISFY THEIR INFORMATION NEEDS.

There is little doubt that individuals are very likely to consult the most convenient human sources before they appeal to an institutional one. When an information need arises, one's memory is most likely to be checked first before seeking other sources for information; in other words, we look inward to see if we can answer the question. If this fails, we might attempt to answer the question by using our own powers of observation, if practical (Krikelas 1983). Failing this, individuals attempt to seek the information from external sources, human or institutional. The research suggests that when faced with an information need, people are more likely first to seek individuals rather than institutions (Chen and Hernon 1982). This means that individuals are more likely to contact their doctors, clergy, coworkers, or neighbors before coming to the library. The quality of the information may or may not be as good, but people are the preferred sources of information.

PEOPLE SELDOM SEE LIBRARIANS AS A SOURCE OF INFORMATION.

There is discouraging evidence that when individuals have an information need, they do not think of libraries or librarians as a primary source of information. Chen, in a large study of information seekers in New England, for example, found that only 3 percent of the individuals with a recent information need identified the library as a possible source for resolving that need (Chen and Hernon 1982). Durrance (1989), reporting on reference user studies, noted that even library users themselves do not wish to trouble staff with questions and think of reference service as only for simple questions.

These findings may have some disturbing implications for librarians. Durrance (1989) suggests, pessimistically and consistent with Chen's observations, that people perceive the library as the solver of their problems rather than librarians. She notes that we speak of "library users" rather than the "librarian's clients" (p. 165). Indeed, the librarian often appears to be transparent, with the patron perceiving the library as a collection of books and materials, not a source of information specialists. Ironically, the impersonality of the library may be aggravated by the new networked technologies that give the appearance of requiring even less human mediation. This is something we need to think about—how do we make ourselves more visible? This lack of visibility may encourage people to continue to underestimate the importance of the librarian in the information transfer process. In addition, if people really prefer human rather than institutional sources of information, emphasizing the librarian rather than the library might increase individual use of the library. In other words, "humanizing" the library may well reduce resistance to its use.

INFORMATION SEEKING IS A DYNAMIC PROCESS.

Studies suggest that the search for information generally goes through a variety of phases beginning with an undefined notion that there is a need for information, which is referred to as an "anomalous state of knowledge (ASK)" (Belkin, Brooks and Oddy 1982, p. 62). Generally, as the process proceeds, the search becomes more and more defined and the area to be explored narrows. The search strategy will vary depending on the nature of the inquiry itself, and as the query becomes narrowed the strategy and type of information sought will vary (Rouse 1984).

Kuhlthau (1991) has proposed that an information seeker generally goes through a six-stage process, which she refers to as the Information Search Process (ISP). The stages are explained in an abbreviated fashion below.

*Stage 1: Initiation*: This stage is characterized by uncertainty as the information seeker realizes that he or she has a need for some knowledge or understanding. The need is still unfocused; the individual has not yet defined the topic or the approach to be taken and may discuss possible courses of action with others.

*Stage 2: Selection*: The information seeker begins to focus on a particular topic and begins to explore the best approaches for meeting the information need. Some tentative attempts to gather information on the topic begin.

*Stage 3: Exploration*: The information seeker begins serious exploration of the topic, gathering information to provide orientation. The information seeker may still have a considerable sense of confusion or doubt because the information may appear to be contradictory. At this point, the information seeker may still not be able to articulate precisely the type of information required to meet the information need.

*Stage 4: Formulation*: This stage is critical as the seeker begins to establish a clear focus for the exploration and feelings of uncertainty begin to diminish. Rather than just collecting information, the seeker begins to evaluate critically the information obtained, accepting some information and discarding information that appears to be irrelevant. The information seeker becomes more confident in the search and the search process.

*Stage 5: Collection*: The focus is now clear, and the information seeker collects only information related to the defined topic. The seeker is able to articulate clearly the type of information needed, the search process becomes more effective, uncertainty is reduced, and the seeker's confidence is increased further.

*Stage 6: Presentation*: The search for information is now complete, although the success of the search may vary depending on factors such as the availability of information, the effectiveness of the information system used, and the skills of the searcher. At this late stage, some of the information obtained may turn out to duplicate previous information. Attention is turned to summary, synthesis, and reporting of the information gathered.

Information search processes, like the one proposed above, reveal the essentially personal, as well as dynamic, nature of information seeking. The problem context in which people search for information provides its own frame-of-reference, and the meaning and relevance of the information is largely dictated by this frame-of-reference rather than some objective measure. Analysis of information needs within this personal context is sometimes referred to as a sense-making approach to information seeking (Dervin 1983). Such an approach suggests that developers of information systems understand not only the internal aspects of an information system, but the importance of responding to the particular problem environment that the user brings to the system. Indeed, if the relevance of a piece of information can be determined only by the user, evaluating information systems requires that the user constantly be consulted to determine if the information retrieved will satisfy the patron's needs.

INDIVIDUALS HAVE SIGNIFICANTLY DIFFERENT ABILITIES IN SEEKING INFORMATION.

It should come as no surprise that some people are very good at seeking information and others are a good deal less skillful. Obviously, there are significant differences in intelligence, analytical ability, and manual dexterity. This has a substantial effect on the capacity of individuals to seek information effectively and can also have a substantial effect on the shaping of library services. Generally speaking, the more varied the users' abilities, the more flexible the information system must be to accommodate these variations. Hence, in a specialized library, where the users might be highly educated and familiar with the organization of the literature and the technologies to search it, the system need not be very flexible. But, in a public library, where the patrons range from highly educated individuals to those who are barely literate, the library needs to be highly flexible.

Not only do individuals vary in abilities, but different groups of individuals use different information strategies. This has led to studies of how specific groups such as the elderly or the economically disadvantaged seek information. For example, they have found that the information-seeking ability improves with age. For those of us who are aging, this seems quite promising, if a bit surprising. But unfortunately, although these skills improve with age, our ability to process information tends to decline with age. In other words, we can find the information, but we can't understand it!

PEOPLE WILL USE THE LEAST EFFORT IN SEEKING INFORMATION.

Sometimes referred to as the "Principle of Least Effort," this finding suggests that people will seek the most convenient source to meet their information need, even when they realize that this source may produce information of lower quality than other sources. Such a finding, although not surprising, can be unnerving when considering the roles of libraries and librarians. There is little doubt that many view libraries as complicated places. Often finding information in libraries *is* a complicated process. It is certainly more convenient to ask one's neighbor or friend than to drive to the library. The problem is exacerbated when one considers that even if a library is used, varying quality of the information makes it critical that the best sources of information also be the most convenient. Libraries need to design their collections and services so that convenience and quality are one and the same for the user (Mann 1993).

In addition to the findings noted above, information scientists have investigated a variety of factors that impair or prevent information seeking. These barriers include the following.

*Physical aspects.* It is known that the location of a library has an impact on its use. Libraries that are geographically remote or difficult to reach are bound to create significant problems for those seeking information. Similarly, libraries that are difficult to enter or negotiate, especially for those with physical disabilities, will have restricted use. No doubt, collections with a poor physical arrangement or poor signage will also exacerbate the problems of information access.

*Policy and procedural aspects.* Often libraries create rules, regulations, and procedures that inhibit the use of materials and services. Sometimes there are very good reasons for these rules, but they can have undesired effects. Restrictive circulation or reference policies; inadequate operating hours; limited use of meeting rooms; restricted use because of age, poor training, or poor scheduling of library staff; inadequate or inappropriate allocation of fiscal resources—all can be impediments to information seeking.

*Economic/financial aspects.* The ability of the library to afford the latest and best information technology and other information resources has a direct impact on the ability of information seekers to find what they need. Even when such resources are available, library economics have sometimes significantly altered the direction of library services to a "fee-for-service" perspective. As the costs of electronic access increase, this problem is bound to increase, and those with minimal financial resources may well receive a lower quality of service. In addition, the financial status of users has a bearing on their familiarity with and knowledge of electronic information technologies. More affluent individuals are more likely to own computers or to attend schools where computers are common. Such individuals will likely find using libraries now and in the future easier and more satisfying. This is a troubling trend if one assumes that access to information should not be dependent on one's financial resources.

*Legal aspects.* Laws and regulations governing the flow of information, such as copyright law, inevitably affect the dissemination of information. Similarly, laws governing the restriction of certain types of information or images, such as those governing access to sexually explicit or violent materials to children and adults, limit the types of information that can be made available. This situation is likely to worsen because there is growing concern over the accessibility of such information on the Internet.

*Social aspects.* A troubling but common finding in studies of library users is that those most likely to use libraries have more formal education, tend to have higher incomes, and are white. There may be many reasons for this, but some may relate to the way members of minority groups perceive the library. If libraries are perceived as aristocratic, authoritarian institutions, unfriendly and unresponsive to minorities, then these groups are bound to have diminished enthusiasm for libraries as sources of information.

Similarly, there are now many social pressures placed on libraries to restrict access to some of the information within them. Organized groups, especially those with a religious agenda, have attempted to influence not only the availability of specific materials, but also library policies (for further discussion see Chapter 5).

In addition, information technologies tend to be "less friendly" to women and older individuals. The extent to which socialization and generational characteristics affect access to such technologies needs to be addressed if access is to be effected.

### Area 2: Information Storage and Retrieval

A central area for research and development in information science is the issue of information storage and retrieval and the systems that support it. Harter (1986) defines an information retrieval system as "a device interposed between an end-user of an information collection and the collection itself. The purpose of the system is to capture wanted items and filter out unwanted items from the information collection" (p. 245). This highlights a central concept of information retrieval: relevance. This concept can be difficult to understand, and much has been written on the subject (Saracevic 1975). There are at least two aspects of relevance: relevant to the user and relevant to the topic. In the former, it is clear that the user defines the context for relevance. An item retrieved from an information system is relevant if the user believes that it helps to meet his or her information need. In the latter case, an item is relevant if it can be shown that it is about the subject, regardless of a given user

(Pao 1989). Relevance forms the basis of much evaluation of information systems. Systems that retrieve relevant items and avoid the retrieval of irrelevant items (sometimes referred to as "false hits" or "false drops") naturally are considered more effective.

It was the information retrieval research in the 1960s that constituted the "first flowering of information science as a science" (Rayward 1983, p. 353). Certainly, this is a critical area for libraries. With the increasing number of information technologies employed by libraries, the effectiveness of these technologies in retrieving the desired information is critical. Systems without computers can also be considered information storage and retrieval systems—libraries, for example, can be conceived as just such a system. But generally, the focus in information science is on computerized information systems. Among the areas studied in information storage and retrieval are the following:

EVALUATION OF INFORMATION RETRIEVAL SYSTEMS

Evaluating an information retrieval system is a very complex task. By what criteria are such systems to be evaluated? Two basic concepts are **recall** and **precision**. Within any given system, it is critical to know if all the available items relevant to a particular search were found; the degree to which this is accomplished is a measure of **recall**. With poor recall many items that might have been useful were not located. On the other hand, it is also important to know if **only** the relevant items were found. Sometimes, many irrelevant items are found. This is difficult and time consuming for the searcher, who must then review all of the items—including those that were not relevant—to find the relevant ones. The degree to which the system finds only the relevant items is a measure of **precision**. The formula for each is noted below:

$$\text{Recall} = \frac{\text{number of relevant documents retrieved}}{\text{total number of relevant documents in the file}}$$

$$\text{Precision} = \frac{\text{number of relevant documents retrieved}}{\text{total number of documents retrieved in the file}}$$

However, these measures are somewhat controversial. They emphasize quantitative, not qualitative aspects, and there are many ambiguities associated with what one might define as "relevant" (Froehlich 1994). More recent approaches have emphasized the responsiveness of the system to the user's needs and psychological characteristics. This type of evaluation places greater emphasis on the searcher's knowledge, cognitive process, and problem to be solved. This will be discussed further below.

SEARCH RETRIEVAL MODELS

An information storage and retrieval system is not useful unless there are search strategies that permit information to be quickly and effectively retrieved. The search models in use vary considerably. The most common search strategy in library settings is the **Boolean logic** model. In the Boolean model, an individual can search a database by combining terms with a variety of logical operators including *and*, *or*, or *not*. With this method, multiple terms can be included in the search simultaneously; this permits highly flexible search strategies compared to manual-searching operations. Other operators can also be employed to further limit searches. For example, retrieval models may permit searching by author, title, year of publication, and journal title. Such models play a crucial role in the discipline and will continue to demand time and attention. Unless effective searches can be performed, information cannot be extracted from an information system.

DATABASE AND FILE STRUCTURE

Database design, the structure of the information, and how it is presented to the user all have a significant effect on the user's ability to retrieve the information. For example, how is the information represented to the user? What types of information are available (numerical, textual, video, audio), and what vocabulary is used? Are the words used in the search process highly restricted, or is the language relatively open? What fields and subfields are searchable; how are the records searched (e.g. by author? title or keyword? subject?)? Can the search be narrowed by date, language, or publisher? Do the records contain abstracts, full text, or images? The usefulness of the database for any given user depends on the answers to these questions. Further discussion of this issue can be found in Chapter 6, "Information Organization."

COMPUTER-HUMAN INTERFACE

Information systems, and certainly systems for libraries, are designed to satisfy human information needs. The point of contact between the human and the computer is called the **computer-human** interface. In the early development of computers, little attention was paid to this area; only a small number of individuals used computers and they tended to be very knowledgeable with the technical languages of computer systems. As computer use became more widespread, especially when the personal computer became commonplace, it became necessary to pay more attention to creating successful searches for the average citizen. Today, the computer-human interface is considered a vital aspect in the success or failure of a computer system (Shaw 1991).

For an information system to function effectively, it must make the user comfortable and make the process of searching as easy as possible. This means that designers of information storage and retrieval systems must understand the way that humans approach computers and how they search for information. This understanding permits computer designers to create, or strive to create, "user-friendly front-ends," which allow users to sit down in front of the computer screen and satisfy their information needs with a minimum of jargon, confusion, or technical knowledge. Some of the issues in exploring computer-human interfaces include screen display features such as color and windows; speed of response; interaction functions such as commands and menus; post-processing functions such as downloading; help systems and messages; graphics capabilities; training time required; user satisfaction, and error rates when using the system (Shaw 1991).

One important area in the exploration of computer-human interfaces is **cognitive research**, which explores how the user's knowledge and the knowledge contained within the information systems can be matched effectively. Knowledge, on a variety of levels, affects the use of information systems. Allen (1991) has identified four such levels:

- **world knowledge**: a person's world knowledge may affect the information they search for and their search strategies. Factors such as ethnicity, gender, and nationality have all been shown to influence the use of information systems.
- **systems knowledge**: the extent and type of knowledge that users possess about information systems and their expectations of the systems affect their ability and manner of use.

- **task knowledge**: the users' particular information goals or needs affect their use of the systems. How users define the information problem to be resolved and the process by which information problems are defined, refined, and resolved have a direct impact on the use of the information systems.
- **domain knowledge**: the users' familiarity with the actual subject will affect their use of the systems. Experts are bound to use information systems differently from the way naive users do.

In addition, cognitive research explores how a user's problem-solving techniques are applied to information systems, how the user proceeds with the information search process, how users judge the relevance of information, how memory affects information users and how users learn to use information systems, and the relationship between cognitive ability and the ability to use an information system (Allen 1991).

Exploring these cognitive areas provides some guidance into how to design the information systems themselves. Understanding how people think, what they know, and how they approach information problems can help system designers create knowledge models within their systems that more closely match the methods and data by which users can meet their needs. This helps designers create what is commonly referred to as "user-friendly" systems or effective "gateways" for information access.

Closely related is the issue of how the user communicates with the computer. For this issue, information science draws upon the field of linguistics. A crucial area of study is **natural language processing** (NLP), which attempts to develop user interfaces that allow users to employ their "natural" language to have their queries answered. In other words, using NLP they should be able to ask a computer a question in the same way they would ask another person, or reference librarian, a question. This eliminates the need for the user to use the "right" term selected by the database developers. Lee and Olsgaard (1989) observe that use of NLP requires that at least four areas be addressed: (1) speech recognition: the computer should be able to hear and understand a question being asked of it through a voice recognition system; (2) command recognition: the computer should be able to understand the command without use of an artificial language or vocabulary; (3) content analysis and representation: the computer should be able to understand the actual meaning of a document. This involves understanding the context in which the language is used. Given the subtleties and ambiguities of language, this represents a major challenge in NLP; and (4) system interaction: the system has to be able to take the natural language query and relate it to the database so that correct information can be retrieved.

ARTIFICIAL INTELLIGENCE (AI) AND EXPERT SYSTEMS

Artificial intelligence is an extremely broad field, and much of the research and application lie outside the realm of librarianship or even of information retrieval in general. Among the many fields of artificial intelligence are machine translation, robotics, expert systems, natural language interfaces, speech understanding, knowledge acquisitions and representation, and pattern matching. One of the most intriguing areas of information storage and retrieval lies in the continuing attempt to develop machines that think like people—or even better than people. There is little doubt that the concept of an actual "thinking machine" has been an attractive concept for years, as any decent survey of science fiction would attest. How many times have we witnessed on a movie screen a computer ready to take over the world, a computer that knows everything and can answer in a friendly voice, like the Enterprise's computer on Star Trek, or an android (robot) that even looks much like us and mimics our thoughts and actions. Work in artificial intelligence is intended, at least in part, to create computers that mimic human thought processes, judgments, and sometimes human actions in the hope that computers can provide invaluable information, perform valuable services, and even render judgments that would assist humans. These activities might be in industrial production (robotics for manufacturing), in game-playing (chess programs), or even in assisting medical diagnosis or legal practice. Sometimes these systems possess considerable power and are referred to as **expert systems**. Expert systems are "computer programs which inform, make recommendations, or solve problems in a manner and at a level of performance comparable to that displayed by a human expert in the field" (Vedder 1990, p. 4).

In libraries, artificial intelligence might be applied to reference functions such as identification and retrieval of documents or data, cataloguing and authority control, and library instruction through computer assisted instruction (CAI) (Smith 1987). In addition, work in developing "expert search intermediaries" would assist users in searching online systems without the need for human intermediaries (Smith, p. 55). To date, the development of artificial intelligence for information retrieval and library applications is still in its early stages, but its potential highlights the need for information professionals to follow its developments.

*Area 3: Defining the Nature of Information and Its Value*

There are many theoretical and practical discussions in information science concerning the fundamental object of the field—information. Perhaps the most conspicuous debate deals with distinguishing among at least three basic constructs: data, information, and knowledge. A fourth construct—wisdom—is also added from time to time. This debate will not be settled here; rather, one perspective, albeit a conventional one, will be advanced in abbreviated form to provide a basic understanding of the distinctions among these concepts. Although such discussions may seem unnecessarily abstract, a critical examination of these concepts can lead to a deeper understanding of the purposes of institutions like libraries.

### DATA

The term *data* is sometimes used synonymously with information, but it also has a more characteristic use, as the building blocks of information and knowledge; it refers to the material out of which information is created. In this sense, data are commonly seen as numbers, letters, or symbols, which may or may not be processible by a computer. The term often implies that meaning is as yet absent, or unassigned, as in *raw data*. Hence, the numbers stored in a computer file are referred to as a data set.

### INFORMATION

Attempting to understand the meaning of the term *information* is more complex, perhaps in part because the term has had a very long etymological history. There are many definitions that persist today, including highly technical ones in the telecommunications industry, law, and genetics, as when DNA is described as passing on genetic information. These more abstract, technical, or metaphorical uses are not addressed in this discussion, but it is important to know that they are part of this definitional milieu.

Many of the historical uses of information have found their way into common usage or are suggestive of current usage. Early senses of the term, for example, suggested that information involved a "forming" or "moulding of the mind" (*Oxford English Dictionary* 1989, p. 944). In this early sense, the soul might be "informed." Although this is not a current usage, it is suggestive of our current concern with the power of information. One hears the phrase "information is power," and certainly many are concerned that the information our citizenry receives from television and other media is a critical component in the shaping of our attitudes. Other senses of the term information are more directly accepted by contemporary society. For example, information can be seen as an activity, namely, "the action of informing" or the "communication of the knowledge or 'news' of some fact or occurrence" (*Oxford English Dictionary*, p. 944). This is what is meant by the phrase "for your information." Information can also be seen as that which is being communicated. It is the "knowledge communicated concerning some particular fact, subject, or event; that which one is apprised or told; intelligence, news" (*Oxford English Dictionary*, p. 944). To say that the library or information center is in the information business plays on both these latter senses of the term. Libraries both inform their users and provide them with information.

Although the terms information and data are often used synonymously, a greater understanding of information science can be gained by noting their distinctive characteristics. Commonly, library and information science sees information as, at the least, an aggregation, organization, or classification of data, and perhaps more importantly, as *meaning* that is assigned to data. In other words, information possesses meaning, (data being its "raw" state) and this seems to also imply that some type of human understanding and processing has occurred. Somewhat more restrictive definitions of information argue that information must not only contain meaning, but that meaning must be previously unknown to the recipient of the information; in other words, it is something new. Some definitions suggest that the information must also be true or accurate, or that it must be conveyed from one person to another, i.e., communicated. Clearly libraries and information centers are constructed for humans, and one can see them as possessing data which are then processed either by staff or patrons—in this sense meaning arises within the walls of the library or information center.

KNOWLEDGE, WISDOM, AND COGNITIVE AUTHORITY

Knowledge is sometimes used synonymously with information, but it is also defined as a **cohesive** body of information; or information that is **integrated** into a larger body of knowledge; that is, it is a body of interrelated information. Knowledge is applied or potentially applicable to some end. From a library perspective, one presumes that knowledge as well as information is gained through libraries—that is, users gain an understanding of the interrelationship of the information obtained and its applicability to a particular setting. Such a view recognizes the obligation of libraries and librarians to make connections whenever possible so that information becomes knowledge to the user.

Although not always part of the discussion, wisdom is also an important notion. One way of understanding wisdom is as knowledge applied to human ends to benefit the world. In this sense, wisdom is the only one of the above terms that is laden with the values of human progress. One can apply knowledge to immoral ends, but wisdom is wisdom because there is a beneficial end to its application. The goals of libraries as a social institution are to benefit the members of society and the society as a whole.

In summary, there appears to be a conceptual ladder: data are raw and unprocessed; information is processed data from which meaning arises and is communicated; and knowledge is further processed information that is organized and interrelated and more broadly understood and applied. Wisdom is knowledge applied to the benefit of humanity. Despite the seeming simplicity of this hierarchy, one should accept these distinctions with great caution. Notably, for libraries, the question of what constitutes knowledge is a very important one, for libraries rely on bodies of knowledge, or knowledgeable works, to perform many of their question-answering functions. That is, although libraries are full of information, when librarians attempt to respond to a query, the knowledgeable or authoritative work is the one that is preferred. In this sense, librarians rely on a canon of authoritative literature to provide the most dependable responses.

This is a thorny question, after all—how does something come to be accepted as knowledge in our society, knowledge that we may end up putting on our shelf to refer to and transmit to others? Wilson (1983) has observed that most of the "knowledge" we acquire does not come from direct experience (first-hand knowledge), but from what he refers to as "second-hand" knowledge: "We mostly depend on others for ideas, as well as for information about things outside the range of direct experience . . . Much of what we think about the world is what we have second hand from others . . . ". (p. 10). That which makes one infer that one item is knowledge and another mere information or speculation is referred to as **cognitive authority**. We believe those sources we think are cognitive authorities—others we reject. What sources have the greatest cognitive authority for librarians? Are they those prepared by famous publishers like Harvard University Press or the *New England Journal of Medicine*? Are they those prepared by major reference book publishers like R. R. Bowker or H. W. Wilson? Are librarians in danger of censoring materials because they regard some authors or publishers as low in cognitive authority (although other groups may not regard them as such)? Although librarians often characterize themselves as objective information providers, their attitudes toward what constitutes knowledge has a profound effect on their ability to serve the entire citizenry.

VALUE OF INFORMATION AND VALUE-ADDED PROCESSES

Part of understanding the nature of information is trying to understand its value. Although information has had value over the centuries, attempts to determine its monetary value have arisen as its critical value has become more prominent. With the industrial society evolving into an information-based society, the concept of information as a product, a commodity with its own value, has emerged. The increasing complexity of the society and its reliance on information have only made the concept of information as a commodity more prevalent. As a consequence those people, organizations, and countries that possess the highest quality information are likely to prosper economically, socially, and politically. This was recognized nationally by the 1991 White House Conference on Library and Information Science, which identified "Information for Productivity" as one of its national themes.

For the field of information science, the attention to the value of information has spawned a variety of investigations into the economics of information; the costs of information and information services; the effects of information on decision-making; the savings from effective information acquisition; the effects of information on productivity, sometimes referred to as "downstream productivity"; and the effects of specific information agencies (such as corporate, technical, or medical libraries) on the productivity of organizations. Obviously many of these areas overlap, but it is clear that information has taken on a life of its own, outside the media in which it is contained. Information has become a recognized entity to be measured, evaluated, and priced.

There is another sense of value that is critical to library and information science, that is the notion of value-added functions. Value-added functions are those performed by librarians and information scientists to increase the value of the information by making it more accessible.

Much of the important work in this area has been developed by Robert Taylor (1986). Taylor sees libraries as document-based systems, which are simply one part of the broader rubric of information systems. He identifies a variety of functions that librarians or information scientists perform to enhance the value of information by increasing its accessibility. A condensation of some of the processes that relate both to information systems in general and to libraries in particular include the following:

*Access processes*: processes that help narrow the search for information. These processes include the classification system, indexes, and subject headings. In addition, there are processes that reduce larger amounts of information into manageable quantities for summary and review; these include abstracts, summaries, and graphs.

*Accuracy processes*: processes that decrease the possibility of error in the data or information provided. These processes include the employment of standards to ensure consistency, completeness, and accuracy of bibliographic records; the use of high quality sources to select materials; and the employment of weeding processes to remove inaccurate materials.

*Browsing processes*: processes that permit the user to browse a "neighborhood" of information. Such processes include classification systems that group items of a similar subject or author together. Library classification systems accomplish this purpose, as does the system of subject headings that permits grouping catalog records by subject. Physical book arrangement can also foster browsing, as do book displays or special exhibitions of materials. These processes permit serendipitous discovery of related information.

*Currency processes*: processes that ensure that the materials or data provided are up-to-date. Among these processes are those that continuously review materials (weeding) and order later editions. They also include processes that employ the most recent indexing terms, abstracting terms, and subject headings to reflect current thinking.

*Flexibility (Adaptability) processes*: processes that adapt to the needs and abilities of the user, that provide a variety of methods or techniques to find information. Processes that assist the patron in analyzing, interpreting, and evaluating information fall within this scope as well because such activities provide means of maximizing the usefulness of the information search and the information itself. Obviously human intermediaries, such as librarians, play a vital role in this process as they assist information seekers with various search strategies and as they provide information on those sources that are considered reliable as well as those that are less so.

*Formatting processes*: Processes that affect the physical arrangement and presentation of information. This function often focuses on the arrangement of a particular electronic record on a computer screen. It can also have an institutional context as well, that is, how the institution provides for guidance to the arrangement of its information. In libraries this would include the use of signs and graphics to guide patrons to the appropriate information or services.

*Interfacing processes*: Processes that provide assistance to the user in understanding and using the system. Computer-based systems have screens and navigation systems that facilitate users' access to information contained in them. In libraries, the fundamental interpreter of the system is the librarian. Also known as information intermediaries, librarians perform reference interviews and help dispel the "mystery" of libraries through their knowledge and guidance. Interface processes also include special services that the library staff provide such as orientations, story hours, and summer reading clubs.

*Ordering processes*: Processes that provide basic organization to the collection. These processes include those dividing the collection by subject area, format, or type of user and those separating types of materials such as encyclopedias and other reference works from the rest of the collection.

*Physical access processes*: Processes that improve physical access to library collections or computer databases including circulation systems, check-out desks, study areas, shelving and shelf-reading, and computers that permit searching remote databases and other library collections throughout the nation and world.

Taylor identifies many other value-added processes that could be applied in institutional settings such as libraries, and it is obvious that many of these processes overlap conceptually. For example, ordering processes can also be seen as flexibility processes. Despite the fact that these value-added services play a critical role in locating information, the systems that provide these services, including libraries, are often underestimated in terms of their importance. The reason may well be, at least in part, that by making the information search easier, these processes are transparent. The user doesn't necessarily struggle to find the information (perhaps they simply ask the librarian) and, therefore, they underestimate the complex design of the information system that makes that search so easy. To the extent that such functions are invisible to the information seeker, librarians and other information providers need to find ways to increase the user's understanding of the importance of these processes. Perhaps the status of information professionals would increase if these value-added processes were made more prominent.

*Area 4: Bibliometrics and Citation Analysis*

Wallace (1989) defines bibliometrics as "the application of quantitative methods to the study of information resources" (p. 10). Such a field explores patterns in the production of knowledge as well as the patterns of its use. Examples of the direct use of bibliometric approaches for libraries include (1) Explorations concerning the use or circulation of library materials. Studies of which items circulate or fail to circulate can provide valuable information to the library regarding future purchases or reveal deficiencies in the library's organization or practices. (2) Studies of how materials are used **inside** libraries can provide valuable insights into the information-seeking behavior of patrons and the use of reference materials. (3) Studies of the obsolescence (aging) of library materials can reveal the currency of library collections and the patterns that govern the use of aging materials. (4) Studies of collection overlap, which often involve comparing the collections of two or more libraries to reveal duplications, can help in planning cooperative collection development, revealing unique features of different library collections, and reducing unnecessary expenditures for materials.

Bibliometric studies can also provide a broader understanding of entire disciplines, revealing which authors are most productive within a discipline and which countries or languages produce greater amounts of material within a field. Sometimes consistencies are so great that bibliometric "laws" can be established. Among the most common is Lotka's Law, named after Alfred Lotka. Lotka (1926) observed that with a body of literature, there are a few authors who contribute a large number of publications, a larger number of authors who contribute a smaller group of publications, and then many authors who contribute a few or only one publication. This relationship was expressed as $(1/n^2)$, where n is the number of contributions. Hence, the number of authors making three contributions in a field would be one-ninth $(3^2)$ of the total number of authors. The number of authors making four contributions would be one-sixteenth $(4^2)$. The pattern quickly becomes obvious; far fewer authors will be contributing a large number of contributions. Unlike actual physical laws, Lotka's law is not a perfect description of how authors and publications are related within a discipline, but generally it is a good estimate.

Another law that is frequently mentioned is Bradford's Law or the Bradford distribution, based on the work of Samuel Bradford (1934). Bradford's law deals with the concept of "scatter," which describes in a quantitative manner how articles within a particular field are distributed among periodical titles. What Bradford found is that given a body of journal literature in a particular area (e.g. engineering), the distribution throughout the various journals is not even, nor is the literature consulted equally. Although the distribution is not even, it *is* predictable. Most notably, he found that the spread of journal articles could be placed into three zones. The first zone was the nucleus of the field in which most articles appeared in a relatively small number of journal titles. A second zone contained the same number of articles spread out in a substantially larger number of journals. A third zone contained the same number of articles but scattered among even more titles. This relation was expressed as "$1:n:n^2$." That is, if there were a total of 1,500 articles, the first 500 might be found in ten journals (Zone 1); the next 500 might be found in fifty journals (Zone 2). Thus produces a ratio of Zone 1 to Zone 2 of 1:5. The next 500 articles should therefore be of a ratio of $1:5^2$ or 1:25. This means that Bradford's law would predict that the 500 articles of Zone 3 would be scattered among (10x25) or 250 journal titles. This regularity suggests that there is a predictable scatter, and such regularity can have a significant impact on the selection and development of library collections. Obviously, in selecting materials for library collections, the crucial selections would be those found in the nucleus, or Zone 1, of a discipline. As with Lotka's law, this regularity has its exceptions, but nonetheless it holds for many disciplines and represents an important bibliometric finding.

A related area of bibliometrics is citation analysis. Citation analysis deals with the frequency and pattern of citations (e.g. references cited in articles and books). There are various ways to analyze the patterns of citations. Among them are direct citation, bibliographic coupling, and cocitation. Direct citation analyzes the items cited by authors. Bibliographic coupling and cocitation are closely related but distinct concepts. As Smith has observed:

> Two documents are bibliographically coupled if their reference lists share one or more of the same cited documents. Two documents are cocited when they are jointly cited in one or more subsequently published documents. Thus in cocitation earlier documents become linked because they are later cited together; in bibliographic coupling later documents become linked because they cite the same earlier documents. The difference is that bibliographic coupling is an association intrinsic to the documents (static) while cocitation is a linkage extrinsic to the documents, and one that is valid only so long as they continue to be cocited (dynamic) (Smith 1981, p. 85).

Among the information that can be revealed by citation studies is identification of which works and which authors are most often cited within a given discipline and why items are cited. For collection development or selection in libraries this can be very useful in that it identifies works that may well be influential. Works that are cited frequently are likely to be requested by those reading the article in which the citations appear. Frequently cited authors may be individuals whose works the library may wish to include. The same might be said for frequently cited journal titles. As with other bibliometric practices, citation analysis may be useful beyond the instrumental uses of libraries. It may, for example, help explain which ideas and thinkers tend to influence the conceptual development within a discipline. It also has been used to identify which disciplines appear to be active and whose work is playing a central role in that discipline.

*Area 5: Management and Administrative Issues*

The growth of information technologies has placed additional burdens on the managers of libraries and other information organizations. Given the initial and continuing expenses of these technologies, making the wrong decisions can be expensive in terms of time, money, productivity, and human resources. As information services play a more central role, demands for accountability will grow. This accountability will require increasing levels of sophistication in measuring library services. Among the issues that information scientists have addressed in trying to cope with these managerial burdens are the following:

### IDENTIFYING AND SELECTING INFORMATION TECHNOLOGIES

It is often assumed that the introduction of information technologies always results in increased productivity—this cannot be assumed. Administrators must be able to determine which processes lend themselves to effective computerization and which do not. Once the processes to be computerized are identified, the appropriate technology must be identified and installed. The essential steps are: (a) identify appropriate computer vendors; (b) develop criteria and establish decision-making structures for comparing and evaluating vendors; (c) develop time-tables for implementing automation; (d) plan on-site visits and demonstrations; (e) develop and implement training and orientation on automated systems for staff; and (f) conduct post-implementation evaluation to determine if the technologies are performing effectively.

### DEALING WITH HUMAN FACTORS IN TECHNOLOGY

Although information science often focuses on the technology itself, the application of most technologies requires human participation. Over the last two decades, it has become increasingly obvious that how people deal with computers can have a significant effect on how effective they are. Similarly, it has become clear that technologies can have significant effects on the people who use them. For this reason, information science explores how technologies can be effectively implemented, what factors generate resistance or acceptance of technologies, and what aspects of technologies have the potential to create physical problems for people. This latter area has spawned a field called ergonomics, which explores the fit between people and machines. This will be discussed further in the next chapter.

DEVELOPING MANAGEMENT INFORMATION SYSTEMS/INFORMATION RESOURCES
MANAGEMENT (IRM)/RECORDS MANAGEMENT

Organizations increasingly rely on information to perform their functions. Managing information inside organizations has many purposes: for record maintenance and oversight (which has spawned an entire subfield referred to as records management); for decision-making; and for strategic and tactical planning. The nature of the information can be extremely varied: data, text, images, sound, or multimedia. Making the best management decisions relies, in part, on an organization's ability to acquire, access, and evaluate information in a timely fashion. As organizations have become increasingly complex and their reliance on rapid access to high quality information has grown, the field known as information resources management (IRM) or information management has emerged. Managing information has become a task with the same significance as managing the fiscal and human resources of an organization.

IRM is much more than file maintenance. It requires that one view information as the life blood of the organization. As such, each aspect of the organization needs to be considered in terms of how it produces, organizes, selects, and disseminates information for use by its members. Among the major objectives of IRM are (1) ensuring that the relevant documents are made available for decision making; (2) developing and implementing cost/benefit analysis of information provision; (3) creating an environment in which IRM and the information manager are perceived by management and administration as a major contributor to the organization; (4) assisting in the evaluation and implementation of information management technologies; (5) defining responsibility and accountability for information management, preservation, and disposal; (6) creating an environment in which the corporate managers recognize properly organized and accessible information as vital for critical corporate decisions (Levitan, 1982).

From these objectives it is clear that IRM has many aspects and responsibilities. The need to ensure that the correct information be provided in a timely manner and the acquisition of appropriate, cost-effective information systems are basic to this activity. In addition, there are political and educational components, including getting organizational leaders and staff to recognize the importance of information and the value of the individual who organizes that information and then training staff in the creation and use of information. The growth of new positions, such as chief information officers (CIOs), is testimony to the increasing recognition of how important IRM is to the survival of organizations.

MEASUREMENT AND EVALUATION OF LIBRARY AND INFORMATION SERVICES

Most information services take place within an organizational context, and administrators and managers need the means to determine whether their organizations are, in fact, accomplishing what they set out to do. Such information is critical not only in evaluating current activities, but also in planning for staffing, planning future services, and determining the direction of collection development. It also provides political and economic justification for budget requests. To this end, information science is concerned with how to measure and evaluate information services.

Some typical targets of measurement and evaluation include collections; services, including reference and document delivery; programs; and staff. Among the most common measures for evaluating information services are *user* and *use* studies. These studies are usually conducted through questionnaires, focus groups, interviews, or analysis of available data such as circulation or interlibrary loan data. The focus of these studies is usually on some aspect of the collection or services provided and the satisfaction of the user with those collections and services. Although user and use studies may appear the same and are interrelated, they focus on different aspects. A user study focuses on the individual or group of individuals. It might examine demographic features such as age, income, sex, and level of education and analyze these in relation to library use. It might focus on the reasons individuals use an information service or where they sought information before coming. Such studies attempt to answer the question: who is using the library and why? An off-shoot of user studies is nonuser studies. Nonusers can provide vital information in evaluating a library for they can reveal organizational inadequacies that prevent full use of library services. Perhaps individuals or groups of individuals do not know that there are library services to help them; perhaps they consider the library unfriendly, or as not having the materials or services they need.

Use studies on the other hand, focus on what is used. They might look at the subjects consulted (e.g., fiction/nonfiction, specialized subject areas); the number of items used; where they were used (e.g. in-house or checked out); the types of materials used (AV, print, computer disks), types of services used (reference, children's), the types of programming used, or whether a librarian was consulted. Such information can provide valuable planning information. As might be expected, because of the close connection between users and uses of libraries, it is common that both are studied and cross-analyzed. Hence, libraries might look not only at which parts of a collection are used most, but also, who uses that collection.

There are many ways to measure library services and different ways to measure them. Perhaps the best known measures of library performance are found in the public library world. These are measures developed by the Public Library Association (PLA, a division of ALA) and are referred to as the "output measures" for public libraries (PLA 1987). The measures were intended to provide guidance on measuring public library performance and suggest methods of data collection. In addition, they help provide consistency and comparability among libraries. Many of these are per capita measurements, that is, they attempt to determine uses per person among the potential user community. Hence there is a circulation per capita measure which determines how many circulations per person occurred in a given year. There are also fill rate measures, which attempt to measure the percentage of successfully filled requests of a particular type. A title fill rate measure would determine the percentage of times a request by title was filled. The recommended measures include those for program attendance; library visits; registration; in-house use of materials; reference transactions; title, subject, author, and browser fill rates; turnover rate (the average number of times a book was circulated in a given year); and document delivery. As an extension of these general output measures, the Public Library Association (PLA) worked with the Young Adult Library Services Association (YALSA) to create output measures specifically designed for young adults (Walter 1995), and with the Association for Library Service to Children to create output measures for children's services (Walter 1992). Academic libraries lack generally adopted output measures and rely in part on standards set by the Association of College and Research Libraries (1986).

There has been considerable debate over the value and validity of the output measures, but they clearly dominate measurement activities among public libraries. Some of the output measures could equally apply to other types of libraries, but others have limited application. Some measures that can be useful are obsolescence studies (aging of the collection), shelf availability (whether the item sought is on the shelf), reference satisfaction, cost-effectiveness, and cost-benefit measures. Some types of libraries have an easier time than others in measuring and evaluating their services using these measures. The more generalized the activities and purposes of a library, the more difficult it is to measure its effectiveness. As a rule public libraries, notwithstanding the output measures, are more difficult to assess than special libraries because the purposes and activities are not as clearly defined. This is especially true in trying to measure productivity, cost-effectiveness, and cost-benefit ratios (Koenig 1990).

## SUMMARY

The field of information science has much to offer when one is considering how to improve information services. The growth of new information technologies has provided a considerable impetus to research in information science, and the efforts of information scientists have contributed much to our understanding of how information is generated, organized, disseminated, and used. Librarians can make good use of much of this research and also contribute to it.

A central value underlying this field is the desire to study how to make information accessible and usable. Information science is designed in large part to satisfy individuals' information needs. As such it has much in common with the purposes of libraries and librarianship. An understanding how to define information needs and wants, how individuals behave when they search for information, how information systems can best be designed and used to satisfy information needs, is critical if librarians are to continue to perform their jobs effectively in the future. To a large extent, librarians must rely on information scientists as a source for this understanding. As the field of information science grows, so should the librarian's interest in it. A strong partnership can only benefit those who use library services.

## REFERENCES

Allen, Bryce L. "Cognitive Research in Information Science: Implications for Design." In *Annual Review of Information Science and Technology (ARIST)* 26 (1991): 3–37.

Allen, Bryce L. *Information Tasks: Toward a User-Centered Approach to Information Systems.* New York: Academic, 1996.

Association of College and Research Libraries. "Standards for College Libraries, 1986." *College and Research Libraries* 47 (March 1986): 189–200.

Bates, Marcia J., Deborah N. Wilde, and Susan Siegfried. "An Analysis of Search Terminology Used by Humanities Scholars: The Getty Online Searching Project Report Number 1." *Library Quarterly* 63 (January 1993): 1–39.

Belkin, Nicholas J., Helen M. Brooks, and Robert N. Oddy. "ASK for Information Retrieval." *Journal of Documentation* 38 (1982): 61–71.

Bradford, Samuel C. "Sources of Information on Specific Subjects." *Engineering* (1934): 85–86.

Brittain, J. M. "The Distinctive Characteristics of Information Science." *Theory and Application of Information Research: Proceedings of the Second International Research Forum on Information Science.* Edited by Ole Harbo and Leif Kajberg. London: Mansell, 1980.

Broadbent, Elaine. "A Study of Humanities Faculty Library Information Seeking Behavior." *Cataloguing and Classification Quarterly* 6 (Spring 1986): 23–37.

Bush, Vannevar. "As We May Think." *Atlantic Monthly* 176 (July 1945): 101–108.

Chen, Ching-Chih and Peter Hernon. *Information Seeking: Assessing and Anticipating User Needs.* New York: Neal-Schuman, 1982.

Debons, Anthony. *The Information Professional: Survey of an Emerging Field.* New York: Dekker: 1981.

Dervin, Brenda. "An Overview of Sense-Making: Concepts, Methods, and Results to Date." Paper presented at the International Communication Association Annual Meeting, May 1983, Dallas, Texas.

Durrance, Joan C. "Information Needs: Old Song, New Tune." In *Rethinking the Library.* Washington, D.C.: U.S. GPO, 1989, 159–178.

Froehlich, Thomas J. "Relevance Reconsidered—Towards an Agenda for the 21st Century." *Journal of the American Society of Information Science* 45 (April 1994): 124–134.

Harter, Stephen. *Online Information Retrieval.* Orlando: Academic Press, 1986.

Koenig, Michael E. D. "Information Services and Downstream Productivity." In *Annual Review of Information Science and Technology* 25 (1990): 74–76.

Krikelas, James. "Information-Seeking Behavior: Patterns and Concepts." *Drexel Library Quarterly* 19 (Spring 1983): 5–20.

Kuhlthau, Carol C. "Inside the Search Process: Information Seeking from the User's Perspective." *Journal of the American Society of Information Science.* (1991): 361–371.

Lee, Chingkwei Adrienne and John N. Olsgaard. "Linguistics and Information Science." In *Principles and Applications of Information Science for Library Professionals.* Edited by John N. Olsgaard. Chicago: ALA, 1989, 27–36.

Levitan, Karen B. "Information Resources Management." *Annual Review of Information Science and Technology (ARIST)* 17 (1982): 227–266.

Lotka, Alfred J. "The Frequency Distribution of Scientific Productivity." *Journal of the Washington Academy of Sciences* 16 (1926): 317–323.

Machlup, Fritz and Una Mansfield, eds. *The Study of Information: Interdisciplinary Messages.* New York: Wiley, 1983.

Mann, Thomas. "The Principle of Least Effort." In *Library Research Models: A Guide to Classification, Cataloging, and Computers.* New York: Oxford University, 1993, 91–101.

Meadows, A.J. *Communication in Science*. London: Butterworths, 1974.

*Oxford English Dictionary*, 2d ed. Oxford: Clarendon Press, 1989.

Pao, Miranda Lee. *Concepts of Information Retrieval*. Englewood, Colo.: Libraries Unlimited, 1989, 54–55.

Public Library Association. *Output Measures for Public Libraries*. 2nd ed. Chicago: ALA, 1987.

Rayward, Boyd. "Library and Information Sciences," In *The Study of Information: Interdisciplinary Messages*. Edited by Fritz Machlup and Una Mansfield. New York: Wiley, 1983, 343–363.

Rouse, William B. "Human Information Seeking and Design of Information Systems." *Information Processing and Management* 20 (1984).

Saracevic, T. "Relevance: A Review of and a Framework for the Thinking on the Notion in Information Science." *Journal of the American Society for Information Science* 26 (1975): 321–343.

Shaw, Debora. "The Human-Computer Interface for Information Retrieval." *Annual Review of Information Science and Technology (ARIST)* 26 (1991): 155–195.

Shera, Jesse H. and Donald B. Cleveland. "History and Foundations of Information Science." In *Annual Review of Information Science and Technology*, Vol. 12. Edited by Martha E. Williams. Knowledge Industry, 1977, 249.

Smith, Linda C. "Artificial Intelligence and Information Retrieval." In *Annual Review of Information Science and Technology (ARIST)* 22 (1987): 41–77.

———. "Citation Analysis." *Library Trends* 30 (summer 1981): 83–106.

Taylor, Robert S. "Professional Aspects of Information Science and Technology." *Annual Review of Information Science and Technology*. Vol. 1. Edited by Carlos A. Cuardra. New York: Wiley, 1966. 15–40.

———. "Question–Negotiation and Information Seeking in Libraries." *College and Research Libraries* 29 (May 1968): 178–194.

———. *Value-Added Processes in Information Systems*. Norwood, N.J.: Ablex, 1986.

Van Styvendaele, J. H. "University Scientists as Seekers of Information: Sources of References to Periodical Literature," *Journal of Librarianship* 9 (October 1977): 270–277

Vedder, Richard G. "An Overview of Expert Systems." In *Expert Systems in Libraries*. Edited by Rao Aluri and Donald E. Riggs. Norwood, NJ: Ablex, 1990.

Wallace, Danny P. "Bibliometrics and Citation Analysis." In *Principles and Applications of Information Science for Library Professionals*. Edited by John N. Olsgaard. Chicago: ALA, 1989, 10–26.

Walter, Virginia A. *Output Measures and More: Planning and Evaluating Public Library Services for Young Adults*. Chicago: ALA, 1995.

———. *Output Measures for Public Library Services to Children: A Manual of Standardized Procedures*. Chicago: ALA, 1992.

Wellisch, Hans. "From Information Science to Informatics: A Terminological Investigation." *Journal of Librarianship* 4 (July 1972): 157–187.

Wilson, Patrick., "The Face Value Rule in Reference Work," *RQ* 25 (summer 1986): 468–475.

———. *Second-Hand Knowledge*. Westport, Conn.: Greenwood, 1983, 10.

# 3

# Redefining the Library: The Impacts and Implications of Technological Change

Obtaining current and accurate information is central to our economic, political, and social well-being, as well as to our ability to compete in the global marketplace. Because libraries have been a major source of information for centuries, they have held a special place in the life of the community. The growth of electronic information technologies has challenged this role and resulted in considerable instability and uncertainty among librarians. Librarians have been forced to redefine and restructure library services, and in the process, the library itself. New information technologies have revolutionized information access, reducing the distinction between the physical library collection and the information stored beyond its walls. Some have said that the emergence of such technologies will lead to the emergence of the "virtual library," where information is accessed remotely without the need of a physical library at all. Only time will tell.

There is no doubt, however, that the increasingly critical need for information and its increasingly electronic nature have produced competitors and alternatives to traditional library practice. These competitors also recognize that information is a valued commodity and that both profit and power can be acquired if its dissemination can be controlled. Electronic information technologies stimulate and promote intense competition in the information marketplace, and as such, libraries must understand their capacities and limitations.

It is very tempting to accept uncritically the belief that new information technologies inevitably lead to progress. Librarians are no more immune than others to this belief. After all, the excitement generated by such technologies is often considerable, and one is often made to feel "behind the times" when doubts are raised. Perhaps librarians have additional reasons to be accepting. They may embrace technology because they think it will raise their status and image and put them on the cutting edge of change. As a consequence, librarians sometimes fail to demand evidence that the technologies adopted actually have an overall beneficial effect on library service (Bushman 1990). The alternative to this uncritical acceptance is not to become a Luddite, however, lamenting all new technologies and pining for the old days of print materials and card catalogs. Rather, we must all remind ourselves that technological developments need to be evaluated objectively and critically, in the same manner that other new techniques or devices are evaluated. Technological developments produce both positive and negative changes. The fact that the consequences of new technologies can be both good and bad is not to say that their use should be discouraged; only that they should be applied appropriately and their negative as well as positive effects anticipated and, when necessary, ameliorated.

## INFORMATION TECHNOLOGIES IN THE TWENTIETH CENTURY

Understanding the historical development of information technologies in the twentieth century helps in this evaluative process. The term *technology* has very broad application and can be defined in many ways. For the purposes of this discussion, *Webster's* (1970) provides a sound working definition: "a technical method of achieving a practical purpose" (p. 2348). As such, the term can be applied to non-electronic tools as well as electronic ones. Given this definition, it is clear that technologies have been around in libraries for many years. A prime example is the manual card catalog of the nineteenth century. This technology allowed us to consult a significant body of knowledge by systematically scanning physical representations of books and other materials, that is, the catalog cards, albeit with varying success. Some would argue that even today the manual card catalog has some distinct advantages over electronic ones (Baker 1994). In addition, the nineteenth century also saw the introduction of the electric light in library stacks, an addition that undoubtedly helped many locate materials without burning down the library. It also saw the development of important intellectual technologies such as the Dewey Decimal Classification System, which is discussed in greater detail in Chapter 6.

The following historical overview is a thumbnail sketch from 1900 forward and is intended to provide a basic outline of these developments and to provide a framework for discussing the issues that are now facing our field.

*Developments in Microphotography: 1900–1960*

The first half of the twentieth century was a very fruitful period for technological development. Major improvements in communications and transportation were especially notable. These included the growth and expansion of telephone services, photo technologies, improvements to airplanes and automobiles, development of the cathode ray tube, diode, triode, and photoelectric cell. It also saw the development of "punch cards" that could be used for mechanical sorting—the forerunner of computer technologies (Buckland 1996).

In terms of their effects on libraries, perhaps the most notable developments in the first half of the century related to the new photographic technologies, especially microphotography. This technology permitted the reproduction of print documents (reprography) onto film (microforms). The physical format was usually a roll of film, the microfilm; or a rectangular card, the microcard. As an alternative to paper, microphotography had many advantages: it could provide much more information in a more compact medium and it was lighter and easier to store. In addition, it proved to be an exceptional medium for the preservation of materials that were likely to deteriorate over time, such as newspapers, magazines, and documents. By the 1920s, there were tremendous successes in reducing print to microform as well as in developing equipment to read the microforms. The potential of microphotography for the library led at least one enthusiast to suggest that the actual book be photographed and attached to the back of the catalog card. Hence, once the user found the right catalog card, the item was literally on the back of the card! (Rider 1944).

Reprography saw additional advances in the 1960s with the development of duplicating machines, most notably the photocopier. This was a tremendous addition to the arsenal of reprographic devices, yet unless one reflects on it, the effect copying equipment has on society is easily lost. The ability to make multiple copies of individual pages had a profound effect on the ability to provide documents over considerable distances and to allow many more individuals to possess the intellectual content of a document simultaneously. (And resulted probably in a great increase in paper consumption as well!) Although not as dramatic as the invention of the printing press, it certainly revolutionized communications for libraries because it permitted them much greater flexibility in the distribution of published materials. In essence, as De Gennaro (1989) observed, "Libraries became publishers of single copies on demand" (p. 42).

*First Application of Computers to Libraries: The 1960s*

Our contemporary sense of technology deals with electronic devices, especially computers. Although the notion of computers has been around more than a hundred years, their application to libraries did not begin in earnest until the 1960s. It is during this time that one encounters the term library automation, although it was first known as "library mechanization." Bierman (1991) defines library automation as "the application of computer and communication technologies to traditional library processes and services" (p. 67).

The 1960s was largely a period of big mainframe computers, punch cards, and mechanical sorting machines. These applications were typically used by small groups of researchers. The first applications of online information retrieval developed in the early 1960s. These were prototype systems, usually consisting of a small database and one terminal. One of the major developers of early online systems during this time was the System Development Corporation (SDC) in California, which produced some of the earliest computers for simple full-text searching and document retrieval (Hahn 1996). There was also another major commercial competitor, the Lockheed Missiles and Space Company, which made major contributions to computerized information retrieval. Working primarily with government agencies such as NASA, Lockheed developed the DIALOG system around 1964. By the early 1970s, Lockheed realized the commercial potential of an online search service and in 1972 created the Lockheed Retrieval Service. Most people simply know it as DIALOG, now a division of Knight-Ridder Information Services.

The rationale for the application of computers to library processes was simple: computerization would increase efficiency of library services, produce costs savings, and reduce the size of staff. Among the typical uses of computers in libraries during this time were creating book catalogs and generating purchasing orders.

The most significant library application of technology during this period was the creation of a standardized bibliographic format that could be read and manipulated by a computer. Machine Readable Cataloging or MARC, created by the Library of Congress, became a standard for the creation of bibliographic records. MARC allowed bibliographic data to be entered, stored, and disseminated electronically on computer tapes. (See Chapter 6 for further discussion of the MARC format.) Once records were centralized in this fashion, the first major use of the tapes was to generate catalog cards. The uses of these computer generated tapes, however, quickly expanded as its potentialities were grasped by support agencies linked to libraries known as bibliographic utilities.

Historically, the most prominent bibliographic utility was the Ohio College Library Center (OCLC), incorporated as a not-for-profit corporation in 1967. In 1981 it changed its name to the Online Computing Library Center. OCLC offered access to the MARC database, which was supplemented by the cataloging efforts of the OCLC member libraries. OCLC loaded the MARC tapes and made these records available to member libraries. The libraries could locate and examine the bibliographic record, make changes for their local institutions as needed, and then electronically order catalog cards to their specifications from OCLC. In a short time the cards would arrive at the library, ready for filing. In turn, their bibliographic records would be entered into the OCLC database. In effect, this created an online shared cataloging network. The advantages of OCLC quickly became clear to many libraries, and in 1972, OCLC opened its membership to nonacademic libraries as well (Grosch, 1995). This led to tremendous growth in membership and increased cooperation among different types of libraries and among regional library networks.

Over the decades, OCLC services have grown, offering interlibrary loan and document delivery, acquisition systems, serials control, electronic publishing, communications access, and reference services. But its early contribution was primarily in the area of shared cataloging. Other bibliographic utilities appeared. For example, major research libraries formed a group called the Research Libraries Group (RLG). This group created the Research Libraries Information Network (RLIN), offering access to a tremendous bibliographic database and thousands of research records. Today, it is difficult to imagine the major changes that were created by these utilities. The impact on some cataloging departments, for example, was substantial, resulting in a reduction in the number of catalogers.

While libraries were introducing these changes, other developments were occurring, such as the computerizing of specialized bodies of knowledge for scientific and medical purposes. The National Library of Medicine (NLM), one of the great special libraries in the world, was confronted with a common problem in the sciences—the rapid expansion of scientific and technical knowledge. For years NLM had been indexing the medical literature manually, but this was becoming extremely cumbersome and costly. The decision to input bibliographic citations on computer tapes led to a computerized version of its medical index, *Index Medicus*. At first, the computer tapes were used to produce a paper copy of the index, but it was not long before it became obvious that the tapes themselves could be searched, creating a searchable database that is one of the great achievements of the decade.

Other events occurring in the 1960s would have even greater impact for the future. In 1969, the Defense Advanced Research Projects Research Agency (DARPA) within the Department of Defense developed a computer network called ARPANET at the University of California at Los Angeles. The network was developed to improve government-sponsored research by electronically linking organizations at different sites and allowing them to share research and data (Tenner 1994). One of the fundamental innovations of this system was the first practical use of a new technology to break information messages into discrete packets, which could be sent independently of one another across "packet-switching" networks. These packets could be reassembled at the receiving computer. Such a method increased reliability and speed. This process substantially improved transmission of research data and analysis. Although ARPANET membership was restricted to institutions with defense-related contracts, this network was the genesis of what would become the Internet, and it advanced development of key features such as file transfer, remote access of data, and electronic mail (Bishop 1990).

These advances had little effect on libraries in the 1960s. Library automation at that time focused primarily on the creation of computerized bibliographic records for catalog card production. Some attention was paid to automating basic maintenance functions including the creation of book catalogs and generating purchase orders, but there remained considerable skepticism on the part of librarians that automation could be applied practically to most library functions and services

(Grosch 1995). The knowledge base, however, was expanding and the application of computers was inevitable.

*Use of Online Information Technologies for Reference: The 1970s*

The increasing sophistication of computer technologies, including the development of the minicomputer, made online interactive capabilities a reality (Grosch 1995). The application of online computer access for information retrieval, replacing card files and print indexes, represents one of the most significant breaks from the past. Major information-dependent institutions, such as the military and business and industry, quickly recognized the potential for these capabilities. Consequently, commercial vendors developed a variety of databases and made them available through telephone lines. Thus, a library in Chicago could access databases that were created and made available by a vendor in Los Angeles. Although these vendors did not necessarily design their services for libraries, it was clear that libraries would be substantial users of the systems.

Libraries quickly created online services for library patrons. Most early online services were developed in academic libraries, primarily because the databases generally available at that time were scientific and technical in nature. Because of the cost and sophistication of these early systems, academic libraries created specifically-designed services, often with their own separate facilities or space and a special, trained staff to conduct online searches. Most online searches were mediated by a trained librarian or an information specialist because the cost of a search depended in large part on what database was being searched and how long it took to perform the search. Even then, libraries often had to pass at least part of the costs on to the individual patron—a practice that runs counter to the normal practice of libraries in providing free services, and which has caused continued consternation.

Associated with the development of online access was the creation of search strategies that could exploit the unique flexibility of computerized access to information. Perhaps the most prominent development in this area was Boolean searching, which permitted one to search a database using logical connectors such as *and, or,* or *not*. Such logical techniques permitted very sophisticated searching by narrowing the search and obtaining more precise access to large bodies of knowledge in a much shorter period of time. Another strategy involved keyword searching. The computer searched for a particular word or phrase anywhere in the bibliographic record, including an abstract. This strategy was very different from searches that required certain subject terms or searches that were limited to titles or authors.

In addition to the use of computers for reference purposes, the 1970s also saw the beginning of early attempts to automate library circulation, serials control, cataloging, and acquisition systems. These systems were a lot more complex than anticipated, and they did not reach maturity until a decade later.

*The Maturing of Local Electronic Information Technologies and the Growth of the Internet: The 1980s*

The 1980s saw a remarkable revolution in information access with the development of the Compact Disk—Read Only Memory (CD-ROM). One small, 4 1/2" disk could contain all, or a great percentage, of the contents of standard reference tools, such as the *Reader's Guide to Periodical Literature*. The disks, along with updates, were sent to the library by an information vendor. They were operated on computer equipment that ran on software also provided by the vendor. CD-ROMs had several distinct advantages over online searching. First, the CD-ROM was locally stored; for all practical purposes the computer databases were in the library. There was no need for a telephone line; all the user had to do was come to the library. Second, the disks could hold a tremendous amount of information, which could be consulted at one time. Third, CD-ROMs had the flexibility of Boolean searching. The material could be searched by author, title, and subject, and by one term or multiple terms, similar to online access. Fourth, CD-ROMs provided the computing power of online searching at a fixed cost. This was very helpful in the financial management of libraries. Costs for online searching were indeterminant, depending on the frequency of use and length of time per search, and so budgeting for these services was difficult. CD-ROMs, on the other hand, had known annual subscription costs.

In addition to radical changes in information access, the 1980s saw substantial developments in automating internal processes such as online catalogs, circulation systems, and acquisitions systems.

### THE DEVELOPMENT OF ONLINE COMPUTER ACCESS CATALOGS (OPACS)

These systems permitted access to the bibliographic records of the library, similar to the manual card catalog. However, the system could be searched by author, title, subject, and sometimes combinations of these terms. In addition, some systems could be searched by call number or ISBN number. There was no longer any need to buy catalog cards or hire individuals to file them. The introduction of OPACs meant the eventual removal of the card catalog, the opportunity for remote access, and a change in the physical environment of the library. It also meant major investments in hardware, software, and computer maintenance.

THE DEVELOPMENT OF ONLINE CIRCULATION SYSTEMS

Once the materials of the library could be accessed electronically, it seemed a logical step to create a system that would control the circulation of these materials. Although the 1970s saw very primitive developments in this area, it was in the 1980s that commercial vendors developed automated circulation systems in earnest. These systems, referred to as "turn-key" systems, were introduced with little modification from one library to another. These systems were relatively inexpensive, and although supposedly one could simply "turn the key and start the system," it was seldom that smooth. In addition, there were costs associated with the time it took staff to prepare the materials for the system, such as barcoding books and converting the library's records into machine-readable format. Staff needed additional time to weed the collection, as well, since there was little reason to spend money to input old, unused materials.

For the most part, automated circulation systems were designed so that staff could check out the materials for the patron. During the 1980s, however, some academic libraries implemented systems that enabled patrons to check out their own books. These systems were known as "self-initiated services." They could also track overdue items, send out recall notices, and produce reports on the circulation of library materials. Such systems helped in analyzing how the library collection was being used and, therefore, in planning.

AUTOMATED ACQUISITIONS SYSTEMS

The 1980s also saw the burgeoning of systems designed to help libraries acquire materials. Some of the larger book vendors, such as Blackwell North America and Baker and Taylor, were quite active in developing these systems. The acquisition system was directly connected to the vendors. The library would order its materials through terminals in the library, and the materials would be sent to the library. The acquisition system could monitor budgets, setting limits so that a particular department could not exceed its budget, and produce reports for analysis and evaluation. It might also include a serials check-in system so that the cumbersome tasks of checking in magazines and other periodicals could be performed without labor-intensive activity. In addition, an automated acquisition system permitted the library to create an electronic profile of its needs, and the vendor could automatically send materials that matched the profile without the library ordering each item. This saved time for the library and for the vendor, who did not have to process so many individual orders.

### INTEGRATED LIBRARY SYSTEMS

The result of performing so many basic library functions by computer was the growth of what is called Integrated Library Systems (ILS). ILS consists of the computerized integration of six key functions: acquisitions, serials, cataloging, online catalog (OPAC), circulation, and collection management. Among the companies that have developed such systems are Innovative Interface, Inc. (III), Data Research Associates (DRA), Geac Computers, Inc., VTLS, Inc., and Ameritech Library Systems. Through ILS, the library could reduce duplication of effort and coordinate and share information more efficiently through the departments that process and use library materials.

*The Linked System Project/Linked Systems Protocol*

As online catalogs proliferated, it became obvious that there would be a great advantage if the computers of various libraries and other information organizations could be made to "talk" to each other. Because various developers had created systems that were incompatible with each other, this had proved an elusive goal. The incompatibility problem led to the creation of the Linked System Project. The participants in this project included the American Library Association, OCLC, the Research Libraries Information Network, the Western Library Network, and the Library of Congress with funding from the Council on Library Resources. Their efforts produced the linked systems protocol (LSP), otherwise known as the Z39.50 standard (National Information Standards Organization 1994).

The protocol is a national standard for bibliographic information retrieval that sets standards so that different automated systems can be linked together electronically. With the development of this protocol, authorized users could consult not only their own online catalogs, but the online catalogs of countless other libraries and information organizations. In essence, the LSP permits us to think of our nation of libraries as one library collection (Buckland and Lynch 1987, 1988). Although there was much concerted effort toward the development of this protocol in the 1980s, it wasn't until the 1990s that the protocol, in conjunction with major improvements in telecommunications technologies, made significant gains in linking online bibliographic systems. These accomplishments contributed to the next evolutionary advance, the Internet.

*The Internet*

The Internet is a term applied to an electronic network that permits access to thousands of computer networks. The use of the Internet has grown quickly in the last few years and is available in over one hundred countries (*World Almanac* 1997). There were approximately 64 million adult users of the Internet in the United States in 1999, up from 53.5 million users in 1998 (Mediamark, 1999). According to data reported from the Emerging Technologies Research Group, nearly three-quarters of Internet users consider the Internet indispensable, and 60 percent of those who use the Internet for business purposes use it daily (Emerging Technologies Research Group 1997). There is an additional 55 million adults who indicate either that they intend to begin using the Internet in the next year or that they would like to learn more about it. This suggests that the number of U.S. users is likely to grow substantially in the near future (Emerging Technologies Research Group 1997).

The Internet is the product of a marriage between the technology perfected by the Department of Defense's ARPANET and the National Science Foundation (NSF). In 1984, NSF was establishing national supercomputing centers to provide high-speed computing for research purposes at major research sites, including several universities. These supercomputing centers could perform some of the most advanced research in the world. Given the importance of these centers, there was a need to facilitate communication among them. Consequently, NSF needed a "high-speed telecommunications backbone." At the same time, funding from the Department of Defense for ARPANET was beginning to decline. An agreement was reached wherein NSF would establish a civilian network (NSFNET) using the ARPANET technology. This electronic backbone now serves as one of the essential components of the

Internet. The NSF also played an important role in increasing participants by encouraging faculty and students at universities to participate and by inviting universities to join the network for a flat, reasonable fee.

As computing power became more and more important for research, there was a need to develop faster and faster means of electronic communication. The issue became a popular political one in the 1990s as the importance of research and computer technologies for national productivity and international competitiveness became a matter of public discussion in the political arena. The Bush administration (with strong support from then Democratic Senator Al Gore) introduced legislation—the National High Performance Computing Act of 1991—to develop an "information highway" that could drastically increase the amount of transmittable information. The goal of this legislation was not only to maintain and further develop an extremely efficient electronic highway for the transmission of information, it also mandated the creation of the National Research and Education Network (NREN). NREN's purpose was to provide electronic links and access to federal agencies, industry and business, libraries, and educational institutions. This linking provided access not only to the institutions themselves, but to the information resources contained within them. In essence, what was being proposed was a virtual library, where resources could be consulted from countless sources at a tremendous speed—the speed that only electronic access could provide. The research and educational implications of such a network are manifest. The outgrowth of this legislation was the creation of the National Information Infrastructure (still today more a concept than a reality), the policy implications of which are discussed in more detail in Chapter 4.

Although the early development of the Internet was funded by the government, the 1980s and '90s witnessed increased participation by those with a significant stake in its development and use. These participants include the telecommunications industry (e.g. telephone, television, and cable industries) on which much of the highway relies and will rely in the future. With the shift in political attitudes in the 1990s toward greater privatization and less reliance on government support, the Clinton administration emphasized more corporate participation in the Internet's development, with the government providing limited financial assistance and some regulatory relief (Gomery 1994). This trend is expected to continue.

The Internet is, in essence, a network of many networks. These computer networks are able to "talk" to each other using standardized practices referred to as communication protocols (Tenant 1992, p. 1). The protocol used on the Internet is referred to as the Transmission Control Protocol/Internet Protocol (TCP/IP), which was originally developed by ARPANET.

There are several fundamental features of the Internet: electronic mail, remote login, and file transfer.

Electronic mail (e-mail) permits an Internet user to communicate electronically with individuals or organizations. Messages can be sent locally or worldwide. The benefits for both personal and professional communication are immense, as ideas can be easily and quickly exchanged. The potential for collaboration among scientists and other researchers is clear. Electronic mail can also be employed to communicate with multiple individuals simultaneously. There are different models for multiple individuals accessing messages sent on e-mail. For example, information can be centralized by posting a message on a bulletin board, which individuals can access as needed. Another model is a Listserv. Listservs usually deal with a particular topic or area of interest, and interested individuals can subscribe. (In some cases, membership to a Listserv is restricted.) There is usually an administrator who handles the membership and other administrative functions. Listservs permit individuals to receive messages from and send messages to all subscribers. As messages are sent to the Listserv they are also distributed to all the subscribers on the mailing list. Thus, a common message can be distributed to thousands of individuals, providing information and often promoting further discussion and responses from Listserv members. (See Appendix I for a selective list of Listservs for library and information science.)

Remote login allows an individual to access thousands of computer systems located anywhere in the world. A user can search an electronic database or library catalog anywhere in the world by following the necessary standardized protocols referred to as *Telnet*. Internet protocol (IP) addresses are established for each remote computer system and through Telnet a user can connect with a remote computer. Tenant (1992) identifies the significant advantage of remote login:

What makes this application truly remarkable is that ease and speed of access are not dependent upon proximity. An Internet user can connect to a system on the other side of the globe as easily as . . . he can connect to a system in the next building. In addition, since many Internet users are not at present charged for their network use by their institutions, or at least are not charged by the level of their use, cost is often not a significant inhibitor of usage. Therefore the barriers of distance, time and costs, which are often significant when using other forms of electronic communication, can be reduced in the Internet environment (p. 2).

The last feature of the Internet is **file transfer**. A logical feature of such a system is the ability to transfer files from one computer to another. Consider the many types of information that could be usefully transmitted: reports, numerical data, sounds, and images. To this end, a protocol referred to as the *File Transfer Protocol (FTP)* has been developed to allow users to copy electronic files. Such transfers can occur from one computer to another or make large numbers of electronic files, sometimes referred to as "archives," which anyone can access for the purpose of downloading these files whenever convenient.

In addition, various navigation tools or "browsers" have been developed that improve access to the Internet, and undoubtedly many more will be developed in the future. These tools assist the user in gaining access to the many resources on the Internet. Traditionally, these browsers have been text-based, that is they could not transmit video, sound, or images. Of these types, perhaps the best known is Gopher, developed at the University of Minnesota. Accessing the Internet and the browsers must be accomplished through telecommunication packages. One of the first of these was Kermit, which permitted a user to access electronic networks and transfer and download information. The next emphasis on Internet resources evolved with the development of the World Wide Web (WWW or "The Web"), developed by the European Particle Physics Laboratory (CERN) in Switzerland in 1989.

*The World Wide Web*

The vastness of the Internet is intimidating and its lack of organization, coupled with the quantity of information available, can be overwhelming. The Web is not the same as the Internet, nor is it a particular computer program. Rather, it is an interface and navigation tool that provides a means of structuring Internet documents and relating them to other documents so that maximum use can be made of Internet resources (December and Randall 1995).

Originally, the Web provided a hypertext environment in which to transmit scientific information among researchers. Subsequently, the types of information and applications expanded markedly and became extremely useful for business, industry, students, and the general population.

In a hypertext environment, documents have visible links to other documents. The links are highlighted or otherwise identified in the text of the document and are referred to as hypertext links. This means that publications on the Internet can be linked by highlighting ideas within the texts of these publications. In addition, a hypermedia environment is created. That is, traditionally Internet resources are transmitted as written text; in the hypermedia environment, sound, video, graphics, and illustrations can also be transmitted. Hence, individuals who prepare Internet documents can integrate sound, motion, and graphics into their materials, and users can download these documents, including the images and sound. In order to interact with the Web its developers created a special protocol known as HTTP (HyperText Transfer Protocol). In addition, a special language HTML (HyperText Markup Language) was created to prepare documents for use on the Web. With HTML a document is divided into various elements, such as headings, titles, lists, addresses, and paragraphs. Each element has a special HTML tag. A particular document is then coded appropriately, e.g., the beginning of the document is identified by a heading tag, the title of the document by a title tag, etc. A document usually has at least tags for the head, body, and paragraphs (NCSA 1997).

Navigation on the Web is provided by graphical Web browsers. Examples of such browsers are Netscape, Mosaic, and HotJava. The purpose of such browsers is to display Web documents and allow the user to use the hyperlinks (December and Randall 1995). When a highlighted item is selected by the user, the user is linked to other items in that publication or to other publications denoted by the highlighted idea. In this way, a user can move from one part of a publication to another, or from one publication to another, through multiple links within the document merely by moving the computer mouse to the highlighted term.

The popularity of the Web is manifest and its use has grown very rapidly since 1995. Estimates as to how many individuals currently access the Web vary widely. The *World Almanac* (1999) estimates that 200 million people had access to the Web and there were 800 million Web pages. What is clear is that Web use is constant. Interestingly, nearly half of all adult Web users use it daily (Emerging Technologies Research

Group 1997), and it is used heavily for general information gathering, work, and education. It is used somewhat less for entertainment and shopping (GVU 1997). The impact of Web use may also have a significant impact on the use of other media. For example, about one-third of adult Web users use the Web instead of watching TV (GVU).

Librarians quickly recognized the advantages of the Web. With access more manageable, the great stores of information on the Internet become a more practical source for assisting patrons. In a 1997 survey, it was found that more than 60 percent of public libraries offer some access to the Web, and nearly two-thirds of public library systems in metropolitan areas offer Web access in at least one branch ("Sharp . . . " 1998). At the same time, the proliferation of Web sites and the popularity of the Web for both library practitioners and the public at large has highlighted some serious concerns. Of particular concern is the quality, or lack thereof, of the information contained on the Web. Traditionally, librarians select the materials for their collections using criteria that help establish the authority and accuracy of the material. This is especially true of the reference materials. When patrons enter a library, they can generally have confidence that the information materials that they consult have been reviewed for authority and accuracy. This is not the case, however, with Web sites. It is often difficult to establish authority for Web sites and, for all intents and purposes, all Web sites are available anyway. This substantially increases the chance that patrons may access incomplete or inadequate information. Librarians have begun to address this issue by establishing their own Web pages for their libraries, which guide the patron to specific electronic sites that have been examined in a manner similar to other materials selected by the library. This is not necessarily to say that access to other sites is prohibited, although that may be the case. Rather, it demonstrates the traditional concern of information professionals to guide the patron to information that is timely and accurate.

## THE IMPACT OF INFORMATION TECHNOLOGIES: THE 1990s AND BEYOND

> In the world of computing, anything over 5 years old is very old, any-
> thing over 10 years old is ancient, and anything older than that is grounds
> for both nostalgia and disbelief (December and Randall 1995, p. 35).

The 1990s saw the introduction, integration, and use of many of the information technologies mentioned above in libraries. A visit to a local public, school, or academic library may well reveal the co-existence of print, AV materials, CD-ROMs, OPACs, online circulation and acquisitions systems, and access to the Internet and World Wide Web. This is not to say that all libraries possess each of these features, but there is little doubt that in the near future they will be incorporated into most American libraries.

The impact of information technologies on the library cannot be overestimated. The means of information production, organization, and dissemination have undergone a major transformation in recent years, with computer technologies emerging as a dominating force. The significance for libraries of these transformations are broad and deep, and it is important to reflect on some of the more profound effects.

### Impact on the Library Environment

New technologies have forced a major redesign of the library's physical environment. The card catalog has been removed in many libraries and in its place are online computer access terminals (OPACs). These devices have completely different physical requirements: they may not only be placed in a centralized area but also dispersed throughout the library. The situation is similar with electronic reference tools such as CD-ROMs. Instead of using shelving, they require terminals. The installation of such devices often requires the removal or moving of tables, chairs, desks, or shelving.

Because of the electronic character of these technologies, their implementation has also led to significant alterations in the wiring of libraries and the placement of electrical outlets and lighting. It can be quite expensive and complicated to redesign the electrical systems of buildings that were built fifty or a hundred years ago, and many libraries have made an uneasy accommodation. In some libraries electrical wires are taped to library floors and stretched to distant outlets.

These technologies have also led to new furniture with significantly different design because of health concerns that may arise among those who use these devices over long periods of time. In all, the library from the outside may appear quite similar as a physical structure, but inside there has been substantial redesign. As these technologies increase, more changes will follow.

*Impact on Local Service*

On a service level, the various electronic technologies have had considerable impact. Consider for example, three technologies: CD-ROMs, online catalogs, and personal computers.

### CD-ROMs AND ONLINE REFERENCE ACCESS

CD-ROMs have transformed a book-oriented reference process into a matter of electronic access. They involve continuing costs including the costs of updating the service itself as well as the costs of hardware, software, wiring, space, and furniture. In addition, the increased training and personnel expenditures for operation and maintenance of these products are needed.

For automated online databases the organizational impact may be even greater because cost control over such databases is less predictable. Automated online databases are behind the creation of new offices (systems offices), new positions (database searchers), and new policies and procedures including those related to patron access rules and fees for services. The concept of subsidized browsing (materials are made available at no charge to the user, a traditional hallmark of public library service) has been replaced or is in direct competition with a fee-for-service arrangement that has gained prominence because of the great difficulty in controlling costs. Even with fee-for-service approaches, the true costs are not usually recovered, only the direct costs.

### ONLINE CATALOGS

The online catalog, which permits computer access to the library's holdings, has created a shift in communication capabilities within a library. Often these catalogs not only give basic bibliographic description but also indicate holdings. For example, they may indicate which branches own copies of a given book; they may even indicate circulation status. Such information may affect circulation rates. In addition, it has increased the need for bibliographic instruction for patrons unfamiliar with the

OPAC and has increased the opportunity to share information and services among independent libraries.

The microcomputer has had a profound effect on library operations. What was once the province of the typewriter has now been transformed into an electronic device that can perform a multitude of operations.

*Word processing*: The flexibility of word processing, compared to the capabilities of the manual typewriter, has revolutionized the activities of both professional and support staff. In many cases, secretarial and clerical workers are no longer needed to type letters because most individuals can generate the finished product themselves.

*Statistical analysis*: The ability to use sophisticated statistical packages on microcomputers has increased the power of the organization to analyze and report data.

*Desktop publishing*: The ability to produce high quality internal and external publications has changed how public relations and communications are handled within and outside the library. Informational and promotional materials, as well as reports for internal use, can now be generated using sophisticated publication techniques. The ability to perform desktop publishing has not only generated new functions for library departments, it has created a new skill level for support employees.

*Local network communication*: Communications within organizations have been revolutionized because software has been developed to permit personal computers to talk to each other. These systems, known as local area networks (LANs), permit the transmission of electronic records and e-mail and the use of computer software packages by multiple users of personal computers simultaneously.

## The Impact of Automated Networks and the Internet

One of the most profound impacts of technology is the ability of libraries to reach beyond their walls to access information remotely and to act cooperatively with other libraries in an electronic environment. Even if one were to set aside the most recent developments, the Internet and the

WWW, the potential of electronic networking has been exploited in many ways. These include various libraries sharing online catalog information, coordinating collection development, coordinating the circulation of materials from other libraries, providing and using cooperative reference services, and resource sharing using the fax. Such networks are often semi-independent organizational entities. Automated networks have not only improved access to information, but they have reduced some costs by reducing duplication of materials and human resources. Interestingly, automated networks have also led to some organizational changes including the appointment of new staff such as network liaisons and more interlibrary-loan and document-delivery personnel—even the creation of new departments. In addition, the networks as semi-independent units need their own administrative policies and procedures, which often affect the internal policies, practices, and staffing of libraries which are members of the network. One of the most profound of these organizational changes in libraries is the result of the creation of bibliographic networks or utilities, such as OCLC. For example, in many public and academic libraries, the staffing of cataloging departments has changed, reducing the number of professional catalogers and increasing reliance on support staff.

Sometimes there may be a tendency to exaggerate the effects of technological developments, and it is too early to assess the impact of the Internet and National Information Infrastructure (NII) fully at this time. Nonetheless, other major innovations involving communications in the recent past, such as the television and radio, have had substantial effects. There is little doubt that although the specific effects of the Internet and the NII may be unpredictable, they are bound to be equally significant.

Part of the impact may arise from the fact that the NII is expected to affect all citizens. In President Clinton's 1994 State of the Union Address, for example, Clinton indicated that he wanted each library in the United States to be connected to the NII by the year 2000. McKenna (1994) has identified eight "opportunities and benefits" that the Internet can have on libraries and library services. They have been adapted and expanded below:

*Leadership opportunities:* For years librarians have provided bibliographic instruction, both formal and informal, to patrons to help them fully exploit the resources of the library. With the Internet, librarians serve as teachers, introducing the Internet to schools, businesses, academic institutions, and the public-at-large.

*Cost and time savings*: Electronic access creates new forums for continuing education and professional development for librarians. Electronic access provides a means of promoting current discussions and information of vital concern. Some Listservs, electronic conferences, and electronic bulletin boards have been designed specifically for librarians. An important side benefit for the organization is that the availability of information electronically can reduce the normal training costs associated with continuing education by eliminating travel costs.

*Question answering services*: Obviously, one of the great benefits of the Internet is that there is a great deal of information contained there. With the development of effective Web-browsers and additional techniques for ordering information on the Internet, the Internet should become increasingly valuable as a source of answers to questions posed by library users.

It is important to understand how reference services change as the library collection evolves from reliance on physical items in the collection to remote access. This requires a new way of looking at service: the key is relating the user to the entire world of information rather than to items in the local collection. It requires librarians to master an entirely new domain of knowledge. This transition does not mean that local library collections are ignored; user needs will require libraries to maintain substantial local collections of physical items. In addition, except for select special libraries whose information sources are now almost entirely available electronically, the poor organization of Internet resources makes the transition problematic. However, as the organization of the Internet continues to improve and librarians increasingly become information seekers on the Internet, bibliographic instruction will evolve into Web-site instruction.

*International interlibrary loans*: It has been the goal of major library organizations, like the International Federation of Library Associations (IFLA), to increase the exchange of materials on an international level. Obviously, this could be a great help, especially to those needing difficult-to-find materials or to countries with minimal library resources. Because the Internet provides access to library catalogs from around the world, verifying materials for interlibrary loan and access to these many collections will become much easier.

*Document delivery services:* For a variety of reasons, many individuals or organizations are willing to pay a fee to obtain documents quickly, and many of these services can now be found on the Internet. Not surprisingly, librarians have developed a growing interest in using these services, as well, to assist patrons in getting materials quickly. The Internet, therefore, will improve librarians' ability to obtain needed materials more effectively.

*Online transactions:* Internet access to major bibliographic utilities may provide more efficient access to and use of bibliographic records. Given the dependence of many libraries on such bibliographic utilities, this type of access may well improve the efficiency of technical service and circulation functions.

*Government information:* The Internet is a natural network to make government information on political issues, legislation, hearings, government documents and regulations available to individuals and local communities. The information is available much more rapidly than through the use of print, and the potential for improving the public's awareness of important political issues is therefore significantly increased.

*Information sharing:* The common standard that has been set for transferring information throughout the Internet (Z39.50) has increased the ability of librarians and other information systems to share data. Sharing data will increase a library's ability to access remotely information that it does not possess in its own collection.

Given this great potential, the role of the librarian significantly increases. Fred Weingarten of the American Library Association has identified at least five roles for libraries and librarians on the NII (Weingarten 1996). These are summarized below:

*On-ramp of first resort:* The NII will continue to change and grow, and even well-educated citizens may not have the technological resources or knowledge to exploit all the information pathways available. The librarian will provide the advanced knowledge and technology to serve even the most demanding information seekers.

*On-ramp of last resort:* Universal access to all citizens, although desirable, will not be likely for many years to come. Libraries will be an information safety net, for those who have neither the skills nor means to use the information highway.

*Navigator/guide*: The Internet is not well-organized nor is it convenient to use: it is highly complex, requiring considerable knowledge on the part of the user to conduct effective, comprehensive searches. Many individuals will look to librarians as information intermediaries, as conduits to get the information that patrons want and need.

*Archivist/depository/authenticator:* The Internet is changing the concept of "publishing." Ostensibly, print versions are more stable, and it is fairly easy to preserve at least one copy. Electronic information can be quite transitory, and usually it can be altered or updated much more easily than print. Librarians may be among the few to perform an archival function, preserving early or first versions and verifying which version is being accessed.

*Organizer of the public-information space*: Among the many parts of the Internet are sections that contain public information, such as governmental information. Given the complexity, variety, and volume of governmental information, librarians can help promote its use by effectively organizing and making this information accessible to the public.

The future impact of the Internet and Web will also be shaped by research and development. Late in 1996, the Clinton administration proposed the Next Generation Internet (NGI). The NGI is designed to deal, ironically, with the success of the Internet, which has experienced such rapid growth that it is possible that its current technology cannot handle the expanding uses. There is particular concern that the original function of the Internet, to promote communication among researchers, has been adversely affected by the amount of commercial traffic. According to the Clinton administration, the NGI has three basic goals:

> (1) Connect universities and national labs with high-speed networks that are 100–1,000 times faster than today's Internet . . . (2) Promote experimentation with the next generation of networking technologies . . . (3) Demonstrate new applications that meet important national goals and missions . . . (National Coordination Office for Computing, Information, and Communications 1997, p. 2).

It is expected that developments with the NGI will have significant effects on health care research and services, national security intelligence activities, distance education, energy research, biomedical research, manufacturing, and environmental monitoring (National Coordination Office for Computing, Information, and Communications 1997).

*Impact of Technology on the Library Collection*

No doubt one of the major challenges of electronic access to information is the need to define what the library collection is. Traditionally, that has been fairly easy. The library collection was the group of physical objects either available for consultation by staff and patrons inside the library or available for circulation outside the library. From time to time one might borrow materials on interlibrary loan, but interlibrary loans represented a very tiny proportion of the library's service and was not enough to confound the basic notion of what the collection was.

Today, a vast amount of available information is remote, residing in computer databases or on the Internet. Although the potential of such resources has not even begun to be taken advantage of, clearly much information may be obtained using computer networks. Presuming that libraries will remain as sources of information, the very concept of the library collection is being transformed. In this new environment, the library collection consists of at least two parts: the items and information contained within the library (stored as physical objects or electronically), and information stored electronically (and sometimes physically) outside the library either as data or documents. This reconceptualization of the library collection raises many issues which can only be briefly mentioned:

FINANCIAL IMPLICATIONS

Information obtained electronically from outside the library may involve the loss of control over costs because there is often a cost per use. Again, this is quite different from the traditional library cost model in which the item is purchased and the cost remains the same no matter how often the item is used. Other factors to take into account include the costs of telecommunications, access to databases, downloading, and compensation concerning copyright, as well as the costs of the hardware and software to access these external sources of information. This requires new perspectives on the allocation of resources and new attitudes toward which items will be collected locally and which will be remotely accessed.

The fact that costs of information access may increase significantly has prompted libraries to institute additional fees for library services. Some fear that charging fees for electronic information delivery, especially in public libraries, may lead to a serious erosion of the "free library ethic" and a blurring of the distinction between commercial vendors and not-for-profit institutions. (De Gennaro 1989). Libraries are not unaware of these ethical issues, and some libraries have tried to subsidize or partially subsidize these costs, especially for users who may not be able to afford the fees. However, libraries may not be able to withstand the fiscal pressures forever. This issue will be discussed further in Chapter 4.

IMPACT ON SELECTION AND ACQUISITIONS OF INFORMATION RESOURCES FOR
THE LIBRARY COLLECTION

As noted above, traditionally library collections have consisted of physical items that were provided by vendors, publishers or producers of books, AV, or serials. Collection development involved the selection and acquisition of materials through these publishers and vendors. At its most basic level, electronic technologies have changed the way that these traditional materials are identified and ordered. Vendors are creating automated systems that permit selectors to access their databases and identify items, consult tables of contents, and read reviews. These systems also permit placing orders, and in some cases, downloading essential bibliographic material for cataloging purposes. These electronic processes not only streamline acquisition and selection processes, but they can also provide fiscal control and financial reports. Automated systems can also reveal which items or subject areas are circulating and which are out on interlibrary loans. These data can also be used for collection development and planning. In addition, electronic technologies have increased the number of information resources for selectors; for example, e-mail and Listservs provide advice and information on material selection.

Vendor acquisition and selection processes have become so sophisticated that in some instances major collection development responsibilities are shifted to vendors. The Hawaii State Library, for example, which is responsible for the library collections of all public libraries in that state, signed a contract with a major vendor, Baker and Taylor, to select all materials for these collections ("Hawaii Hands . . . " 1996). Significant concern, however, was expressed in Hawaii concerning the outsourcing of selection, and especially the lack of input by librarians ("Hawaii Bills . . . " 1997). Ultimately, this resulted in the cancellation of the contract.

Selection is changing in other ways as well. The knowledge and skills for collection development are expanding. For example, in selecting local electronic resources such as CD-ROMs one must not only know the contents, but also understand both hardware and software and be prepared to address issues such as screen display, response time, postprocessing activities (e.g. downloading), leasing and pricing arrangements, and vendor evaluation.

But perhaps more significant in the long run is the effect on the collection. The new electronic resources provide access to information outside the walls of the library. As most, if not all, of the texts, sights, and sounds become available on the Internet, how does the librarian deal with the issue of collection development? Given that information on the Internet is available for consultation and downloading at the local library, then this information becomes, for all intents and purposes, part of the library collection. But in this situation, to what extent can the library apply its traditional notions of selection? If the library is unable to apply these traditional controls over the collection, then it must address additional questions, such as the following:

- What are the "selection criteria" for libraries and information centers for information available on the Internet?
- How does one select browsers?
- To what extent does the library staff control access to the content of the Internet? What policies are needed to balance intellectual freedom issues with protection of vulnerable clientele such as children?
- To what extent does the library staff create interfaces that guide patrons to particular Web sites?
- How does the library staff decide if a particular information resource should be made accessible in print, AV, or electronic format? When should the same information be available in multiple formats?
- What responsibility does the library staff have to make available only information that they feel is accurate or reliable?
- To what extent are librarians responsible for evaluating information for the patron?
- To what extent should libraries or information centers warn patrons that the information available may be inaccurate, biased, or incomplete?
- How will the library or information center subsidize or charge for fee-based information?

In addition, remote access to electronic information creates entirely new issues regarding collection evaluation. It is no longer enough to examine the local collection to determine if it is meeting users' needs. Rather, there will be much greater attention to whether the library can provide adequate access to the needed information. As De Gennaro has observed, "In the future, the size of a library's collection of conventional materials will matter far less than it does now. The question is no longer how many volumes a library has, but how effectively the library can deliver needed resources from a wide variety of sources to users via the new technology" (De Gennaro 1989, p. 42).

PRESERVATION

Preservation seems a relatively easy concept when considering print materials. Among the measures one would take would be encouraging the purchase of materials printed on acid-free paper; maintaining proper humidity, temperature, and other environmental controls; ensuring the use of preservation-quality materials for repair and storage of materials, applying mass and individual de-acidification techniques to deteriorating items of importance.

Electronic media raise important new issues. For example, the impermanence of electronic records is an important quality of the media itself, for it is the ability to make alterations quickly that often make them so appealing. Yet which iterations are to be preserved and how? Similarly, much electronic information is vulnerable to damage and deterioration over time. How does one preserve compact disks? We often think of books as delicate, but CD-ROMs can also be damaged and then the content is no longer accessible. Electronic information stored on floppy disks represents another preservation challenge. Such data often needs to be refreshed over time; otherwise, the data may be corrupted. Given the vast amount of information stored on such disks, how can it be effectively preserved? Preservation of electronic media also implies that the equipment also be preserved. Having CD-ROMs is of little use, if the software and hardware to use this medium is not also available.

The issue becomes even more difficult when one considers the information on the World Wide Web. It is likely that much of the information on the Web will not exist a year or two from now. If the marketplace determines what is preserved, then probably only material of commercial value will remain (Coyle 1994). Obviously this is not the traditional basis for preservation of library materials. Who will take responsibility for determining what will be preserved and how it will be preserved? These are just a few of the challenges that will face the preservation officers of today and tomorrow, as their electronic collections increase in proportion to their traditional print holdings.

### THE CHALLENGE TO THE LIBRARY AS A PHYSICAL PLACE

Over the past few years, library automation has undergone a shift in its direction. Attention has changed from in-house processing of traditional tasks to the use of computing and telecommunications tools to develop the "library without walls" . . . , using technologies to expand services, resources, and relationships between libraries and resources around the world (Whitney and Glogoff 1994, p. 321).

The notion of a library without walls is an exciting prospect for many in that it conjures an image of the breaking of physical barriers to permit total freedom of access to all information throughout the world. Computers seem to be a suitable means for removing these walls.

The growth of scientific and technical information and the increasing need to harness this information toward technological progress helped spawn a major revolution in computerized access to information. The movement toward greater computerization seems irresistible. As more and more information is accessed remotely or provided by organizations that exist to provide information through telecommunication lines and electronic databases, the obsolescence of the library is considered a possibility—even a desired end for some (Birdsall 1994). Does this presage the end of the library as a physical place to be visited? Is it to be replaced by the virtual library?

To some extent, the answer to these questions depends on how we perceive the purpose of libraries, a subject that will be covered in more detail in Chapter 8. Birdsall (1994) has noted that those who envision the end of physical libraries rely more on a research and academic model than on the traditional service model prevalent throughout the history of American libraries and represented more by the public library than the academic one.

There is a significant political advantage to emphasizing the electronic aspects of information access. These networks seem to resolve some of the basic political liabilities that libraries as places have often had, e.g., duplication in collections or unequal access due to wealth of particular communities. In addition, politicians and community leaders are as much taken by the "bells and whistles" of technology as anyone else. By the same token, there is much activity that goes on in a library as a place—story hours, adult programming, collaboration with librarians in the research process, and access to print and audiovisual materials. Libraries have often been perceived as community centers—as centers of education. Their presence has served as a material symbol of cultural and educational values for many years. It is unclear how electronic networks could serve in this social capacity. No doubt, the tension between increasing remote access to information and access to physical objects or electronic files in a physical place will remain a dynamic one for a long time to come.

*Impact of Technology on Human Resources Issues*

During the 1960s and '70s, when automation was introduced into libraries, little attention was paid to the effect on staff. Indeed, a major argument regarding the desirability of its implementation was that it would reduce dependence on library staff. However, the experiences of the last two decades have made it clear that the reaction of staff to the introduction and implementation of automation plays an important role in its effective use and the retention of valued employees.

In fact, the introduction of new technologies has generated considerable perturbation in the workplace and especially in regard to human resources. These can be examined from two perspectives: effects of technology on the organizational structure and human responses to the introduction of technologies.

IMPACT ON THE POSITIONS AND ORGANIZATIONAL STRUCTURE

Whenever new technologies are introduced in an organization, they often bring the need to hire new people with different knowledge and skills. Automation has stimulated the hiring of such individuals and brought up a variety of issues and problems. For example, as computer technologies are integrated into library functions, libraries have hired systems experts to maintain and enhance the system, to train others in the use of the system, report on the system's operation, and make recommendations for new systems as needed. Depending on the size of the library and the sophistication of the system, additional systems staff have been retained. The individuals hired for these positions are often quite different from library staff both in terms of knowledge and disposition. The organizational culture from which they come may also be different. The result is potential estrangement of certain staff or conflict within the organization, which in turn may affect organizational productivity.

In addition, the introduction of these new positions with special technical expertise has often required the creation of new job descriptions and new job classifications that have unique relationships to the traditional organizational structure. New reporting lines have been established, which can lead to resentment or concern. For example, the head of a systems department might report directly to the library director or other high-level administrative position. These seemingly privileged lines of communication may make other managers uneasy and suspicious. Similarly, compensation for new technically oriented classifications is problematic. The marketplace for individuals with computer expertise is often substantially more lucrative than the marketplace for librarians. To recruit and retain talented individuals with computer expertise, it may be necessary to pay these individuals more than librarians. Such a distortion of the traditional pay structure can affect the morale of other staff.

The relationship between support and professional staff has also been deeply affected by new technologies. The professional level of library work is becoming more intellectually labor-intensive and less physically labor-intensive as it consists of locating information electronically rather than retrieving it physically from the collections. (American Council of Learned Societies 1990). This increased emphasis on the intellectual aspects of the work suggests that librarians are and will be performing substantially different tasks from those performed in the past and will require new skills as the information environment becomes increasingly complex. A variety of competencies have been suggested for information professional in this dynamic situation, including knowledge of new information technologies, substantial adaptability and flexibility, creativity, ability to manage change, willingness to take risks, increased ability to plan and supervise, increased skills in determining the information needs of users, ability to create and maintain information systems, strong interpersonal skills, leadership, and vision (Bailey 1991; Tees 1991). No doubt, there will be significant organizational challenges as qualified individuals must be identified, hired, and retained.

Support staff are also experiencing changes in their work. They, like the professional librarians, must also be adaptable and flexible and be able to learn new things quickly. Support staff may well be providing basic reference services using electronic technologies or developing strong skills in desk top publishing or information management systems. As support staff acquire new, complex technical skills, they are also likely to demand greater status and pay and want to be treated in a collaborative manner rather than in the context of the traditional superior/subordinate relationship. The result is that many support/professional staff tensions have been magnified as these technologies have been introduced. The recognition of the significant contributions of support staff and the responsibility of motivating and rewarding these workers constitute fundamental management challenges for library administrators and staff.

Organizations are changing in other ways as well. Some of the activities that have traditionally been performed by libraries are now being outsourced to other organizations. For example, automated acquisitions have also permitted vendors to supply some materials already processed and cataloged, and even re-bound to specification. This effectively reduces the need for library departments devoted to these activities. The extent to which outsourcing will become an integral part of library processes is yet to be seen, but electronic technologies are bound to increase the percentage of this activity in the future.

Finally, the organization is changing as some of the duties performed by employees will be performed by the users themselves. For example, technology makes certain functions much easier for the patron to perform, essentially eliminating the need for librarians as intermediaries in some cases. These are sometimes referred to as patron-initiated service systems. Examples include self-checkout of local materials; direct interlibrary loan and document delivery; and electronic systems that permit renewal, recalls, and holds on materials or access to Internet resources.

THE IMPACT OF TECHNOLOGIES ON THE PHYSICAL AND PSYCHOLOGICAL
CONDITION OF WORKERS

The effect of technologies on people can be profound, and since new technologies are introduced regularly, it is important to understand the many potential reactions to their presence in the workplace. One concern is the physical impact of electronic technologies. Experience with employees working with computers has revealed that a variety of physical symptoms, some quite serious, can arise: carpal tunnel syndrome, repetitive motion disorders, headaches, neckaches, vision problems, joint pain, numbness in limbs, and fatigue. More controversial findings have suggested that there may be serious side effects from extensive exposure to electromagnetic radiation from the computer. These problems have highlighted the field of ergonomics, which devotes itself to studying the fit between people and machines. Ergonomic studies have revealed the need for carefully redesigning workspaces so that lighting is appropriate for video display terminals; chairs provide proper support for arms, legs, neck and back; and keyboards and desks are designed and placed at appropriate heights to minimize injury to hands and arms. In addition, employers are discovering that employees working all day on computers need frequent breaks to maintain their productivity.

Similarly, employers are concerned with the negative psychological reactions from employees when new technologies are introduced. Their reactions are sometimes described as technostress or resistance to change. Technostress is "a condition resulting from the inability of an individual or organization to adapt to the introduction and operation of new technology" (Brod 1984, p. 30). The introduction of new technologies sometimes creates irrational fears, but many of the fears are perfectly rational and need to be anticipated and dealt with. There are, for example, natural fears of job loss, of being able to master new training, of technical jargon, of physical harm, and fear that computers will be used to inappropriately monitor work. Such fears often produce symptoms of technostress.

Regrettably, the symptoms of technostress are not uncommon and can be quite serious. They include mental fatigue, combativeness, depression, increased errors and bad judgments, panic, resistance to change, and feelings of helplessness. These undesirable responses can cause loss of productivity and morale not only among the particular workers experiencing the problem, but also among those who work with or rely on the work of those employees. The causes of technostress are many and varied and include poorly designed or inadequate computer hardware and software, poor lighting or wiring, noisy equipment, poor training, poor organizational communication, and existing feelings of job insecurity and fragmentation. Dealing with these factors can diminish the unproductive responses of workers encountering new technologies.

Experience has revealed that there are a variety of steps libraries can take to alleviate negative psychological responses to change. These include the following:

(1)   Involving staff from the beginning in the planning and acquisition of new technologies. Keeping secrets only leads to the proliferation of rumors and a feeling of being left out. Ideas should emerge from the staff itself,

which increases commitment and reduces the feeling that the technology is being imposed.

(2) Demonstrating to the employees that there are direct beneficial consequences from the change. After all, self-interest is a strong motivator: if the change helps the employees do their needed work, it is more likely to be greeted positively.

(3) Communicating to staff the progress of technological changes and providing time to adjust. This should include plenty of time for learning how to operate and use new technologies, opportunities to make mistakes without penalties, and chances to receive and provide feedback on the effectiveness of or any problems with new systems. For technological change to work well, there must be open communications in both directions.

(4) Refraining from ridiculing critics. There are bound to be people who will resist technological change. Although they sometimes can be difficult, they also can serve a vital purpose: they can reveal inadequacies that should be remedied. Criticizing these individuals may simply build resentment and fear on the part of others.

(5) Ensuring staff they will not lose their job or be reduced in rank or pay following the change. After all, resistance is bound to arise if one feels that one's interests are being threatened.

## *Impact of Technology on the Traditional Mission of Libraries*

It has been the traditional mission of public, academic, and school libraries to serve all their constituents' information needs, regardless of their background or economic standing. Does the introduction of electronic technologies alter that mission?

It is a common belief that technologies themselves are value-neutral, that it is the uses to which technology is put that dictate the values. But there are those who argue that this is not so, that technologies have significant social, political, and economic impact, and their development and use is promoted by select groups to serve their own purposes. This concern has been reflected professionally with the creation of the Progressive Librarians Guild (PLG) in 1990, an affiliate of the Social Responsbilities Round Table of ALA. Among the PLG's stated concerns is "our profession's rapid drift into dubious alliances with business and the information industry, and into complacent acceptance of service to the political, economic, and cultural status quo (Progressive Librarians Guild 1998, p. 1). As John Bushman (1990) has observed, "the implementation of technologies is not democratically controlled; it serves the interests of the people who control them" (p. 1029). It is hard not to argue that the computer revolution has been developed and exploited by the educational and economic elite, and that many of the electronic resources developed are designed for research and development, business and industry, academics and their students. Is it possible that the information resources on which libraries are spending so much money are specifically designed to cater to these groups and that the social mission of libraries is deteriorating as fewer resources can be devoted to this end?

## SUMMARY

As new information technologies provide increasingly greater access to information, libraries will undoubtedly continue to acquire them. Continuous change will be an inherent part of this process. In such a dynamic environment, many questions need to be answered:

How will new technologies affect the mission of libraries?
How will electronic publications and information be evaluated and selected?
How will access to electronic information be provided, controlled, and paid for?
How does technology affect the employees of the organization, and how can it be implemented for maximum productivity?

There is no doubt that the concept of the library is changing—some say it is in transition from "collection to connection." The extent to which this transition will actually occur and its impact on library services is yet to be fully determined. There is no doubt that libraries of the future will be looking for new skills and abilities among its employees and will be continually emphasizing retraining and continuing education as new technologies are introduced. The new technological environment is one in which professional and support staff each need significant skills, and there are many types of professionals (e.g. systems operators and librarians) working to provide information services. There are many unknowns regarding the future of libraries and how they will be affected by technology. What we do know is that change will be a natural and continuous part of that world.

REFERENCES

American Council of Learned Societies. *Scholars and Research: Academic Libraries in the 21st Century*. ACLIS Occasional Paper, No. 14. New York: ACLS, 1990.

Bailey, Martha J. "Characteristics of the Successful Information Professionals of the Future: Branch Libraries/Information Centers." In *Future Competencies of the Information Professional*. SLA Occasional Papers Series, Number One. Washington D.C.: SLA, 1991.

Baker, Nicholson. "Discards." *New Yorker* (April 4, 1994): 64–86.

Bierman, Kenneth J. "How Will Libraries Pay for Electronic Information?" *Journal of Library Administration* 15 (1991): 67–84.

Birdsall, William F. "Breaking the Myth of the Library as Place." In *The Myth of the Electronic Library: Librarianship and Social Change in America*. Westport, Conn.: Greenwood, 1994, 7–29.

Bishop, Ann P. "The National Research and Education Network (NREN): Promise of a New Information Environment." *ERIC Digest* (November 1990) EDO-IR-90-4.

Brod, Craig. "How to Deal with 'Technostress'." *Office Administration and Automation* 45 (August 1984): 28–47.

Buckland, Michael K. "Documentation, Information Science, and Library Science in the U.S.A." *Information Processing & Management* 32 (1996): 63–76.

Buckland, Michael K. and Clifford A. Lynch. "The Linked Systems Protocol and the Future of Bibliographic Networks and Systems." *Information Technology and Libraries* 6 (June 1987): 83–88.

——. "National and International Implications of the Linked Systems Protocol for Online Bibliographic Systems." *Cataloging and Classifications Quarterly* 8 (1988): 15–31.

Bushman, John. "Asking the Right Questions about Information Technology." *American Libraries* 21 (December 1990): 1026–1030.

Coyle, Karen. "Access: Not Just Wires." Paper presented at the annual meeting of the Computer Professionals for Social Responsibility (CPSR). San Diego, October 1994.

December, John and Neil Randall. *The World Wide Web Unleashed 1996*. Indianapolis: Sams, 1995.

De Gennaro, Richard D. "Technology and Access in an Enterprise Society." *Library Journal* 114 (October 1, 1989): 40–43.

Emerging Technologies Research Group. *The 1997 American Internet User Survey* [Online]. Available at *http://etrg.findsvp.com/internet/overview.html* (July 1, 1997).

Gomery, Douglas. "In Search of the Cybermarket." *The Wilson Quarterly* (summer 1994): 9–17.

Grosch, Audrey N. *Library Information Technology and Networks*. New York: Marcel Dekker, 1995.

GVU (Graphic, Visualization, & Usability Center). *7th WWW User Survey* [Online]. Available at *http://www.gvu.edu/user_surveys/survey-1997-04* (June 30, 1997).

Hahn, Trudi Bellardo. "Pioneers of the Online Age." *Information Processing and Management* 32 (1996): 33–48.

"Hawaii Bills Address Outsourcing." *American Libraries* 28 (June/July 1997): 30.

"Hawaii Hands Collection Development to Baker and Taylor." *School Library Journal* 49 (June 1996): 10.

McKenna, Mary. "Libraries and the Internet" *ERIC Digest* (December 1994) Syracuse, ERIC Clearinghouse on Information and Technology.

Mediamark Research. "64.2 Million American Adults Regularly Use the Internet." (Online) Available at *http://www.mediamark.com/mri/docs/prcs_s99.htm* (March 21, 2000).

National Coordination Office for Computing, Information, and Communications. Next Generation Internet Initiative [Online]. Available at *http://www.ccic.gov/ngi/background.html* (December 28, 1997).

National Information Standards Organization. "Information Retrieval: Application Service Definition and Protocol Specification." Bethesda, Md.: NISO, 1994.

NCSA (National Center for Supercomputing Alliance). *A Beginner's Guide to HTML* [Online]. Available at *http://www.ncsa.uiuc.e . . . /WWW/HRMLPrimerPl.html* (July 3, 1997).

Progressive Librarians Guild. "Progressive *Librarians Guild" [Online]*. Available at *http://home.earthlink.net/~rlitwin/PLG.html* (January 6, 1998).

Rider, Freemont. *The Scholar and the Future of the Research Library: A Problem and Its Solution.* New York: Hadham, 1944, 99. Cited in Buckland, 65.

"Sharp Increase in Internet Use at Public Libraries." *American Libraries* 29 (January 1998): 11.

Tees, Miriam H. "Competencies for the Mid-Sized Special Library," *In Future Competencies of the Information Professional.* SLA Occasional Paper Series, Number One. Washington D.C.: SLA, 1991.

Tenant, Roy. "Internet Basics." *Eric Digest* (October 1992):EDO-IR-92–7.

Tenner, Edward. "Learning from the Net," *Wilson Quarterly* (summer 1994): 18–28.

*Webster's Third New International Dictionary.* Springfield, Mass.: G & C Merriam, 1970.

Weingarten, Fred W. "Five Great Roles for Libraries and Librarians within the NII." *American Libraries* 27 (January 1996): 17.

Whitney, Gretchen and Stuart Glogoff. "Automation for the Nineties: A Review Article." *Library Quarterly* 64 (July 1994): 319–331.

*World Almanac and Book of Facts, 1999.* New York: World Almanac Books, 1999.

# 4

# Information Policy: Stakeholders and Agendas

## INFORMATION POLICY STAKEHOLDERS

The importance of information in our society can hardly be overestimated. As we increasingly recognize the critical nature of information, policies that affect information creation, organization, use, and dissemination become equally critical. This chapter is devoted to a discussion of the major information-policy issues with special attention to national policies that affect libraries. Institutions such as libraries, museums, and archives also create information policies that can affect the citizenry's access to information. The information policies specifically created by libraries have a significant effect on their collections and services, and Chapter 5 is devoted entirely to this subject.

Information policy is any law, regulation, rule, or practice (written or unwritten) that affects the creation, acquisition, organization, dissemination, or evaluation of information. Most often, information policy is discussed in terms of governmental legislation. This legislation usually focuses on areas such as information technologies for educational and industrial uses, telecommunications, privacy issues, computer regulations and crimes, copyright and intellectual property, and government information systems (Burger 1993).

In American society, discussion of information policy highlights a fundamental tension between entrepreneurship and democracy. Under capitalism, information can be viewed as a commodity, a form of property that can provide a competitive edge. Insofar as such information can be held privately, there is a strong incentive for individuals to dis-

93

cover new information and apply it to products and services that both advance society and increase personal wealth. On the other hand, the democratic values of society promote information as a right. Democratic traditions promote the free flow of ideas as essential if a free society is to prosper. This is not to say that capitalism and democracy are incompatible; it is to suggest that information policy in a democratic society requires a balancing of social, economic, and political interests.

Not surprisingly, there are a variety of stakeholders in the information policy process, stakeholders who are deeply concerned about information from a legal and political perspective. These stakeholders include business, government, information producers and disseminators, and the public.

### Business and Industry

Because information is critical to competition, business and industry are very active in influencing policies that will affect the dissemination and restriction of information. Business and industry have special interests in both the discovery of new knowledge and the organization of current knowledge.

POLICIES AFFECTING THE DISCOVERY AND EXPLOITATION OF NEW KNOWLEDGE TO IMPROVE PRODUCTIVITY AND PROFITS.

Business and industry have a strong need to control knowledge and to protect proprietary information, such as new inventions or discoveries. Patent and copyright laws are needed as well as laws that permit the restriction of an employee's use of protected knowledge even after separation from employment. For example, employers can use a "no competition" clause in contracts so that an employee cannot reveal secret information about an employer's processes or inventions. Similarly, organizational policy may prevent an employee from working for a competitor. Such restrictions are needed to maintain a competitive edge with domestic and foreign competitors and to ensure organizational survival.

THE ORGANIZATION OF CURRENT KNOWLEDGE FOR PURPOSES OF ACCESS.

Organizations need access to information to prosper. The extent to which government policies permit easy and inexpensive access to information can have a substantial effect on an organization's ability to function effectively in competitive national and international environments.

### Government

Political bodies are well aware that information is essential for decision-making and action. Local, state, and federal governments are in the business of collecting, organizing, and evaluating information. The federal government does this through government hearings, the information-gathering activities of executive offices such as the Department of Labor or Department of State, the FBI law-enforcement investigations, or by the CIA's political-military assessments. Government is also in the business of disseminating and controlling information. To this end, the government promulgates regulations to restrict information, such as information affecting national security, and plays a role in selecting what information is published and made available to the public (or the press) and what information is not. Laws such as the Freedom of Information Act and the National Security Act form part of the process that defines the role of government in the dissemination and control of information.

### Information Producers, Disseminators, Transmitters, or Telecommunicators

Although these stakeholders could be considered part of business and industry, they form a critical subgroup that takes a special interest in information policy because of the profound effect such policies might have on them. Information producers and disseminators include the telecommunications businesses such as American Telephone and Telegraph (AT&T) and Ameritech; the television, cable, and radio industry; producers of videos and audio tapes; the print and publishing industry; the computer industry, including database producers and vendors; and, of course, libraries. One can imagine any number of laws and regulations that can either promote or diminish the effectiveness of such organizations. Laws affecting competition, pricing of services, the right to tape programs, taxation, postal rates, and royalties and laws concerning libel or invasion of privacy could all have profound implications for these organizations. Libraries as information disseminators have a special role and exercise a special interest because they are among the few whose motivations are not profit-oriented.

### The American Citizen and Those Organizations that Represent their Interest

In a democratic society, each citizen is a major stakeholder. The manner by which information flows in our society has a direct effect on our ability to make informed judgments and to take deliberative action. The subtlest shift in policy may affect the extent to which we receive accurate, up-to-date, and sufficient information, and who receives this information. For American citizens, defining rights to information is a critical function. Dowlin (1987) argues, for example, that citizens have rights to information that would help them deal with their environment including information related to their health, safety, careers, and their government including information on political issues and candidates.

A fundamental value that underlies the transfer of information in a democratic society is the right of individuals to information, and with it comes the expectation that information policies will support that value. The extent to which information policies promote or diminish these rights is a critical consideration. Individual citizens, however, do not always have a significantly strong voice. Consequently, a variety of organizations try to represent the public's interests on information policy issues, including the American Library Association, the American Civil Liberties Union, and Computer Professionals for Social Responsibility. Clearly, there can be a vigorous clash of interests, and this produces a dynamic and sometimes unsettling tension in our society.

## THE POLITICO-ECONOMIC CHARACTER OF INFORMATION

Fundamental to our understanding of information policy is the fact that, whether we like it or not, information is being reconceptualized from something merely useful for improving understanding to something that can be seen as a commodity in and of itself. This reconceptualization could potentially threaten the existence and well-being of libraries. This transformation has been fostered, in large part, by computers with dramatically increased capacity to store and process information and by the increasing sophistication of telecommunications, which permits computers to transmit data throughout the world almost instantaneously.

The value of having the right information at the right time, or the value of depriving others of information to gain an advantage, has become so obvious, that it was inevitable that individuals would see the economic and political value of information. Hence, information becomes a commodity—something to be bought, sold, or controlled in and of itself. The economic characterization of information can be seen in the use of the common metaphor, "information marketplace." This change has been likened in significance in at least one commentary, Louis

Vagianos and Barry Lesser (1989), to the profound changes created with the invention of the printing press. To equate this change with the invention of printing might be hyperbole, but it is certainly a change with troubling implications. The view of information as a commodity could create for information providers like libraries an uneasy and potentially unethical accommodation with the economic "haves"—to the great disadvantage of the economic "have nots" (Blanke 1989).

Once the metaphor of the economics of information takes hold in the public consciousness, it is an easy assumption that all information should have economic value or price. The result may be that social, cultural, and creative knowledge, traditionally provided for free, may be curtailed or extinguished. The economic advantage of information may be becoming so powerful that those who are advantaged by its creation, dissemination, use, and control may not wish public institutions like libraries to have much of a role in the process. In the future, librarians may not serve as major players in defining how and at what price information will be used. The diminution of the library's role may be accelerated because the technology of information is blurring the traditional model of library work, a model that presupposes a depository to organize and disseminate information. Vagianos (1989) argues, in fact, that the "standalone depository is at an end" (p. 10). The more others perceive that information has less and less to do with libraries and more and more to do with technology and telecommunications, the less libraries will be perceived as important in the information policy process. Similarly, as information technologies spawn an increasing variety of information channels such as electronic networks and the Internet, the temptation to think of information as a commodity, rather than a right, intensifies.

What, then, are some of the major information policy issues facing librarians and citizens today?

*Protecting the Privacy of Citizens*

There is growing concern that unauthorized individuals can gain access too easily to records with information on our health, financial affairs, or buying habits. Consequently, there is an interest in protecting a citizen's privacy from third party intrusions—from individuals or governments. Federal and state governments have promulgated legislation attempting to define a citizen's right of access to files maintained about them and the rights of others to access these same files. These are broadly referred to as Privacy Acts and Public Records Acts. Some acts are designed to protect privacy in specific areas, such as the Right to Financial Privacy Act of 1978, which deals with protection of financial records; the Electronic Communications Privacy Act of 1986, which deals with the privacy of cellular phones; and the Communications Assistance for Law Enforcement Act of 1994, which in part deals with the privacy of cordless phones and data communications (Science Applications International Corporation 1995).

Privacy has become a particularly important information policy issue for libraries because of governmental attempts to obtain borrowing information on individuals through their circulation records. This has led to the creation of many state "Confidentiality of Circulation Records" statutes that provide fairly complete protection against third party access to borrowers' records, while still providing limited access by governmental agencies for specific reasons.

*Promoting the Freedom of Information*

Certainly, the need to protect the privacy of citizens is vital, but it is also vital that citizens have a right to information regarding governmental activities. This balance between privacy and public records is constantly being tested and redefined. Ironically, some of the same acts that serve to protect an individual's privacy are also ones that ensure rights of access when legitimate interests arise. For example, the protection of a citizen's right to government information is also defined in Public Records Acts, the most prominent being the first of these acts, the federal Freedom of Information Act of 1966. This act was meant to ensure that governmental records that were not specifically protected by national security or other valid reasons would be made available for inspection by members of the public. The intent was to prevent governments from withholding information merely because they thought that the information would be embarrassing or would be a political liability. The federal act was followed by many state acts, which define the records to which the public has access and usually exempts specific records from public access. These might, but do not necessarily, include law-enforcement investigation records, adoptions, and personnel or medical records.

*The Production and Control of the Flow of Government Information*

In recent years, there has been a systematic attempt to reduce the amount of material being produced by the federal Government Printing Office (GPO) to make production more efficient and to reduce the budget for this agency. One major change is the shift from paper printing to the use of electronic photographic formats, including microfiche and CD-ROMs. The decision to use other formats as a matter of government information policy may have significant implications for the use of such materials. Although production in electronic formats may increase flexibility for searching, it may also present a barrier to many citizens who want to access it. Knowing how to use computers and peripheral equipment is but one possible obstacle for some citizens. Increased costs for using electronic media may be another barrier because libraries may be unable to afford the different peripherals and software required to run a multitude of different electronic systems.

The emphasis on cost consciousness is highlighted by what appears to be increasing control of information dissemination by the Office of Management and Budget (OMB). Its "Circular A-130, Management of Federal Information Resources" requires cost-benefit analysis of government information activities, and requires reliance on the private sector to disseminate government information and recover costs by charging users (American Library Association 1991). If the information decision-making of the OMB is strictly centered on financial aspects, the philosophical, pedagogical, and social benefits, which are not easily measured, may be underestimated. The end result will be the publication of material that makes a profit, not necessarily the publication of material of most value.

The trend toward the privatization of information and removing the responsibility for producing documents from the Government Printing Office (GPO), may be equally problematic. This trend was accelerated during the Reagan Administration, but it has continued. Since 1982, one of every four of the 16,000 publications produced by the government has been eliminated (American Library Association 1991). The privatization of public information has far-reaching effects, and there are arguments for this trend on both sides. These arguments have, in part, been summarized by a major federal governmental commission, the National Commission on Libraries and Information Science (NCLIS 1981, pp. vii–ix). NCLIS is a "permanent federal agency charged with advising the President and the Congress on policy matters relating to library and information services" (White House Conference 1991).

(1)   Our society is founded on the traditional view that individual freedom and initiative, expressed through competitive private enterprise, are the best means of supplying the products and services needed by society;

(2)   Government entry into the marketplace can have a chilling effect on private sector investment in the generation, collection, and distribution of information;

(3)   When the government enters the marketplace, it interferes with the ability of the market mechanism to allocate resources to the optimum production of goods and services;

(4)   The private sector, if not threatened by the anti-competitive effects of government in the marketplace, can widen the distribution of government information as well as information from other sources.

On the other hand, NCLIS has also identified the reasons why privatization is not desirable:

(1)   There is a need to ensure equitable, open access by the general public to information that has been generated, collected, processed, or distributed with taxpayer funds;

(2)   To participate fully in our democratic society, citizens must be informed and aware, regardless of their ability to pay for needed information;

(3)   Information needs that are not served by the marketplace must be met by the government;

(4)   The government has a role to play in stimulating the development of information as a resource for dealing with societal problems.

The concern over private publication of public information might be expressed in another way: private publication relies on a profit motive. This means that information that does not have a sufficiently clear market for making a profit may not be published. If the basis for publication is projected sales, a considerable amount of information may be restricted. Even if an item with poor sales potential is published, the price is bound to be high, which also may make access or acquisition prohibitive. This is exemplified in the publication of the *Federal Statistical Directory*. When published privately, the price tripled in the first year and was more than five times more expensive in the second. At the same time, it was removed from the Depository Library Program, which prevented Depository libraries from acquiring it at no cost (American Library Association 1988). Furthermore, private publishers are permitted to copyright their version of the material even though the Government Printing Office cannot. Information produced privately is also exempt from the Freedom of Information Act. Such conditions may seriously restrict the ability of individuals to consult these documents, or even after consultation, to easily and inexpensively disseminate the information to others.

*National Security Issues*

An important area in which the government wants to restrict information as a matter of policy is information that could threaten the security of the nation. This, of course, seems intuitively reasonable. Nonetheless, there has been considerable controversy over the government's attempt to classify information that some would consider merely politically embarrassing. In addition, the government has, on several recent occasions, attempted to *re*classify information that had already become public in an attempt to further restrict information. Security issues have also arisen concerning the dissemination of scientific information through conference presentations. This has been especially notable in the areas of cryptography.

An odd turn of events regarding information policy and national security affected libraries in the 1980s. Unbeknownst to the library community, in the 1970s the Federal Bureau of Investigation launched a program known as the Library Awareness Program. This program was initiated because U.S. intelligence agencies had become concerned about foreign agents gathering unclassified scientific and technical information that could give them a technological edge. They believed that libraries were a fertile source for such information (Schmidt 1987). They also believed that libraries could be a source of recruitment for foreign agents. Consequently, the FBI began making inquiries in libraries around the country regarding the use of libraries by foreigners. Librarians became aware of it in June 1987, when two FBI agents came to the Math and Science Library at Columbia University. According to Schmidt's account, these agents asked a clerk questions about the use of the library by foreigners. A librarian who heard the conversation referred the agent to the head of the library. The head librarian reported this contact to the New York Library Association Intellectual Freedom Committee, which in turn reported it to the ALA. This led to an ALA investigation and subsequent congressional hearings. The FBI agreed to discontinue the program but did not guarantee that it would not be started again.

National security is an important issue in our society, but so is our concern that the rationale of national security not be employed simply to suppress embarrassing information or to impede the free flow of ideas unnecessarily.

### Transmission and Control of Information across National Boundaries

The ability to disseminate information globally has raised some important questions. In a world in which satellites can instantaneously transmit information, in which substantial electronic computer storage is both practical and economical, and in which this information can be transmitted and retrieved by microcomputers in homes around the world, the globalization of information raises deep issues about the impact of the spread and control of such information. Although there may be many reasons to control dissemination of information, the United Nations has asserted an underlying principle that is familiar to all Americans. In its Universal Declaration of Human Rights, Article 19, it states,

> Everyone has the right to freedom of expression and opinion. This right includes freedom to hold opinions without interference and to seek, receive, and impart information and ideas through any media regardless of frontiers.

The international exchange of information is sometimes referred to as transborder data flow (TDF) and concerns itself primarily with the flow of digital information across borders for storage or processing in foreign computers. There are a variety of personal, economic, national, and sociocultural issues to be dealt with, which can only be briefly identified here.

PERSONAL ISSUES

Because individual records throughout the world are stored on computer systems, it has become common to transmit this information to various organizations both private and governmental. Attempts have been made, especially in Europe, to control the unnecessary transmission of personal information across national borders so that individual rights are protected at the same time that necessary information can be transmitted (Bortnick 1985).

## ECONOMIC ISSUES

The information industry is worth billions of dollars, and nations naturally compete to dominate this market. This leads to international issues such as tariff and trade regulations that restrict or encourage the flow of information and information technologies. Similarly, different countries may impose special standards on equipment or insist on a pricing structure inconsistent with the producer (Bortnick 1985). Of considerable interest is placing tariffs on the information itself, not just on the equipment or information products used to transmit it.

## NATIONALISTIC ISSUES

The concerns over national issues related to TDF have grown over the years. Among those is the fear of a foreign national dominating the information resources of one's country. Over the years, this has usually meant the domination of the United States, but it could also imply other countries and multinational corporations. There is always a temptation on the part of a country to jump ahead by importing technologies, software, and information from another country. This usually means adopting the hardware, software, language, and cultural assumptions of the country that provides these means. Similarly, the importing of information technologies may inhibit a country's ability to create its own infrastructure to produce its own technologies. As nations become increasingly dependent on the technologies of another nation, this may be perceived as a potential threat to their sovereignty. Similarly, countries may define public and private information differently. Information readily and legally available in one country may not be legally available in another (e.g., information on drugs or sexuality). Given the ease by which electronic information can be transmitted, this can generate much national concern.

Another concern is the protection of national-security information from electronic intrusion by another country. Electronic storage of highly sensitive governmental information is now common in many countries, and the fear that the information may be accessed and transmitted across international borders is a common and important concern.

SOCIOCULTURAL ISSUES

Technologies transform fundamental values, assumptions, and activities within society. The introduction of such technologies that are not consistent with these values and assumptions may create social and cultural dislocations that are unanticipated and undesired. Could the introduction of information technologies increase the capacity of government leaders to control their populations? Could such technologies change the economic basis of a society from rural to urban? Could devoting fiscal and human resources to building a technological infrastructure divert needed resources from other vital activities?

The importation of new technologies from one country to another can also raise serious concerns about undue cultural influence or dominance. There is a fear that such technologies can influence populations through the messages that are received. Thus a developing nation, for example, may fear the influence and effect of technologies imported from a Western nation, especially in terms of the developing nation's own culture and traditional values.

## Attempts to Control Artistic and Other Individual Expression

The government has attempted in a variety of ways to control the flow of certain types of information and expression. It has restricted information that is harmful to national security, libelous, slanderous, or which could incite individuals to violence. Among the other categories it has tried to limit are artistic expression, expression in opposition to the U.S. government, and sexually explicit materials.

### ARTISTIC EXPRESSION

There is a long history in the United States of attempts to censor books, plays, and works of art. The suppression of such material has been of great concern to libraries. Although some works that were suppressed have been of questionable artistic merit, there are many other items that have reached the status of literary classics such as James Joyce's *Ulysses* and J.D. Salinger's *Catcher in the Rye*. Usually, it is obscenity statutes and postal regulations that have been used to regulate this type of information. Today, other tactics are also being used to limit artistic expression. Most notably, pressure has been put on funding federal programs such as the National Endowment of the Arts (NEA) because of objection to the content of some of the projects funded. Funding for NEA has been held up periodically and provisions of NEA law have been changed in an attempt to prevent what some view as offensive content. It is doubtful that attempts to use information policies to suppress artistic expression will abate in the near future. Attempts to regulate the content on the Internet through legislation (such as Communications Decency Act, recently ruled unconsitutional) is another example of this continued scrutiny.

### EXPRESSION IN OPPOSITION TO THE U.S. GOVERNMENT

A variety of State Department, postal, and import regulations have been used to bar either speakers or information from entering the United States when the information provided is considered contrary to the interests of the U.S. government. Foreign nationals, for example, have been prevented from speaking at conferences, e.g., members of the Irish Republican Army (IRA). Similarly, films considered to be propaganda have been prohibited. Some years ago this happened to a Canadian film on acid rain that was in opposition to the Reagan administration's view that acid rain was not a serious problem.

### SEXUALLY EXPLICIT MATERIAL

Federal, state, and local laws usually prohibit the production, importation, and mailing of obscene materials. These federal laws have shaped a complex, sometimes opaque, policy. It is clear, for example, that child pornography is not permitted in our society. On the other hand, explicit sex-education books showing nude children might also be construed as obscene under the laws. Information policy on sexual information remains a confused matter because of court interpretations on obscenity laws. Since determination of obscenity is based on community standards, it is hard to know what material can be restricted and what cannot. What is clear is that laws are used to try to define and restrict such material.

## Copyright or Intellectual Property Rights

One of the most complex legal and ethical issues facing information creators, disseminators, organizers, and users is the issue of copyright and intellectual property. Intellectual property includes a variety of products including patents, trademarks, and publications (print, electronic, and audiovisual). Of course, a major issue in the field of library and information science is the copyright of publications. Central to this concern is determining to what extent the creator or publisher of information can control the copying and use of that information by others. This has been further complicated with the development of the Internet, which is changing our notion of "publication." Does something become a publication once it is available on the Internet? Given the ease with which versions can be changed, which version is copyrighted and how can it be protected?

ALA considers this such a serious issue that one provision of its Code of Ethics is specifically devoted to respect for intellectual property rights, and the Association of Research Libraries has its own statement on this issue as well (Appendix A).

It is important to realize that the purpose of the copyright law is based on the power granted to the federal government in the U.S. Constitution. It states that the Congress has the power to "promote the Progress of Science and useful Arts, by securing for limited Times to Authors and Inventors the exclusive Right to their respective Writings and Discoveries" (U.S. Constitution, Article I, Section 8, Clause 8). The basic idea is that by rewarding individuals for their creative efforts, the society benefits.

This benefit cannot be assumed in each and every case, and from a constitutional perspective, information policies must consider a balance between the interests of those who deserve to profit from their ideas and creations and the rights of individuals to have access to and use of information. This balance can be very difficult to obtain, especially given the political power of the for-profit sector. Sometimes, it seems as though the current attitude is that the copyright law is primarily to protect the economic interests of publishers and producers. This tension has created considerable controversy. Librarians find themselves in the center of this controversy since they depend on authors and producers of information to maintain the reservoir of knowledge so critical to library functions. On the other hand, librarians also have a strong conviction that information access, either physical or electronic, should be available at minimum or no cost to the user. Hence librarians favor very generous copying privileges, and producers favor restricted ones.

The constitutional objective of promoting developments in the useful arts and sciences and rewarding creators for their original ideas is codified in federal law through the U.S. Copyright Act, its most recent version being passed in 1976. The act does not deal with the ideas themselves, but with ideas once they are "fixed" in some form—they may be fixed in a variety of formats, including print, a phonodisk, or a computer disk. Generally, copyright ownership resides with the author of the work, unless it is turned over to another individual or organization, such as a publisher. The Copyright Act protects eight categories of works:

- literary works;
- musical works, including any accompanying words;
- dramatic works, including any accompanying music;
- pantomimes and choreographic works;
- pictorial, graphic, and sculptural works;
- motion pictures and other audiovisual works;
- sound recordings; and
- architectural works. (17 U.S.C. Section 102[a] [1988 & Supp V 1993])

Copyright interpretation has been complicated because so many documents are now made available in an electronic environment. In fact, by the late 1970s it had become clear to information producers and disseminators that the development of new technologies had raised a variety of critical issues. The 1976 Copyright Act does not explicitly identify electronic works such as floppy disks and compact disks as works protected by copyright legislation. However, the act itself does state that

Copyright protection subsists, in accordance with this title, in original works of authorship fixed in any tangible medium of expression, now known *or later developed* [italics mine], from which they can be perceived, reproduced, or otherwise communicated, either directly or with the aid of a machine or device (17 U.S.C. 102).

The House Report (1976), however, describing the legislative intent of the Copyright Act, reveals that a broad meaning was to be given to the concept of a "literary work" that would be protected by the act. In fact, the concept includes "computer databases, and computer programs to the extent that they incorporate authorship in the programmer's expression of original ideas . . . (House Report 1976)." Thus, ideas fixed in media such as CD-ROMs, floppy disks, digital tape, and optical and compact disks are all subject to the copyright law (Information Infrastructure Task Force 1995).

The exclusive rights of the copyright owner are considerable. They include the rights

(1)  to reproduce the copyrighted work in copies or phonorecords;
(2)  to prepare derivative works based upon the copyrighted work;
(3)  to distribute copies or phonorecords of the copyrighted work to the pub-

lic by sale or other transfer of ownership, or by rental, lease or lending;
(4)  in the case of literary, musical, dramatic, and choreographic works, pan-
     tomimes, and motion pictures and other audiovisual works, to perform
     the copyrighted work publicly; and
(5)  in the case of literary, musical, dramatic, and choreographic works, pan-
     tomimes, and pictorial, graphic, or sculptural works, including the indi-
     vidual images of a motion picture or other audiovisual work, to display
     the copyrighted work publicly. (17 U.S.C. Section 106 [1988 & Supp. V
     1993])

As might be expected, those who produce original works, or who purchase the rights to reproduce such works, wish to restrict copying privileges by others. Librarians, on the other hand, wish to disseminate information as freely as possible. This is usually accomplished by loaning the material or making copies (or permitting others to make copies) of materials. The right to perform these functions is currently defined under two doctrines in the copyright law, the Right of First Sale and the doctrine of fair use.

### RIGHT OF FIRST SALE

The Right of First Sale is the fundamental right that permits libraries and others to loan copyrighted materials to others. Under this right, the owner of a lawfully made copy is authorized "without the authority of the copyright owner, to sell or otherwise dispose of the possession of that copy . . . " (17 U.S.C., Section 109 [a] [1988]). The model by which libraries operate today and have operated in the past, is that they purchase an item (book, periodical, film, etc.), and once they have purchased it, they can subsequently loan that item without remunerating the copyright owner. The Right of First Sale supports the fundamental notion of "subsidized browsing" so important to libraries. That is, library funds are expended to purchase the item, hence, subsidizing the use by the library patrons. It is critical to keep this in mind, because electronic dissemination of information is substantially altering this notion. The implications of this will be discussed below.

### FAIR USE

The doctrine of fair use, which has been developed over many years, identifies uses of copyrighted material that fall outside the control of the copyright owner. When an individual makes a copy under the fair-use doctrine, he or she is not required to get permission from the copyright owner. The complexity and subtleties involved in interpreting when a use is "fair use" are tremendous, and there is little doubt that with the introduction of electronic access, the issue will become even more complicated. The key provision of the Copyright Act is Section 107, which identifies four specific criteria that must be considered when determining whether a use constitutes "fair use." They are

(1) the purpose and character of the use, including whether such is of a commercial nature or is for nonprofit educational purposes;
(2) the nature of the copyrighted work;
(3) the amount and substantiality of the portion used in relation to the copyrighted work as a whole; and
(4) the effect of the use upon the potential market for or value of the copyrighted work (17 U.S.C. Section 107).

As a rule, the fair-use doctrine is more likely to apply when the use is noncommercial (used for educational or research purposes) and would have little effect on the profits of the copyright owner. There are many restrictions, however. For example, copying of films, videocassettes, and sheet music has more severe restrictions.

Librarians depend heavily on the fair-use doctrine in making copies for users or permitting patrons to make copies for themselves. An area of particular concern, however, for publishers is librarians making copies for interlibrary loan purposes, especially copies of periodical articles. Librarians, of course, would like to make such copies freely, but it is natural that the publishers should be concerned with loss of subscription income. The copyright law addresses this issue by permitting libraries to make individuals copies of most copyrighted works, but not "in such aggregate quantities as to substitute for a subscription to or purchase of" a copyrighted item (17 U.S.C. 108 [g][2]). The law, however, does not clearly identify how much copying is too much. Fortunately, the issue was subsequently addressed by the National Commission on New Technological Uses of Copyrighted Works (CONTU). This commission was created while the 1976 Copyright Act was being drafted primarily to deal with the effects of computers on copyrighted works. However, it also agreed to address the issue of photocopying as well (CONTU 1978).

CONTU consisted of members from the legal profession, librarians, journalists and writers, consumer organizations, publishers, business executives, and officials of the Library of Congress and Copyright Office (CONTU 1978). The end product of their deliberations is known as the "CONTU Guidelines on Photocopying under Interlibrary Loan Arrangements" (CONTU 1978, p. 54). In an attempt to balance the interest of periodical publishers with those of libraries, CONTU attempted to clarify what was meant by "aggregate quantities as to substitute for a subscription . . . " (17 U.S.C. 108 [g] [2]). In doing so, they established a guideline that permitted libraries to make as many as five copies from a given periodical in a given calendar year (CONTU 1978). The guideline applies only to requests for periodical articles published within the last five years. The CONTU guidelines were subsequently incorporated as part of the legislative history of the 1976 Copyright Act (CONTU 1978). As such, they play an important role in guiding library photocopying practices for interlibrary loans.

For copying activities that exceed "fair use," a mechanism has been established to assist in the payment of royalties to publishers. This is the Copyright Clearance Center (CCC). This center licenses photocopying by corporations and other institutions by creating agreements with a wide variety of journal publishers. Royalty payments are made to the CCC, which then grants the right to make copies of the material. The doctrines of fair use and Right of First Sale have served as important foundations defining the rights of access to information for many years.

*Telecommunications Legislation*

There is no doubt that our society is becoming increasingly reliant on telecommunication systems to create, organize, and disseminate information. The dynamic character of the National Information Infrastructure (NII) has led legislators to recognize the need for new legislation to address the new issues that have arisen as this infrastructure has increased in sophistication. The result is the Telecommunications Act of 1996, signed by President Clinton on February 8, 1996. Interestingly, it was signed at the Library of Congress. Two aspects of the act have direct effects on libraries. One deals with the cost to libraries and other educational institutions to use telecommunication lines for access to the Internet. Under what is known as the Snowe-Rockefeller-Kerry-Exon provision, the legislation authorizes reduced rates for libraries, schools, and health care providers for access to the Internet. The implementation of these rates is through the Federal Communications Commission which on May 7, 1997, created new rules that mandate substantial discounts of between 20–90 percent for schools and libraries ("FCC Approves . . . " 1997).

Another provision of the act, known as the Communications Decency Act (CDA), subjected a person who knowingly transmitted or displayed materials that might be construed as "indecent" to minors to fines and criminal penalties. Indecency was construed very broadly to include words as well as images. This provision was challenged by the American Library Association and other organizations, and the Supreme Court declared this section of the law to be unconstitutional and a violation of the First Amendment. Justice John Paul Stevens, writing for the majority of the Court, noted that the

> CDA lacks the precision that the **First Amendment** requires when a statute regulates the content of speech . . . As a matter of constitutional tradition, in the absence of evidence to the contrary, we presume that governmental regulation of the content of speech is more likely to interfere with the free exchange of ideas than to encourage it. The interest in encouraging freedom of expression in a democratic society outweighs any theoretical but unproven benefit of censorship (*Janet Reno v. American Civil Liberties Union et al.*)

Although this provision was successfully challenged, the passage of the CDA reflects a strong desire on the part of some to control materials sent through telecommunication lines and to punish those who send undesirable materials (whatever that means). It is likely that new versions of the CDA will be proposed in the future.

It is understandable that this legislation prompted a strong reaction from the electronic community. In fact, it generated a new "Declaration of Independence" from one of the founders of the Electronic Frontier Foundation (EFF), a group that devotes its energies to promoting freedom on the Internet. On February 10, 1996, John Perry Barlow published electronically "A Declaration of the Independence of Cyberspace" (Barlow 1996). It raises a variety of critical issues of intense interest to the new electronic community and demonstrates the impact of national information policies (see Figure 4.1).

In a way, one might describe this declaration as a "counter-information policy." It demonstrates something new about the electronic community—a belief that this community is extra-national, perhaps even extra-physical: it is not in three-dimensional space at all, but cyberspace. As such, there is a denial of conventional laws, rights, and practices. It is a new "social contract," in essence, a new society. The consequences of such a view are not known at this time, but given the fact that the Internet was designed with great flexibility, so that it could withstand even a nuclear attack, the difficulties in controlling such "independents" may well prove quite formidable.

---

**Figure 4.1**
**A Declaration of the Independence of Cyberspace**

Governments of the Industrial World, you weary giants of flesh and steel. I come from Cyberspace, the new home of the Mind. On behalf of the future, I ask you of the past to leave us alone. You are not welcome among us. You have no sovereignty where we gather.

We have no elected government, nor are we likely to have one, so I address you with no greater authority than that with which liberty itself always speaks. I declare the global social space we are building to be naturally independent of the tyrannies you seek to impose on us. You have no moral right to rule us nor do you possess any methods of enforcement we have true reason to fear.

Governments derive their just powers from the consent of the governed. You have neither solicited nor received ours. We did not invite you. You do not know us, nor do you know our world. Cyberspace does not lie within your borders. Do not think that you can build it, as though it were a public construction project. You cannot. It is an act of nature and it grows itself through our collective actions.

You have not engaged in our great and gathering conversation, nor did you create the wealth of our marketplaces. You do not know our culture, our ethics, or the unwritten codes that already provide our society more order than could be obtained by any of your impositions.

You claim there are problems among us that you need to solve. You use this claim as an excuse to invade our precincts. Many of these problems don't exist. Where there are real conflicts, where there are wrongs, we will identify them and address them by our means. We are forming our own Social Contract. This governance will arise according to the conditions of our world, not yours. Our world is different.

Cyberspace consists of transactions, relationships, and thought itself, arrayed like a standing wave in the web of our communications. Ours is a world that is both everywhere and nowhere, but it is not where bodies live.

We are creating a world that all may enter without privilege or prejudice accorded by race, economic power, military force, or station of birth.

We are creating a world where anyone, anywhere, may express his or her beliefs, no matter how singular, without fear of being coerced into silence or conformity.

Your legal concepts of property, expression, identity, movement, and

## Figure 4.1 (cont.)

context do not apply to us. They are based on matter. There is no matter here.

Our identities have no bodies, so, unlike you, we cannot obtain order by physical coercion. We believe that from ethics, enlightened self-interest, and the commonweal, our governance will emerge. Our identities may be distributed across many of your jurisdictions. The only law that all our constituent cultures would generally recognize is the Golden Rule. We hope we will be able to build our particular solutions on that basis. But we cannot accept the solutions you are attempting to impose.

In the United States, you have today created a law, the Telecommunication Reform Act, which repudiates your own Constitution and insults the dreams of Jefferson, Washington, Mill, Madison, DeToqueville, and Brandeis. These dreams must now be born anew in us.

Your increasingly obsolete information industries would perpetuate themselves by proposing laws, in America and elsewhere, that claim to own speech itself throughout the world. These laws would declare ideas to be another industrial product, no more noble than pig iron. In our world, whatever the human mind may create can be reproduced and distributed infinitely at no cost. The global conveyance of thought no longer requires your factories to accomplish.

These increasingly hostile and colonial measures place us in the same position as those previous lovers of freedom and self-determination who had to reject the authorities of distant, uninformed powers. We must declare our virtual selves immune to your sovereignty, even as we continue to consent to your rule over our bodies. We will spread ourselves across the Planet so that no one can arrest our thoughts.

We will create a civilization of the Mind in Cyberspace. May it be more humane and fair than the world your governments have made before.

---

Reprinted with permission: John Perry Barlow, Electronic Frontier Foundation 1996.

*Education Legislation*

There are various library- and education-related legislation and policy statements that have a considerable effect on the information infrastructure, including libraries. Among the most notable items are the National Education Goals, the Higher Education Act, and the Elementary and Secondary Education Act.

NATIONAL EDUCATIONAL POLICY

Educational policy, for obvious reasons, has a significant effect on libraries. Because national policy influences the legislative agenda, it also significantly affects funding priorities for federal agencies. If libraries wish to partake of funds provided by the federal government, their programs and activities must reflect the priorities set by these funding bodies. A critical educational policy that affects libraries is the *National Education Goals* adopted by the United States Department of Education.

These goals and their implementation through a program titled Goals 2000: Educate America take as a basic assumption that the nation's schools will need considerable support and cooperation from community and other grass-roots organizations (U.S. Department of Education 1994). The formation of coalitions and partnerships is identified as an

---

**Figure 4.2**
**National Education Goals**

- All American children will start school ready to learn;
- At least 90 percent of our students will graduate from high school;
- Our students will demonstrate competency in challenging subject matter and will learn to use their minds well, so they may be prepared for responsible citizenship, further learning, and productive employment;
- American students will be first in the world in science and mathematics achievement;
- Every adult will be literate and have the knowledge and skills necessary to compete in a world economy and exercise the rights and responsibilities of citizenship; and
- Every school will be safe and drug-free and offer a disciplined environment conducive to learning.

essential aspect of helping the nation reach these goals. One natural part-
ner in helping to obtain these goals is the library. Children from preschool on must be given the opportunity and skills to survive and prosper in an increasingly complex and competitive world. Because these
goals so clearly implicate libraries in the national educational agenda,
the libraries' participation and proactive approach to assisting children
seems both natural and politically beneficial to both libraries and those
they serve.

### HIGHER EDUCATION ACT OF 1965/1992

The Higher Education Act of 1965 (HEA) was passed to support the
educational programs of colleges and universities. Title II was designed
to improve the quality of college library service. Grants were provided
for books and other materials and for training and research demonstration projects. Aside from assisting in the acquisition of library materials,
the grant has provided funding for many types of training programs
including cable-TV training, library technical education, development
of library curricula, and support for minority students in doctoral programs (Krettek 1975). HEA has also supported programs at the Library
of Congress to purchase scholarly materials for use by academic and
research libraries.

HEA was reauthorized in 1986 and most recently in 1992. The current titles of the law deal with such areas as promoting partnerships
among academic institutions, other state agencies, and primary and secondary schools serving low-income and disadvantaged students; assisting colleges and universities that serve a large number of minority students; providing funds to pay students who work for their local communities; encouraging individuals to become teachers and providing
continuing education and training for current teachers; promoting international studies; providing assistance to improve the physical facilities of academic institutions; providing financial assistance to graduate
students in need; increasing the number of minority students in science
and engineering; promoting the participation of urban academic institutions to help solve urban community problems; and increasing the
number of Native Americans attending academic programs.

Title II of the 1992 Act is currently titled Academic Library and Information Technology Enhancement (20 U.S.C. 1021). The provisions of
this title focus on assisting libraries in the acquisition of technologies;
promoting the education and training of individuals in library and in-

formation science, especially in institutions that serve a large number of minority students; promoting research and development in the improvement of library services; and maintaining and strengthening the major library research collections (20 U.S.C. 1021, Sec. 201.).

### ELEMENTARY AND SECONDARY EDUCATION ACT 1965 / IMPROVING AMERICA'S SCHOOLS ACT OF 1994

The Elementary and Secondary Education Act of 1965 (ESEA) was created to supplement state and local support to improve the quality of education for elementary and secondary schools, both public and private. Much of the act has been devoted to helping support programs for children with special needs or low income. Title II was the first provision designed to enhance the collections of school libraries and includes monographs, periodicals, and AV materials. At the time of the original passage of the act, nearly one-third of the students in school attended schools without libraries. ESEA helped resolve this problem by providing monies for textbooks, library resources, and other instructional materials. Since its enactment, funds have been used for development of curriculum and instruction, staff training and development, selection and purchase of instructional and library materials for pupils and teachers, setting of educational standards, demonstration of media programs; support of special-education programs, support for at-risk children, materials for bilingual studies, and support for the acquisition of materials in areas of social problems (Krettek 1975).

In 1994, the Improving America's School Act was passed as the reauthorization of the ESEA. This act contains a variety of provisions focusing on contemporary issues facing elementary and secondary education. Among the purposes identified for support are the following: (1) encouraging equal access to a quality education, especially for children in poverty; (2) encouraging parental participation in schooling; (3) upgrading the quality of instruction through professional development programs for teachers, administrators, and other school staff; (4) promoting the development and implementation of technology throughout school systems, using technology to enhance curricula and instruction and for administrative support; (5) providing funds to prevent violence and drug abuse in schools by supporting local organizations and agencies and helping them to develop and improve their violence- and drug-abuse programs; (6) encouraging the use of magnet schools to improve equal access to a quality education and reduce the effects of discrimination on minorities; (7) promoting innovative education programs and practices; (8) developing effective bilingual education programs; (9) ensuring that Native Americans, Native Hawaiians, and Alaskan Natives receive a high quality education while respecting their native cultures; (10) encouraging the coordination of health and social service agencies with school systems; (11) providing funds for improving the physical facilities of schools; and (12) providing technical assistance to school systems and other agencies in developing, administering, and implementing their educational programs (U.S. Department of Education 1997).

*Library Legislation*

THE LIBRARY OF CONGRESS

Some of the most critical library legislation deals with the activities of the Library of Congress (LC). LC was established in 1800 and is the closest thing the United States has to a national library (especially in conjunction with the National Library of Medicine, the National Agricultural Library and the National Archives). LC is one of the great repositories of the world with more than 118 million items, an operating budget exceeding $391 million, and staff of more than 4,100 individuals. Its stated mission is "to make its resources available and useful to the Congress and the American people and to sustain and preserve a universal collection of knowledge and creativity for future generations (*lcweb.loc.gov/ ndl/mission.html*). In 1999 alone, LC undertook more than 540,000 research assignments through its Congressional Research Service. It also provides limited services to the general citizenry; for example, it provides materials to the blind and physically handicapped. More than 22 million audiovisual and braille items were circulated in 1999 to more than 764,000 users. The use and collection of LC for 1999 is summarized in Figure 4.3 (Library of Congress 1999).

The programs funded by the Congress and implemented by the Library of Congress are many and varied. As developers of MARC, for example, LC transformed and made uniform the bibliographic record, which in turn has greatly accelerated the development of bibliographic utilities. Similarly, the considerable repository of materials at LC is primarily the result of the federal Copyright Law, which requires that publishers deposit two copies of each item published at the Library of Congress. Although LC is not required to retain material sent to it, this fed-

**Figure 4.3**
**Summary of Selected Data Concerning the**
**Library of Congress for 1999**

| | |
|---|---:|
| Number of on-site patrons and visitors | 2,000,000 |
| Number of items in collection | 118,993,629 |
|     Cataloged books | 18,024,002 |
|     Nonclassified items | 91,540,443 |
| Audio materials (disks, tapes, talking books) | 2,396,808 |
| Maps | 4,523,049 |
| Microforms | 12,555,509 |
| Visual materials | 13,371,794 |
| Electronic transactions per month | 80,000,000 |
| Number of staff | 4,194 |
| Total appropriations | 391,660,000 |

Source: "Library of Congress Year at a Glance—Fiscal Year 1999." (*Library of Congress, Public Affairs office 1999*)

eral law provides a means of creating a central repository for much of the material printed in the United States. The historical and research implications are manifest.

Recently, with the continuing concern over the growth of federal spending, the Library of Congress has come under serious scrutiny by the legislative branch. The Joint Committee on the Library of Congress, which has oversight over the Library, commissioned Booz-Allen & Hamilton and the Price Waterhouse accounting firms to conduct a review of the management and financial condition and practices of the Library. ALA considered the recommendations, including decentralizing the library collection, a serious diminution of the Library's role and mission and a threat to concept of the Library of Congress as a "national library." In part, this may be because of an overly optimistic conception of the National Information Infrastructure as being able to perform the function LC has performed over the years (American Library Association 1996). Clearly, this trend will need careful and continued monitoring.

THE DEPOSITORY LIBRARY PROGRAM

The federal government not only seeks information in great quantities, it produces great quantities. As the nation's largest printer, the government produces publications in monumental number and variety. The Depository Library Program is intended to make a selected, albeit substantial, number of these documents available to the citizenry by providing more than 1,300 libraries with copies of this material. These libraries are both public and academic, and some receive more complete sets of these documents than others. Nonetheless, such a program makes vast quantities of information available for public consumption. For example in 1999, the Government Printing Office (GPO) printed and distributed more than 40,000 titles in paper, microfiche, and electronic format. Of these items, approximately 16,000,000 copies were distributed to the depository libraries (GPO 1999). Because of the importance of the depository program, recent attempts to reduce funding for this program have concerned many people. In addition, as mentioned above, with the movement toward privatization of government information, such materials may not find their way to depository libraries. This would result in a reduction of available information to the citizenry.

Complicating this issue is the fact that more and more government information is being produced in electronic formats. There is some doubt as to whether it is possible to provide information free of charge given the costs of electronic formats and whether it is possible for the current depository system to accommodate the new responsibilities created by electronic dissemination of this information (Office of Technology Assessment 1988). This problem may become even more dramatic, because there is now a formal initiative to convert the print-based Depository Library Program to one that is almost entirely electronically based. Only twenty-four core titles will remain in print form at the completion of the project, October 1998. ALA has expressed both concern and support for this program, hoping that adequate funding will be provided to ensure access to government records and advocating free access to such electronic materials.

THE LIBRARY SERVICES ACT, THE LIBRARY SERVICES AND CONSTRUCTION ACT, AND THE LIBRARY SERVICES AND TECHNOLOGY ACT

Since 1956, the federal government has passed legislation to foster improved library services in the United States. Originally this legislation was meant to redress the considerable inequalities evident in library services to cities compared to those in rural areas. Consequently, the Library Services Act addressed the needs of public libraries serving fewer than 10,000 people. Funds were funnelled through the state library agencies. The restriction on size of libraries to be served was removed in 1964, and the legislation's name was changed to the Library Services and Construction Act (LSCA). To date, LSCA has been the largest single provider of federal assistance to libraries (Molz 1990). As the title change reflects, the funding was expanded to include not only improving library services, but also library construction. Over the years, a variety of titles (sections) have been added to the bill for potential funding. Until very recently, the titles included funding for public library services (Title I); construction (Title II); interlibrary cooperation (Title III); services for Indian tribes (Title IV); foreign-language materials acquisition (Title V); and library-literacy programs (Title VI). Programs under LSCA were administered by the Department of Education.

In the 1990s regular politically partisan attempts have been made to remove or reduce funding from various titles with varying success. In 1995 and 1996, concerted efforts were made to change the legislation to de-emphasize construction in favor of developing information technologies. The resulting legislation, however, did not clearly reflect these desires. On October 1, 1996, the Library Services and Technology Act (LSTA) was signed by President Clinton. Funds for construction remained the same, while there were decreases in funding for resource sharing and increases in funding for public services, especially for programming for children and literacy (*Slolist* 1996). LSTA reorganized the programs under the old LSCA, placing them under a newly formed Institute of Museum and Library Services rather than under the Department of Education. Despite this reorganization, one hopes that these changes will serve libraries equally well.

NATIONAL COMMISSION ON LIBRARIES AND INFORMATION SCIENCE ACT AND
THE WHITE HOUSE CONFERENCE ON LIBRARY AND INFORMATION SCIENCE

Created in 1970, the National Commission on Libraries and Information Science (NCLIS) is a non-partisan, independent agency, charged by Congress to assess continuously the problems that face libraries and to find ways to harness the potential of libraries. NCLIS consists of fifteen members, including the Librarian of Congress. Molz (1990) notes that it operates under four "rubrics": "access to information; information technology and productivity; improving library and information services; and policy, planning, and advice" (p. 21).

NCLIS serves in part as a national planning agency for libraries in the United States, although it does not really have significant formal powers. It also serves as the planning agency for the White House Conferences on Library and Information Science (WHCLIS). These conferences convene delegates from each of the fifty states as well as from seven U.S. Territories and the Native American community. They begin at the local level with preconference forums held in every state and are comprised generally of four categories of participants: library and information professionals, friends and supporters, government officials, and members of the general public (White House Conference on Library and Information Science 1991). Out of these forums, the delegates to the national conference are selected. There have been two such conferences since the commission's inception, and their recommendations serve as part of the national agenda for libraries. The last WHCLIS Conference was mandated by the Congress in 1988 and held in 1991. The conference had three fundamental themes:

*Library and Information Services for Democracy*: The conference recognized that there is an increasing reliance on information and that the potential for the creation of an information elite is also growing. If democratic institutions rely on an informed electorate and if, in a democratic society, information is power, then it becomes critical that literacy be promoted throughout the population and that the average citizen be able to access information effectively.

*Library and Information Services for Literacy*: The conference acknowledged that the U.S. ranked forty-ninth in literacy among 158 member countries of the United Nations and that there were nearly 23 million functionally illiterate adults with reading skills below the fourth-grade level. The conference also reported that there were an additional 35 million individuals classified as "semi-literate," who possessed reading skills below the eighth grade level. The delegates recognized that this problem is exacerbated by increasing numbers of children living in poverty, a dropout rate of high schoolers over 30 percent, and increasing diversity, both racial and cultural, all of which make the challenges to educate the country's young people even more difficult. Under these circumstances, libraries must play an ever-increasing role in promoting literacy.

*Library Information Services for Productivity*: The conference recognized that the economic system was being transformed from a labor-intensive one to an information-based one, and information has become a resource. This produces the need for well-trained "knowledge workers" who have the requisite skills to maintain their productivity in an information society. Similarly, business and industry will rely on information to maintain their competitiveness. This means the efficient and effective use of information technologies to continue leadership in a worldwide marketplace.

Within these three themes, nine areas of concern were identified. Together they represent a very good summary of the many issues facing libraries today: (1) Availability and Access to Information; (2) National Information Policies; (3) Information Networks Through Technology; (4) Structure and Governance; (5) Service for Diverse Needs; (6) Training to Reach End Users; (7) Personnel and Staff Development; (8) Preservation of Information; and (9) Marketing to Communities. The conference produced ninety-five final recommendations, some of which were identified as priority recommendations. Below is a synthesis of some of the priority recommendations and suggestions for implementing them (A complete list of priority recommendations is found in Appendix B):

- *Promoting student learning and literacy* by supporting demonstration grants to schools and library media centers for services to children and young adults, giving grants for information technologies including the networking of school libraries, developing partnerships with day care centers and other such agencies, developing partnership programs with schools and public libraries, creating family-literacy demonstration programs, and providing grants to library schools to educate librarians in children's and YA services. Special attention should be directed to literacy initiatives to the disadvantaged.

- *Building an education information network* by creating the National Research and Education Network (NREN), which would allow libraries and educational institutions to share their information and resources more effectively.

- *Providing sufficient support for information sources* by providing strong funding to support libraries and other educational institutions and encouraging the private sector to provide support for such institutions as well.

- *Developing model library-marketing programs* by assisting libraries in promoting themselves as key resources for educational, business, and personal needs.

- *Developing a national preservation policy* by providing funding to support strong programs in preservation training, developing a program to pre-

serve nonpaper materials, providing increased funding to support regional preservation centers, and developing and implementing new technologies to preserve library materials.

* *Improving rural services* by networking rural areas so that information
readily available to higher-density population areas can be available
equally to those in rural ones.

* *Amending copyright provisions* by recommending new copyright legislation to reflect the new developments in information technologies.

* *Protecting intellectual freedom* by encouraging Congress to enact national
information-policy legislation designating libraries as education institutions, identifying libraries as essential for a democratic society, and
protecting the freedom to read.

* *Reducing barriers for special groups* by recommending that Congress provide funding for programs to serve multicultural and multilingual groups
including Native Americans, providing funds for populations with special needs and those not traditionally served, and eliminating physical
barriers that present a problem for individuals with disabilities.

* *Ensuring access to information* by guaranteeing full and timely access to
public information. This involves ensuring that the Freedom of Information Act contain provisions to open all nonexempt records to public
scrutiny, reducing postal rates for libraries, providing low-cost access to
telecommunications services, and promoting better information access
to rural areas.

## INFORMATION POLICY ISSUES IN THE NETWORKED ELECTRONIC ENVIRONMENT

There is an initial temptation to focus on the technical aspects of the
new information technologies, but it quickly becomes clear that policy-
making and planning for future uses of these technologies are crucial
activities. Most notably, we have entered the age of the networked environment: an environment that breaks down the geographic barriers of
the past. The single most important development is the envisioning of a
National Information Infrastructure (NII), sometimes referred to as the
information highway or the National Data Highway. This exciting concept is promoted by politicians, scholars, researchers, business leaders,
and the military. Such a highway not only provides access to networks
around the world, but access to the information contained in those net-

works, which can be accessed, modified, or downloaded from almost anywhere in the world.

The United States already has an information infrastructure (Chapter 1) consisting of various communications channels and devices (radio, TV, publishers, etc.), but currently, there is no systematic integration of these channels. The NII would create just such an integration, and its potential has not been lost on the U.S. government. Among the benefits that have been projected for the NII are that it can

1.  Create jobs, spur growth, and foster U.S. technological leadership;
2.  Reduce health-care costs while increasing the quality of service in underserved areas;
3.  Deliver higher-quality, lower-cost government services;
4.  Prepare our children for the fast-paced workplace of the twenty-first century; and
5.  Build a more open and participatory democracy at all levels of government (Information Infrastructure Task Force 1993, p. 13) .

To foster the development of the NII, in 1993 the White House created the Information Infrastructure Task Force (IITF), the purpose of which was to "articulate and implement the Administration's vision for the NII" (Information Infrastructure Task Force 1993, p. 19). It is notable that the Task Force was chaired by Ronald Brown, the late Secretary of Commerce, and Bruce Lehman, Assistant Secretary of Commerce and Commissioner of Patents and Trademarks. Such leadership clearly put economic and business concerns at the forefront.

A variety of committees were appointed to execute the purpose of the task force, including a Telecommunications Policy Committee, which dealt with formulating policies on telecommunications issues such as universal service; an Information Policy Committee, which dealt with intellectual property and privacy and access to government information; and an Applications Committee, which promoted the application of information technologies in business, industry, government, and public services such as libraries. In addition, by executive order, the White House created the United States Advisory Council on the National Information Infrastructure, which is intended to solicit advice from the private sector.

Actually, the concept of the NII is a general one with very fuzzy boundaries. As a concept it arose slowly from an evolution in information technologies including the Internet and the political realization that a coordinated and effective information infrastructure was essential if the United States was to prosper, compete economically on the international level, and remain militarily secure in the next century. It is not to be assumed, however, that the NII is a single, unified, and systematically developed system. Rather there are many features to this infrastructure that have their own histories and independent evolution.

## Major Policy Issues on the NII

Although many issues in the development of the NII are technical, there are very serious policy implications as well. At this point, it is difficult to determine exactly what the ultimate effect will be on society as a whole, and libraries in particular. Several bodies have begun to develop principles or statements of rights and responsibilities regarding use of the NII. Two of these, Principles for the Development of the National Information Structure, and the EDUCOM Bill of Rights and Responsibilities for Electronic Learners can be found in Appendixes C and D.

As the Information Infrastructure Task Force developed its recommendations, there was some concern that their direction was unduly slanted toward business interests and that the public interest was not being fully represented. In 1993, representatives from fifteen organizations associated with libraries and other information-related activities met in Washington, D.C., at a forum sponsored by the Council on Library Resources, the National Science Foundation, and the American Library Association. The purpose of the meeting was to review many of the major policy issues raised by the development of the NII. This group developed a set of six principles, called the Principles for the Development of the National Information Infrastructure (NII) (Appendix C). Six basic areas were identified: First Amendment and Intellectual Freedom, Privacy, Intellectual Property, Ubiquity, Equitable Access, and Interoperability. A brief discussion of these six areas as well as additional concerns related to the development of the NII provides a critical perspective for understanding the important policies issues that have arisen.

## First Amendment/Intellectual Freedom

Freedom of speech is one of the primary rights accorded to each citizen. This freedom not only protects the right to express oneself, but also to receive information as well. The NII can certainly be perceived as a new and vital forum to express and hear the opinions of others. In addition, the Internet has been characterized by some as the last area where a "frontier" spirit reigns. It is a highly individualistic and attractive channel of communication; people have felt free to express themselves on any subject in any manner they see fit. Clearly, there is a strong interest in assuring the rights of free speech on the Internet. This implies not only that the content of what people say be protected, but also that the system permit free and open access to the network so people are able to express themselves and that the system be designed so that effective two-way communication is available. In addition, the network should ensure that, despite its increasing privatization, there will be "public spaces" on the NII in which people can express themselves freely on the issues of the day.

At the same time, some serious questions have been raised regarding uncontrolled speech on the Internet and the appropriateness of some of the subjects discussed, especially those that involve sexual and alternative lifestyle topics, e.g., homosexuality, bestiality, sado-masochism. Explicit sexual images as well as language can also be found. Similarly, some individuals have expressed highly unflattering opinions about other individuals on the Internet. This type of vituperative expression is referred to as *flaming*. Such issues raise a whole range of questions: (1) Who should have access to the Internet? (2) Should children have access at the same level as adults? (3) Should certain types of expressions or subjects be restricted or excluded on the Internet? (4) What are the legal liabilities involved if individuals send or download questionable material on the Internet? (5) Do obscenity laws apply in the Internet environment? Currently, there are a variety of laws being proposed to regulate certain types of expression on the Internet. No doubt this will be a continually evolving aspect as First Amendment rights are applied to the electronic environment.

*Privacy*

Marc Rotenberg (1994), from Computer Professionals for Social Responsibility (CPSR), has stated that " . . . protection of personal privacy may be the single greatest challenge in facing the developers of the National Information Infrastructure" (p. 50). Internet communication involves many different activities including sending and receiving e-mail messages, transmitting and downloading files, participating in electronic discussion groups, and commercial activities involving the purchase and sale of goods and services. These activities take place in the privacy of one's own home or in the work setting. Many Internet users are under the impression that their identities are confidential; in reality, they can usually be discovered easily. To what extent are our communications protected and private? Who can read our electronic messages and under what circumstances? CPSR has proposed a "Code of Fair Information Practices" (Rotenberg 1994) for the NII, which includes the following:

---

### Figure 4.4
### Code of Fair Information Practices

1. The confidentiality of electronic communications should be protected.

2. Privacy considerations must be recognized explicitly in the provision, use, and regulation of telecommunication service.

3. The collection of personal data for telecommunication services should be limited to the extent necessary to provide the service.

4. Service providers should not disclose information without the explicit consent of service users. Service providers should be required to make known their data collection practices to service users.

5. Users should not be required to pay for routine privacy protection. Additional charges for privacy should be imposed only for extraordinary protection.

6. Service providers should be encouraged to explore technical means to protect privacy.

7. Appropriate security policies should be developed to protect network communications.

8. A mechanism should be established to ensure the observance of these principles.

---

Reprinted with permission: Marc Rotenberg 1994. (Originally published in Rotenberg, Marc. "Code of Fair Information Practices." *Educom Review* March/April 1994, p. 51.

*Intellectual Property*

As noted above, traditionally, intellectual property has been protected by copyright laws (as well as patent and trademark law). The properties being protected were physical representations. Today, with electronic access, either online or through CD-ROMs, the producers of information tend to retain control of the information (the intellectual property). Traditionally, the creator of the information sold a physical item (book, periodical), which under the doctrine of the Right of First Sale could then be loaned as many times as the item would sustain the uses. But online access and CD-ROM databases generally do not circulate, and the copyright law generally has less impact under these circumstances. Under what conditions then is access to this type of information controlled? Generally, databases and CD-ROM access are regulated as much, if not more, by licensing and leasing agreements than by copyright. It is not uncommon for such agreements to be negotiated before these services are provided. The agreements set forth the conditions under which the library may disseminate the information and provide a very different context for the dissemination of information than in the past. Because these agreements are mutually agreed upon, they are governed by contract laws, a fundamentally different set of laws. Most notably, where the intent of copyright law had the primary objective to advance developments in the arts and sciences, the basis of contract law has no such idealistic motive. Rather, contract law is written to benefit the parties who enter into the contract; benefits to the society at large are entirely incidental. For the producers and distributors of the information there is no need to consider the social issues at all—merely the economic ones. Because libraries often must sign a licensing agreement before they can gain access to the information in a particular product, they exercise far less control over their ability to disseminate this information than under the Right of First Sale. Indeed, if a library discontinues its lease on an information product, it can lose its access to the information, both current and retrospective. Control of the intellectual property thus remains and resides with the producer of the information, and although the fair use doctrine still applies, these rights can be limited by the contracts that libraries sign. The extent to which this control will be maintained in the future may well depend on the policies and practices to be established in the years to come regarding use of information on electronic networks. To address this problem, six library associations—the American Library Association, the Association of Research Libraries, the

American Association of Law Libraries, the Association of Academic Health Sciences Libraries, the Medical Library Association, and the Special Libraries Association—developed a group of fifteen principles when negotiating licenses for electronic resources (American Library Association, "Principles," 1998). Among the issues that are addressed are the need for clear statements in the agreement concerning the nature of the access rights obtained, liability or lack thereof for unauthorized use, protection of users' privacy and confidentiality, rights to make archival copies, and protection of rights under the current copyright law (ALA "Principles," 1998).

The implications for network access however remain unclear. The development of digital technologies and the tremendous advances in the development of electronic networks have created an entirely new situation when it comes to copying information. Today, all types of information, visual, audio and print, can be digitized and stored electronically. This information can then be uploaded, downloaded, and otherwise made available on electronic networks. This information can then be copied many times without loss of quality in copying and sent to literally hundreds or thousands of individuals. The many intellectual-property issues that have arisen with the NII prompted the Clinton administration to address potential legislative changes to the Copyright Act. Consequently, the Working Group on Intellectual Property Rights, a subcommittee of the Information Infrastructure Task Force (Department of Commerce), was created to review the implications of electronic access on copyright issues. Their report, *Intellectual Property and the National Information Infrastructure* (1995), constitutes an important analysis of current thinking on this issue. The report's recommendations, some of which are major, and their suggestions for legislation have caused much controversy and discussion and resulted in the proposed NII Copyright Protection Act (H.R. 2441), which has been developed primarily by copyright owners. ALA and other organizations are currently involved in attempting to ensure that NII access not be too restrictive and thus impair legitimate and open access to information.

Similarly, control over intellectual property in the electronic environment is also an international issue. There have been previous international treaties on intellectual property including the Berne Convention for the Protection of Literary and Artistic Works (1971), and the Rome Convention for the Protection of Performers, Producers of Phonograms and Broadcasting Organizations (1961). But recent development in networked communication technologies have made it clear that these treaties are inadequate for the dramatically changed information environment. To this end, the World Intellectual Property Organization (WIPO), an agency of the United Nations, has been active in developing the legal and administrative controls over intellectual property disseminated across international boundaries. In December 1996, at a WIPO conference held in Geneva, a new WIPO Copyright Treaty was adopted. This treaty deals with literary and artistic works, including works of an electronic nature. Among its central features is that it extends copyright protection to computer programs, including their copying, distribution, and rental (WIPO 1997). Interestingly a major issue for debate at the conference was whether accessing a Web page, which requires that the computer store the data in RAM on a temporary basis, constituted making a copy—and hence requiring permission from the copyright owner. After much debate and controversy, the treaty did not grant copyright to this type of temporary storage. In other words, the copy must be fixed or distributable in a tangible form (Blum 1997).

*Universal Access*

The NII is rapidly becoming one of the primary channels of communication in the United States. If developed properly, it should provide a wide range of information services to homes, offices, organizations, and governmental agencies. A major issue is whether the Internet will continue to be open to all or will be foreclosed to only those who have the means to afford it. As commercial and private interests increase, there may be a temptation to exclude marginal users. Thus, public access to information on the Internet at little or no cost becomes a major political issue.

If one presumes that in a democratic society access to information is essential, then the Internet should, to a large extent, be barrier free. This means that use of the system should incur minimum or no cost to the average user. It also implies that the protocols required to use the Internet be simple enough so that most people can learn how to use it quickly and effectively. It further suggests that a wide variety of information sources be available and that the integrity (accuracy) of that information be high. There is little point to universal access if the information itself is questionable. Users may be especially vulnerable in electronic information systems because there is a tendency for the naive user to accept what is found on electronic networks.

How will ordinary citizens gain access to the rich sources of information on the Internet? Currently, the cost to connect to the Internet from home is considered modest by many, but for the poor it may be prohibitive. What types of information should be made readily available to all citizens at no cost, and how will they be able to access it? These are important questions that must be addressed.

*Equitable Access*

Services and products in this society are not equitably distributed. Geographic, social, and economic conditions often lead to inequitable access. Rural areas, for example, often have far inferior access to goods and services, including information services. Equality of access will require that diverse groups have a voice in the construction and governance of the NII, and that access to basic services be available and affordable for all.

In addition, it is important to consider the types of information that should be available to all on an equitable basis. For example, because the Internet can be a critical component in encouraging an informed citizenry, the network has a great obligation to make information concerning the government and government officials readily accessible. Conversely, the network should make it easy for all citizens to provide feedback to their federal, state, and local government and officials. It is not only governmental institutions that provide access: access to information in public institutions such as university, school, and public libraries should also be equitable. Other types of information that might be available to all include legal records, census data, statistical information and reports issued by the government, and information on various social services. Unfortunately, information on the Internet, especially for those unable to pay, may be significantly restricted as proprietary interests are balanced against the interests of the free flow of information.

Among the vital questions that arise are the following: Under what circumstances should the right of use and access be denied? What is the role of public institutions, such as public, school, and academic libraries, in providing open and equitable access to the Internet? How can information concerning government activities be effectively communicated to all citizens?

*Interoperability and Stability*

The amount of information that is available on the Internet is tremendous, but this does not mean that it is easy to access this information. The policies governing the design of the NII must ensure high levels of reliability, possess a wide array of functions, and permit easy access to information. The NII must be a system that is adaptable so that new functions can be added as they are developed, and it must also be able to withstand heavy use, natural disasters, and attempts to sabotage the system. In addition, if the NII is to work to maximum advantage, the various computer networks should be able to function seamlessly and promote effective transmission of information between the various networks.

The ability of computer systems to communicate with each other is called *interoperability*. Among many requirements, a key to attaining interoperability is the acceptance of national standards. Many of these standards are currently under development by the American National Standards Institute (ANSI) and the National Information Standards Organization (NISO). One of the most important standards adopted by ANSI is NISO standard Z39.50. The standard was developed with the cooperation of librarians and computer scientists and establishes rules for the search, location, and communication of certain types of information between computer networks. Its focus is on the search for and transmission of bibliographic and abstracting information and, therefore, has a critical impact on information retrieval functions. Without it, the sharing of electronic information so vital to librarians and researchers would be nearly impossible. The participation of librarians in the setting of these standards has given them the opportunity to have significant input into information transfer standards. Continued participation should provide an opportunity for leadership into future developments (Ward 1994).

There are many other standards that are being addressed including those related to the ordering of materials, interlibrary loan, and standards for the search, location, and transmission of video images, audio and video clips, and numerical data. Additional standards for bibliographic control are also being developed and improved for all types of media, periodicals, microfilms, technical reports. Obviously, the potential for an extremely efficient and effective system of information transfer is possible if and when good standards can be created and accepted by database producers, networks, and users.

*Governance*

Part of the difficulty and strength of the Internet lies in the fact that the Internet is not centrally managed; rather, it runs primarily on the cooperative efforts of its users, many of whom are responsible for maintaining one of the thousands of networks that are connected to the Internet. This has been described by one writer as "agreeable anarchy" (Tenner 1994).

The government has been an active participant in the development of the Internet, and it continues to have an interest, especially in balancing the interests of the citizenry with the obvious commercial interests involved. Overall, however, governance is, in many ways, based on a participatory design in which both users and producers of information coordinate their efforts. There is an Internet Activities Board (IAB) that serves a coordinating function for the design, engineering, and management of the system. Among the issues the IAB deals with are creation of Internet standards, network planning, and problem-solving (Computer Professionals for Social Responsibility 1993). Despite their good efforts, the effectiveness of the Internet relies greatly on those who maintain and improve the networks connected to it; their active participation and coordination drives the effective functioning of the system.

Because the NII will be playing such a vital role for information in the future, it is important that libraries participate actively in the information policy process, which will often occur at the national level. McKenna (1994) has made several recommendations to librarians as they compete in this dynamic political environment:

> Librarians need to take an active role during formulation of national policy and legislation to ensure that libraries receive adequate funding to be major players in the National Information Infrastructure (NII).
>
> Librarians need to take an active role in new legislation being proposed concerning intellectual property and copyright in an electronic environment.
>
> Librarians need to have significant influence on the evolution of Internet services and need to be prepared to share their ideas with administrators and project planners (p. 4).

*The Role of Government*

Although the federal government has recognized the increasing importance of the private sector to the development of the NII, it still has a significant role to play in NII development. To this end, the federal government has created an "Agenda for Action," which outlines the principles and objectives that it has adopted (Information Infrastructure Task Force 1993). Below is a brief summary of these major principles and objectives:

*Promote private sector investment.* Government policy suggests that the private sector bear the primary responsibility for the development of the NII and also be its chief benefactor. With more than $50 billion dollars invested each year by U.S. companies on the telecommunications infrastructure (the Government investing nearly $2 billion), government energies will be directed toward establishing appropriate tax and regulatory policies to encourage further private sector investment.

*Extend the "universal service" concept to ensure that information resources are available to all at affordable prices.* This concept has been discussed above and was part of the 1996 Telecommunications Act. The government recognized this concept previously when dealing with telephone communications under the Communications Act of 1934, which promoted telephone service for all citizens. Underlying the concern for universal access is the fear that allowing only the privileged to access information on the NII would only exacerbate the divisions between the information "haves" and "have nots."

*Act as a catalyst to promote technological innovation and new applications.* This will be accomplished, in part, by continuing to fund research and to support legislation that promotes the development of the NII. In addition, because the private sector has a large vested interest in such developments, research partnerships will be fostered. It is also recognized that some developments do not necessarily have profit-making potential for the private sector; these might include education- and health-related areas as well as the direct provision of government services. Resources for development in these areas will come from the government alone.

*Promote seamless, interactive, user-driven operations of the NII.* As has been noted above, the need for the many and varied computer networks that comprise the NII to operate effectively is crucial if its potential is to be realized. The government views such a system as open and interactive, promoting the view that users should be able to easily develop new services and applications that can be offered through the NII. To this end, participation of government agencies in encouraging standards-setting is vital.

*Ensure information security and network reliability.* Although it is crucial that the system be as open as possible, it is manifestly important that security and reliability also be maintained. Users must be confident that the system will properly route information to the appropriate sources and prevent interlopers from appropriating or reading files to which they have no authorized access. The role of government includes exploring means of protecting the privacy of citizens and investigative agencies, as well as promoting the development of appropriate encryption (code) technologies.

*Improve management of the radio frequency spectrum.* Wireless technologies will play a critical role in providing worldwide access to the NII. To this end, government policies are expected to broaden access to the various radio frequencies to promote use by the private sector and also to ensure access to radio frequencies for minorities, women, and rural areas.

*Protect intellectual property rights.* As noted previously, copyrights and other intellectual property rights are significantly affected by electronic access. Government policy is directed toward balancing the interest of the citizenry to free access to information while protecting the rights of creators and distributors so that they fairly profit from their efforts. Issues of policy interest include examining current copyright and other intellectual property laws to see if modifications are necessary, to offer recommendations regarding their modification, and to explore the means to identify copyright ownership on the NII and a means of remuneration for use.

*Coordinate with other levels of government and with other nations.* Internally, the United States is a multitude of political jurisdictions (federal, state, county, local) each with its own laws and regulations. As a consequence, energies must be devoted to scrutinizing those regulations that create barriers to the development of the NII. Given the national and international nature of this infrastructure (Global Information Infrastructure [GII]), there is a strong need to identify problematic laws and regulations within the various jurisdictions, to coordinate information policies, and to reduce burdensome regulations. Similarly, if the NII is to reach its maximum potential as a worldwide resource, it is necessary to identify international and national trade regulations that inhibit distribution of information technologies, to promote policies that increase the exportation of communication technologies, and to ensure that standards are set.

*Provide access to government information and improve government procurement.* The NII provides not only a tremendous opportunity to share information in general, it also provides a unique opportunity for the government to share the vast amounts of information that it collects each year. Therefore, it has been suggested that the government actively promote increased accessibility to government information through the NII. This involves converting information stored in traditional formats to electronic ones, making the electronic information available on the Internet, promoting citizen access by keeping costs to a minimum, increasing the use of e-mail, and fostering the development of new information technologies through federal procurement of them, creating a lucrative market for continued development.


## SUMMARY

As the value of information increases, there will be more and more stakeholders, each trying to maneuver governmental information policies to serve their needs. Librarians, like all other participants, must actively monitor the information-policy climate and aggressively make their case for the values that they strive to preserve. Because librarians are generally oriented toward service rather than profit, their voice is democratic and represents a vital advocate for the tradition of an open marketplace for ideas. There has been a long tradition of library and education legislation that has supported the role of libraries in this process. But the growth of electronic technologies and the emphasis on the NII as an economic stimulus have created competitors more interested in gain than in universal access. This may be both just and natural in a capitalistic society, but it makes it doubly important that libraries have a place in the information policy debate.

## REFERENCES

American Library Association. "Less Access to Less Information by and about the U.S. Government: XVII: A 1991 Chronology: June–December." Washington, D.C.: ALA, 1991.

————. *Newsletter on Intellectual Freedom.* March 1988.

————. "Principles for Licensing Electronic Resources." [Online] Available at *http: www.ala.org/washoff/ip/license.html* (January 7, 1998).

"ALA Lead Plaintiff in Lawsuit to Fight Communications Decency Act." ALAWON. 5, no. 5 (February 26, 1996).

Barlow, John Perry (Internet message): "The Life of Mind." Davos, Switzerland: The Cyberspace Society List. Electronic Frontier Foundation, February 8, 1996.

Blanke, Henry T. "Librarianship and Political Values: Neutrality or Commitment?" *Library Journal* 114 (July 1989): 39–43.

Blum, Oliver. "The New WIPO Treaties on Copyright and Performers' and Phonogram Producers' Rights." [Online] Available at *http://www.voncerlach.ch/wipo.htm#2A* (January 1997).

Bortnick, Jane. "National and International Information Policy." *Journal of the American Society for Information Science* 36 (1985): 164–168.

Burger, Robert H. *Information Policy: A Framework for Evaluation and Policy Research.* Norwood, N.J.: Ablex, 1993.

Computer Professionals for Social Responsibility. *Serving the Community: A Public Interest Vision of the National Information Infrastructure.* Palo Alto, Calif.: CPSR, 1993.

"Congressional Oversight Committee Reviews Library of Congress." ALAWON 5, no. 28 (May 17, 1996).

CONTU (National Commission on New Technological Uses of Copyrighted Works). *Final Report. July 31, 1978.* Washington, D.C.: GPO, 1978.

Dowlin, Kenneth E. "Access to Information: A Human Right?" In *Bowker Annual*, 32nd ed. New York: Bowker, 1987, 64–68.

"E-mail message." ALAWON 5, no. 2 (February 1, 1996).

"FCC Approves Telecom Subsidies for Libraries, Schools." *American Libraries* 28 (June/July 1997) 12.

Government Printing Office. "What is the GPO?" (Online) Available at *http://www.access.gpo.gov/public-affairs/5–99facts.html*

House Report. *House Report No. 94–1476, Copyright Act. In United States Code: Congressional and Administrative News.* 94th Congress-Second Session 1976. St. Paul: West, 1976, 5659–5823.

Information Infrastructure Task Force. *Intellectual Property and the National Information Infrastructure.* Washington D.C.: IITF, 1995.

————. *The National Information Infrastructure: Agenda for Action.* Washington D.C.: IITF, 1993.

*Janet Reno v. American Civil Liberties Union et al.* Cited in Citizen Internet Empowerment Coalition. "Supreme Court Opinion" [Online]. Available at *http://www.ciec.org/SC_appeal/opinion.shtml*, June 26, 1997.

Krettek, Germaine. "Library Legislation, Federal." In *Encyclopedia of Library and Information Science*. Vol. 15. New York: Marcel Dekker, 1975, 337–354.

Library of Congress. "Library of Congress Year at a Glance—Fiscal Year 1999. Public Affairs Office, 1999.

McKenna, Mary. "Libraries and the Internet." *ERIC Clearinghouse on Information Technology*, Syracuse University, 1994.

Molz, R. Kathleen. *The Federal Roles in Support of Public Library Services: An Overview*. Chicago: ALA, 1990.

National Commission on Libraries and Information Science. Public Sector/Private Sector Task Force. *Public Sector/Private Sector Interaction in Providing Information Services*. Washington, D.C.: NCLIS, 1981.

Office of Technology Assessment (OTA). *Informing the Nation: Federal Information Dissemination in an Electronic Age*. Washington, D.C.: OTA, 1988.

Rotenberg, Marc. "Privacy and the National Information Infrastructure," *Educom Review* (March/April 1994): 50–51.

Schmidt, C. James. "Rights for Users of Information: Conflicts and Balances among Privacy, Professional Ethics, Law, National Security." In *Bowker Annual*, 32nd ed. New York: Bowker, 1987, 83–90.

Science Applications International Corporation (SAIC). *Information Warfare: Legal, Regulatory, Policy and Organizational Considerations for Assurance*. Washington, D.C.: Pentagon, 1995.

*Slolist@winslo.state.oh.us* (State Library of Ohio Listserv). October 18, 1996.

Tenner, Edward. "Learning from the Net." *The Wilson Quarterly* (summer 1994): 18–28.

U.S. Department of Education. "H.R. 6: Improving America's Schools Act of 1994." [Online] Available at *http://www.ed.gov/legislation/ESEA/toc.html* (June 22, 1997).

———. *Goals 2000: Educate America*. Washington, D.C.: DOE, 1994.

Vagianos, Louis and Barry Lesser. "Information Policy Issues: Putting Library Policy in Context." In *Rethinking the Library in the Information Age*. Washington, D.C.: GPO, 1989, 9–42.

Ward, Maribeth. "Expanding Access to Information with Z39.50." *American Libraries* 25 (July/August 1994): 639–641.

White House Conference on Library and Information Science. *Information 2000: Library and Information Services for the 21st Century*, Washington, D.C.: GPO, 1991.

WIPO (World Intellectual Property Organization). WIPO Copyright Treaty. [Online] Available at *http://www.wipo.int/eng/diplconf/distrib/94dc.htm* (April 23, 1997).

# 5

## Information Policy as Library Policy: Intellectual Freedom

### LIBRARY INFORMATION POLICIES

The general subject of information policy bears a specific relationship to the field of library and information science. Although not usually discussed in this context, the fact is that the policies and practices that are established and implemented by libraries regarding the creation, organization, use, and dissemination of the knowledge contained within libraries are themselves information policies, and they have tremendous impact on the accessibility of information contained within those libraries.

### ORGANIZATION OF MATERIALS AND COLLECTIONS

At the very center of library function is the ability to organize library collections so that they can be easily accessed by patrons and librarians. The policies affecting this organization are, therefore, some of the most important information policies that a library establishes. Generally, as a matter of policy, libraries use one of two basic types of information organization for their materials: the Dewey Decimal Classification (DDC) or the Library of Congress Classification System. These systems and related systems such as the Library of Congress Subject Headings and the use of the Anglo-American Cataloguing Rules (AACR2) will be discussed in the chapter on the intellectual organization of libraries (Chapter 6).

*Selection and Collection Development Policies*

Although selection and collection development policies are not commonly thought of as information policies, they are, in fact, the guiding forces in determining the nature and type of information that is provided to library users. Libraries generally employ two basic information policies when building their library collections: collection development policies and selection criteria. These are very closely related but distinct.

A collection development policy takes a broad view of the collection. It answers such questions as What is the fundamental mission(s) of the library? What subjects should be collected and in what depth should each of the subjects be collected? What types of formats should be included in the collection and what should be the balance among these formats? Who are the library users and what types of materials and services should be provided to meet their needs? and What cooperative relationships should be established with other libraries and other information providers? Answers to these questions provide considerable direction to the library. A collection development policy serves many purposes: (1) as a planning tool to determine the use of monetary resources and staff; (2) as a guide to selectors in developing their collections; (3) as a means to ensure that collections are developed consistently over time and through changes of staff; (4) as a means to train new library staff; (5) as a statement of philosophy; and (6) as a defense in case of challenges to library materials (not an uncommon occurrence in many libraries.)

Selection criteria, on the other hand, are used to select individual items or small groups of items. Obviously, the individual selections should be consistent with the wider objectives of the collection development policy, but there remains a need to assess each item to determine if it is of sufficient quality, even if it seems to fit within the parameters established by the collection development policy. Selection criteria may vary in complexity from library to library, but there are some conventional criteria.

*Authority*: Knowledge and reputation of the author or of the organization producing the item.

*Appropriateness*: Match of the item to the intended users. For example, is the age level appropriate?

*Accuracy or timeliness*: The accuracy of the content and its currency.

*Physical characteristics*: The quality of the binding, paper, or material on which the information is stored. The size and quality of the print.

*Collection fit*: The contribution the item makes to the collection; the appropriateness of the item in relation to the collection development plan; the balance it provides to other points-of-view.

*Demand*: The popularity of the item and likelihood of use by library patrons.

*Content:* The quality of the information or narrative and the clarity of its organization.

*Special characteristics*: The availability of such features as indexes, bibliography, notes, prefaces, introductions, teacher guides, and interpretive material.

There are many other criteria that might be applied depending on the nature of the work and the format. New selection challenges have arisen as more and more information products become available on CD-ROM or on electronic networks. The rise of these new information technologies has forced libraries to consider information policies that address the balance of items that will be possessed physically by the library, e.g., books, periodicals, videos, and in remote locations, information that will be accessed electronically, e.g., searches of databases from networks or information vendors, such as DIALOG (Knight-Ridder). In addition, the decision to access information electronically through sources such as the Internet raises a variety of information-policy issues regarding the library's responsibility to control access to some types of information that would not otherwise be selected by the library, e.g. certain sexually explicit electronic files or the use of age restrictions on users of these networks.

## Service Policies as Information Policy

The policies that a library establishes to encourage or discourage library use are also information policies. Even the simplest of policies can have significant implications for information access. For example, the establishment of library hours can be seen as an information policy because it affects when individuals can have access to the information. More obvious policies include

- **circulation policies**: these policies include length of loan periods and renewal policies. They may also include the designation of some materials as noncirculating, requiring that the materials be used inside the library;
- **reference policies**: these policies include those affecting the types of services provided and the restrictions on such services. Examples are policies that set a time limit for the provision of reference service to an individual patron or a restriction based on the type of research (e.g. restricting service provided to students doing their homework or restricting the answering of contest questions). They may also include reference philosophy issues such as the belief that reference service should be primarily instructional, assisting the patron to learn how to get to information (quite common in academic and school libraries), in contrast to the belief that reference service means getting the patron the answer (more common in public-library adult-reference service or in special libraries). Such policies affect the nature of library service and the type of information provided.
- **personnel and staffing policies**: library service remains a labor-intensive activity. Therefore, the type and size of the service staff has a direct effect on the quantity and quality of information services that can be provided. If a library decides to hire subject experts in a particular field, e.g., business or genealogy, this will affect the use and depth of service provided. The same may be said if knowledgeable children's librarians are hired to develop in-depth children's services.

Perhaps one of the most controversial and important information policies facing libraries concerns charging fees for services. Although fees have been part of many libraries' practices for years, the practice has increased substantially since the development of electronic access. Today, about 70–80 percent of public libraries charge some user fees. The debate over charging has been recognized as a fundamental issue by professional associations and in the library community. The arguments for and against fees have been well summarized by the National Commission on Libraries and Information Science (1985).

PRO-FEE ARGUMENTS

1.  Charging fees increases recognition of the value and importance of library services.
2.  Fees encourage efficient use of public resources. Those who benefit from a given service should pay for its associated costs. An efficient pricing

system allows the consumer the flexibility to choose from a variety of public goods and services and pay an amount that is in proportion to the amount consumed.

3.  Fees promote service levels based on need and demand. The willingness of the public to pay for a service is a good indication of the public's demand for the service.

4.  Fees encourage management improvements. Examples of such improvements include increased productivity, better time management, better organization and control, and the establishment of a management plan based on staffing, equipment, and available resources. Accurate financial control is an ongoing responsibility for the departments that administer fee based facilities.

5.  Fees limit waste and over-consumption. Setting a fee can lessen inefficient or wasted use of public facilities. Fees have a rationing effect on user consumption. Indeed, a pricing plan may be structured to limit "peak load" situations or encourage use in off hours.

6.  Fees enhance investment in ongoing maintenance and repair of public facilities. Fees improve the level of facility maintenance in providing revenue dedicated to maintaining the service.

7.  Fees encourage a better understanding of the financial limitations of the local government. Pricing public facilities indicates that there are financial limits to what government can provide.

8.  Premium service should be provided only to those willing to pay a premium. Users should be given the choice of having these services. These are services not traditionally provided by the library.

9.  The tradition of charging for services is part of American culture. Users pay fees for other public resources and services such as bridges, highways, museums and parks.

10.  Fees control growth of and lower demand for service. If service demand is greater than capacity to meet that demand, fees help to discourage "frivolous" use of services.

11.  Escalating service costs make user fees a necessity. Information has economic value. "Free" access to information is not the same as "without charge." Adopting a no fee policy forces substantial limits to service. "Free" services are unrealistic in times of tight budgets.

12.  Most library users can afford to pay a fee. The public library serves a relatively young, educated, middle-income segment of the population. Low-income persons make limited use of the library. A fee-based library would relieve the poor of the tax burden associated with the free library.

13.  Without fees, public and academic libraries could not serve the larger community or non-residents. Fees for nonresidents are equitable since this group does not pay the taxes levied on residents. Fees for non-students are equitable because this group pays no tuition.

14.  Fees cover only a small portion of the total costs of service provision.

15.  Fees for most services are simple and inexpensive to collect.

16.  Local policy may require libraries to charge for services.

1.  Library services are a public good. Free access is a fundamental right of each citizen.
2.  The American tradition of free library services is damaged by charging fees. The introduction of fees is the beginning of the end of free library services.
3.  Fees are illegal. (In some states, laws prohibit the charging of fees in some municipal or other public agencies. Lawyers need to be consulted.)
4.  Fees are discriminatory. Only those who can afford to pay may use special services. Fees negate equal access to information. They discriminate against those users who either lack the resources to pay for services, or are unwilling to pay for services. An individual's access to information will be based on ability to pay rather than need.
5.  Fees represent a form of double taxation. Users are charged first by taxes to operate public services and then by charges for special services.
6.  Libraries will place emphasis on revenue-generating services. Libraries will shift from nonrevenue producing services to those which generate revenue, even if the nonrevenue services are vital to a part of society which cannot afford the fee.
7.  Fees will have the long-term effect of reducing public support for libraries.
8.  Fees might not be used to support library services. Revenues received from fees may be returned to the general revenue fund and allocated for non-library uses.
9.  The social benefits of library services are difficult to measure, therefore a fee cannot be efficiently assigned. Fees charged have been set by tradition and habit and not out of any analysis of market demands or costs.
10. It is difficult to define special and basic services and to distinguish between them. Should citizens be expected to pay extra for better fire department equipment, or additional police security assistance? Services once viewed as special are now viewed as basic.
11. Private and public sector markets are separate and should remain separate. The private sector should charge fees, reap profits and compete in whatever manner is appropriate. Public funded libraries should provide services out of their budgets and should not provide services for a fee.
12. The costs of administering and collecting fees outweighs the financial benefits of fees.
13. Most users have little need for fee-based online services. Users don't need a speedy response; they simply want an answer. Fee-based online services are really a convenience for the librarian, not the user.
14. If the service cannot be provided without a fee, the service should not be provided.
15. Improvements within library management and delivery of services would diminish the need for fees.
16. There is considerable staff resistance to fees.

17.   Charging for a service subjects libraries to liability risks because of the responsibilities implicit in providing a service for a fee (pp. 9–10.)

*Preservation as Information Policy*

Libraries have many purposes and one of the oldest is the preservation of the human record. Unfortunately, for a number of reasons many library materials are deteriorating. These include (1) poor environmental conditions, such as unstable temperatures or improper levels of humidity; (2) improper handling of materials by patrons and library staff; (3) natural disasters such as fire and flood; and (4) the presence of insects that damage materials. Perhaps the most prominent reason, however, involves the nature of the materials themselves. Most print materials published since the 1850s are printed on paper that is highly acidic. This acidity was introduced by the process used to make the paper. As the years pass, the acid slowly breaks down the paper, making it dry and brittle. The result is that the paper literally crumbles, whether it is being used or not. Many libraries, especially research libraries that maintain materials for many years, are suffering severely from this deterioration, and there is far too little money available to restore or preserve most of these materials. As a consequence, a substantial part of the written record may eventually be lost.

The preservation policies that are established by libraries are critical information policies because in many ways they are decisions as to what ideas or materials will continue to exist. Libraries, for example, may have policies on what materials will be microfilmed or repaired. They may have a disaster plan in case of unpredictable natural events like fires. Recently, the federal government increased funding for the preservation of scholarly materials. With the available technologies such as microfilm and emerging technologies such as the videodisc, more materials might eventually be saved. In fact, the Library of Congress has initiated a major project to digitize (convert to electronic data) a sizeable portion of its collection. This is called the National Digital Library Program (NDLP) and is a cooperative effort with the private sector. The costs involved are considerable; digitizing a page can cost between $2 and $6. The NDLP target is to have about 5 million items digitized by the year 2000. Currently the program is focusing on about 200 special collections representing unique items such as photos, sound recordings, maps, and personal papers (Lamolinara 1996).

*Intellectual Freedom as Information Policy*

Most prominent among the information-policy issues for libraries are those related to intellectual freedom. Intellectual freedom issues are implicated in librarianship when a variety of activities are performed, such as selecting materials, not selecting or weeding materials, classifying materials, physically locating materials in the collection, establishing reference-service policies, or establishing administrative policies such as those requiring confidentiality. Concern for the protection of intellectual freedom is certainly as important now as it has ever been. Some have noted that attempts to censor library materials have been on the rise since the 1980s, and what has become most prominent has been the increased number of groups, in contrast to individuals, that are systematically attempting to influence the character of library collections (Abbott 1990). Groups such as Family Friendly Libraries, the Christian Coalition, and Focus on the Family have been active in placing pressure on libraries regarding their materials. Of course, such attempts do not only come from politically conservative groups. Consequently, the array of materials that have been challenged over the years and more recently is quite varied. In 1999, among the most challenged books were J.K. Rowling's *Harry Potter* series, Phyllis Reynolds Naylor's *Alice* series, Walter Dean Myers, *Fallen Angels*, Margaret Atwood's, *The Handmaid's Tale*, Alice Walker's, *The Color Purple*, and David Guterson's, *Snow Falling on Cedars*. There were also perennial favorites such as Maya Angelou's, *I Know Why the Caged Bird Sings*, Judy Blume's, *Blubber*, John Steinbeck's, *Of Mice and Men*, and Robert Cormier's, *The Chocolate War*, which was the most challenged book of fiction for 1998 (American Library Association 2000). Movies have also been challenged. Sex and violence in movies are of major concern, but there have also been some surprises such as *Snow White*, *The Little Mermaid*, and *My Friend Flicka*. In addition, there have been broad-based attempts to create legislation that would have the effect of limiting the range of materials and services that could be provided through library collections and services.

Attacks on works such as those noted above highlight a fundamental value of most library and information work: the need to preserve intellectual freedom and the responsibility to resist censorship. Censorship is an act or set of acts by government, groups, or individuals (including librarians) to restrict the flow of information or ideas, usually because the content is considered offensive for political, religious, or moral reasons. The Code of Ethics and the ALA Library Bill of Rights (discussed below) place libraries securely within this context. However, intellectual freedom is a much larger concept than censorship. It deals with protecting the free flow of ideas or information. It is based on the fundamental belief that the health of a society is maintained and improved when ideas can be created and disseminated without governmental, political, or social impediment. Such an idea is hardly innocent; in some cases, it may lead to the propagation of heinous ideas with deleterious results. Such a view presumes, however, that the best way to combat a bad idea is not to suppress it, but to produce a better idea, and that the only alternative to censorship is tyranny. It presumes that the generation of good ideas is increased when there is unimpaired freedom to do so. There are those who fear that some ideas may be so clearly harmful that they should be restricted. These individuals are prone to acts of censorship.

As an issue, censorship and the protection of intellectual freedom are of prime importance to many libraries and the profession as a whole. On its surface, it seems obvious that the former should be inhibited and the latter promoted. Regrettably, the situation quickly becomes opaque. The protection of intellectual freedom is, in fact, one of the most difficult aspects of library work and is the cause of much professional controversy. At the root of the problem are what librarians often perceive as conflicting moral, ethical, personal, social, and legal obligations. Some of these obligations form powerful motivators to restrict access to some library materials, while other obligations serve as countervailing forces, encouraging unrestricted access. By making these forces more explicit, perhaps a better understanding can be reached as to why librarians sometimes have a difficult time making decisions on this issue.

### OBLIGATIONS THAT TEND TO RESTRICT ACCESS

*The obligation to act in accordance with one's personal values.* Each individual, through childhood training and experience, has developed certain moral precepts that form one of the bases for action. Information providers do not surrender these precepts just because they pass through the doors of the library. This is not to say that information providers should impose these precepts, but it is clear that certain circumstances that occur within libraries are more likely to evoke an interest in applying them than others. A common example would be the distribution of materials that promote bigotry. Librarians could believe that providing such material would be harmful, especially to children, and be inclined to restrict access.

*The obligation to protect, preserve, and maintain the values of one's community and those of the society as a whole.* As already noted, libraries and librarians do not exist outside the context of the society of which they are a part. Quite naturally, librarians and the libraries perceive themselves as part of the community. Many librarians not only work in the community but also live in it and participate in its many social, political, recreational, and cultural activities. Similarly, most libraries, public and school in particular, depend on local communities in terms of dollars and local friends and boosters. If a librarian values the community, then there is a general feeling that the collection and services provided should reflect its needs and desires. Indeed, the librarian may feel that the promotion of such values is both necessary and worthwhile. Under such circumstances, purchasing materials that represent values substantially different from the community's or that would offend a significant number of community members may seem inappropriate and a source of unnecessary conflict. This would tempt the librarian to restrict such materials.

*The obligation to protect children from harm.* Few obligations are as indisputable as the obligation of members of the society (no matter what their profession or job) to protect from exploitation those who are defenseless or vulnerable. What group would fall more clearly into this category than children? The society even recognizes that many groups dealing with children—teachers, health-care workers, social workers, university researchers—are obligated to monitor harm done to children and to report such harm to authorities. Although most librarians, as a rule, are not required by law to monitor such harm it is unreasonable to presume that librarians have no stake in caring for and protecting children. Indeed, a central historical tradition of library work is nurturing children and developing their minds through exposure to books and other library materials. Can one reasonably say that if one believes that books and other library materials can improve children, that they cannot also harm them? This is a common argument by those who wish to restrict materials to young people, and it can be an attractive argument for librarians in some instances.

*The obligation to protect the survival of the library.* There are few obligations dearer to the librarian than the preservation of the library as an institution, and the survival of an institution is an important factor in ethical decisions. Generally, actions that would threaten the library's survival are anathema to librarians. They are therefore put in the position of making an economic and political calculation when making decisions about the selection, organization, and dissemination of library materials when they fear that the existence and use of certain materials would threaten the fiscal and political support of the community. Libraries are commonly threatened in this way by those who wish to restrict materials. Citizens, for example, may threaten to campaign against current or improved funding for library services.

### OBLIGATIONS THAT TEND TO INCREASE ACCESS

The obligations that tend to restrict access are not trivial; in fact, they enlighten us regarding the realistic pressures that many librarians face in performing their work. But there are other obligations that are taken quite seriously by librarians and which often lead them to resist the temptation to restrict access to materials.

*The obligation to protect the rights of patrons to free access to ideas and information in a democratic society.* A value held dear by many librarians is the importance of providing information to those who seek it. This view may be held deeply on both a professional and personal level and often reflects a complementary belief in democracy as the most effective form of government. Holding such a belief entails that the citizenry be educated in order to make informed choices and that being informed means being able to read and view materials with different points of view. In order to make good citizens, the library must provide a variety of ideas. It is a premise of democratic societies that opposing points of view are aired, not suppressed, and that it is up to the people to make a decision. Such a viewpoint means that materials that are considered heinous and patently false may be part of the collection because they represent a point of view present in the society. Swan (1986) notes that we have a commitment to protect the flow of information, whether it is true or false, because a citizen's search for truth in a democratic society means exposure to all types of ideas and freedom of expression requires that the untrue be heard as well as the true. Indeed, sometimes what is considered false in one generation becomes the truth of another. In this sense, the suppression of untruths can be dangerous to the flow of ideas. Indeed, falsehoods can often be quite useful in the learning process.

This obligation is also viewed by librarians as an obligation to preserve and support the First Amendment of the U.S. Constitution. It is well understood by most librarians that the First Amendment plays a central role in the establishment, maintenance, and protection of libraries and their patrons. The First Amendment forms the foundation of the right that publishers and creators of materials have to produce the products central to libraries. The First Amendment, however, not only provides people with the right to express themselves, it establishes a corollary right to receive expressions protected by that amendment. The library is a primary place for citizens to receive this information, hence the First Amendment protects patrons in the use of libraries and helps defend librarians in their selections. This was recently recognized in an important appellate court decision in 1994 in which the court recognized that libraries were "limited public fora," where the expression of ideas is fundamental to the library's purpose (*Kreimer v. Bureau of Police* 1991). As such, librarians feel that restricting access to library materials contravenes the letter and spirit of this amendment, and restrictive actions taken by themselves and others diminishes its authority and effect.

*The obligation to educate children.* As noted above, librarians feel strongly that a critical purpose of most libraries is to advance the education of the young. Although some feel that this process requires that some ideas be restricted, others would argue that children who are free to explore ideas become healthy adults and better educated citizens. In addition, many librarians feel that the obligation to restrict access rests with the parents alone and that librarians should not attempt to displace this obligation. The obligation to educate children is usually accomplished in libraries through careful collection development, responsive reference services, entertaining and educational programming, and cooperation with outside agencies such as schools and social-service agencies.

Of course, what is meant by education can be a complex concept. Those who wish to restrict access to ideas might argue that education means inculcating the values and behaviors of the majority of the society into the young. Others contend that education involves exposing the young to many different points of view and giving them the decision-making skills to make up their own minds. This argument was a fundamental issue in one of the most important Supreme Court cases on school censorship, *Island Trees v. Pico* (1982). For contemporary librarianship, the obligation to educate children generally has meant that access to information should be unrestricted, and this has been supported by a variety of formal statements from the American Library Association (ALA). For example, in the document "Kids Need Libraries," which was prepared by the ALA prior to its participation at the White House Conference on Library and Information Services in 1990, a set of needs for children was clearly identified (Mathews, Flum, and Whitney 1990). These needs include the following:

### Kids Need

- The belief in a worthwhile future and their responsibility and desire to contribute to that future.
- A positive sense of self-worth.
- The ability to locate and use information and the awareness that this ability is an essential key to self-realization in the Information Age.
- Preparation to use present-day technology and to adapt to a changing technological world.
- Equal access to the marketplace of ideas and information.
- The ability to think critically in order to solve problems.
- The ability to communicate effectively—to listen, to speak, to read, and to write.
- Preparation to live in a multicultural world and to respect the rights and dignity of all people.
- The desire and ability to become lifelong learners.
- Creative ability to dream a better world (pp. 33–37).

These needs strongly imply unimpeded access to materials and information available in libraries, but they also suggest that the librarian plays a critical role in guiding children so that they become thoughtful, well-informed citizens with abilities to discover the information they need for themselves.

*The obligation to preserve the values of one's profession.* Through formal library education and on-the-job-training, most librarians and library employees become acquainted with the accepted professional standards of library service. In terms of intellectual freedom, these are best expressed in the ALA's Library Bill of Rights and its interpretations. These obligations are also reiterated in the Code of Ethics of both the ALA and the American Society for Information Science (ASIS).

When such doctrines are properly taught, the library worker develops a strong obligation to provide a wide range of materials that are openly available to all, including children. The preservation of professional values can form a powerful source of resistance when attempts to restrict materials are made—so powerful that some librarians prefer to lose their positions rather than sacrifice these principles.

Central to the preservation of professional values in libraries is the conviction that the selection of materials is based on professional judgement rather than personal interest. Although personal preferences are hard to avoid, what distinguishes professional judgement from personal bias in the selection process are reasonably objective criteria on which selection judgements are based. These criteria usually include the factors listed under Selection and Collection Development Policies above. Lester Asheim (1954) has characterized the difference between selection and censorship in the following way:

> To the selector, the important thing is to find reasons to keep the book. Given such a guiding principle, the selector looks for values, for virtues, for strengths, which will overshadow minor objections. For the censor, on the other hand, the important thing is to find reasons to reject the book. His guiding principle leads him to seek out the objectionable features, the weaknesses, the possibilities for misinterpretation . . . The selector says, if there is anything good in this book let us try to keep it; the censor says, if there is anything bad in this book, let us reject it. And since there is seldom a flawless work in any form, the censor's approach can destroy much that is worth saving (pp. 95–96).

Upholding professional values by selecting a wide array of materials for reasons unrelated to personal liking or taste is crucial. The breadth of library collections is a reflection of that belief.

## Research on Censorship and Intellectual Freedom

Many librarians respect the principles of intellectual freedom, but find it much more difficult to practice it in the real world for a variety of reasons. Almost any debate over censorship, intellectual freedom, and libraries will provoke discussion over at least some of the obligations noted above. Although the basic value of intellectual freedom is strong in the library profession, individual librarians often feel ambivalent. This ambivalence may, in part, be based on the historical roots of the profession. In the nineteenth and well into the twentieth century, there was little doubt that librarians felt it was their duty to restrict access to library materials or to refuse to acquire materials that were deemed to have an unfortunate effect on patrons—adults and children. The library literature is replete with admonitions of librarians to obtain only the most wholesome materials. As Dewey (1876) noted, "only the best books on the best subjects" were to be collected (p. 5), and there was considerable debate as to whether patrons should be exposed to such works as romances. The women who were hired as librarians at the end of the nineteenth century were expected to represent the values of polite middle-class society and to steer individuals from good to better books (Garrison 1972).

Interestingly, the ambivalence of librarians toward intellectual freedom has been documented in research on librarians for many years. Serebnick (1979) in reviewing the research drew some informative conclusions: Censorship in the schools and public libraries was reported in the research as early as the 1950s. The source of school censorship was not just principals and parents, but to a large extent the librarians themselves, often without prompting. In many cases, the librarians simply did not buy books if they thought they would be controversial, or at the least would restrict their access (Eakin 1948; Fiske 1959). In other words, much censorship was self-imposed, associated with the belief that books could actually harm the children.

Serebnick also found that there was considerable ambivalence on the part of librarians, and subsequent research has supported this. Studies of senior-high-school librarians and public librarians in the Midwest in the 1960s and '70s revealed that a significant proportion of librarians had weak or wavering views about censorship and that there was little correlation between asserting a belief in intellectual freedom and actually censoring materials (Farley 1964; Busha 1971). Again, much of the censorship was self-imposed and occurred more often with materials that had pictures than with those that were unillustrated. The propensity to restrict materials was greatest among school librarians, followed by public, and then academic librarians; librarians with the stronger educational backgrounds were less likely to restrict materials (Pope 1973).

More recent research has focused on challenges in schools and provides an enriched perspective on censorship issues. One study, titled *Limiting What Students Shall Read*, conducted by the Association of American Publishers in 1981, focused on a large sample survey of 1,891 public elementary- and secondary-school librarians, library supervisors, principals, and district superintendents using mail and telephone surveys. Many challenges to library materials were reported. Nearly one-third of the librarians reported at least one challenge in the previous year, and in 30 percent of the challenges the material was altered, restricted, or removed. Perhaps a bit different from previous research was that a large percentage of the challenges came from outside: more than 50 percent of the challenges came from parents. About 10 percent of the challenges came from teachers, and 6 percent from the school-board members (Association of American Publishers 1981). In a subsequent study, Hopkins (1993) sampled more than 6,500 U.S. school systems. She found that challenges came from both within and outside of libraries. Challenges from within, especially by principals, were the most problematic, because the item was least likely to be retained in this circumstance. In addition, the political aspect of protecting library materials was also highlighted as Hopkins noted that support from media and outside groups played a significant role in protecting materials from removal. Librarians were found to be most supportive of intellectual freedom when they had a high level of confidence in their own abilities.

*Major Concerns of Those Who Wish to Censor Materials*

The movement to censor library materials remains unabated today. What is it that bothers people so much that they believe that people, especially children, should not be able to obtain certain materials in libraries?

OFFENSIVE SUBJECTS

Probably the single most important factor that prompts a desire to censor is content. Content issues can be broken down into two categories: offensive subjects and offensive language. In terms of offensive subjects, two of the greatest concerns are sexual content and violence. This is not to suggest that these are the only themes that lead to censorship attempts. Other content areas are those that appear to undermine the "traditional family," are antireligious, are anathema to authority, are antidemocratic, or offend various groups such as African Americans, Asians, or Native Americans.

*Sexual content*: Many individuals are concerned that sexual subject matter is inappropriate in libraries, especially if that material is available to minors. Some may argue, for example, that sex-education materials should be provided by the parents, and children's access to them in the library should be restricted. Similarly, some argue that certain materials promote "perverse" sexual behaviors and adversely affect the attitudes of young people. This was the central focus of the debate over *Daddy's Roommate* and *Heather Has Two Mommies*, which were written for children and dealt with the family life of homosexual couples. But objections do not stop with minors alone; sexual materials that are too explicit, Madonna's book *Sex*, for example, may not be seen as acceptable for anyone, even adults. For this reason, it is common for censorship issues to arise over sex-education materials or any materials that have sexually explicit images, words, or lyrics.

*Violent content:* A second content issue is violence. Certainly, this is a subject of great concern to most people. Does exposure to violent behavior in books and films promote unacceptable behavior? There is some evidence that regular exposure to violence may, in fact, harden us (Huesmann 1986). Watching people get shot and stabbed over and over diminishes the shock of these disturbing actions. We are less shocked by such explicit violence than we were in the 1950s or 1960s. Are libraries promoting our insensitivity to violence by making available materials that harden us to violent acts? In addition, there is concern in the psycho-social literature that regular exposure to violent material might make us more likely to commit violent acts or, at least, increase our levels of aggressiveness. Libraries, as has been mentioned before, are imbedded in the society. As this society grows ever more concerned with the violence within it, people are searching for those aspects that might promote or foster this violence. Some find library materials to be one of those factors, and their contention may have greater power than they otherwise might because the fear of violence is so prevalent in our world.

*Offensive Language*: Another common area of concern is the language contained in materials. The language used in print and AV materials has become progressively colorful over the years. Today, explicit sexual slang and profanity are commonplace in many works. The use of such language, it is feared, serves as a role model for subsequent behavior, especially for young people, and like violence, there is concern that we become used to this type of language in everyday speech.

CONCERN WITH FORMATS

Although the censorship of print materials has been around for thousands of years and continues today, the focus of much concern is within the realm of audiovisual materials. Perhaps what underlies this concern is that the visual medium is especially effective; our visual senses are among the strongest. Therefore, we may be more deeply and immediately affected by what we see on the screen compared to what we read in a book. Recently, audio materials have also been under attack. Lyrics from rap music have been particularly vulnerable to requests for limitation and removal. The attempt to suppress material by 2 Live Crew is but one example. One argument is that the combination of the words and music makes the message much more powerful than the use of the words alone. It is hard to deny that music can sometimes intensify an experience; that is why movies have musical accompaniments at strategic parts. Whether it actually produces deleterious effects, however, has yet to be demonstrated.

### CONCERN FOR CHILDREN

The most heated censorship debates often center around those affecting children. This is reasonable, because it is presumed that young people are the most vulnerable to undesirable influences and need to be protected. As a historical footnote, the first obscenity case in English law occurred around 1860. The court was concerned with the effects of obscene materials on "vulnerable minds." Interestingly, this case did not deal with sexual materials but with anti-Catholic pamphlets. Our fear of the harmful effects of ideas on youth goes back even further, to classical Greek times: the reason that Socrates was put to death was for corrupting the youth of Athens. Today, even those individuals who are resistant to censorship in general may experience qualms when it comes to permitting materials with adult themes to be circulated to the young.

Defending unrestricted access to such materials is probably the most difficult intellectual freedom task that libraries perform, and the matter is further complicated by legal concerns. Although obscenity statutes are quite common in the United States, they are seldom useful as selection criteria. However, approximately forty-eight states now have what is referred to as "Harmful to Minors" statutes. These statutes attempt to create an obscenity standard for youth that is easier to meet than the standards set for obscenity for adults. See Figure 5.1 for an excerpt from one such law from the *Ohio Revised Code* for the State of Ohio:

---

## Figure 5.1
## Sample of Harmful to Juvenile Statute
## (Ohio Revised Code)

### Section 2907.31

(A)   No person, with knowledge of its character or content, shall recklessly do any of the following:

    (1)   Sell, deliver, furnish, disseminate, provide, exhibit, rent, or present to a juvenile any material or performance that is obscene or harmful to juveniles;

    (2)   Offer or agree to sell, deliver, furnish, disseminate, provide, exhibit, rent, or present to a juvenile any material or performance that is obscene or harmful to juveniles;

    (3)   Allow any juvenile to review or peruse any material or view any live performance that is harmful to juveniles.

(B)   The following are affirmative defenses to a charge under this section that involves material or a performance that is harmful to juveniles but not obscene:

    (1)   The defendant is the parent, guardian, or spouse of the juveniles involved.

    (2)   The juvenile involved at the time of the conduct in question, was accompanied by the juvenile's parent or guardian, who, with knowledge of its character, consented to the material or performance being furnished or presented to the juvenile.

    (3)   The juvenile exhibited to the defendant or to the defendant's agent or employee a draft card, driver's license, birth record, marriage license, or other official or apparently official document purporting to show that the juvenile was eighteen years of age or over or married, and the person to whom that document was exhibited did not otherwise have reasonable cause to believe that the juvenile was under the age of eighteen or unmarried.

(C) (1) It is an affirmative defense to a charge under this section, involving material or a performance that is obscene or harmful to juveniles, that the material or performance was furnished or presented for a bona fide medical, scientific, educational, governmental, judicial, or other proper purpose, by a physician, psychologist, sociologist, scientist, teacher, librarian, clergyman, prosecutor, judge, or other proper person.

### Section 2907.01 (Defining "Harmful to Juveniles")

(E)   Any material or performance is "harmful to juveniles," if it is offensive to prevailing standards in the adult community with respect to what is suitable for juveniles, and if any of the following apply:

    (1)   it tends to appeal to the prurient interest of juveniles;

(2) it contains a display, description, or representation of sexual activity, masturbation, sexual excitement, or nudity;

(3) it contains a display, description, or representation of bestiality or extreme or bizarre violence, cruelty, or brutality;

(4) it contains a display, description, or representation of human bodily functions of elimination;

(5) it makes repeated use of foul language;

(6) it contains a display, description, or representation in lurid detail of the violent physical torture, dismemberment, destruction, or death of a human being;

(7) it contains a display, description, or representation of criminal activity that tends to glorify or glamorize the activity, and that, with respect to juveniles, has a dominant tendency to corrupt.

---

There are many vagaries that are associated with such a law, and one can see how its application could be troublesome to a librarian. The librarian is not just confronted with the natural fears of people who believe that some books might have the tendency to corrupt, but with the possibility that an irate citizen or public official might employ legal means to restrict or eliminate library materials from the shelves.

## The Information Policies of the American Library Association

As can be seen by the previous discussion, librarians struggle with their perceived obligations—personal, professional, and organizational. In addition, the society itself is attempting to come to grips with its many problems and influences. In response to these pressures, ALA has established over the years a variety of policies meant to guide librarians in protecting the rights of their patrons. Most of these policies have been created by ALA's Intellectual Freedom Committee (IFC). The IFC was created in 1940, one year after the first version of the Library Bill of Rights was passed. The purpose of the IFC was to help promote and protect the values espoused by the Library Bill of Rights. It has accomplished this task primarily by developing policies and written interpretations of the Library Bill of Rights over the years (ALA 1996). These policies have provided national guidance to the library community on some of the most complicated issues that face librarians. Given the tremendous burden of this responsibility, in 1967, an administrative unit called the Office of Intellectual Freedom (OIF) was created. The OIF was established to relieve the administrative burden on the IFC and to coordinate intellectual freedom activities. OIF is responsible for implementing the intellectual freedom policies that are adopted by ALA. It also presents conference programs, collects data, and generally promotes the concept of intellectual freedom. Policy making remains in the jurisdiction of the IFC (ALA 1996).

Copies of the policies promulgated by the IFC and passed by ALA Council as well as background on them can be found in OIF's *Intellectual Freedom Manual* (ALA 1996). Below is a brief discussion of some of the major ALA information policies. They have been broken down into four basic areas: philosophical foundations, access issues, modification of materials, and administrative aspects.

PHILOSOPHICAL FOUNDATIONS

*Library Bill of Rights.* The fundamental obligations of libraries and library professionals are clearly defined by the central document of the American Library Association: the Library Bill of Rights (see Figure 5.2).

These provisions, first adopted in 1948 and revised on numerous occasions, create a positive obligation to select materials for the entire community and to reject censoring of materials based on the characteristics of the author (Section 1); to select materials with a wide array of viewpoints and to reject censoring materials due to doctrinal disapproval of content (Section 2); to reject censorship and to cooperate with others to fight the abridgement of free speech (Sections 3 and 4); to provide library materials and services by all individuals regardless of their characteristics (Section 5); and to permit equitable access to library facilities (Section 6).

Understanding how to apply the Library Bill of Rights is not always easy, especially when one is attempting to balance the entire range of obligations noted above. This has been recognized by the ALA, which has consequently issued a variety of formal interpretations to assist librarians. Many of these will be noted below.

*The "Freedom to Read Statement" and the "Intellectual Freedom Statement."* The *Freedom to Read Statement* was originally adopted in 1953 and revised in 1972. It was jointly prepared by ALA and the American Book Publishers Council. It is a philosophical statement directed at both publishers and librarians and concerns itself with how important reading is to our democratic society and the inadvisability of permitting suppression of ideas because they may be considered controversial or immoral. Among the key points argued in this statement are that the great-

---

**Figure 5.2**
**The Library Bill of Rights**

The American Library Association affirms that all libraries are forums for information and ideas, and that the following basic policies
should guide their services.

1.  Books and other library resources should be provided for the
    interest, information, and enlightenment of all people of the
    community the library serves. Materials should not be excluded
    because of the origin, background, or views of those contribut-
    ing to their creation.

2.  Libraries should provide materials and information presenting
    all points of view on current and historical issues. Materials
    should not be proscribed or removed because of partisan or
    doctrinal disapproval.

3.  Libraries should challenge censorship in the fulfillment of their
    responsibility to provide information and enlightenment.

4.  Libraries should cooperate with all persons and groups con-
    cerned with resisting abridgement of free expression and free
    access to ideas.

5.  A person's right to use a library should not be denied or abridged
    because of origin, age, background, or views.

6.  Libraries which make exhibit spaces and meeting rooms avail-
    able to the public they serve should make such facilities avail-
    able on an equitable basis, regardless of the beliefs or affilia-
    tions of individuals or groups requesting their use.

—Adopted June 18, 1948. Amended February 2, 1961, June 27, 1967,
and January 23, 1980, by the ALA Council.

---

Reprinted with permission from the American Library Association est diversity of views, both unorthodox and orthodox, are in the public's interest; that the possession of materials does not constitute an endorsement of the ideas contained within them; that librarians should not permit the labelling of works as subversive or dangerous; and that it is the responsibility of publishers and librarians to protect peoples' freedom to read, to oppose censorship, and to provide access to a diversity of ideas. Perhaps the document's most notable assertion is the recognition of the importance of the freedom to read, its promise, and its dangers:

> We do not state these propositions in the comfortable belief that what people read is unimportant. We believe rather that what people read is deeply important; that ideas can be dangerous; but that the suppression of ideas is fatal to a democratic society. Freedom itself is a dangerous way of life, but it is ours.

The *Intellectual Freedom Statement* expresses the position of the ALA Council and the Freedom to Read Foundation, which is closely associated with ALA. The document closely parallels the *Freedom to Read Statement*, asserting the importance of our freedom of expression and through seven propositions asserting the need for diverse collections and the obligation to resist attempts at censorship by individuals or groups. In addition, there is a statement of professional concern regarding the fact that library professionals are often subjected to threats of legal, financial, or personal pressures to bow to censorious attempts. The statement reasserts our obligation to resist such attempts.

*"Freedom to View Statement."* In response to the growing interest in AV materials, the Educational Film and Video Association adopted a statement in 1979 protecting the rights of viewers and creators of AV materials. Titled the *Freedom to View Statement*, this document (Figure 5.3) parallels in many ways the rights asserted in the Library Bill of Rights.

ACCESS ISSUES

*"Restricted Access to Library Materials."* Although it is clear that preventing individuals from exposure to materials considered offensive by simply not selecting them is censorship, can the library simply restrict access to materials it believes are problematic? The interpretation *Restricted Access to Library Materials* indicates that such an action places a barrier between the patron and the collection. When libraries try to restrict access to various areas of the library using techniques such as closed shelv-

---

### Figure 5.3
### Freedom to View

The FREEDOM TO VIEW, along with the freedom to speak, to hear, and to read, is protected by the First Amendment to the Constitution of the United States. In a free society, there is no place for censorship of any medium of expression. Therefore, we affirm these principles:

1. It is in the public interest to provide the broadest possible access to films and other audiovisual materials because they have proven to be among the most effective means for the communication of ideas. Liberty of circulation is essential to insure the constitutional guarantee of freedom of expression.

2. It is in the public interest to provide for our audiences, films and other audiovisual materials which represent a diversity of views and expression. Selection of a work does not constitute or imply agreement with or approval of the content.

3. It is our professional responsibility to resist the constraint of labeling or prejudging a film on the basis of the moral, religious, or political beliefs of the producer or film maker or on the basis of controversial content.
4. It is our professional responsibility to contest vigorously, by all lawful means, every encroachment upon the public's freedom to view.

—Drafted by the Educational Film Library Association's Freedom to View Committee, and adopted by the EFLA Board of Directors in February 1979.

---

Reprinted with permission from the American Library Association

---

ing (shelves available only to staff), "adults only" sections, or restricted shelving areas, it is *de facto* suppression of ideas. But aren't there some legitimate reasons to restrict access to some materials? The association recognizes that it is acceptable to restrict access to materials for special reasons such as to protect materials from mutilation or theft, but these should not be used as a pretense for censorious activity.

*Free Access to Libraries for Minors.* Although the temptation to restrict access is usually most powerful when young people are involved, and it is perfectly reasonable that librarians, as noted above, feel a special concern for children, ALA, through the promulgation of its policy *Free Access to Libraries for Minors* clearly states that library materials are not to be restricted on the basis of the patron's age. Hence reading areas restricted to adults, collections limited to adults or teachers, or restricted access to interlibrary loan all would constitute a violation of the ALA Library Bill of Rights because they restrict access to library materials. In this policy, ALA also asserts a key position in regard to access for young people:

> The American Library Association opposes libraries restricting access to library materials and services for minors and hold that it is the parents—and only parents—who may restrict their children—and only their children—from access to library materials and services (*Intellectual Freedom Manual* 1996, p. 92).

In other words, the library does not serve *in loco parentis* (in the place of the parent), and the focus of responsibility for controlling the reading, viewing, or listening habits of children is vested with the parent alone.

*Access for Children and Young People to Videotapes and Other Nonprint Formats.* Because of the growing prominence of nonprint formats, ALA established a second interpretative document entitled, *Access for Children and Young People to Videotapes and Other Nonprint Formats,* in 1989. This document reaffirms the association's stand that materials should not be restricted on the basis of the patron's age and specifically rejects policies that set minimum age limits or the costs of nonprint materials as a reason for restriction. Libraries are also cautioned about the inappropriateness of using Motion Picture Association of America (MPAA) ratings as a means of restricting access, but it also protects the inclusion of such ratings when they appear on the film or video from the distributor. Removal of such ratings would constitute expurgation.

*Economic Barriers to Information Access.* Over the years, libraries have charged fees for a variety of reasons, but these fees have generally been minimal. With the increasing number of formats, expanding demands to purchase new technologies, and serious constraints on library budgets, libraries have experienced increasing temptations to charge substantial fees for library services. This policy affirms that free access to information is the fundamental mission of publicly-funded libraries, and that fees ipso facto create barriers to such access. The policy states unequivocally that access to information in whatever format should be provided equitably and that charging fees for materials, services, and programs is anathema to the concept of free and equal access. Ability to pay, according to this policy, should not govern ability to know.

*Access to Library Resources and Services Regardless of Gender or Sexual Orientation.*  In recent years, discussion of sexual orientation has become commonplace, and there have been continuing efforts of various groups to advocate for the rights of gays and lesbians, as well as other groups. Consistent with ALA's general philosophical stand on free and equal access to libraries, the association asserts the rights of individuals to use libraries regardless of sexual orientation. In addition, this policy explicitly rejects the nonselection of materials because of the sexual orientation of the creator.

*Access to Electronic Information, Services, and Networks.*  There is no doubt that the Internet has become a major source of information for librarians and library users. This has raised some very important issues for libraries, because the databases that can be accessed may contain controversial or "adult" material. The potential and real problems that have arisen prompted ALA to create a new interpretation of the ALA Library Bill of Rights in 1996 directly addressing this issue. It is clear that the policy reflects the consistent position of ALA regarding the right of access to information for all library users. This policy asserts that "users should not be restricted or denied access for expressing or receiving constitutionally protected speech." It also asserts that access should not be limited because some content may be controversial and that minors have equal rights of access to electronic-information sources. Similar to earlier interpretations, this places the burden of restricting access to information on the parents of minors rather than on the librarian. In addition, the policy asserts that users of electronic-information services and networks in libraries should have their rights to privacy and confidentiality protected.

*Access to Resources and Services in the School Library Media Program.*  Schools are especially common locations for attempts to restrict information. In part this is a reflection of the *in loco parentis* (in the place of the parent) function of schools. Parents expect schools to protect their children from harm; indeed, schools are legally obligated to do so. Some parents believe that this harm extends to exposure to "unhealthy" materials. Access to the NII has exacerbated the problem because there is a general lack of control over the content of materials on it.

Because of the high probability that schools will experience attempts to restrict access, the ALA has recognized the importance of specifically addressing the problems of school-library media centers. The policy notes that the underlying value of intellectual freedom should be sustained by school libraries and that the ALA Library Bill of Rights applies in these settings. ALA recognizes the school library as a place where different sides of an issue should be available and where the collection should reflect the heterogeneous society in which schools exist. Access to the collection should be free and open, and attempts to restrict materials should be resisted. It places the burden of broad collections, reflecting diverse points of view, directly in the hands of the school librarian.

### MODIFICATION OF MATERIALS

*Expurgation of Library Materials.* Sometimes a librarian may be tempted to alter library materials rather than restrict the item itself. This might mean obliterating text or altering or excising a photograph. Any attempt to alter material in this way is considered to be expurgation of library materials and, hence, is a type of restricted access. As such, it is considered a violation of the ALA Library Bill of Rights.

*Statement on Labeling.* It is normal to organize materials by classifying them. For example, we label some books "history," others as "science." This is not generally a concern to the ALA insofar as the labeling does not attempt to restrict access to such materials. ALA's concern is with affixing a prejudicial label to materials or separating materials through a prejudicial system. For example, labelling materials "Adults only" or "Teachers only" would have a tendency to restrict access. As noted above, placing MPAA ratings on videos unless already provided by the distributor, is considered a violation of this policy.

### ADMINISTRATIVE ASPECTS

*Challenged Materials.* From time to time, individuals challenge materials in the library, insisting that the materials be removed or restricted. Challenges can produce very difficult times for a library because of the potential of political pressure as well as the possibility of unpleasant

media exposure. Nonetheless, such attempts can threaten the dissemination of ideas and as such challenge the basic principles of intellectual
freedom. The policy on challenged materials asserts that libraries should
have a clear materials-selection policy and that materials that conform
to that policy should not be removed simply because individuals place
legal or extra-legal pressures on the library. Rather, the library should
protect such materials and insist, at the least, on an adversary hearing
so that such requests can be closely scrutinized. This is not to say that a
library should never remove materials that it has selected, but doing so
under pressure should be avoided.

*Policy on the Confidentiality of Library Circulation Records.*  When individuals take out a book from a library, it is normally assumed that no one
else has access to the information regarding what was checked-out, i.e.,
to the circulation record. Underlying the privacy of circulation records
is the belief that if individuals think that their reading habits can be
scrutinized, they might feel pressure or embarrassment. This can create
a chilling effect on an individual's use of the library, and essentially re-
stricts the right to use the library and the ideas contained within.

From time to time such information is, in fact, requested. Usually
this is done by an arm of law enforcement: a police officer or prosecutor.
In some cases, FBI agents have requested circulation records. ALA policy
asserts that any records that associate an individual with particular
materials are confidential and should be released only after a subpoena
has been issued and after the library is satisfied that the subpoena is
properly issued. This means that libraries should usually insist on a court
hearing to ensure that they are required to turn over the records.

*Guidelines for the Development and Implementation of Policies, Regulations,
and Procedures Affecting Access to Library Materials, Services, and
Facilities.*  These guidelines, adopted in 1994, were prompted by a court
case known as the "Kreimer case," which involved the rights of a homeless individual who was removed from the library for inappropriate behavior. There was much debate over this issue because the library community felt that it was important to ensure the rights of each individual
to use the library, even those who may behave differently. At the same
time, the library community wanted to ensure that an individual's behavior could be controlled so that others could use the library effectively as well.

Because the case was so controversial, the library community looked to ALA for guidance on the development of rules and regulations regarding patron behavior. The guidelines presented make it clear that patron-behavior rules should be no more restrictive than absolutely necessary, should be consistent with constitutional protection of citizens, and should be consistent with the ALA Library Bill of Rights and the mission of the library. It further condemns focusing on specific groups of people, such as children or the homeless, and asserts that guidelines should be clearly written and that an appeal procedure be available.

These information policies are only some of the policies and statements made by the ALA addressing the dissemination of information by libraries. ALA also takes professional positions on national and international issues that affect the information rights of its citizenry and those of the world.

## SUMMARY

Libraries are critical information providers, and part of their function is to make information policies. The policies that they adopt on the selection, organization, and dissemination of the information they possess determine in large part their effectiveness. Few such policies are as important as those related to intellectual freedom and resistance to censorship. Libraries represent a special forum: a place where library users should be able to find a broad range of points-of-view on topics of interest. Some of these topics may be quite controversial, and there may be a tendency on the part of the public, and library staff as well, to consider restricting access or even removing some of these materials for fear of public response or the effects these materials may have, especially on the young. These concerns have been exacerbated as video formats have become a larger part of library collections. Although some of the concerns may have merit and tempt librarians to restrict access to library materials, there are also countervailing professional obligations and policies that provide guidance. The intellectual freedom policies, adopted by the ALA, serve as both a philosophical and instrumental foundation for the practices of libraries and librarians. The task of defending intellectual freedom is a very difficult one. Libraries and librarians have often been subjected to intense pressures as they defend items in their collection. There is little reason to believe that these problems will dissipate. On the contrary, with the increasing use of the Internet, it is likely that the problems will increase. Only a firm understanding of the principles of the profession can provide the necessary rationale to protect patrons' rights to read and view the library materials of their choosing.

## REFERENCES

Abbott, Randy L. "Pressure Groups and Intellectual Freedom." *Public Library Quarterly* 10 (1990): 43–61.

American Library Association. "Banned Books Web Site" [Online]. Available at *http://www.ala.org/bbooks/challeng.html*

——. *Intellectual Freedom Manual*, 5th ed. Chicago: ALA, 1996.

Asheim, Lester. "The Librarian's Responsibility: Not Censorship but Selection." in *Freedom of Book Selection*. Edited by Frederic Mosher. Chicago: ALA, 1954: 95–96.

Association of American Publishers, American Library Association, and Association for Supervision and Curriculum Development. *Limiting What Students Shall Read*. Washington, D.C.: Association of American Publishers, 1981.

Busha, C.H. "The Attitudes of Midwestern Public Librarians toward Intellectual Freedom and Censorship." Unpublished dissertation. Indiana University, 1971. Cited in Serebnick (1979).

Dewey, Melvil. "The Profession," *Library Journal* (June 15, 1989): 5. Reprint of article in *American Library Journal* 1 (September 1876): 5.

Eakin, M. L. "Censorship in Public High School Libraries." Master's Thesis, Columbia University, 1948. Cited in Serebnick (1979).

Farley, J.J. "Book Censorship in the Senior High Libraries of Nassau County, N.Y." Unpublished dissertation. New York University, 1964. Cited in Serebnick (1979).

Fiske, Marjerie. *Book Selection and Censorship: A Study of School and Public Libraries in California*. Berkeley: University of California Press, 1959. Cited in Serebnick (1979).

Garrison, Dee. "The Tender Technicians: The Feminization of Public Librarianship." *Journal of Social History* 6 (winter 1972–1973): 131–156.

Hopkins, Dianne McAfee. "A Conceptual Model of Factors Influencing the Outcome of Challenges to Library Materials in Secondary School Settings." *Library Quarterly* 63 (January 1993): 40–72.

Huesmann, L. Rowell. "Psychological Processes Promoting the Relation between Exposure to Media Violence and Aggressive Behavior by the Viewer." *Journal of Social Issues* 42 (1986): 125–139.

*Island Trees Union Free School District v. Pico* 102 S. Ct. 2799 (1982).

*Kreimer v. Bureau of Police for the Town of Morristown, et al.* 765 F. Supp. 181 (D.N.J. 1991).

Lamolinara, Guy. "Metamorphosis of a National Treasure." *American Libraries* (March 1996): 31–33.

Mathews, Virginia H., Judith G. Flum, and Karen A. Whitney. "Kids Need Libraries: School and Public Libraries Preparing the Youth of Today for the World of Tomorrow," *School Library Journal* 36 (April 1990): 33–37.

National Commission on Libraries and Information Science. "The Role of Fees in Supporting Library and Information Services in Public and Academic Libraries." Washington, D.C.: NCLIS, 1985. In *Fees for Library Service: Current Practice and Future Policy.* Vol. 8 of *Collection Building* (1986): 3–17.

Pope, M. J. "A Comparative Study of the Opinions of School, College, and Public Librarians Concerning Certain Categories of Sexually Oriented Literature." Unpublished dissertation, Rutgers University, 1973. Cited in Serebnick (1979).

Serebnick, Judith. "A Review of Research Related to Censorship in Libraries." *Library Research* 1 (1979): 95–118.

Swan, John. "Untruth or Consequences." *Library Journal* 111 (July 1, 1986): 44–52.

# 6

## Information Organization: Issues and Techniques

Information tends to have an entropic character: it does not organize itself, rather, it has a tendency toward randomness. Unless there are ways to organize it, it quickly becomes chaos. The primary purpose of organizing library collections is to meet the various information needs of library users. Given the amount of knowledge that is currently available and its projected growth, librarians and other information providers have logical, albeit sometimes complex, ways to arrange and to promote retrieval of information within their libraries as well as outside library walls.

Considering the vastness of today's information, and the inevitable and explosive growth of knowledge in the future, it is daunting to consider the task of organizing it so it is accessible. Existing in its unorganized state, it is, for all intents and purposes, impossible to access except by accident and serendipity. Libraries and other information organizations cannot operate in this manner, and although the issue of how knowledge is organized in society is an interesting one, the crucial concern for librarians is how information is organized within a library or within a database. A library's fundamental purpose is to acquire, store, organize, disseminate, or otherwise provide access to the vast bodies of knowledge already produced. Organizing knowledge in libraries means organizing many types of information and media: information stored in physical items such as books, video recordings, or pictures; it means organizing virtual information, that is, information stored electronically in words, sounds, or images. It also means organizing the records that serve as representations of these items, such as catalog cards or the electronic bibliographic records in library computerized catalogs.

The notion of knowledge organization within a library can be very broad. For example, access to knowledge can be organized by the media used to record that knowledge, e.g., print or audiovisual; by user, e.g., children, adults, vision-impaired; by genre, e.g., westerns, mysteries, fiction, nonfiction, or even by size, as with "oversize" shelving. Obviously, except in the smallest of collections such general forms of organization are usually not sufficient to locate most information effectively, but they do constitute useful forms of organization within a library.

The library itself can be viewed as one type of information-retrieval system. Its content is a database, which is organized in such a way as to produce effective access to that content. Any information retrieval system has at least two parts: a database and a system for retrieval of the database. The database of the library would be its contents: the books, periodicals, audiovisual materials, and other items in the collection. The system would include the hardware, software, rules, policies, and management used to effect retrieval of the information in the database. The library catalog might also be considered an information-retrieval system in itself. The database is the content or information (the electronic records or the cards in a manual system and the descriptions of the items in the catalog), the retrieval system would be the hardware, management, software, rules, policies, and procedures by which the catalog records are prepared (file preparation) and manipulated for access purposes. Classification schemes can also be seen as information-retrieval systems. For example, the content is the classification scheme and the numbers that stand for the content; the retrieval system is the alphabetical and numerical rules that govern the system. Indeed, Marcia Bates has argued that a reference book itself is a retrieval system (Bates 1986). As can be seen from these examples, a library is not only an information-retrieval system, but it relies on many other information-retrieval systems that function within it.

Although it is sometimes difficult to locate information or items in libraries, what is truly remarkable is that despite the incredible range and diversity of information they contain, the right information is frequently located. This is due in large part to the intricate systems and techniques that have been developed to organize the content of libraries. These systems and techniques have been developed and implemented by catalogers, archivists, information-retrieval system designers, bibliographers, and indexers, all of whom assist information seekers by designing effective systems to retrieve information.

An important aspect of knowledge retrieval, and one that constitutes an important focus of this chapter is the concept of access points. Those designing information systems or those who make these systems available create the access points. The access points are employed by users of these systems, including librarians, to locate the desired material or information. There are many types of access points in a library. They can be access points in a bibliographic record, such as author, title, and subject headings, or they can be something as basic as a library sign naming a subject area or indicating the range of classification numbers located in a shelving range. Access points can also be human, such as access provided at the reference desk by a reference librarian. All of these provide points of access to the library collection. Knowledge retrieval involves much more than just these access points: Other important aspects of knowledge organization and retrieval include shelf arrangement and indexes and bibliographies as systematic summaries and pointers to full texts.

Libraries, in order to accomplish their purposes, employ various intellectual tools, sometimes referred to as intellectual technologies. These tools help arrange knowledge in such a way as to promote retrieval of that knowledge. Effective organization of knowledge, however, is extremely difficult to accomplish: the organizing principles must be relatively easy to apply, easy to understand by both information professionals and users, and they must reflect, to the greatest extent possible, the way that people ordinarily seek out information.

But even in the best of organizational systems, the individual information seeker is an essential variable. Individuals seek information with their own mental constructs, and no system can account for each of these constructs. In other words, no particular organization of information will satisfy each information seeker's needs perfectly (Mann 1993). Nonetheless, libraries, through their intellectual tools, provide an efficient means of retrieving a vast amount of information.

It is obvious that in this brief chapter a complete or sufficient discussion of knowledge organization is unattainable. The primary discussion, therefore, will center on the intellectual tools that promote retrieval of information. There are many such tools and those discussed in this chapter are ones that play a prominent role in the organization of the knowledge contained within libraries, although many of them play equally important roles in other types of information systems. The intellectual tools that will be discussed are (1) classification systems, (2) controlled vocabulary including thesauri and the Library of Congress Subject Headings, (3) the library catalog including the Anglo-American Cataloging Rules (AARC2), (4) indexes, abstracts, and bibliographies, (5) electronic databases. These tools are not mutually exclusive; indeed, some rely heavily on others. For example, the library catalog and electronic databases rely heavily on controlled vocabulary. These have been selected as influential tools that affect how knowledge is organized in libraries.

## CLASSIFICATION SYSTEMS

A method fundamental to information access in libraries is through disciplinary and subject access. Although the concepts of discipline and subject are closely related, they are distinct. Put very simply, a subject is what an item is about; a discipline is a related body of knowledge that defines a particular approach. Take for example, the subject of the origin of humans. A book on the origin of humans that examines it from scriptural text is likely to be placed within the discipline of religion; a book on the same subject (the origin of humans) that focuses on physical processes and evolution is likely to be placed in the biosciences: same subject, different disciplines. Despite these differences, however, disciplines and subjects share many similarities when it comes to searching for information. Two basic systems that provide such access will be considered here: classification systems and controlled vocabularies.

One of the fundamental organizing principles libraries employ is called classification. Classification "is the act of organizing the universe of knowledge into some systematic order" (Chan 1994, p. 259). This organization provides "a descriptive and explanatory framework for ideas and a structure of the relationships among the ideas" (Kwasnik 1992, p. 63). Classification schemes attempt to identify knowledge and the interrelationships among knowledge. In this way, one is "connected" not only to a specific item, but also to other items on the same subject or items on related subjects. Good classification systems reflect the inter-connectedness of ideas; they not only help searchers locate material but also help them to think about related aspects of their search and identify those materials that embody those aspects.

Generally, libraries conceive of the universe of knowledge in terms of broad-based classification systems that are discipline oriented. Of course, items in a collection can be and are classified using many organizational principles that are not discipline based, for example, by author, as in a typical fiction collection. However, it is clear that classification by discipline is a fundamental and dominant intellectual technology for the arrangement and retrieval of items and information in libraries.

Among their many uses, classification schemes perform a direct and critical function: they provide a basis for the physical arrangement of library materials. There is a close relationship, of course, in how items are physically arranged on the shelf and the intellectual principles used to organize the knowledge contained within those items. Library classification schemes provide a means of organizing full texts—the items on the shelf (Mann 1993). Such classification systems function in at least two helpful ways: (1) they help to locate specific items on the shelf; and (2) they serve as a means to place items treating the same or related subjects in the same area (this is referred to as *collocation*). Hence, as classification systems provide for the physical arrangement of library materials they also permit the grouping of like materials within the same area, thereby providing a means of discovering items of interest through browsing.

Two classification systems dominate in American libraries: the Dewey Decimal Classification (DDC) and the Library of Congress Classification (LCC). These schemes were devised originally to organize books—the traditional medium for information. In more recent times they have been adapted for use with other media. These classifications will be briefly discussed below because of their ubiquity and importance in American librarianship. Suffice it to say, these systems are quite complex, and the superficial discussion below is meant only to identify a few of their major characteristics.

## Dewey Decimal Classification

The most common library classification system is the Dewey Decimal Classification (DDC), which has formed the foundation of library organization since 1876, when it was first proposed by Melvil Dewey. DDC was devised to arrange items and collections of items in a logical fashion using Arabic numerals. It is the most widely used classification system in the world; it is used in 135 countries and translated into more than thirty languages. It is certainly the classification system best known by most library users in the United States. Ninety-five percent of all U.S. public and school libraries and a quarter of all college and university libraries use this system (Dewey Decimal Classification 1996).

The DDC divides knowledge into *classes*; these classes represent traditional academic disciplines. There are ten main classes that are intended to encompass the universe of knowledge. Each of these main classes is assigned a specific numerical range. The main classes are as follows:

---

**Figure 6.1**
**Dewey Decimal Classification**
**Main Classes**

| | |
|---|---|
| 000 | Generalities |
| 100 | Philosophy, parapsychology and occultism, psychology |
| 200 | Religion |
| 300 | Social Sciences |
| 400 | Language |
| 500 | Natural sciences and mathematics |
| 600 | Technology (Applied Sciences) |
| 700 | The arts |
| 800 | Literature (Belles-lettres) and rhetoric |
| 900 | Geography, history, and auxiliary disciplines |

---

Each item that falls within the scope of one of these classes is assigned a number within that range. The number assigned is called a *class number*. The internal logic within a main classification is hierarchical: that is, within a main discipline or class, there are various subclasses or subdivisions, and the subclasses are variously subdivided with greater and greater specificity. Each subclass is assigned a range of numbers within the range of the main class. For example, the items classed in the 640s deal with Home economics and family living. Items in the 641s deal with Food and drink, while those items dealing with household furnishings would be classed in the 645s (Dewey Decimal Classification, p. 640). The class number becomes longer as the subclass of the discipline becomes more specific. To this end, decimals are used. Hence, the number 795 applies to Games of Chance; 795.4 applies to Card Games; 795.41 applies to "Games in which skill is a major element"; and 795.412 applies to Poker, except in my own case in which skill is not involved

(Dewey Decimal Classification, p. 794). The length of the decimal notation can extend to many digits, reflecting highly detailed subdivisions of a discipline.

The DDC is a remarkable system of library organization and has served library users for more than a century. Obviously, both the physical and intellectual organization of library collections is directly affected by this system. Interestingly, although DDC affects the physical location of items in the collection, a key feature of this system is that it provides for "relative location" rather than a fixed one. Before DDC, books in libraries were numbered based on physical location in the library. Books had only one fixed location. In DDC, the numbers assigned to books are not related to a particular place, but in relation to other books (Chan 1994). Hence, the actual physical locations of materials could change as long as the books remained in appropriate relation to each other (any shelver shifting books will tell you this!).

This is not to say that DDC is without problems. Among the problems is that the system is a closed one. The range of numbers is limited between 000 and 999, and the disciplines they designate have already been assigned. As new disciplines arise, they must be accommodated within the existing ten classes, and in many cases this is not easy. Disciplines that were undeveloped or unknown at the time the DDC was created are today often crowded into narrow ranges. In the twentieth century a major problem arose with the growth of the social sciences. More recently, the rise of computer technologies, which, of course, were unanticipated in Dewey's time, have also necessitated considerable modifications. DDC has been revised many times to reflect needed changes, but the changes themselves can cause problems because altering classification practices may entail substantial work on the part of libraries. A second problem is that DDC places heavy emphasis on knowledge created and disseminated in European and North American culture. This reflects the nineteenth-century biases from which the system emerged. DDC tends therefore to accommodate with some difficulty these other bodies of knowledge. Of course, these problems are not solely those of DDC: most other classification systems also share these difficulties because they also reflect the times in which they are created.

*Library of Congress Classification*

The Library of Congress Classification (LC Classification) was developed at the turn of the century to deal with the ever-growing size of the

Library of Congress's collection. Although DDC and other existing classification systems influenced the development of LC Classification, the system is unique and was developed for the practical purposes of organizing and accessing the Library of Congress collection. Other libraries that tend to adopt LC classification are often academic libraries with large collections. LC Classification is an alpha-numeric system. Each class number begins with one to three letters followed by one to four integers. Decimals can be used to expand the class. The letters represent the main class and subclass divisions followed by the integers that further subordinates the discipline. Hence a notation that begins with the letter P deals with language and literature, while the letters PT stands for German literature.

There are twenty main classes:

---

### Figure 6.2
### Library of Congress Main Classes

| | |
|---|---|
| A | General Works |
| B | Philosophy; Psychology and Religion |
| C | Auxiliary Sciences of History |
| D | General and Old World History |
| E-F | American History |
| G | Geography; Maps; Anthropology; Recreation |
| H | Social Sciences; Economics and Sociology |
| J | Political Science |
| K | Law (General) |
| L | Education |
| M | Music |
| N | Fine Arts |
| P | Language and Literature Tables |
| Q | Science |
| R | Medicine |
| S | Agriculture |
| T | Technology |
| U | Military Science |
| V | Naval Science |
| Z | Bibliography; Library Science |

There are specific subclasses for a variety of the main classes. For example, under the class K (law), there are specific schedules for laws of the United States, Germany, United Kingdom and Ireland, Latin America, and Canada.

## CONTROLLED VOCABULARY

A second crucial intellectual technology is controlled vocabulary. According to Meadows, a controlled vocabulary is "a list of preferred and nonpreferred terms produced by the process of vocabulary control" (NISO, Z39.19–1993, p. 35). Vocabulary control is "the process of organizing a list of terms (a) to indicate which of two or more synonymous terms is authorized for use; (b) to distinguish between homographs; and (c) to indicate hierarchical and associate relationships among terms in the context of a thesaurus or subject heading list" (NISO, Z39.19–1993, p. 38). Decisions regarding which terms will be used to refer to authors, titles, or subjects are referred to as authority control. With authority control, one term is selected for use. The list of accepted terms used in a controlled vocabulary is referred to as an authority list. Such vocabularies, however, consist of more than just the words or vocabulary itself, they consist of rules for assigning terms, methods for describing relationships among terms, and a means for changing and updating terms (Meadows 1992).

Controlled vocabularies play crucial roles especially when seeking subject-related information, but they provide consistency in the assignment and use not only of subject terms or headings, but also of author and titles terms as well. Controlled vocabularies are vital for effective use of indexes and thesauri and are essential for the collocating function of the library catalog. When using the subject headings in a card catalog or online catalog, one is experiencing a controlled vocabulary; when consulting the index terms in the volumes of *Reader's Guide to Periodical Literature*, one is experiencing a controlled vocabulary; when searching a computerized bibliographic database, such as ERIC, one is using a controlled vocabulary. Every time one encounters a well-prepared index at the back of a book, it is a controlled vocabulary at work.

Controlled vocabularies provide important information to the user. The following are some of the issues they deal with.

**Synonymy**: A variety of terms can mean the same thing. Organizers of information must select and consistently apply the same term so that

searchers can retrieve information effectively. (Of course, those selecting such terms also can create references from synonymous terms to the
one selected for use, e.g., *see* references in the library catalog.)

**Hierarchical relationships**: Controlled vocabularies can reveal when
a concept identified by a term is also contained within a larger concept
also identified in the thesaurus, e.g., references to *broader terms* or *narrow terms*.

**Associative relationships**: Controlled vocabularies help identify
related terms (concepts) that could serve to broaden and enrich an information search.

**Homographs**: Sometimes, terms spelled the same way may represent different concepts. Controlled vocabularies reveal this ambiguity
and refer information seekers to the appropriate terms.

Obviously, this type of information provides valuable information
and it is easy to see why controlled vocabularies are important in databases and in libraries. Consider the problem of synonymy in the library
catalog. Suppose there were no vocabulary control for the subject headings in a library catalog. Catalogers could choose any terms they wished
to describe the contents of the items they catalog. Consider if, when creating catalog entries on aircraft, catalogers could choose any number of
terms such as aircraft, airplanes, planes or flying machines to describe
the content of various items on this subject. A catalog user would then
need to look in at least four places to find all the material, *if* the user
could think of each of these terms and any others that might seem reasonable. Clearly, if different terms are assigned to describe the same content in different items, it becomes very difficult to retrieve those items.
Controlled vocabularies reduce error and ambiguity and guide the user
to the proper place. This guidance is provided in part by showing relationships between terms in a controlled vocabulary. Hence, when consulting a given term, the controlled vocabulary may suggest terms that
are broader or narrower or give the proper equivalent term used by the
controlled vocabulary. Examples of these relationships will be discussed
further in the context of the Library of Congress Subject Headings.

*Thesauri*

A critical tool intended to promote retrieval of information through the
use of a controlled vocabulary is the thesaurus. A thesaurus is "a controlled vocabulary of terms in natural language that are designed for

postcoordination" (NISO 1993, p. 1). Indexers and catalogers use such a vocabulary to determine precisely what terms to assign as access points to a record or document. Users of indexes, catalogs, and databases can use thesauri to locate the proper terms for searching or to discover related terms and subjects. According to the National Information Standards Organization, thesauri accomplish four purposes: they (1) translate the language of authors and indexers into a fixed vocabulary that can be used for indexing and information retrieval; (2) help ensure consistency when assigning headings and index terms; (3) reveal relationships between terms, and (4) assist in the information retrieval of information and documents (NISO 1993). As can be seen from these purposes, thesauri play critical roles in structuring access as well as in assisting in retrieval itself.

Thesauri usually consist of a core list of index terms, usually single words but sometimes combinations of words, phrases, or names. Terms in a thesaurus are sometimes referred to as descriptors. The terms comprising the core list are the ones determined to be acceptable for use to gain access to the information system (e.g., catalog, database, index). Associated with these terms are additional terms that are not used for direct access to the information system, but which, if consulted first, will direct a user to the appropriate term for use. These are sometimes referred to as cross-references or lead-in terms. Such an expansion is critical to a thesaurus because individuals trying to gain access to a particular information system are usually not aware of the terms that were selected. Rather they come with their own vocabulary and their own ideas as to which terms reflect the subject matter. As with controlled vocabularies, the terms selected are also enriched by notations about other associated terms and their relationships. Although thesauri have been in existence for many years, they have become especially important in the use of automated information-retrieval systems. Such thesauri provide a wide variety of available terms for those assigning terms to documents for access and for searchers seeking information. Examples of such thesauri include the *ERIC Thesaurus* and *INSPEC Thesaurus*.

## Subject Headings (LCSH)

The importance of the Library of Congress Subjects Headings (LCSH) is unquestioned, and its influence is worldwide. LCSH is best known for its applications to library catalogs and serves as an authoritative source of subject headings not only for library catalogs but for many indexes.

Among its significant advantages is that it controls terms for the information organizer (e.g., cataloger or indexer) and the information seeker (the user or librarian).

Subject headings have a special relationship to the classification system and provide an additional means of retrieving information. Classification puts subjects into the context of disciplines. For example, information on horses can appear in an animal (biology) class, in sports (horse racing), and in pets. Subject headings, in contrast, list subjects outside the disciplinary context, so a search on horses retrieves items about horses regardless of their disciplinary context. As a by-product, subject headings act as a kind of index to the classification scheme. That is, by identifying a subject through a subject heading, one also discovers the classification number or numbers assigned to that subject.

The LC subject headings are developed by the Library of Congress to provide subject access to the collections of the Library of Congress. They are widely used, in part because they are one of the few *general* (nondisciplinary) controlled vocabularies in English. LC uses these headings in MARC records (discussed below), which in turn means that all other libraries and other organizations that use the MARC records also have the advantage of the LC subject headings. The dominance of these subject headings highlights the importance that these headings provide effective and complete access to library collections.

The subject headings list contains many different types of headings, listed in an alphabetical arrangement.

Among the types of headings used are (1) single nouns or terms, e.g., "Lifeguards"; (2) adjective with a noun, e.g., "Life-saving apparatus"; (3) prepositional phrases, e.g., "Life-Saving at Fires"; (4) compound or conjunctive phrases, e.g., "Lifting and carrying"; (5) phrases or sentences (see Figure 6.3). The headings can also include a variety of subheadings under important terms. These subheadings can take many forms such as division by time, e.g., nineteenth century; geography, e.g., France; or form of item, e.g., dictionary.

Decisions made by the Library of Congress regarding the terms used to denote a particular subject can dramatically affect the ability of a library user to locate the information or item desired. For this reason, there is a *syndetic* structure to the LCSH subject headings. A syndetic structure is one that links related terms, a structure that is common in such vocabularies generally. The use of related terms allows a searcher to identify those subjects that may relate to the one under investigation as well as identify the "correct" term used by the Library of Congress.

# Figure 6.3

Survival swimming
**Life-saving apparatus**
VK1460-VK1481
BT    Survival and emergency
        equipment
NT    Emergency vehicles
        Immersion suits
        Life-boats
        Life-preservers
        Life rafts
        Life-saving nets
        Line-throwing guns
        Line-throwing rockets
        Submarine rescue vehicles
—**Law and legislation** *(May
    Subd Geog)*
**Life-saving at fires** *(May Subd
    Geog)* TH9402-TH9418
BT    Fire-escapes
        Fires
        Rescue work
Life-saving nets
    *TH9418*
BT    Life-saving apparatus
**Life-saving stations** *(May Subd
    Geog)*
VK1460-VK1471
BT    Life-saving
NT    Lifeboat service
Life science engineering
    USE Bioengineering
**Life science publishing** *(May
    Subd Geog)*
BT    Life sciences
        Publishers and publishing
        Science publishing
**Life sciences** *(May Subd Geog)*
UF    Biosciences
        Sciences, Life
BT    Science
NT    Agriculture
        Biology
        Life science publishing
        Medical sciences
        Medicine
—**Bibliography**
RT    Life sciences literature
—**Moral and ethical aspects**
    USE Bioethics
Life sciences ethics
    USE Bioethics

**Life sciences libraries** *(May
    Subd Geog)*
UF    Libraries, Life sciences
BT    Scientific libraries
NT    Agricultural libraries
        Biological libraries
        Medical libraries
—**Collection development**
*(May Subd Geog)*
BT    Collection development
        (Libraries)
**Life sciences literature** *(May
    Subd Geog)*
QH303.6
BT    Scientific literature
RT    Life sciences—
        Bibliography
NT    Agriculture literature
        Biological literature
        Medical literature
**Life skills** *(May Subd Geog)*
    Here are entered works that
discuss a combination of the
skills needed by an individual to
exist in modern society,
including skills related to
education, employment, finance,
health, housing, psychology, etc.
UF    Advice-for-living books
        Basic life skills
        Competencies,
        Functional
        Coping skills
        Everyday living skills
        Functional competencies
        Fundamental life skills
        Living skills
        Personal life skills
        Problems of everyday
        living, Skills for solving
        Skills, Life
BT    Interpersonal relations
        Social learning
        Success
NT    Conduct of life
        Self-help techniques
        Social skills
        Study skills
        Survival skills
—**Handbooks, manuals, etc.**

UF    Life skills guides
SA    *subdivision* Life skills
        guides *under classes of
        persons and ethnic groups*
—**United States**
NT    Hispanic Americans—
        Life skills guides
        Vietnamese Americans—
        Life skills guides
Life skills guides
    USE Life skills—Handbooks,
        manuals, etc.
**Life span, Productive** *(May Subd
    Geog)*
UF    Productive life span
        Work life
        Working life
BT    Age and employment
        Aged
        Life cycle, Human
        Mortality
        Occupations
Life span prolongation
    USE Longevity
Life stages, Human
    USE Life cycle, Human
**Life style** *(May Subd Geog)*
HQ2042-HQ2044
    Here are entered theoretical
works on an individual's distinc-
tive, recognizable way of living,
and the behavior that expresses it.
UF    Counter culture
        Lifestyle
        Social environment
        Style, Life
BT    Human behavior
        Life cycle, Human
        Manners and customs
        Quality of life
NT    Living alone
**Life support systems (Critical care)**
*(May Subd Geog)*
RC86.7
BT    Critical care medicine
**Life support systems (Space en-
    vironment)**
UF    Man in space
BT    Bioengineering
        Environmental engineering

## Figure 6.3 (cont.)

Human engineering
Space flight—Physiologi-
cal effect
Space medicine
NT  Closed ecological systems
(Space environment)
Extraterrestrial bases
Space cabin atmospheres
Space ships
Space suits
Space vehicles—Oxygen
equipment
Space vehicles—Water-
supply
Life tables
USE Mortality—Tables
Life testing, Accelerated
USE Accelerated life testing
Life time light (Portrait
sculpture)
USE Strong, Brett-Livingstone,
1953-
Life time light
Life without death (Tale)
USE Youth without age and
life without death (Tale)
**Life zones** *(May Subd Geog)*
QH84
UF  Biogeographic zones
Zones, Life
BT  Biogeography
Ecology
NT  Crop zones
Hybrid zones
**Lifeboat crew members** *(May
Subd Geog)*
BT  Life-saving
Lifeboat service
**Lifeboat service** *(May Subd Geog)*

BT  Life-boats
Life-saving stations
NT  Lifeboat crew members
Lifecare communities
USE Life care communities
Lifecycle, Human
USE Life cycle, Human
**Lifeguards** *(May Subd Geog)*
GV838.72-GV838.74
UF  Life guards
BT  Life-saving
Swimmers
**Lifeline earthquake engineering**
*(May Subd Geog)*
BT  Earthquake engineering
Lifelong education
USE Continuing education
Lifestyle
USE Life style
**Lifjell (Telemark fylke,
Norway)**
BT  Mountains—Norway
Lifoma (African people)
USE Foma (African people)
Lifou language
USE Dehu language
**Lift (Aerodynamics)**
UF  Aerodynamic forces
BT  Aerodynamic load
Aerodynamics
RT  Drag (Aerodynamics)
NT  Flaps (Airplanes)
Ground-cushion
phenomenon
Stalling (Aerodynamics)
—Computer programs
**Lift fans**
UF  Fans, Lift
Lifting fans

BT  Air jets
Fans (Machinery)
RT  Ground-effect machines
NT  Fan-in-wing aircraft
**Lift irrigation** *(May Subd Geog)*
BT  Irrigation
**Lift net fishing**
SH344.6L5
UF  Dip net fishing
Lift nets
BT  Fisheries
Fishing nets
Lift nets
USE Lift net fishing
Lift-off from the moon
USE Artificial satellites—
Lunar launching
Lift stations
USE Pumping stations
Lifters, Vacuum
USE Vacuum lifters
Lifthrop family
USE Liptrap family
**Lifting and carrying**
T55.3L5
UF  Carrying weights
BT  Materials handling
NT  Slings and hitches
Vacuum lifters
Weight lifting
**Lifting and carrying (Jewish
law)**
BT  Jewish law
Prohibited work (Jewish
law)
Lifting fans
USE Lift fans
**Lifting-jacks**
TJ1430-TJ1435

To this end, major terms are linked to other subject terms or phrases. These links can be to broader terms (BT), narrower terms (NT), or to the equivalent terms, which are the accepted terms (USE). For example, for the subject heading "Life-saving apparatus" there is a reference to the broader term "Survival and emergency equipment" and to the narrower term "Emergency vehicles." For the term "Life science ethics," the LCSH subject headings indicate that the term used in the catalog is "Bioethics" (USE). Indexers and catalogers use this structure to provide the helpful "see" and "see also" references in catalogs and indexes.

The Library of Congress Subject Headings, although dominant, are not the only subject headings in common use. Smaller public libraries, for example, use the *Sears List of Subject Headings*. This is a simplified list, similar to LCSH, but the terms and structure are less complex. On the other end of the spectrum is the highly technical Medical Subject Headings (MeSH) created by the National Library of Medicine for searching *Index Medicus*, a database of medical materials.

Over the years, however, critics have expressed concern that some of the headings employed are inadequate. One criticism suggests that the subject headings reflect a cultural bias. Perhaps the most notable and outspoken professional advocating this view is Sanford Berman, head cataloger of the Hennepin County (Minneapolis, Minn.) Public Library. Berman has argued for many years that the "LC list can only 'satisfy' parochial, jingoistic Europeans and North Americans, white-hued, at least nominally Christian (and preferably Protestant) in faith . . . and heavily imbued with the transcendent, incomparable glory of Western civilization (Berman 1971, p. ix)." Berman has repeatedly exposed subject headings that suggest racial or religious prejudices and stereotypes. LC recently made modifications to headings considered discriminatory largely in response to Berman's criticisms (University of Illinois 1996). Berman has also suggested that there aren't nearly enough "people helping descriptors," or popular terms, rather than the formal terms often devised by LC (Berman 1981, p. 96). As a consequence, people may approach the catalog with a popular term only to find that there is no such term, and they may be unable to locate the correct synonym. Among other concerns are that the subject terms have an academic bias that is unconducive to applications in public libraries. Also, there is concern that the subject heading terms become outdated quickly. Newer items stored under outdated terms may not be located, because the user is using the more modern term in the search. The need to use the latest editions of the LCSH to obtain effective access to the information contained in the catalog and hence in the collection itself becomes obvious.

## THE LIBRARY CATALOG

One of the fundamental limitations to collections of physical objects (such as books or periodicals) is that they can only be in one place at one time: only one physical arrangement of materials or group of materials can exist at a time. In order to overcome this limitation and to increase the modes of access, the library arranges representatives or surrogates of that knowledge in alternative arrangements. Historically, the surrogates were first organized only by author. With the development of card technology and the ability to produce duplicate cards, title and subject access were added to author access. Today, catalog records provide fundamental access to the library collection by author, title, and subject. Hence, if books are arranged alphabetically by author's last name on the shelf, the surrogates can be simultaneously arranged by subject, title, or discipline. A catalog that arranges records in one alphabetical file is called a *dictionary* catalog. Catalogs that have separate subject catalogs are called *divided* catalogs. Catalogs that arrange their records by classification number are called *classified* catalogs. While card catalogs may have separate physical files, one electronic catalog can provide the same search options, and more, and perform the search far more efficiently.

The library catalog, whether physical cards (the manual catalog) or electronic records, is an important intellectual technology that attempts to present much of the knowledge in the library in a systematic fashion. A catalog lists materials that comprise a collection, which in libraries usually focuses on the book collection. The records in a catalog are surrogates for the materials in that they represent items in the collection. Classification numbers on the cataloging record combined with the classification number on the material itself effect retrieval of materials in a library collection.

The library catalog is critical for libraries because it represents a large proportion of the total knowledge contained in the library collection or information system. In fact, the contemporary library catalog also may provide access to electronic indexes and other information-retrieval tools that expand the library resources far beyond its own collection.

Among the earliest and most influential attempts to define the purpose of the catalog was made by Charles Ami Cutter, who developed what he terms the "objects" of the catalog in his *Rules for a Dictionary Catalog* (1904).

---

**Figure 6.4**
**Cutter's Objects of the Catalog**

Objects

1. To enable a person to find a book of which either
   (a) the author
   (b) the title           } is known
   (c) the subject
2. To show what the library has
   (d) by a given author
   (e) on a given subject
   (f) in a given kind of literature
3. To assist in the choice of a book
   (g) as to its edition (bibliographically)
   (h) as to its character (literary or topical)

---

Cutter, Charles Ami. *Rules for a Dictionary Catalog*. Washington, D.C.: GPO, 1904, p. 12.

Cutter's first two objects describe the two basic access functions of catalogs: the finding function and the collocation function. Hence, the catalog is designed to locate items and to bring items of similar characteristics (such as author or subject) together. As Tillett observes, " . . . a library catalog should facilitate finding a desired item and should enlighten us about related items by displaying, in one place, all items that share a common characteristic, be it author, title, or subject, and informing us of relationships to other materials" (Tillett 1991, p. 150). The objectives of the catalog were reaffirmed by the International Federation of Library Associations (IFLA) at the International Conference on Cataloguing Principles in 1961, which included fifty-three countries. At the conference the "Statement of Principles" (or "Paris Principles") were adopted, which established basic principles for access. The function of the catalog as described in the "Statement of Principles" is shown in Figure 6.5.

---

**Figure 6.5**
**Functions of the Catalogue**

2.  Functions of the Catalogue

The catalogue should be an efficient instrument for ascertaining

2.1  whether the library contains a particular book specified by
(a) its author and title, *or*
(b) if the author is not named in the book, its title alone, *or*
(c) if the author and title are inappropriate or insufficient for identification, a suitable substitute for the title; and

2.2  (a) which works by a particular author and
(b) which editions of a particular work are in the library.

---

International Federation of Library Associations, "Statement of Principles: Adopted at the International Conference on Cataloguing Principles, Paris, October, 1961." Annotated Edition by Eva Verona. London: IFLA, Committee on Cataloguing, 1971, xiii.

The goal of a catalog is not only to permit individuals to find items that they already know exist, but also to help them find items of which they were previously unaware (Layne 1989, p. 188).

The catalog as an intellectual technology provides more than an access function, however; it also provides systematic description of items in the collection. Some of the descriptive functions of the catalog include

1.  To state significant features of an item; to identify an item.
2.  To distinguish one from other items by describing its scope, contents, and bibliographic relation to other items.
3.  To present descriptive data that responds best to the interests of most catalog users, and,
4.  To provide justification for access points, that is, to make clear to users why they have retrieved an item, e.g., to discover that a particular person authored or illustrated or adapted a particular work (Carlyle 1996).

These descriptive functions provide valuable information by supplying needed information about the item and ensuring that the item is actually the one sought. This leads naturally to a discussion of a key element of catalogs and other information organizing tools—the bibliographic record itself.

## BIBLIOGRAPHIC RECORDS (FOR PRINT OR MACHINE-READABLE CATALOGS)

A fundamental aspect of designing information systems for retrieval is the creation of records that represent the items needed. These representations are sometimes referred to as surrogates. The content in these records is referred to as the bibliographic description. The entire record is referred to as the bibliographic record. Such information representations can be found in a variety of locating tools, including the library catalog, bibliographies, indexes, and abstracts. The records in these tools are intended to represent the actual item of knowledge in one way or another. A bibliographic record consists of a series of data elements (e.g., author, title, place and date of publication, subject heading). Those elements that are created specifically for retrieval to bibliographic records are called access points or index terms. It should be noted that calling records surrogates implies that they always serve to guide the user to another item—the item referred to by the surrogate. But in reality, this is not always the case. There are times when a bibliographic record can, in and of itself, provide the information needed, and in this sense can be seen itself as part of the body of knowledge to be retrieved.

Some bibliographic records contain just a little information, while others may be quite detailed, but their purpose is always the same: to represent a unique item, for example a particular version or edition, sometimes referred to as a manifestation of the same work. For example, there are many versions or manifestations of *Alice in Wonderland*. A bibliographic record has to provide sufficient information to distinguish one manifestation from another and relate the particular item being described to other items.

The actual construction of bibliographic records is a complex task, and there is considerable discussion as to how much and what type of information is needed to represent an item. In fact, surrogates must reflect subtle intellectual distinctions. For example, there is a distinction between a particular book (the physical object) and the "work," which is embodied not only in a particular book but in many books. Hence, the work *Moby Dick* is embodied in many books of the same name, including many editions or translations. Creating a bibliographic record requires that the physical character of the book and the intellectual character of the work be properly described and differentiated. As Lubetzky has observed, "a *book* is not an independent entity but represents a particular *edition* of a particular *work* by a particular *author* . . . " (Lubetzky 1985, p. 190).

The creation of bibliographic records is guided by codes that provide standards or rules for the creation of such surrogates. The common process for providing bibliographic descriptions is called descriptive cataloging. Traditionally, these descriptions were found on catalog cards; today, they are more likely to appear on an online catalog screen, but the principles are the same.

There are two major factors that have dramatically affected descriptive cataloging over the last two decades. First is the economic advantage realized by shared cataloging efforts, and second is the use of computer technologies in the cataloging process (Delsey 1989). Cooperative efforts for standardized cataloging depend heavily on computerized bibliographic utilities such as OCLC, and this cooperation is promoted primarily through the efforts of the Library of Congress through its National Coordinated Cataloging Program. In this program, responsibility for descriptive cataloging is shared among the Library of Congress, designated libraries, and bibliographic utilities such as OCLC and the Research Library Group (RLG). Obviously, if one standard computer-generated record can be created for use by all or most libraries, significant fiscal and human resources are saved.

Bibliographic utilities and libraries rely on codes and standards to help make consistent their bibliographic descriptions. Codes that standardize bibliographic descriptions are important: standardization makes it easier for individuals to use a variety of information systems and databases and makes production of bibliographic records more economical since only one standard record need be generated. The movement for standardization has increased substantially in the last few decades, with major interest being generated on the international level. Primary activity for the international standardization for descriptive cataloging is currently being promulgated by the International Federation of Library Associations (IFLA). In 1971, for example, IFLA promulgated, through its program for international standardization, the International Standard Bibliographic Description for Monographs (ISBD(M)). In the years following, standards were subsequently developed for serials ISBD(S), printed music, maps, and other nonbook materials. These standards identify the key components for bibliographic description, the punctuation, and the preferred order for the components. Fortunately, these standards have been incorporated in individual cataloging codes including AACR2. IFLA has continued these standardization activities through its Universal Bibliographic Control program.

Similarly, major constituencies involved in the creation of cataloging records are also working to improve bibliographic access. Most notably, in 1992 the Library of Congress, OCLC, and the RLG formed the Cooperative Cataloging Council to "facilitate an increase in the number of mutually acceptable bibliographic records available for use by the cooperative community" (Cromwell 1994, p. 415). This cooperative was succeeded by the Program for Cooperative Cataloging (PCC) in 1995. Of course, perfect standardization may not be possible, or even desirable, as variations in languages, cultural values, types of users, and purposes of institutions may be sufficiently great to create a need for variation in bibliographic description.

Today, there is considerable discussion regarding the need for various levels of cataloging. Given the economic stresses felt by libraries and the differences in library patrons' needs for detailed bibliographic description, some have argued that not all items have to be described with the same detail. They point particularly to research that suggests that patrons use only a few elements of the bibliographic description when searching for information, most notably, author, title, publisher, and place of publication (Svenonius 1990). These findings are somewhat controversial, but it is common for libraries to use more than one level of description, notably minimal-level cataloging and full-level cataloging. The minimal level was designed for materials considered to be less important than others and to help speed up the cataloging process, especially when backlogs were present (Cromwell 1994). The use of the minimal level remains controversial, although its use is commonplace, and there has also been an attempt to create a level of cataloging somewhere between minimal and full. This level is referred to as core-level standards, developed by the Cooperative Cataloging Council, which attempts to identify the essential elements of a bibliographic record requiring greater description than minimal level, but less than full (Cromwell 1994). These standards share a similar purpose in their creation: to accommodate the tremendous budget problems of libraries, to speed up the cataloging process for some materials, to reduce backlogs, and to make items available more quickly to users. But there is ongoing concern that less description is likely to mean a substantive decrease in the quality of information provided to the searcher. The importance of such a concern cannot be overestimated.

*Anglo-American Cataloguing Rules*

The primary code used to create bibliographic description for library catalogs is the *Anglo-American Cataloguing Rules* (*AACR*). They are not the first rules proposed for cataloging. Indeed, AACR is descended from a set of rules proposed by Antonio Panizzi for the British Museum library in 1841. The American Library Association promulgated rules for descriptive cataloging in 1908 and revised them several times. The Library of Congress used its own internal rules for description until the 1960s, when there was a strong interest in developing international standards for cataloging and in accommodating the use of computers. The first code designed specifically to accommodate these interests was the *Anglo-American Cataloguing Rules (AACR 1)*, promulgated in 1967. These rules recognized the importance of the "Paris Principles" written in 1961 and were developed with these principles in mind. *AACR1* included rules for choosing access points for description (the method for describing the material) and for cataloging nonbook materials.

Although the intention was to create international standards, the practices of American, Canadian, and British libraries varied on many points (actually a separate edition was issued for British libraries), and as might be expected, the rules needed to undergo constant revision and enhancements. This ultimately led to a major revision of *AACR1* in 1974 by international representatives from various national library associations and representatives from Canada, Great Britain, and the United States. The resulting revision is called the *Anglo-American Cataloguing Rules Second Edition (AACR2)* and incorporates International Standard Book Description (ISBD) standards. Although the code continues to be modified, *AACR2* represents an international standard for bibliographic description.

## BIBLIOGRAPHIES, INDEXES, AND ABSTRACTS

In addition to classified arrangements and library catalogs, there are other tools that represent common and important additions to the librarian's arsenal of organizing devices in the library. These tools not only play an important role in identifying and locating materials in the library; they also extend one's retrieval capabilities beyond those of the classified collection or library catalog. Among these are bibliographies, indexes, and abstracts, which can come in print, microform, and electronic formats. The effectiveness of these tools relies heavily on their ability to apply many of the intellectual technologies previously described, most notably the principles involved in controlled vocabulary, including the assignment of subject headings or descriptors.

A bibliography is a list of materials or items usually restricted in some way, such as by subject, form (e.g., periodicals), or coverage (e.g., items published before 1900). As a rule, bibliographies are intended to lead the user to the sources they identify. Bibliographies centralize bibliographic information: they are another form of collocation. Some include a brief note or summary of the contents and are referred to as annotated bibliographies. There are basically two types of bibliographies: systematic bibliography and analytical bibliography. Systematic bibliographies generally focus on a particular subject or are designed for a particular purpose. They are sometimes further subdivided into enumerative bibliographies and subject bibliographies. The latter is self-explanatory; it is a bibliography in a particular subject area. Enumerative bibliography is designed to provide an extensive list of items, but not necessarily on a specific subject. A catalog is an enumerative bibliography, as is a national bibliography. Analytical bibliography (also known as descriptive bibliography) is a list of items that carefully focuses on the physical aspects of the item so that historical and comparative analyses can be effected. In such bibliographies careful attention is paid to the physical characteristics of various editions, and they identify any characteristics of the item that would permit a scholar to place the item in its historical or aesthetic context (Bates 1976).

An index is "a systematic guide designed to indicate *topics* or *features* of documents in order to facilitate retrieval of documents or parts of documents" (NISO Z39.4–199X-1995, p. 8). This very broad characterization is especially appropriate for automated indexes. Such indexes consist of five components: terms, rules for combining terms, cross-references, a method for linking headings, and a particular order of headings, or search procedure (NISO Z39.4–199X-1995). More simply, an index can be viewed as an alphabetized list of items that direct the searcher to further information. It can point to content within a given work (e.g., an index in the back of a book) or to items located outside the work (such as a periodical index). For example, when a searcher uses an index in the back of a book, the index term provides the appropriate section or page numbers within the work where information denoted by the term is provided. Indexes can provide retrieval information for most types of materials, including books, periodical articles, and dissertations. Other indexes have features much the same as bibliographies, for example, periodical indexes such as *Reader's Guide to Periodical Literature* or the *Social Science Citation Index*. These tools provide bibliographic citations arranged under various index terms. These terms might include, but are not limited to, subject terms, author names, article or book titles. Some indexes are devoted to a specific discipline, such as *Art Index*, while other indexes are considerably more general, such as *Magazine Index*; some are devoted to a single publication like the index for *National Geographic* or the *New York Times Index*. Given the proliferation of journals and the tremendous increase in the number of published articles over the years, the periodical index provides an essential pathway for the location of up-to-date material.

There are two major methods of indexing: precoordinate indexing and postcoordinate indexing. In precoordinate indexing, the indexer coordinates all the indexing terms at the time of the indexing. That is, the control over the combining of terms or indicating relationships between terms is done prior to the information seeker's use of the retrieval system. Postcoordinate indexing permits searchers to coordinate index terms of their own choosing (within the bounds of the controlled vocabulary) at the time of searching. This is most common in (although not exclusively restricted to) electronic information-retrieval systems in which the searcher selects combinations of search terms and connects them by logical operators, such as the Boolean terms *and*, *or* or *not*. Obviously, postcoordinate indexing permits great flexibility when using electronic indexes.

An abstract is "a brief, objective representation of the contents of a primary document, or an oral presentation" (NISO Z39.14–199X, p. 1). Whether prepared by the author or not, it is a form of surrogate that summarizes the contents of a document so that readers can determine if the document is appropriate for their purposes. Because of their abbreviated character they can serve many useful purposes. For example, abstracts serve as a current awareness tool, a quick way to stay up-to-date; they also provide information seekers with access to a large body of literature that can be scanned quickly, including material in foreign languages (Pao 1989).

An abstract usually includes a bibliographic citation indicating where the entire text of item can be located. It can be quite detailed or brief, but generally it attempts to describe key aspects of the document. There are two varieties of abstracts: *informative abstracts* and *indicative abstracts*. Informative abstracts represent and summarize the content of all major aspects of the material. Indicative abstracts briefly summarize what the document is about and include results when they are significant. Abstracts, however, are neither critical nor evaluative (Pao 1989); this differentiates an *abstract* from an *annotation*, which is a "brief comment or explanation about a document or its content" (NISO. "American National Standard for Writing Abstracts." (Z39.14–1979), p. 7.) or a *review*, which is usually a more extensive summary of a document that includes evaluation and comment. Tools that arrange abstracts so that they can be accessed by index terms are especially useful knowledge location tools. Such tools often arrange the abstracts by broad classifications or subjects. The tools operate like periodical indexes except that they also contain abstracts, providing the searcher with even more information to help decide if consulting the full text would be helpful. Examples of such tools would be *Psychological Abstracts* or *Library and Information Science Abstracts*.

The intention of bibliographies, abstracts, and indexes is to centralize bibliographic information for materials that may exist in a variety of physical locations, to arrange it in a systematic way, and often to provide the information needed to locate the items for use. As such they represent important finding tools for both the librarian and the library user. But it also must be kept in mind that such tools have their limitations as well. They often reflect the cultural or theoretical biases of their authors or, due simply to economic limitations, are not complete. Some tools, notably those published as books, may quickly become outdated, especially in disciplines that change rapidly or in which new information is produced at a rapid pace. Few periodical indexes and abstracts are comprehensive; they seldom index *all* periodicals that might have an article in the pertinent subject area. Hence, some journals may not be indexed or only partially indexed. This is not to underestimate the importance of these tools. Rather, it highlights the complexity of trying to represent large bodies of knowledge. Information professionals must understand that all intellectual technologies and tools have their deficiencies; our confidence should not be placed entirely in any one item.

## SHELF ARRANGEMENT

The manner in which a library physically arranges its items plays a critical role in the ability of the user to retrieve the desired information. The arrangements must take into account a wide variety of subjects, formats, and uses. Theoretically, a library could assign accurate and highly precise classification numbers to items, but arrange the materials on the shelf randomly, ignoring the benefits of the classification system. Such randomness might promote serendipity but is hardly efficient retrieval!

Of course, shelf arrangement in libraries is not random and reflects a variety of organizational models. The models that predominate in libraries are alphabetical, numerical, and disciplinary. Clearly, most library collections begin with the premise that items of the same subject or from the same discipline are shelved together.

The proximity of subjects is effected through the use of the major classification systems (DDC and LC). Because the disciplines are designated by numerical notations (Dewey) or alpha-numeric notations (LC), subject proximity is created through the alphabetical/numerical sequences. Alphabetical arrangement predominates in fiction collections in public libraries, which are usually arranged in alphabetical order by author's last name and not generally classified by number. It should also be noted that discipline affects the arrangement even when the numbers for the disciplines are not sequential. For example, one might place language materials and literature close together (grouping 800s and 400s in Dewey), perhaps because users of one are also frequent users of the other. This suggests, as noted above, that other models of knowledge organization may also operate in libraries as well. These models are usually more general, but certainly are quite common. For example, collections may be organized by (1) type of materials: indexes, general reference materials, periodicals; (2) format: videocassettes, audiocassettes, computer software, microforms, print materials; (3) user: children's, young adult, adult, vision-impaired.

## THE ORGANIZATION OF KNOWLEDGE WITHIN ELECTRONIC INFORMATION-RETRIEVAL SYSTEMS

Electronic information-retrieval systems include a wide variety of tools. The online catalog is an example of such a system, as are periodical indexes, CD-ROM databases such as *Psychological Abstracts*, the Internet, and online databases such as the more than 600 databases accessible through Knight-Ridder Information Services. Understanding their basic structure is critical, because these systems are integral components of information access in libraries and other information centers and will continue to grow in importance as they are accessed both within the library and remotely through the Internet.

*Records and Fields*

The foundation of electronic databases is in many ways similar to the card catalog: it is the record. A record is the information stored concerning a particular document. Each record refers to a document and consists of a series of fields. Fields are units of information within a record, that is, each field is a special area into which a specific category of information is added. Hence, in a bibliographic record there may be an author field, title field, an issue or volume field, a subject heading or descriptor field, and perhaps a field for special comments or notes. Database designers create these records and fields, but they do not necessarily select the access points to these records. Rather, it is common that the vendors who make these databases available determine which fields will actually be searchable and which ones will simply be displayed. The searchable fields may vary depending on the vendor, but the overall effect is to increase dramatically the number of access points that a searcher can use in locating information sources.

One of the most important developments for libraries regarding the creation of electronic records and fields was the development of MARC. MARC stands for Machine Readable Cataloging and was developed by the Library of Congress in the mid-1960s. The intention was to create a standard machine-readable format for bibliographic description. MARC is in reality a communications tool, designed for the creation and sharing of bibliographic information in a computerized or online environment. Today, MARC is the standard for the creation of bibliographic records.

MARC consists of various fields, also called identifiers or tags, each associated with specific information concerning a bibliographic entity (see Figures 6.6 and 6.7). There are many possible fields, including the basic ones such as author fields, title fields, subject fields, and publisher fields.

Additional fields include those for series, notes, related titles, and physical description. The effect of the MARC format can hardly be overestimated. MARC made possible the first substantive use of computer technologies for libraries—the centralized preparation of catalog cards for libraries—and its development also made possible the establishment of bibliographic utilities such as OCLC. The impact on collection development and resources sharing has been tremendous.

However, the MARC format was developed primarily as a cataloging format, and the organization of knowledge in other types of com-

## Figure 6.6
## Selected MARC Fields

| | |
|---|---|
| 010 | LC card number |
| 020 | International Standard Book Number |
| 050 | Library of Congress Classification Number |
| 082 | Dewey Decimal Classification Number |
| 100 | Personal author main entry |
| 245 | Title proper, subtitle, and statement of responsibility |
| 246 | Variant form of title |
| 250 | Edition statement |
| 260 | Publication information |
| 300 | Physical description |
| 440 | Series |
| 500 | General note |
| 505 | Contents note |
| 650 | Subject heading |
| 700 | Personal author added entry |

## Figure 6.7
## Sample MARC Record with Fields*

| | |
|---|---|
| 020 | ISBN 1-56308-354-X |
| 050 | PS374.P63R67 1995 |
| 082 | 016.813009 |
| 100 | Herald, Diana Tixier. |
| 245 | Genreflecting: a guide to reading interests in genre fiction / Diana Tixier Herald. |
| 250 | 4th ed. |
| 260 | Englewood, Colo.: Libraries Unlimited, 1995. |
| 300 | xxvi, 367 p.; 25 cm. |
| 500 | Rev. ed. of: Genreflecting / Betty Rosenberg, 3rd ed. 1991. |
| 504 | Includes bibliographical references and indexes. |
| 650 | American fiction—Stories, plots, etc. |
| 650 | Popular literature—Stories, plots, etc. |
| 650 | English fiction—Stories, plots, etc. |
| 650 | Fiction genres—Bibliography. |
| 650 | Fiction—Bibliography. |
| 650 | Reading interests. |
| 700 | Rosenberg, Betty. Genreflecting. |

*Record modified

Reprinted with permission, Online Computer Library Center

puter databases designed can be quite different. Abstracting and indexing databases, for example, use a variety of formats. The types of fields
available and the type and number of searchable fields may also be different. The situation, however, is not totally chaotic. Some database producers in common subject areas have agreed to substantially the same
formats. For example, Chemical Abstracts Services (CAS) and Biosciences
Information Services (BIOSIS) use standardized record formats. Nonetheless, there us definitely a need for greater standardization.

STANDARDIZATION OF RECORDS

With the ever-expanding volume of documents the need to standardize
the format and organization of records has become critical. Considerable help in standardization of records as well as other information-related activities is provided by the National Information Standards Organization (NISO). NISO is accredited by the American National Standards Institute (ANSI) to create and maintain technical standards for
information and for other organizations that exchange data. NISO develops standards only after a considerable process of consultation and
participation by individuals and organizations that would be affected
by the standard under development. When NISO believes a consensus
has been reached, a standard is issued (although sometimes not all participants agree with a standard, even when it is issued in its final form).
Compliance with the standard is voluntary, but the use of standardized
formats can be of considerable value, both financial and instrumental.
Among the many standards that are relevant to libraries are the following:

| | |
|---|---|
| Z39.2–1994 | Information Interchange Format |
| Z39.4–199X | Guidelines for Indexes and Related Information Re-<br>trieval Devices |
| Z39.9–1992 | International Standard Serial Numbering |
| Z39.14–199X | Guidelines for Abstracts |
| Z39.18–1995 | Scientific and Technical Reports—Elements, Organiza-<br>tion, and Design |
| Z39.19–1993 | Guidelines for the Construction, Format, and Manage-<br>ment of Monolingual Thesauri |
| Z39.41–1990 | Printed Information on Spines |
| Z39.44–1986 | Serials Holdings Statements |
| Z39.48–1992 | Permanence of Paper for Publications and Documents<br>in Libraries and Archives |

Z39.50–1995      Information Retrieval Application Service Definition
                 and Protocol Specification
Z39.63–1989      Interlibrary Loan Data Elements

*Files*

A file is a group or collection of records that share common characteristics. A library catalog may be seen as a file of works with the shared characteristic that they are contained within the library. Of course, there are many other types of files. Electronic files are referred to as databases, and there are literally thousands of such databases. The way that files are arranged in a database is referred to as file organization. Just like in a physical file, the logical structure of organization within an electronic file determines how well information retrieval can be effected. Generally, storage of files is logically organized around a key field. That is, the collection of records in the file are organized around a single field, e.g., a field containing the record number or the author's name. For example, a common arrangement of files is alphabetical: hence, a database may be arranged alphabetically by author's name. This results in a linear or sequential file. The files arranged by key field is the main file. Of course, database searching for anything but the simplest databases must be much more flexible than being searchable by the key field. This is certainly true of the online catalogs and databases that librarians use. The searching of most files is supplemented through the use of inverted files, which serve as indexes to the main file. An inverted file consists of particular fields that are associated with particular records within the database. Hence, if the key field is an author field, other inverted files may contain title words or subject-heading terms or descriptors. Searching on any of these terms leads to the identification of documents associated with that term. Although there are other ways to organize computers such as list chains and clustered files, the inverted file is the fundamental organization for searching electronic databases (Pao 1989).

SOME ISSUES AND CHALLENGES FACING KNOWLEDGE ORGA-
NIZATION

*Organizing Knowledge on the Internet/World Wide Web*

A current and growing problem facing all seekers of information is how to deal with the deluge of information available on the Internet or World

Wide Web. Of course, a major problem is that the Internet was developed as a decentralized system in which there is minimal control as to content and organization. Obviously, such a system has great advantages in that the freedom to produce and make information available is maximized. But a significant disadvantage is the lack of standardization. It is obvious from the discussion in this chapter that the standardization of information organization can make vast amounts of information accessible. This has been especially true in libraries. Unfortunately, this standardization is not available on the Internet, although a variety of Web browsers have been and are being developed which will, it is hoped, provide some order to the chaos of information currently available. For example, the Dewey Decimal System and the Library of Congress Classification System have been employed by some Web sites to provide subject access to the documents contained within them (Vizine-Goetz and Mitchell 1995). OCLC has expressed considerable interest in finding ways to use DDC as an online organizing tool. Others have proposed that classifications such as DDC might be helpful in providing control over the chaotic condition of the Internet. This certainly makes sense. Anyone who has tried to navigate on the Internet quickly realizes that the information is not only poorly organized—it is chaotic. The application of intellectual technologies such as classification systems might have a tonic effect and provide at least some structure to this unstructured and increasingly riotous environment. (Vizine-Goetz and Mitchell 1995). The participation of librarians in this process and the use of the intellectual technologies commonly used in libraries might help immensely. Others, however, have suggested that these traditional systems assume a permanence and stability to documents that were chiefly characteristics of print materials, while electronic records are characterized by impermanence and fluidity. (Levy and Marshall 1995).

*Keeping Classification Systems and Controlled Vocabularies Up-to-date*

Classifications such as DDC and LC rely heavily on disciplinary approaches, and controlled vocabularies also focus heavily on subject terms. Without a crystal ball, it is difficult to predict new disciplines or significant changes within disciplines such as the emergence of new subdisciplines. Similarly, some disciplines become obsolete. Attempts to respond to these changes can sometimes be quite cumbersome and present major problems to classification systems and thesauri. For example, the introduction of new disciplines or subdisciplines may force the creation of new classification numbers and the alteration of old ones. Policy and economic implications can be considerations for libraries if they decide to adjust their collections and catalog to reflect these changes.

*The Limited Application of Classification Systems for Periodicals and Other Formats*

Mann (1993) has observed that the current use of library classification schemes does not normally provide assistance in retrieving information from certain types of documents: most notably periodical articles and audiovisual materials. Library classification systems themselves have not been used to assign classification numbers to periodical articles (although theoretically this is possible). In addition, the systems themselves were designed for books, and the great advantage of the system was to permit browsing of similar materials in the same location. Other formats can seldom be shelved with the book materials. As a result, the application of classification in libraries generally has not allowed classification schemes to accomplish one of their basic goals when other formats are considered (Mann). It should be noted that this is not a failing of the conceptual scheme of the classification system. The system itself could be used to assign numbers to individual periodical articles or audiovisual materials. Perhaps with the growth of automated indexing of periodical articles, the assignment of classification numbers will become commonplace. But currently, such systems have not been employed for this purpose. Hence, subject access is left to other tools, such as periodical indexes, or it is not provided at all.

*Alternative Communication Formats for Retrieval of Documents in the Online Environment: SGML*

With the growth of information retrieval through online computer systems and the Internet, alternative communication techniques for retrieving documents are being developed. In librarianship, the dominant format has been MARC, which has served as an important tool for bibliographic communications using computers. It has been noted however that the MARC format was developed originally for the electronic production of catalog cards: the MARC format was thus linked to a single record pointing to a single item. Are there other approaches that could make retrieval of electronic documents more effective?

Among the notable alternatives is the development of the Standard

Generalized Markup Language (SGML), which was originally developed in 1970 as the Generalized Markup Language [GML] (Gaynor 1996). SGML provides a standardized means to describe various classes of documents and to identify the elements that comprise each class. Classes are characterized by document-type definitions (DTD), which also identify the structure of the document by identifying the necessary and optional elements. Each element for a class is assigned a code number. Hence, one class of document might be poem, and among its elements might be lines, stanzas, couplets, author, etc. (Gaynor 1996). SGML can describe content as well as structure in a document. For example, it can identify phone numbers, chemical structures, and citations within a document. It also permits the addition of nonbibliographical elements that can provide evaluative and analytical information for electronic documents. Overall, the use of SGML permits an hierarchical structure in which the bibliographical information, analytical information, and the full text itself can be "tagged" for retrieval. In this environment, retrieval could be very flexible and increasingly informative: each element or combination of elements, including whole documents, could be manipulated electronically and retrieved.

The consistent application of SGML in the creation or processing of documents residing in online systems could have dramatic implications for effective retrieval of not only individual documents, but of the individual elements. Nor is this possibility far-fetched. SGML is accepted as both a national and international standard (ISO 8879) and is already being used in projects to improve the encoding and interchange of machine-readable texts for scholars [Text Encoding Initiative]; for increased access to archival, museum, and library finding aids [Berkeley Finding Aid Project]; and for increased retrieval of digital images [Columbia University Digital Image Access Project] (Gaynor 1996). In addition, items in MARC format could be computer "translated" into SGML, making the application even broader for library use. Perhaps, most dramatic, one version of SGML, Hypertext Markup Language (HTML), is the fundamental language used to make documents available on the World Wide Web.

## SUMMARY

As the universe of knowledge expands, the demands placed on systems to organize this universe increase concomitantly. The focus on libraries often falls on the information-giving function. But information cannot be effectively retrieved unless it is properly organized. New information channels, such as the Internet, have produced great excitement, and it is a constant refrain that you can get "everything on the Internet." This, of course is the problem—too much, rather than too little information is there, and the information environment in which it resides is disorganized. The organization of knowledge will continue to be a central issue for those in library and information science who have been dealing with this problem for years. It is hoped, that those who produce and make available the vast new sources of information will recognize the expertise of librarians and information scientists and the technologies that they have developed to gain some control over this ever-expanding universe.

## REFERENCES

Bates, Marcia. "Rigorous Systematic Bibliography." *RQ* 16 (fall 1976): 2–26.
——. "What Is a Reference Book? A Theoretical and Empirical Analysis." *RQ* 26 (fall 1986): 37–57.
Berman, Sanford. *The Joy of Cataloging: Essays, Letters, Reviews, and Other Explosions*. Phoenix, Ariz.: Oryx, 1981.
——. *Prejudices and Antipathies: A Tract on the LC Subject Heads Concerning People*. Metuchen, N.J.: Scarecrow, 1971.
Carlyle, Allyson. "Descriptive Functions of the Catalog." (Unpublished class materials). Kent, Ohio: Kent State University, SLIS, 1996.
Chan, Lois Mai. "General Principles of Classification." In *Cataloging and Classification: An Introduction*. New York: McGraw-Hill, 1994. 259–284.
Cromwell, Willy. "The Core Record: A New Bibliographic Standard." *Library Resources and Technical Services* 38 (October 1994): 415–424.
Cutter, Charles Ami. *Rules for a Dictionary Catalog*. Washington, D.C.: GPO, 1904.
Delsey, Tom. "Standards for Descriptive Cataloguing: Two Perspectives on the Past Twenty Years," In *The Conceptual Foundations of Descriptive Cataloging*. Edited by Elaine Svenonius. San Diego: Academic Press, 1989. 51–60.
*Dewey Decimal Classification and Relative Index*, ed. 21. Edited by Joan S. Mitchell et al. Albany: Forest Press, 1996.
Gaynor, Edward. "From MARC to Markup: SGML and Online Library Systems." *ALCTS Newsletter* (Supplement) 7 (1996): A-D.
Kwasnik, Barbara H. "The Role of Classification Structures in Reflecting and Building Theory." In *Advances in Classification Research: Proceedings of the 3rd ASIS SIG/CR Classification Research Workshop*, vol. 3, Medford, N.J.: Learned Information, 1992. 63–81.
Layne, Sara Shatford. "Integration and the Objectives of the Catalog." In *The Conceptual Foundations of Descriptive Cataloguing*. Edited by Elaine Svenious. San Diego: Academic Press, 1989. 185–195.

Levy, David M., and Catherine C.Marshall. "Going Digital: A Look at Assumptions Underlying Digital Libraries." *Communications of the ACM* 4 (April 1995): 77–84.

Lubetzky, Seymour. "The Objectives of the Catalog." In *Foundations of Cataloging: A Sourcebook*. Littleton, Colo.: Libraries Unlimited, 1985. 186–191.

Mann, Thomas. *Library Research Models: A Guide to Classification, Cataloging, and Computers*. New York: Oxford University Press, 1993.

Meadows, Charles T. *Text Information Retrieval Systems*. San Diego: Academic Press, 1992.

[NISO] National Information Standards Organization. "Guidelines for the Construction, Format, and Management of Monolingual Thesauri." Bethesda, Md.: NISO, 1993.

———. "Indexes and Related Information Retrieval Devices." Bethesda, Md.: NISO, 1995.

Pao, Miranda. *Concepts of Information Retrieval*. Englewood, Colo.: Libraries Unlimited, 1989.

Svenonius, Elaine. "Bibliographical Control." in *Academic Libraries: Research Perspectives*. Edited by Mary Jo Lynch and Arthur P. Young. Chicago: ALA, 1990. 38–68.

Tillett, Barbara B. "A Taxonomy of Bibliographic Relationships." *Library Resources and Technical Services* 35 (April 1991): 150–158.

University of Illinois. "Sanford Berman Recipient of the 1996 Robert B. Downs Intellectual Freedom Award" [Online]. Available at *http://alexia.lis uiuc . . . text/news/downs96.html* (November 18, 1996).

Vizine-Goetz, Diane and Joan S. Mitchell. "Dewey 2000." In *Annual Review of OCLC Research, 1995*. Dublin, Ohio: OCLC, 1996. 16–19.

# 7

# From Past to Present: The Library's Mission and Its Values

Libraries, in one form or another, have been around a very long time. They satisfy a fundamental need of society: the need to have the society's records readily accessible to the citizenry. Now there are so many records a library can not conceivably store them all and although the place where records are stored may change in the future, the society continues to need access to organized information—perhaps more than ever before. Librarians must address the issues of which records should be stored, what types of records, who should have access to them, and for what purpose? Understanding the historical context in which libraries emerged provides a helpful context for answering these questions and offers a useful rudder to guide our course into the future. For this reason, we will make a brief excursion into the past to identify some of the major historical developments that defined the different missions that libraries have undertaken. This will provide a basic context for understanding the mission of present-day libraries and the libraries of the future.[1]

## THE MISSIONS OF LIBRARIES IN HISTORY

Not all societies can have libraries; at least three prerequisite conditions are required for libraries to prosper (Harris and Johnson 1984). First, libraries require *centralization*. Libraries do not prosper in nomadic conditions; there must be a stable "place" for the materials. The centralization of population in cities and towns was a critical precondition for the development of libraries. Even a small stable population such as a university or monastery can serve as a sufficient concentration to produce a library. Second is *economic growth*. Libraries cannot prosper when the primary energies and resources of the community are devoted to subsistence; they require a certain commitment of wealth and time. Similarly, wealth makes individual philanthropy possible, and libraries, in particular American libraries, have relied on philanthropy for much of their development. Finally, libraries require *political stability*. They cannot flourish where the political climate is unstable. In times of revolt and political chaos libraries are bound to be destroyed, and history has seen the destruction of many great libraries when empires fell.

### The Earliest Mission: Maintaining a Records Archive

No one knows when the first library was established, but at least two factors provided a significant impetus for their creation: the invention of writing and the rise of a commercial culture. The earliest written records of a society were found in Sumerian temple libraries in Mesopotamia around 3000 BC. The Sumerian temple library was, for the most part, a commercial archive (Kramer 1961). Temples were the social and economic center of Sumerian communities. They conducted business, managed estates, and lent money. The records of these temples included "commercial accounts, grammatical exercises for young scribes, mathematical texts, treatises on medicine and astrology, and collections of hymns, prayers and incantations" (Dunlap 1972, p. 2). Some historical and literary works as well as early codifications of law have also been found (Harris and Johnson 1984). In addition to temple libraries, there have also been discoveries of municipal and government libraries that held business records as well as deeds, contracts, tax lists, and marriage records (Harris and Johnson 1984).

The form of writing used to record this information is known as cuneiform. It involved impressing a square shaped or triangular-tipped stylus into clay tablets. There is evidence that some of the temples had schools that taught the art of writing and trained clerks to keep records of accounts (Dunlap 1972). Thus, it appears that the initial impetus for writing was primarily for administrative and practical business purposes, not for religious ones (Childe 1965).

Because of the complexity of some of these records and the number of clay tablets that must have been required, Harris and Johnson (1984) suggest that there must have been an organized arrangement for these materials. One wonders about the first librarians. The possibility of a "Marian, the Sumerian Librarian" wandering about some clay stacks gives us pause. We do know that the Sumerians had "Masters of the Books" or "Keepers of the Tablets" who were well-educated scribes or trained by scribes. Sometimes priests served in this capacity (Harris and Johnson 1984). Their specific duties, however, are unknown.

*The Religious and Practical Mission of Egyptian Libraries*

Parallel with the development of early libraries in Sumeria, the Egyptian culture was also producing written records. The form of writing used by the Egyptians is known as hieroglyphics and was pictorial in nature. The writing material was made from papyrus reeds that were flattened, rolled, and stored as scrolls (Jackson 1974).

The earliest Egyptian libraries probably emerged around 2400 B.C. As with Sumerian libraries, they were most often associated with Egyptian temples that were both religious and cultural centers. The libraries stored food, educated scribes, dispensed justice, and served both as historical archives and working libraries for learning the practical, spiritual, and medical arts. One early Egyptian library at Edfu, known as the "House of Papyrus," had a collection of practical and spiritual materials that included writings on administration, magic, astronomy, astrology, and medicine (Thompson 1962; Shera 1976). Egyptian libraries were particularly notable for their medical writings, which included pharmacological information as well as materials on diagnosis and treatment of diseases and surgery (Harris and Johnson 1984).

There were also extensive private collections among royalty and individual, wealthy Egyptians. Palace collections probably contained governmental records as well as philosophical or religious materials. Perhaps the most notable royal Egyptian library was that associated with Pharaoh Ramses II in Thebes between 1200–1300 B.C. This library may have had as many as 20,000 scrolls (Nichols 1964). Legend has it that based on the work of the Greco-Roman historian Diodorus Siculus, the portal above the library was inscribed with the words "Healer of the Soul" (Jackson 1974). Such an inscription suggests the presence of both spiritual and medicinal materials, but evidence is lacking concerning the actual contents.

Egyptian "librarians" were also scribes, often highly placed officials or priests. The Egyptian priest or scribe was held in high esteem because the ability to read and write was so rare. Writing itself may well have been considered a sacred activity, thus giving the scribes considerably more power than today's librarian (Harris and Johnson 1984).

## The Mission of Scholarship and Research

### THE LIBRARY OF ASHURBANIPAL

The mission of libraries was broadened by the Assyrians in Mesopotamia around the eighth century B.C. The Assyrian King, Ashurbanipal, expanded a library begun by his great-grandfather, Sargon II, at his palace in Nineveh. Ashurbanipal believed that the library should not only maintain archival records, but also serve as a current source of reference materials and contribute to the education of future generations (Dunlap 1972). To this end, Ashurbanipal directed a group of scholars and assistants to collect clay tablets produced from other lands. The result was that thousands of tablets were collected on a wide variety of subjects. Many of these tablets were translated from their original language into Assyrian. The collection contained Sumerian and Babylonian materials, including literary texts, history, omens, astronomical calculations, mathematical tables, grammatical and linguistic tables, and dictionaries, as well as commercial records and laws. There is evidence that the collection was organized with the titles arranged by subject and listed in registers. Some of the clay tables had markers to help in locating and shelving them. There is also evidence of a "keeper of the books," suggesting a librarian, but nothing else is known regarding the duties or character of this individual (Jackson 1974).

The library of Ashurbanipal was the greatest library of its time, providing a rich collection of materials and information on Mesopotamia and its culture. At its height, it was estimated to have as many as 30,000 clay tablets, two-thirds of which were collected during Ashurbanipal's reign (Dunlap 1972). Taken as a whole, the Royal Library at Nineveh was a remarkable achievement. The size of the library collection was a direct result of a concerted effort to collect a vast amount of material on a variety of subjects; the collection was developed, at least in part, for future generations; the materials were often translated; the materials were systematically organized, marked, and arranged; and a "librarian" played a significant role in the library's activities. No doubt, part of the reason for the library's existence was to glorify Ashurbanipal's greatness. But all of the characteristics noted above also suggest that the Royal Library can be seen as the first attempt to build a collection for reference and research.

## THE ALEXANDRIAN LIBRARY

Advancing the scholarly mission of libraries was one of the notable contributions of the Greeks to the history of libraries. Two factors contributed to this influence. First, before the fifth century B.C., Greece had been an oral culture, and consequently there was little need for libraries. However, beginning with the teachings of Socrates, Plato, and especially Aristotle, along with the philosophical schools that they established, reading and written records became more commonplace (Dunlap 1972). Second, the values of reading and learning were spread through the conquests of Alexander the Great, although Alexander himself was not directly responsible for the building of libraries.

Following Alexander's death in 323 B.C., his conquered lands were divided among five Macedonian generals, one of whom, Ptolemy Soter (Ptolemy I), was given Egypt. Ptolemy had great respect for learning and he encouraged the emigration of many scholars to Egypt, especially Alexandria, which became a center of culture and learning. Ptolemy and his son Ptolemy Philadelphus (Ptolemy II), with the help and encouragement of Demetrios of Phaleron, founded the Alexandrian Museum and Library. The mission of the library was ambitious—to collect the entirety of Greek literature. To accomplish this, the founder went to great and sometimes questionable lengths. The Alexandrian, like the library of Ashurbanipal before it, aggressively collected materials throughout the known world (Harris and Johnson 1984). In addition, Ptolemy frequently confiscated cargoes of books in ships that came to Alexandria (Hessel 1955). Copies were made of the originals and then the copies were returned to the owners (Thompson 1962). The items were subsequently organized and edited, and many of them were translated into Greek by scholars from many countries.

The collection was stored in two buildings: a major structure called the Brucheion and a smaller library called the Serapeum. This latter structure may have provided some service to students and the public, but the primary purpose of the library was scholarship (Harris and Johnson 1984). The library was used by scholars for general as well as special research. It was divided into ten great Halls, each Hall representing a separate area of learning. There were also some smaller rooms for individuals involved in special studies (Parsons 1952).

The Alexandrian was also notable for its librarians, many of whom achieved great personal fame, such as the scholar Callimachus. Callimachus is especially known for his *Pinakes*, which was the subject catalog of the library holdings. The *Pinakes* contained 120 scrolls with entries for each document including author and title. Because some entries included historical or critical remarks, some library historians regard the *Pinakes* as more than a library catalog, suggesting that it may have also served as a history of Greek literature (Jackson 1974).

The Alexandrian possessed the strength of any great research collection: a tremendous range of material and scholars to collect and maintain the collection. The comprehensiveness of the collection was beyond comparison for its time. At its height it may have contained more than a half-million items (Parsons 1952). Unfortunately, the Alexandrian declined with the decline of the Greek empire and by the third century A.D. suffered badly from pillaging and destruction.

### The Mission of Personal Status and Public Use: The Roman Libraries

With the rise of the Roman Empire, the mission of libraries appeared to shift. The Romans possessed few, if any, libraries during the early years of their history. However, following the conquest of Greece, during which time the collections of Greek libraries were plundered, possessing a library became a symbol of status and rank, as well as personal pride, for many generals and the aristocracy. By the first century A.D. there were a large number of books and private libraries in Rome, and in Roman country houses private libraries abounded. Aristotle's library, for example, was brought to Rome in the first century B.C. by the Roman general Sulla (Thompson 1962). Cicero made his library "the heart of his home" (Hessel 1955, p. 6), and had a library in each of his villas (Dunlap 1972).

As with the Greeks, there also appeared to be some impetus among the Romans to serve the "public" as well. Julius Caesar planned to build the first public library in Rome, but died before it was completed. His consul, Asinius Pollio, is given credit for this accomplishment. Two additional public libraries were created by the emperor Augustus, and by the fourth century A.D. there were as many as twenty-nine public libraries in Rome (Boyd 1915). These libraries were usually associated with Roman temples, but included public records and general literature as well as religious items.

It appears that the materials contained in both the private and public libraries may have been available for borrowing under rare circumstances (Harris and Johnson 1984). One wonders what the penalty for returning materials late might have been? The existence of public libraries, however, should not conjure up the same image as that of the modern public library. It is likely that less than 10 percent of the Roman citizenry could read (Harris, W. 1989), and it is quite probable that access to public library collections was limited to the wealthy and educated classes of Rome. Some library historians have speculated that the public libraries may have served more often as a public forum for recitation of works by Roman authors than as a resource or lending library (Dix 1994; Harris, W. 1989).

For most of the years of the Roman Empire, the Romans recorded their history and accounts using papyrus scrolls, like the Greeks before them. There were some obvious disadvantages to the scrolls; they were bulky and it was more difficult to find one's place because there were no pages. During the first century A.D., due to persecution and the need to record religious text quickly and in readily transportable form, the early Christians abandoned the scroll and replaced it with the parchment codex (book). By the fourth century A.D., the codex was in widespread use and had replaced papyrus scrolls (Thompson 1962).

With the decline of the Roman Empire, the rise of Christianity, and the invasions from Northern Europe, the libraries of the empire were destroyed. Libraries did not entirely disappear from Western Europe, but their form and function changed substantially. As Western Europe plunged into political, economic, and social chaos, the archival and scholarly missions of libraries were sustained through the growth of Byzantine and Moslem libraries and the monastic libraries of Western Europe.

*The Re-emergence of the Scholarly Mission: The Byzantine and Moslem Libraries*

Although the Western Empire was in serious decline by the fourth century A.D., the Eastern Empire under the leadership of the Christian emperor Constantine was flourishing. The center of the Byzantine Empire was the newly founded city of Constantinople. Constantine and the Byzantine culture valued education and writing, and it is in Constantinople that the Imperial Library was founded under the auspices of Constantine's son, Emperor Constantius, in 353 A.D. (Jackson 1974). Although the Eastern Empire was more influenced by Greek culture and traditions than Rome, the Imperial Library contained Christian and Latin works in addition to Greek materials (Johnson and Harris 1984).

By 450 A.D. the library had been expanded to an impressive 100,000 items. Constantinople contained not only the Imperial Library, but a large university library and the library of the leader of the Eastern Church, the patriarch. The mission of these libraries was scholarly and religious, and this mission played an invaluable part in the sustenance of Western society. As Harris has noted, "of the Greek classics known today, at least seventy-five percent are known through Byzantine copies" (Harris and Johnson 1984, p. 83). Without this preservation of materials, the Renaissance would not have been possible.

The same can be said concerning the achievements of the Moslem Empire, which flourished by the middle of the seventh century until 1000 A.D. Because of the respect afforded reading and learning in this culture, libraries became commonplace in private homes, royal palaces, and universities throughout the Moslem world. The caliphs in many of the major cities were scholars and literati (Thompson 1957). Spain had seventy libraries, Baghdad thirty-six, and "every important city in Persia had its library" (Thompson 1957, p. 353).

The earliest major library was the Royal Library in Damascus, which contained materials from throughout the world on a wide variety of topics including medicine, philosophy, history, and literature (Harris and Johnson 1984). Later, during the eighth and ninth centuries, Baghdad became the cultural center for the study of Greek medical, scientific, and philosophical works and "abounded with libraries" (Thompson 1957, p. 351).

In addition, research and learning were furthered by large libraries located in Moslem universities. There were, for example, major universities in Baghdad, Cairo, and Cordoba. The Cairo library may have held more than 200,000 volumes, and the library at Cordoba was reported to contain between 400,000 and 600,000 volumes, larger than the Alexandrian (Harris and Johnson 1984; Thompson 1957). Like the Byzantine libraries, Moslem libraries contained not only Arabic works, but Persian literature as well as Greek and Latin philosophy and science. As such, Moslem libraries made a substantial contribution to the preservation of Western culture by preserving the central works of Western thought. The Western world owes a particular debt to the Moslems for preserving the works of Aristotle, whose works were quite popular, and many of his writings were translated into Arabic for use by Arabic scholars (Harris and Johnson 1984). With the decline of the Moslem Empire, however, the fate of libraries was sealed.

*The Religious Mission: Monastic Libraries of the Middle Ages*

With the fall of the Roman Empire, social and political chaos led to economic instability throughout Western Europe. Inevitably, a decline of libraries followed. Only one major Western institution was able to sustain the critical preconditions for library development, the Christian monastery. Monasteries provided a means of geographically, as well as spiritually, isolating Christian adherents from the disorder that had spread throughout society. These monasteries were well established by 500–550 A.D. The mission of the monastic library was threefold: to provide a place for spiritual reflection, to archive religious texts, and to reproduce religious and sometimes secular texts.

Perhaps the best exemplar of the religious mission of the monastic library comes from the Benedictine Order established in 529 A.D. in Monte Casino, Italy. The monastic life in this monastery and the Benedictine monasteries founded thereafter were guided by the Rules of St. Benedict. One of the rules was that each monk was to be given one book for study each year (Clanchy 1979). Other rules included copying books as a fundamental aspect of monastic life. Copying was done in a special room called the scriptorium. Sometimes copying was used as a punishment for a recalcitrant monk, and the quality of the copy often left much to be desired (Shera 1976).

It should be kept in mind, however, that according to St. Benedict, the purpose of monastic life was to concentrate on spiritual matters and to avoid secular thoughts. Reading and copying books were seen as a means to maintain an ascetic life, not to become educated per se. For example, books were often read to monks when they were dining, but it was not to enlighten them, but to keep their minds from straying to frivolous or worldly matters. The purpose of copying was not to create more useful and instructive texts, but to keep the monks busy (Thompson 1957).

Other monasteries founded in Ireland, Switzerland, Scotland, France, and Britain emphasized books and copying in a different vein. For example, if one were copying religious texts, one would be expected to derive inspiration from them. Many of these monasteries produced fine, illuminated manuscripts intended to reveal the spiritual beauty of God. These works of art reflected the copyist's realization that he was representing sacred words from the scripture. Their physical beauty, however, might also have been fascinating to the laity and may even have served as an early incentive to literacy (Clanchy 1979).

Regardless of whether the purpose of reading and copying books was to learn, to inspire, or to achieve an ascetic life, the fact is that many books were saved and copied during this time, thus preserving the writings of antiquity. One should not, however, give too much credit to the monks. As Thompson has observed, " . . . it is equally true their preservation was as often due to neglect and mere chance as it was to conscious intent . . . the medieval scriptorium was more often a treadmill for meaningless labor than it was a shrine where the expiring flame of literary culture was sedulously preserved" (Thompson 1957, pp. 30–31).

One other aspect of medieval monastic life deserves mention. One could argue that modern library and information science began with another monastic tradition: the Dominicans. Among the rules of the Dominican friars are those related to finding a good location for the library, providing adequate shelving, organizing the library by subjects, marking the spines of books with their titles, replenishing and weeding the collection, establishing hours of operation, and selling duplicate titles (Clanchy 1979). Certainly these are reflective of some of the duties of the modern librarian.

*The Educational Mission of Libraries: Cathedral and University Libraries of the Late Middle Ages*

The mission of Western libraries to educate re-emerged in the late Middle Ages (800–1200 A.D.). With the growth of cities and towns and the improvement in trade and other economic and social conditions, there was a concomitant improvement in the intellectual climate. The increasing respect for learning made fertile conditions for libraries once again.

By 1100, large cathedrals in major cities were the administrative centers for bishops and archbishops and training centers for priests and other religious functionaries (Harris and Johnson 1984). The mission of the cathedral libraries, unlike the monastic libraries, was to support the educational program of the cathedral and encourage study. The cathedral libraries were larger than most monastic ones and were less dominated by religious works (Shera 1976). Although some of the cathedral libraries were substantial, such as those in Verona and Monte Casino, Italy, or at the cathedrals at Rheims and Chartres in France, none were anything resembling the size of the larger libraries of the Moslem Empire (Dunlap 1972).

Although the church continued to be a vital part of the life of the late Middle Ages, it was also a period of transition. The cities were producing a middle class, and there were those among the laity and intellectual aristocracy who did not rely on church teaching to guide their intellectual pursuits (Hessel 1955). These developments, coupled with the dominance of less contemplative and more secularly-involved religious sects such as the Dominicans and Franciscans, spawned the establishment of academic centers in Bologna, Paris, and Oxford. These institutions supported not only theological studies, but also classical and professional instruction in law, medicine, and philosophy. Initially, the first universities did not have libraries; rather, students bought their books from booksellers. The first university library appeared at the University of Paris in the mid-thirteenth century, and subsequently at Oxford and Cambridge among others (Shera 1976). These libraries were often small, well under 1,000 items, but their mission to support and expand the educational mission of the university served as a bridge from the domination of the medieval church to the birth of the Renaissance (Harris and Johnson 1984; Shera 1976).

*The Humanistic Mission and the Re-emergence of the Library for Personal Status*

The period following the Middle Ages was a time of considerable economic, social, and political ferment, with much of it centered in Italy, most notably Venice and Florence. Contributing factors included the rise of secular monarchies, an increased sense of nationalism, a decline in the power of the church, an increase in literacy, an emerging interest in natural sciences, an expanding interest in secular politics, and a re-awakening of the philosophical traditions of ancient civilization, most notably the Greek and Roman thinkers. This fervor for the knowledge of the ancients and for new secular knowledge rather than spiritual enlightenment characterizes much of what is referred to as Renaissance Humanism.

The Renaissance was primarily an aristocratic enthusiasm, and great private libraries were developed by leading literary figures such as Petrarch and Boccaccio, who themselves were sponsored by popes or the Renaissance princes, e.g., the dukes of Urbino and the Medici. These sponsors were passionate book collectors as both a matter of personal vanity and a genuine interest in secular learning. They sent agents throughout Western Europe to locate and retrieve the manuscripts stored in the deteriorating monastic libraries. Sometimes the manuscripts were copied but, at other times, enthusiastic agents confiscated (saved?) these items for posterity by bringing them to their sponsors. As a result, Renaissance libraries were richly appointed and filled with beautifully illuminated texts. They served as places for scholarship, but also as places where aristocrats could "display their sensitivity to classical Latin" (Jackson 1974, p. 107).

Although the Renaissance princes may have taken the notion of the private library as personal aggrandizement to its highest form of ostentatious display, it was hardly a new concept or new mission (remember Ashurbanipal and the wealthy Romans?). One might reasonably contend as Dunlap (1972) does, "Had it not been for the enthusiasm of a few collectors of that age . . . we should certainly possess only a small part of the literature, especially that of the Greeks, which is now in our hands" (pp. 106–107).

*Promoting National Pride: The Mission of the National Libraries*

The growth of secular monarchies and nationalism is consistent with the emergence of a new type of library with a special mission—the national library. Early examples of such libraries arose in the seventeenth century in England, France, Germany, Denmark, and Scotland. The eighteenth and nineteenth centuries saw national libraries in Austria, Italy, Sweden, Norway, Greece, Spain, and Ireland among others (Gates 1976). What distinguishes these libraries is not simply their large collections; rather their special mission was to preserve the cultural heritage of the countries in which they were situated. This meant developing a comprehensive collection of materials by and about the country including books, manuscripts, documents, and other records.

In order to meet this mission, a unique collection development technique was employed: the creation of a "depository" right. That is, some nations passed laws requiring that at least one copy of each item published within the country be sent to the national library. This was accomplished, for example, in England in 1610, when an agreement was made between the Stationers' Company (which licensed publications in England) and the Bodleian Library of Oxford University. This agreement stipulated that one copy of each book published would be given to the Bodleian in return for limited borrowing privileges (Jackson 1974).

In essence, this meant that all items, or nearly all items, published would become part of the national collection. In the United States, this depository right is held by the Library of Congress and, although it is not officially our national library, it is a very close approximation.

*Making Modern Missions Possible: The Printing Press*

If one can identify a single historical development that affected all library collections in a profound way, it would be the invention of the printing press in 1464 in Mainz, Germany. The invention of the printing press had broader effects than those on libraries, but there is no doubt that libraries would never be the same following its genesis, and it is impossible to consider the modern mission of libraries without considering some of the changes that the printing press wrought. Eisenstein (1979) identified many effects of the printing press. Some of these are summarized below:

(1) *The ability to produce an authoritative version*: Before the time of printing, copies were made by hand. This laborious process sometimes produced extraordinary works of art, but more often less-than-perfect versions: copiers made mistakes or even intentionally omitted or amended text. The printing press could produce identical copies.

(2) *The ability to produce more titles and copies*: The sheer volume of printed materials increased dramatically as use of the printing press increased. Obviously hand copying was slow and arduous and, although multiple copies were made, overall they were small in number. In the sixteenth century, after the printing press had had some time to develop, more than 100,000 different books were printed in Europe alone (Harris and Johnson 1984). The implication for libraries is obvious: the size of library collections could increase substantially. In addition, by making more copies available, more collections could develop.

(3) *The ability to cover more subjects:* With an efficient means to produce materials, there was an opportunity to spread many more ideas. For example, in the first decade of printing, ending in 1460, the publications consisted of four typically medieval categories: sacred literacy (Bibles and prayer books); learned literacy (works of grammar and scholastic works such as those of Thomas Aquinas); bureaucratic literacy (official documents such as papal bulls and indulgence certificates); and vernacular literacy (works in the language of the people, notably German readers) (Clanchy 1983). During the second decade of the press, the breadth of subjects increased and spread beyond medieval thinking. Obviously, the communication of different ideas can have a profound effect on society. In fact, one of the earliest effective uses of the printing press was to spread the ideas of Martin Luther, who dissemi-

nated his religious tracts throughout Europe using this method. The effect of the subsequent Protestant Reformation can hardly be overestimated.

(4) *The creation of new techniques for the organization of published materials:* Given the growth in size and subject diversity of library collections, new techniques for organizing and classifying materials became necessary. This eventually led to the complex systems we have today in the Dewey Decimal or Library of Congress Classification System.

(5) *The stimulation of literacy and education for the general population:* When books are scarce, only a few can have access to them. As more books became available, it was inevitable that more people would learn to read. This, in turn, would eventually generate the market for library users.

In sum, the invention of the printing press, coupled with the reawakening of secular and scientific interests during the Renaissance ultimately formed the foundation for the growth in number and size of libraries and consequently for a broader and wider mission for libraries.

## LIBRARIES IN THE UNITED STATES: NEW MISSIONS

As we move to the next period in the development of library missions, it is time to leave the European continent. The seventeenth and eighteenth centuries were formative periods in American life, and as the focus of this book is on the United States, the balance of this discussion will concentrate on American libraries.

There were few libraries in America during the early part of the seventeenth century. The social preconditions were not yet in place: people were struggling for subsistence, there were few urban settings, and there was limited economic development or individual wealth. America was an agrarian society that depended on manual labor and the literacy rate in the general population was low. One of the first libraries to appear was the religious library. In England in the late seventeeth century, the Reverend Thomas Bray, an Anglican clergyman, advocated for libraries devoted solely to religious purposes. To this end, he created the Society for the Propagation of the Gospel, which established parish libraries throughout England. His interest soon spread to America and by the 1700s, seventy parish libraries were established in the United States (Harris and Johnson 1984).

A few private libraries were found in the colonial homes of ministers, doctors, and other prominent citizens. In general, these libraries were less a form of status or recognition, however, and more a resource for practical or spiritual materials to deal with the problems confronting settlers in the New World. Most of these collections were quite small. In addition, there were also a few modest college libraries. Harvard, founded in 1636, possessed a small library of approximately 5,000 volumes by the mid-eighteenth century; Yale, founded in 1700, held around 2,500 volumes by 1750 (Harris and Johnson 1984). The sparsity of college libraries is a reflection of the sparsity of the college educated. By 1775, fewer than one in a thousand citizens had attended any college (Hanson 1989). By 1792, only nine colonial colleges were established that had libraries. The libraries themselves were not located in separate buildings, but in rooms within buildings in which other functions were performed.

The size of the typical collection was small for several reasons: the low number of book titles produced in the United States at the time, lack of fiscal resources, and lack of recognition for the library's role in academic life. The growth of the collection depended primarily on donations. If a college had a library, it was usually open infrequently and usually had no librarian to provide assistance. For example, Harvard did not have a librarian until 1667. When assistance was available, it was usually a faculty member who served only secondarily as a part-time librarian (Harwell 1968). Book selection was accomplished usually by a committee of trustees or faculty members (Hamlin 1981; Shiflett 1994). Professional librarians were generally not part of college staff until the end of the nineteenth century (Hamlin 1981).

*The Mission of Self-Improvement: The Social Libraries of the Eighteenth Century*

As in Europe, the seventeenth and eighteenth centuries in America were a time of considerable political stability and growth in scientific and technical knowledge. With these advances and the development of mechanical technologies, the industrial revolution soon led to the growth of the economy with concomitant growth in individual and community wealth. This in turn meant that some of the more fortunate citizens had more leisure time, time which could be spent pursuing self-development. These were fertile conditions for the emergence of new libraries and missions.

During the first half of the eighteenth century two such library models emerged: the social library and the circulating library. According to

Shera (1965) "the social library was nothing more than a voluntary association of individuals who had contributed money toward a common fund to be used for the purchase of books" (p. 57). Two types of social libraries eventually emerged: proprietary libraries and subscription (association) libraries. Proprietary libraries operated on the principle that those who contributed money for the library actually owned the material purchased, in essence, they were stock holders. In subscription libraries, the fees contributed permitted the participants to use and circulate the collection, but they did not have ownership of the items themselves (Shera 1965). The collections of social libraries were often quite small, as was their membership, many having less than 300 books, and most fewer than fifty members.

The mission of the social library was to assist self-improvement and the search for truth. Many of its members had a genuine love of literature and believed that the common use of such materials led to character improvement and through discussion with others, increased knowledge, as well. One of those who believed in the value of self-improvement was Benjamin Franklin. Franklin is given credit for establishing in 1728 the first, although short-lived, library in Philadelphia, called the Junto. He founded a second library, also in Philadelphia, which he referred to as a "subscription library" in 1731. It survives today as the Philadelphia Library Company.

The social library became quite popular throughout New England in the latter half of the eighteenth century and well into the nineteenth. The mission of self-improvement was not restricted to scientific, technical, or professional pursuits but served whatever group decided to create the collection. Hence, although there were social libraries that had relatively aristocratic and well-educated clients, there were also YMCA libraries, agricultural libraries, "ladies clubs," and mechanics libraries, all developed to meet the special interests of less affluent, and often less educated, members of the community. There were also many general interest social libraries that did not focus on one particular subject but nonetheless met the educational needs of its members. Their collections often contained religious materials, history, travel, and literature (not to be confused with popular fiction, of which there was little in these collections). Although social libraries may have had materials of a more diverting nature, their purpose was not to appeal to mass tastes, but to one's "better angels."

Given the voluntary nature of social libraries, their ability to accomplish their missions was deeply affected by the ability of their members to sustain the library. Often these libraries relied on one or a few bene-factors, and shifting economic times, depressions, wars, and social un-rest led to the relatively quick demise of many. Nonetheless, the legacy of the social library is significant. Not only did the development of li-brary collections for self-improvement become ingrained in America and form the basis of an important aspect of public library service, but the core of many future library collections were the remnants of abandoned social libraries. To those defunct libraries, the American public library owes much for its early inventory.

*The Mission of Mass Appeal: The Circulating Library*

While the social library was attempting to meet the need for self-improvement and edification with informative materials, there was contemporaneously a second mission pursued by a different type of li-brary: the circulating library (sometimes referred to as the rental library). Although England had circulating libraries many years before America, the first circulating libraries in America arose in the 1760s. Their mis-sion was to satisfy public demand and popular tastes, especially the demand for fiction. The popular novels of this time consisted mostly of romances (much like today!) and the appearance of these novels was fairly well established in America by 1790. Although there were few romances by American authors, there was ample supply of popular for-eign novels published by American presses. There may have been as many as 350 foreign titles published in America from 1789 to 1800, com-pared to 35 titles by American authors (Shera 1965). Serving mass tastes appears to have been as profitable in colonial times as it is today; many of these libraries prospered and spread throughout New England.

The distinguishing feature of circulating libraries was their profit-making character. Usually they were associated with another com-mercial enterprise such as a printer or bookstore. From this perspective, the circulating library's purpose, first and foremost, was to make money. The majority of the collection was fiction although there were some hold-ings of literature, history, and theology. Overall, the materials were in-tended for entertainment rather than education. The books were either rented or individuals were charged a membership fee that allowed them to borrow a designated number of materials over a specified period of time.

It is worth noting that circulating libraries often incurred the wrath of certain segments of society who were concerned with the immoral effects of popular reading. As sometimes happens today in public libraries, circulating libraries were suspected of corrupting youth, usually because of the corrupting effects of the popular novels—especially the French ones (Shera 1965).

Just as the social library formed the basis for many early public library collections and provided some of the philosophical underpinnings as well, the circulating library also made several contributions to public library philosophy and service. For example, despite its profit motive, its mission to appeal to popular taste echoes in contemporary public library service. In addition, Kaser (1980) notes that circulating libraries were the first to provide (1) service to women, (2) newspapers and magazines, (3) extended hours of service, (4) reading areas in the library itself, and (5) outreach services including the home delivery of books. These are substantive contributions. The circulating library's survival, however, was ultimately threatened by its low status and competition from tax supported public libraries (Kaser 1980).

*The Library in Support of Commercial Profit: The Rise of Special Libraries for Business and Industry*

Although the circulating library as a money-making venture failed to catch on, its spirit of free enterprise was certainly consistent with a capitalistic economy, one of the central elements of American society. Shortly after the start of the industrial revolution, public libraries started collections for factory workers, technical workers, craftsmen, and managers (Kruzas 1965). Not long thereafter, American business and industry discovered the instrumentality of the library. The roots of the business library go back to the mechanics, mercantile, and factory libraries established at the beginning of the nineteenth century. Generally, however, with the exception of a few law or insurance firm libraries, most libraries associated with private enterprise in the past were used for education, consultation with professional literature, or diversion of its users; its purpose was not to provide direct assistance in conducting business itself.

At the beginning of the twentieth century, however, there emerged a new library whose purpose was the "direct application of recorded information to the practical goals of profit-seeking business enterprises" (Kruzas 1965, p. 109). The purpose of the commercial library was to promote the profitability of the company. Hence, these libraries collected only materials that focused on the direct needs of the enterprise. Interestingly, this led to the collection of materials unfamiliar to many libraries: records, documents, papers, announcements, reports, and, by the 1920s, microfilm. Emphasis was on providing reference service to the organization rather than on collection development itself: providing the information to the individual who needed it was much more important than revealing to the requester where to find the information. This remains a fundamental characteristic of special libraries to this day. The concerns of these types of libraries helped promote the creation of the Special Library Association in 1909, and these libraries also served as a primary impetus for fostering new technologies that would access information rather than documents. As noted in the previous chapter on information science, this shift in emphasis was also an important foundation for the rise of information science and the exploitation of information technologies in libraries.

### The Mission of Supporting Teaching and Research: The American Academic Library

Although the educational mission of libraries emerged as early as the Alexandrian library, the mission of the library in the modern American academic institution did not evolve until the latter part of the nineteenth century when universities were established (Hamlin 1981). There are historical reasons for this late development. From the colonial period to the Civil War, the curriculum of academic institutions followed a classical model. Areas emphasized were theology, philosophy, history, and the trivium of the liberal arts—grammar, rhetoric, and logic (Hanson 1989). The faculty taught from a single text or, at best, a few books. Classroom recitation was strongly emphasized (Hamlin 1981). Such methods produced little need for libraries, and academic collections remained small throughout this period.

Several developments in the mid-nineteenth century substantially changed academic institutions and produced the foundation of modern academic libraries' missions. In particular, the library was recognized as a critical factor necessary to support the curriculum and research for students and faculty. Three important changes led to this recognition; they were changes in the curriculum, the rise of the research model, and the Morrill Land Grant Act of 1862.

### (1) Changes in the nature of the curriculum

Fundamental to the advancement of the academic library was the evolution of teaching methods and subject matter in academia as a whole. With the rise of the sciences and the industrial revolution, the need to change the classical nature of the college curriculum arose. Industry and manufacturing were demanding graduates with practical education rather than an understanding of the classics (Hanson 1989). Realization of the need for change started slowly, but by the 1840s the curriculum often included courses in the natural sciences. In 1850, Brown University began the first elective system, including courses in the sciences and languages (Shiflett 1994). Although the elective system did not spread rapidly, it served as the model for the modernization of the academic curriculum. As the breadth of the curriculum expanded, access to materials became an increasingly important issue, concomitantly increasing the importance of the library. Teaching methods also changed. Seminars, laboratories, and independent study emerged as an alternative to the recitation techniques of the past (Hanson 1989).

The evolution of the academic curriculum and its implication for librarianship were recognized early by Melvil Dewey:

> The colleges are waking to the fact that the work of every professor and every department is necessarily based on the library; text books constantly yield their exalted places to wiser and broader methods; professor after professor sends his classes, or goes with them, to the library and teaches them to investigate for themselves, and to *use* books, getting beyond the method of the primary school with its parrot-like recitations from a single text. (Dewey 1888, p. 136).

## (2)  The rise of the research model

As the classical model of the curriculum changed, there was also a change in the perception of the role of research, which had not traditionally been a part of academia. At the turn of the century at the University of Berlin in Germany, however, a model of the modern university emerged. This model saw the faculty member as an independent researcher. The notion of objective scholarship was promoted and an expansive faculty research agenda was encouraged (Shiflett 1994). Given the obvious need for published resources for research, the library increasingly played a critical role. The reforms in German higher education did not go unnoticed at some of the more prestigious academic institutions in the U.S., and many American students were sent to Germany to study. These individuals, in turn, brought the new concept of research coupled with teaching back with them (Shiflett 1994).

Although these ideas had some effect on American higher education throughout the nineteenth century, it was not until 1876 that this model was explicitly adopted with the founding of Johns Hopkins University. Emphasis was placed on research as a key function of the university. The seminar model of teaching was emphasized and students were encouraged to consult a wide variety of published sources. Soon thereafter, Harvard, Cornell, and Columbia adopted this teaching approach (Jones 1989). The need for a library with current and deep collections was essential to fulfill this function and the result was to increase substantially the importance and centrality of the academic library.

*(3)    The Passage of the Morrill Land Grant Act of 1862*

Although most colleges founded before the Civil War were private and sectarian, by the nineteenth century, it became clear that the higher education of the citizenry was also a matter for the state. Beginning in the East and South, universities were founded in many states including Vermont, Maine, North Carolina, Georgia, New York, Pennsylvania, Massachusetts, and Kentucky. By midcentury, the federal government recognized that it could play an important role by providing grants of land to states for educational purposes. This led to the passage of the Morrill Land Grant Act in 1862, which allocated 30,000 acres of public land per senator or house member for educational use. The act was specifically designed to promote agriculture and the mechanical arts, and the universities founded as a result of the act emphasized applied sciences and technology (Hamlin 1981). The act resulted in the establishment of many major state universities, including The Ohio State University and the University of Illinois.

Fortunately, the growth of the academic library coincided with the systematic development of professional education for librarians, with the founding of the American Library Association (ALA) in 1876, and the establishment of the first library school in 1887 (Jones 1989). As the demands for collection development, selection, and library service grew, there were increasing numbers of trained librarians who could nurture the fertile environment for scholarship and teaching. Although the mission of academic libraries continues to evolve, the need to support the academic curriculum and provide research support for faculty remain the academic library's primary functions.

*Supporting the School Curriculum: The Mission of the American School Library*

There were a few publicly supported schools in Massachusetts and New York during the colonial period, but in general publicly supported schools were a rarity. In the middle Atlantic states and the South, parochial and private schools were more common (Hanson 1989). In general, schools in the colonial period focused on elementary-level education—a level considered sufficient to create a sufficient labor force of manual laborers. There were a few secondary schools in the colonial period, but they were available to only a small number of students preparing for a limited number of colleges (Hanson 1989). It was not until the second half of the nineteenth century that the modern school system began to emerge. In 1852 Massachusetts passed the first compulsory school attendance laws. Other states followed and by 1890, half of the states had compulsory attendance laws. At the same time, more and more schools, including secondary schools, many of which had libraries, were being built.

The earliest attempt to support public school libraries occurred in 1835 when the New York state legislature under the leadership of Governor DeWitt Clinton passed a law that permitted school districts to apply some of their tax receipts to create and maintain school libraries. By 1875, twenty states had passed similar legislation (Knight and Nourse 1969). Unfortunately, many of these efforts to assist school libraries proved unsuccessful. The laws often allocated money for books, but not for administration and maintenance. In addition, sometimes money allocated for books went to teachers' salaries. The result was poorly developed, poorly maintained libraries that were seldom used (Knight and Nourse 1969; Cecil and Heaps 1940). Although these libraries had great potential, they did not perform their central mission. Gillespie and Spirt (1983) suggest, however, that these legislative endeavors to create and maintain public school libraries established the idea that public funds were an appropriate means to support school libraries, and that school libraries could play a useful role in public school education.

By the last decade of the nineteenth century, the number of school libraries, especially in high schools, began to increase substantially, and by 1895 it was estimated that there were from 2,500 to 4,000 school libraries in the country (Knight and Nourse 1969). The earliest example of funding for school libraries with a material effect on curriculum support occurred in 1892 when the state of New York passed legislation providing matching funds to purchase library books for school districts. The books purchased from these funds first had to be approved by the Department of Public Instruction. These approved books consisted of "reference books, supplementary reading books, books related to the curriculum, and pedagogical books for use by teachers" (Gillespie and Spirt 1983, p. 3). Some of them could even be taken out of the library!

New York notwithstanding, public school education in America continued to emphasize rote memorization and teaching from a single text. Consequently, there was little need for, or emphasis on, school libraries. Fortunately, there were several groups that were concerned, among them the National Council of Teachers of English (NCTE), the National Education Association (NEA), and ALA. In 1914 the NCTE formed a standing committee on school libraries and ALA formed a School Library Section (Cecil and Heaps 1940). In 1915 the NCTE conducted a national survey, and the findings expressed serious concern about the adequacy of school libraries. This prompted the NEA and ALA to appoint a joint committee headed by Charles Certain to study the condition of school libraries and develop standards for them. Certain's first report focused on high schools and was published in 1920. The second report focused on elementary schools and was published in 1925. Both reports concluded that school libraries were seriously deficient. The standards prepared by Certain's committee describe the library as "an integral part of the daily life of the school" and included several significant recommendations (Certain 1925, p. 5). First they emphasized the centrality of "materials of instruction," i.e., curricular support. Second, they emphasized a centralized collection. The centralization of materials in the school had been an issue for some years with some arguing for small library collections in each classroom, and others arguing for centralized location and control of library materials. Third, they emphasized library instruction as a duty of school libraries. Fourth, they emphasized the integral character of the school library within the total setting of school life. Certain's reports were significant in that they proposed the first national standards for school libraries and these standards were endorsed by both ALA and NEA (Gillespie and Spirt, 1983).

One should not assume, however, that Certain's report led to the quick development of centralized and modern school libraries, though it certainly made a major contribution. Fortunately, in addition to the report, there were other significant factors that contributed to progress in that direction. Among them were the changes looming on the horizon as a result of the educational reform movement, which Certain (1925) anticipated:

> Modern demands upon the public school presuppose adequate library service. Significant changes in methods of teaching require that the school library supplement the single textbook course of instruction and provide for the enrichment of the school curriculum (p. 1).

The decade of the 1920s was indeed an era of reform in public education. John Dewey and the progressive education movement introduced a variety of new educational theories that contributed to the emergence of the modern school library and its mission (Gillespie and Spirt 1983). Among the new principles of learning advanced by Dewey and the reformers were the following: (1) a child's growth and development, rather than subject matter, should be the central focus of the school; (2) education should involve children learning through a variety of experiences and exploring a variety of subjects; (3) children learn best when they are exploring subjects of interest to them; and (4) schools should be a social experience that teaches the children how to be self-directed (Fargo 1930). These "radical" ideas resulted in a more varied school curriculum requiring access to a much wider range of materials. Responding to children's interests, encouraging exploration, and providing a broad range of experiences could only highlight the importance of a school library. As Fargo (1930) observed:

> With such a program, it is obvious that the library stands in a far more vital relationship to the school than before. Under the older tradition, books other than texts were desirable; in the new school they are indispensable. They are not the accompaniment of the school's activities; they are its warp and woof (pp. 31–32).

Other influences that contributed to the emergence of the modern school library included the encouragement and studies of the U.S. Office of Education, NEA, ALA, the Carnegie Corporation, and the North Central Association of Colleges and Secondary Schools (Cecil and Heaps 1940; Gillespie and Spirt 1983). The combination of changing teaching philosophies and the evaluations and standards developed by NEA and ALA had a substantial impact on establishing the foundations of the school library and its mission—to support the curriculum by providing current and appropriate materials for students and teachers.

*The Mission of Serving the Public: The American Public Library*

The social library and the circulating library each performed a unique mission: the former to educate and enlighten; and the latter to satisfy popular taste. Both of these libraries contributed to the development of the modern public library and its very special mission—the mission of serving the public. The term "public library" refers generically to public support of a library. Using this broad definition, there were approximately 3,600 public libraries in the United States by 1876. Most of these, however, were associated with academic institutions, public schools, or social libraries. As we apply the term today, there were very few public libraries. By 1880, only seven of the sixteen largest cities in the U.S. had municipally supported public libraries. What we mean when we speak of "public" libraries, today, is very specific to certain fundamental characteristics shared by all American public libraries:

1. *Supported by taxes*. They are usually supported by local taxes, although over the years there have been exceptions. The notion of public support through taxation is rare before the nineteenth century. As noted in earlier discussions, prior to this time, libraries were most often sponsored or subsidized by private citizens, religious orders, or royal families.

2. *Governed by a board*. This board is specifically appointed to serve the public interest. Boards have usually consisted of prominent citizens charged with ensuring that the library provides materials that serve the community.

3. *Open to all*. A fundamental tenet is that the library is accessible to everyone in the community. This is not to say that all want to come or all have been made to feel welcome; various groups have not found public libraries friendly or accommodating to their needs. But in principle, the libraries are open to all.

4. *Voluntary*. People are not forced to come; the use of the library is entirely up to them. This distinguishes it from other educational institutions, such as public schools. Its voluntary nature is also part of the underlying social philosophy of the nineteenth century in which self-improvement was considered an important value.

5. *Established by state law*. This point is not generally well understood. During the early development of libraries, serious questions arose concerning whether a town could create a public institution and tax its citizens for its maintenance without the state's approval. As a consequence, a key aspect of the creation of public libraries was the passage of "enabling legislation" on the part of the states that permitted the creation of public libraries on the local level. In rare instances, public libraries are not only "enabled" by state legislation, they are financed by state monies. Such is the case in Ohio today, where 5.7 percent of the state's income tax is earmarked for the funding of public libraries.

6. *Provide services without charge to the user*. Although some public libraries charge a small fee for copying and interlibrary loans, the overwhelming number of services have been provided without fees. This issue may become more problematic in the electronic marketplace, but there is considerable professional resistance to fees for library services.

There is and will continue to be a debate as to when and where the first "public" library in the U.S. was established. Some have suggested that the honor belongs to Peterborough, New Hampshire, because in 1834 "there for the first time an institution was founded by a town with the deliberate purpose of creating a free library that would be open without restriction to all classes of the community—a library supported from the beginning by public funds" (Shera 1965, p. 169). One thing is certain, there is no dispute as to where and when the first *major* public library was established. In March of 1848, the Massachusetts legislature authorized the city of Boston to provide municipal support for a public library. The Boston Public Library, founded twenty years after Peterborough, in 1854, receives credit for being the first major public library. There is no question that the establishment of the Boston Public Library was a landmark in library development. Interestingly, however, there has arisen an informative debate regarding the reason for its founding that touches at the heart of the mission of public libraries. For this reason, some discussion of this debate is worthwhile.

The creation of the Boston Public library can be seen in at least two lights: first, as a natural outgrowth of prevailing social attitudes and developments at work by the mid-nineteenth century; and second, as the result of efforts by a group of specific individuals who, for whatever reason, concluded that a public library was an appropriate institution for the citizens of Boston.

Not only the emergence of the Boston Public library, but that of public libraries in general, can be seen as a natural outgrowth of other institutional developments of the period. For example, urbanization in America had reached a point at which there was considerable centralization of municipal services. As cities matured and prospered economically, their political and bureaucratic structure also matured. Boston was typical of a prospering and stable urban environment, where wealth had accumulated both generally and among specific individuals. In such sophisticated urban settings, it was not uncommon to have a highly developed urban infrastructure provide basic services such as water, sanitation, public health, fire, water, and education. As a result, when the issue of a public library was first raised in Boston, it was perceived from an administrative point of view as a logical extension of city services.

Similarly, by the mid-nineteenth century, there was growing interest in literature in general and in American literature in particular as well as in book production, which served to promote a climate conducive to public libraries. The concept of a public library for Boston was first advanced more than a decade before its establishment by a noted French actor and ventriloquist of the time, M. Nicholas Marie Alexandre Vattemare. Vattemare was especially energetic in trying to promote an exchange of international materials. In the 1840s he proposed that several of the major private libraries in Boston agree to combine into one public institution to facilitate this exchange. This proposal met with some favor from local officials, but the libraries resisted, and M. Vattemare's proposal did not succeed. Nonetheless, the public discussion on this issue continued for some time and helped maintain the necessary political and social momentum that would ultimately produce the desired result more than a decade later.

There were also other more general social forces at work that promoted public library development. For example, it was a time when people believed that individuals could be improved morally and socially by the good efforts of others, as well as by their own efforts. An associated belief was that social institutions could also uplift and improve individuals. Examples of such institutions included the church, but in New England at this time there was, in fact, a declining power of the conventional churches and a strong emphasis on the power of reason. More consistent with the temper of the times, and still evident today, was the belief that public schools were a vital force in the socialization of the population. The concept of the public library was closely allied with this belief, and this relationship was made explicit by Melvil Dewey (1876), who stated that popular education was actually divided into two parts: "the free school and the free public library" (p. 5). He thought of the library as a school and of the librarian as a teacher, and indeed, the librarians of the latter half of the nineteenth century saw themselves as agents of social improvement. Wiegand (1989) characterized this attitude as the "ideology of reading" (p. 100). This ideology held that there was good reading and bad reading; the former led to good conduct, the latter to unacceptable conduct. The implication, of course, was that librarians were to buy only the good reading.

The responsibility to improve people lay not only with social institutions. Members of the upper classes still believed in noblesse oblige and assumed that they too bore responsibility to provide the means by which others could improve themselves. This implied a duty on the part of the wealthy and better educated to improve the poor and uneducated in so far as these individuals wanted to be improved. Thus American philanthropy became one of the critical foundations for the growth of the public library for years to come. Libraries were seen as an ideal institution to help those less fortunate. This was, ostensibly, an underlying reason for the philanthropy of Andrew Carnegie, who asserted in his *Gospel of Wealth* (1889):

> This, then, is held to be the duty of the man of wealth: To set an example of modest, unostentatious living, shunning display or extravagance; to provide moderately for the legitimate wants of those dependent upon him; and, after doing so, to consider all surplus revenues which come to him simply as trust funds, which he is called upon to administer, and strictly bound as a matter of duty to administer in the manner which, in his judgment, is best calculated to produce the most beneficial results for the community—the man of wealth thus becoming the mere trustee and agent for his poorer brethren, bringing to their service his superior wisdom, experience, and ability to administer, doing for them better than they would or could do for themselves (p. 25).

The growth of libraries and librarianship during the nineteenth century was deeply rooted in these beliefs (Nielson 1989). In the 1840s, Boston found itself with numerous individuals who had both the wealth and power to generate a civic interest in libraries. Most notable were the efforts of Charles Ticknor and Edward Everett. Ticknor was the educated son of a wealthy Boston merchant. He assumed that social change was possible if accomplished gradually, and he believed that public schools and libraries could improve social and political stability by promoting the education of the general population (Ditzion 1947). Everett was a Unitarian clergyman, teacher, scholar, and at one point, governor of Massachusetts. A strong advocate of the public schools, Everett's beliefs were less populist and more academic than Ticknor's. He saw in the public library the opportunity for those no longer attending schools to continue their studies. He believed the public library could extend one's education by providing educational materials, not just for scholars, but for professionals and merchants. The efforts of Ticknor, Everett, and others finally convinced the Boston city fathers to appoint a Joint Standing Committee on the Library, which in turn recommended the appointment of a board of trustees. The Boston Public Library opened in the spring of 1854. Its mission was to meet the educational convictions of Everett and the popular needs espoused by Ticknor.

What then can we adduce about the historic mission of the public library? Clearly, it shared the educational mission of American public schools. But in what way was the mission of the public library distinct from the public schools? First, the public library could satisfy the interest in reading and learning for all ages, not just for those who were in school; second, it was a means to self-improvement in an age when self-education was still a vital means for improving one's chances in the society. Third, it was intended to produce more thoughtful people, individuals capable of making balanced and well-reasoned judgements in a democratic society that depended on their judgements at the voting booth. Such citizens would serve as a strong and stabilizing force to the democratic society. The nobility of these objectives is rewarding to those who reflect on the foundations of public librarianship from today's vantage point. Much of this same rationale is used to defend libraries today from attacks of various kinds, both fiscal and philosophical.

Recently, however, this historical account of the motivations of the founders of the Boston Public Library has met with skepticism, most notably from Michael Harris (1973), whose "revisionist" interpretation provides a considerably different perspective. Although few of the facts are disputed, Harris has challenged the notion that it was humanitarian, idealistic, or democratic impulses that prompted the leaders of Boston society to create the public library. Rather, Harris reminds us that the founders were among the Boston "Brahmins," a highly privileged, politically conservative, and aristocratic class that dominated the social, economic, and political life of the city. Harris argues that the founders were far less concerned with making educated democrats than with socializing the wave of immigrants who were flowing into Boston in great numbers. He suggests that the immigrants were perceived as unruly and subject to undue influence by political demagogues and other unscrupulous politicians who could foment political and social instability within the genteel confines of Boston. In other words, the creation of the Boston Public Library was another strategy of elitist aristocrats to maintain class stratification and ensure the social order that had benefited them. By controlling what was taught about the social and political institutions of American society, the immigrants would accept those institutions, institutions that were controlled and shaped by the elites. In this conceptualization of the public library, libraries and librarians are seen as agents of authority and social control, implementing restrictive rules, and generally unfriendly to hoi polloi. How could they be otherwise, run by board members appointed by elites, who were themselves elites? Further, Harris has suggested that the public library collection was not designed for the common person, but catered to the educated and upper classes. He argues that this pattern has been repeated time and again as evidenced by the fact that public libraries then and today are run by elites and attended by a disproportionately large number of upper- and middle-class patrons.

Harris's position has been challenged by other library historians. Dain (1975), for example, noted that there is insufficient historical evidence for some of Harris's strongest assertions. Further, she points out that just because elites created the first public libraries does not mean ipso facto that other classes were not well served by them. She notes that the authoritarian nature of early public libraries was a reflection of all public institutions of the time. She argues that public libraries make earnest efforts to attract a variety of users and offers as evidence the extended hours of operation on Sunday and evenings, information services, open stacks, classification systems, branches, children's rooms and services, meeting rooms for community groups, cooperative activities with schools, interlibrary loan, and special services for immigrants (Dain 1975).

Although Harris's position is controversial, it reminds us that comfortable views of history are not without their problems and that the mission of public libraries had multiple philosophical underpinnings, some of them countervailing and incompatible. Are public libraries the cauldrons of democracy or the tools of social control? Perhaps these missions coexist in a dynamic tension that remains unresolved.

ANDREW CARNEGIE AND THE PUBLIC LIBRARY

The events of the latter half of the nineteenth century probably exacerbated this tension. In many ways Andrew Carnegie personified it. Carnegie was a Scottish immigrant who, through hard work and ingenuity, prospered in the iron and steel industry. He amassed a huge fortune exceeding $330,000,000, 90 percent of which went into charitable trusts. Carnegie's philosophy of stewardship certainly marked him as a prominent exponent of noblesse oblige, but his philanthropy served many. From 1886 to 1919, Carnegie donated $56,000,000 to construct more than 2,000 library buildings, many of them public libraries, in more than 1,400 communities, large and small, in the United States. The communities that requested Carnegie's money often did so as a source of civic pride. The libraries built with Carnegie's largesse were their libraries, not Carnegie's, and their shelves were stocked with materials of local interest, not Carnegie's. In fact, the specifically local character of today's public library collections and services may be a direct result of the special conditions and restrictions that Carnegie required with every donation. First, the money that Carnegie provided was for building construction only, not for the purchase and maintenance of library materials or for staff. This, in essence, guaranteed the local character of library collections. Second, Carnegie required that all recipients of his money must contribute an annual sum equal to 10 percent of the money donated to build collections and hire staff. This created a tradition of shared government support of public libraries and defined local governance. The town, through its appointed board, was in control, not Carnegie. The inevitable result was that the mission of the Carnegie public library was shaped by local interest: library collections did not necessarily reflect the views of Carnegie but of the local community and popular taste. Thus one of the fundamental missions of public libraries, to meet the needs of the local community, may be derived from the Carnegie model of local taxation and local governmental control. Indeed, Carnegie may well have done more to establish this model than the Boston Public Library. After all, Carnegie contributed mightily to making the public library commonplace throughout the United States.

### WOMEN'S CLUBS AND THE PUBLIC LIBRARY

One cannot leave the discussion of the forces that shaped public libraries without noting the significant contributions of women's voluntary organizations, most notably women's clubs. Paula Watson (1994) has conducted considerable research in this area and much of the information that follows relies on her findings.

Women's clubs became commonplace following the Civil War as it became more acceptable for women to seek an education, especially self-education. Some of these clubs were local, while others were affiliated nationally with the General Federation of Women's Clubs. Like similar organizations devoted to education, "the members were imbued with the idea of the importance of books in improving the quality of life" (Watson 1994, p. 235). Their support for improving women's education extended to developing libraries for use by members of their local community. Watson suggests that women's clubs contributed in significant ways to the development of more than 470 public libraries between 1870 and 1930. Although the exact percentage of public libraries established through the efforts of women's clubs in the early part of the twentieth century is unclear, Watson estimates that it may have ranged between 50 and 75 percent of the total. In some instances the clubs provided support for additional materials and club members volunteered as librarians. Some women's clubs were influential at the state level, lobbying for library legislation and the need for state library commissions (Watson

1994). Although many of the members of the women's clubs were aristocrats, or at least middle class, and therefore potentially subject to Harris's criticisms, their contributions to advancing the public library are substantial. Their stated mission of self-education and improvement is firmly in line with the history and values of their era, and the results were salutary.

### MEETING POPULAR TASTES: QUALITY VERSUS DEMAND

It is also worth noting that from the beginning, the public library has been challenged by the mission of satisfying popular tastes. As public libraries proliferated, much discussion arose concerning the popular novel. Charles Ticknor advocated that a collection of popular materials should be part of the library's collection for the entertainment of readers. But serious concerns were raised by others that popular novels would lower morals. It was even suggested by some that too much fiction reading might cause insanity! Should the collection of the library include such diversions? What would be the effect on young people? Some librarians felt that popular fiction might serve to bring less-educated readers into the library where they would then be exposed to a better quality of literature. Even among librarians with serious misgivings, most had at least some popular novels on their shelves. They realized that if they wanted library users, they would need popular fiction. Generally, these collections were not overly stocked with "cheap" novels, but offered works by Flaubert, Zola, Fielding, and Balzac. This did not protect libraries, however, from censorship attacks. The works of these masters were perceived as scandalous at the time.

### SERVING ETHNIC GROUPS AND MINORITIES: A MISSION OF INCLUSIVENESS

During the nineteenth century, America experienced major immigrations from many countries, and in many areas, especially cities, America was a multicultural and polyglot nation. Amidst this influx of new peoples, the concerns regarding the education and socialization of the immigrants was a natural outgrowth of the progressivist philosophy of the times. This philosophy viewed the function of educational institutions as improving society and advancing the democratic tradition (Du Mont, Buttlar, and Caynon 1994). For many, this meant that immigrant groups needed to be assimilated into the American mainstream. Because of their numbers, Europeans were considered to be a particularly difficult challenge (Stern 1991). Libraries were "to furnish fuel for the fires beneath the great melting pot" (Roberts 1912, p. 169). What better group to select and provide the necessary material than librarians? Many librarians took this responsibility quite seriously and numerous articles in professional periodicals offered advice on providing services and understanding the needs of immigrants. Some librarians exhibited an almost missionary zeal in their efforts to bring the benefits of reading to the general public.

Nonetheless, it is true that the public library of the nineteenth century was used primarily by white, middle and upper classes. Ethnic minorities were largely excluded from the benefits of library service (Trujillo and Cuesta 1989). There is relatively limited evidence, however, to determine whether public libraries intentionally excluded ethnic groups, or whether librarians and trustees were simply uninformed as to how to serve them effectively.

It was not until the turn of the century that the library's mission began a systematic effort to provide service to ethnic groups. This was also a time of considerable immigration with more than 20 million arriving in the first quarter of the century (Stern 1991). Although some librarians recognized that each ethnic group had a literature and culture worth preserving and transmitting, the primary emphasis was on integration of immigrants into the American way of life. Library collections and services included books and newspapers written in native languages; programs on U.S. citizenship; classes in English; story hours in native languages; programs on American history and culture; supplementary materials to support school curricula; and help for immigrants in reading letters, sending messages to social service agencies, writing checks, and completing citizenship forms (Stern 1991; Du Mont, Buttlar, and Caynon 1994). In 1917, ALA created a Committee on Work with the Foreign Born whose job it was to collect and disseminate information on how to help educate immigrants on American values and the English language (Stern 1991). The committee produced numerous guides to assist in this process.

Perhaps the most notable organizational response to serving ethnic groups and minorities was the creation of branch libraries in urban areas. Branches provided extension services that could reach special populations, especially industrial workers and those who did not speak English (Ditzion 1947). Branches also offered special services to children. By 1900, many public libraries had a separate room for children's books and services. What better place to educate the first generation of immigrant children in the ways of American life (Du Mont, Buttlar, and Caynon 1994)?

Sadly, there were some minorities and ethnic groups that did not receive much attention from librarians, most notably, African Americans and Hispanics. Prior to the Civil War, the majority of African Americans lived in the South and were forbidden to read. Even after the Civil War, although there were relatively few public libraries in the South, where they existed, African Americans received no library services or severely restricted ones (Trujillo and Cuesta 1989). Even into the 1930s there was considerable evidence that funding for library services to African Americans in the South was not commensurate to the proportion of African Americans in the community (Gleason 1941). There were few services and what was available was often offered only in segregated circumstances: separate branches, poorly funded school libraries, restricted privileges at main libraries, and a few independent African-American libraries (Du Mont, Buttlar, and Caynon 1994). Sometimes the same library served both blacks and whites but had separate entrances, collections, and reading areas. The establishment of black branches was usually funded by the philanthropy of whites or the activities of both black and white churches or civic organizations (Cresswell 1996).

There were a few notable exceptions to this picture, in particular, the work of Thomas Fountion Blue, who pioneered library service to African Americans in Louisville, Kentucky. Blue was a graduate of the prestigious Hampton Institute and Richmond Theological Seminary. He was placed in charge of a segregated branch of the Louisville Free Public Library in 1905. This was the first branch for African Americans in any American city (Josey 1994). His services and library training programs for African Americans were considered a national model (Josey 1970). Nonetheless, in general, public library service to people of color was poor or nonexistent.

Regrettably, ALA was not outspoken on this issue until the 1960s when the Civil Rights movement made it impossible to ignore (Du Mont, Buttlar, and Caynon 1994). Generally, until the 1960s, the association viewed itself as representing a national constituency of librarians, including those in the South, who favored segregation. ALA did not want to be perceived as judging the political or social beliefs of its members and viewed segregationist policies as a local matter. There was also concern that too much agitation on the issue would create more resistance in the South and bring unfavorable publicity to those public libraries who were desegregating quietly (Cresswell 1996; Josey 1994).

The problems, of course, were not only in the South. Evidence that northern libraries also engaged in discriminatory practices was available, but generally overlooked. For example, communities that received Carnegie dollars often spent the money on the provision of service to Whites in the community but not for African Americans; or far less money was spent, resulting in inferior service. As the historian, John Hope Franklin observed, "one searches in vain for an indignant outcry on the part of the professional librarians against this profanation of their sacred profession and this subversion of their cherished institutions (Franklin 1977, p. 13).

It was not until 1961 that the ALA took a firm stand regarding service to African Americans as well as all other citizens, advocating equal library service to all. At the midwinter meeting, the association passed an amendment to the Library Bill of Rights that made clear that an individual's library use "should not be denied or abridged because of his race, religion, national origins or political views." Regrettably, the response of many communities toward opening their libraries to ethnic minorities, especially African Americans, was met with disappointingly strong opposition. In Virginia, for example, the citizens of Danville and Petersburg voted to close their public libraries rather than to desegregate them (Cresswell 1996).

Hispanics experienced a similar lack of quality and quantity in public library services. Haro, in his study of library services to Hispanics (1981), found that libraries are often perceived as one of many Anglo institutions that are designed and controlled by Anglos to serve Anglos.

> While most Mexican Americans, even the poor and illiterate, aspire to better education, the public library is not seen as a vehicle to attain it. The public library is viewed by far too many Mexican Americans, particularly within the lower classes, as an Anglo institution which has never cared about their needs, which does not hire their people, and which engages in the disproportionate distribution of resources to satisfy first the demands of an Anglo society... (Haro 1981, p. 86)

The Civil Rights Movement of the 1960s was a critical turning point in ensuring that African Americans and Hispanics were equally included in the mission of public libraries. The earlier public library movement focused primarily on assimilating ethnic cultures into the American mainstream. The Civil Rights Movement of the 1960s was a struggle for ethnic self-determination (Stern 1991). Groups such as African Americans and Hispanics did not necessarily desire to be assimilated; rather they argued for equal opportunity and rights to the advantages that American society had to offer. The concept of the melting pot was replaced by a concept of a multicultural society.

The focus on minorities and disadvantaged groups in the U.S. produced several pieces of progressive legislation affecting libraries. Most notably was the passage of the Library Services and Construction Act (LSCA) in 1964, which served as the major force in developing library services. LSCA specifically provided funding for libraries to develop services and collections for ethnic, disadvantaged, and underserved groups. Similar funding was provided with the passage of the Higher Education Act for colleges and universities (Trujillo and Cuesta 1989).

Libraries responded to these initiatives by hiring individuals from ethnic groups, collecting reference resources on ethnic cultures and experiences, creating criteria to make library collections inclusive of all members of the community, developing outreach programs to attract minorities, offering information and referral programs for minorities, and building collections that were more responsive to the needs of various ethnic groups.

There was also a significant professional response through library associations and organizations. In the late 1960s a considerable number of ALA members expressed concern that the association had done little to secure open access for all citizens and to address issues of equality and social justice within the profession and in society at large. The ALA response was to create the Social Responsibilities Round Table (SRRT) in 1970. Among SRRT's purposes is "to act as a stimulus to the association and its various units in making libraries more responsive to current social needs . . . "(ALA 1997, p. 135). SRRT has been very active over the years addressing a variety of issues including advocating for international human rights and rights for racial minorities and gays, securing rights for the poor and homeless, and promoting equal rights for women. Their focus has been both on the library profession and on policies and practices of the society as a whole (West 1997).

Additional organizations were established as a result of the turmoil and activities of the 1960s. One such ALA-affiliated advocacy group is REFORMA (The National Association to Promote Library Service to the Spanish Speaking), which was established in 1971. This organization's stated purpose is to foster the development of library collections that include materials written in Spanish as well as materials that are oriented to Hispanics, to encourage the recruitment of bilingual librarians and staff, to develop services and programs for Hispanics, to educate

Hispanics regarding the services and materials available in libraries, and to lobby to maintain library services for Hispanics (Reforma 1997). Similar to REFORMA, the Black Caucus of ALA has worked since 1970 on behalf of African-American librarians and the African-American community. Among its purposes are to encourage ALA to focus on the information needs of the African-American community, to promote services to that community, and to encourage the creation of information resources about African Americans for dissemination to the wider community (Black Caucus 1997).

Stern (1991) has observed that in the last decade there have been changes in emphasis in developing library services to ethnic groups and minorities. He observes that the traditional focus regarding services to ethnic groups has been based on the perception of this community as "disadvantaged." However, since the 1980s the approach has shifted somewhat to serving the "ethnically enfranchised." In this sense, members of ethnic communities are seen "as equal partners with nonethnic residents in the fight to improve the quality of their lives and the communities in which they reside" (Stern 1991, p. 96). Some of the resulting library collections are developed less for self-improvement than to empower.

The public-library mission to serve the various ethnic communities in the United States continues to grow and evolve. The White House Conference on Library and Information Services held in 1991 reaffirmed the need to respond to the needs of an increasingly multicultural society. Its recommendations included providing financial and technical assistance to promote service to multicultural populations and populations with disabilities, promoting outreach services to traditionally underserved populations, and encouraging support for training library and information-science professionals to serve multicultural needs (White House Conference 1991). Today, ALA has a variety of committees and round tables that monitor minority issues in addition to the ones noted above. These include the Minority Concerns and Cultural Diversity Committee, the ALA Office for Literacy and Outreach Services (OLOS), the LITA (Library and Information Technology Association)/ LSSI Minority Scholarship in Library and Information Technology Subcommittee; LITA/OCLC Minority Scholarship Subcommittee, and the Minorities Recruitment Committee of the New Members Round Table (ALA 1997).

Although there have been concerted efforts to provide library services to ethnic minorities, few would argue that the problems of unequal service have vanished. Prominent issues remain including the need for recruitment and retention of a diverse library workforce, concern for the reduction in federal funding for library services to ethnic communities, and the need for good research on the impact of the programs and services that have been developed to serve these communities (Trujillo and Cuesta 1989).

### SUMMARY: SERVING THE PUBLIC

Today's public libraries serve as archives of commercial and historical records; they contain religious and liturgical works and interpretations; they offer a place for students, scholars, academics, and the general citizenry to study; and provide a source for edifying reading. These services reflect the historic missions of libraries in the past: (1) to support the education and socialization needs of society; (2) to meet the informational needs of a broad spectrum of citizens; (3) to promote self-education; and (4) to satisfy the popular tastes of the public. Whether these missions were undertaken to control the masses or to make them more effective citizens will be a subject of continuing debate. Nonetheless, as the missions of the public library have been revealed, they suggest that the modern public library's purposes and practices rest on a rich historical foundation.

## THE MISSION AND FUTURE OF THE MODERN AMERICAN LIBRARY

Today's libraries and librarians confront a host of destabilizing factors: the flood of information, constant innovations in technology, economic and political demands and stresses, as well as numerous social problems. What will be the mission and values of the library in the future? It is clear from history that the mission of libraries is shaped by the societies in which they exist. The values and attitudes that evolve within a given society are the self-same forces and attitudes that mold and shape its institutions. Thus, it is to our advantage to examine some of the influential values and attitudes in today's environment that are likely to shape our future.

*Forces that Shape the Future: Attitudes*

ATTITUDE TOWARD GOVERNMENTAL AGENCIES

The society's confidence, or lack thereof, in government agencies to perform their tasks will have a direct effect on the society's willingness to
continue providing fiscal resources to operate them. Lack of confidence
will produce diminished funding, which in turn will result in shrinking
services, a situation that has been demonstrated in several states over
the last decade, e.g., California. As government funding has declined,
so has funding for libraries. Of course, other factors play a role, including the general health of the economy and individuals' personal financial condition. Nonetheless, as the public demands greater and greater
accountability from its public institutions, libraries will be forced to demonstrate their contribution to the community. Failing to do so may well
affect both the quality of services provided and the means by which
they are delivered. For example, library services and materials may be
offered on a cost-recovery basis with fees being charged directly for services rendered.

ATTITUDE TOWARD EDUCATION

Because libraries are so closely linked with education, the society's attitude toward education is a critical factor in the library's survival. In a
society where learning is highly valued and libraries are perceived as
positive contributions to education, libraries are likely to receive considerable support. It is safe to say, however, that among the general public
there has been a considerable decline in confidence in public-school education. This is a substantial change from the 1950s, when Americans were
much more confident in the ability of their public schools to educate the
young.

Two alternative scenarios for libraries are possible. A loss of confidence in the public schools could lead to decline in confidence and support for all agencies perceived as primarily educational. In this case,
public-library funding and support may suffer. A second alternative may
have the opposite effect: if the public schools are perceived as failing,
citizens may expect the library to strengthen its role in the education of
its citizenry as a substitute for the deficiencies of schools. In this case
libraries may assume greater status and responsibility for encouraging
young people to read, developing their collections to support curricula,
and providing increased educational programming.

There is considerable contemporary debate over the role of government agencies in helping various groups in our society. Libraries have mirrored this ambivalence, going through periods of activism to recruit new groups of people who were not traditional users, and at other times focusing on the library's traditional clientele. Bernard Berelson (1949), in a major study of library use in 1949, concluded that the library should focus on its natural constituency—the better educated, middle class individual who represented the typical user of public libraries at that time. This constituted 10 percent of the adult population. Certainly, there are librarians today who feel that the energies and resources of libraries should be devoted to those individuals who are its most likely users. Underlying this belief is the essentially voluntary and passive nature of libraries; if people want to use a library, they do so. Others have argued that the library should be reaching out to those groups, who, for whatever reason, have not taken advantage of this tax-supported resource. These individuals may have not received adequate education to develop literacy skills or may have been victims of discrimination. The extent to which the society sends a clear message as to how public institutions function in meeting the needs of various groups will help shape the library's direction. Surely, if the library directs its attention to frequent users, it is likely to devote resources to materials and services quite different from those it would use if it attempts to meet the needs of those for whom the library has not been a regular contact.

ATTITUDE TOWARD THE IMPORTANCE OF READING

If the society believes that reading, and by inference, literacy, is important, then it is likely that libraries will have great support. In addition, if reading is considered critical, then the materials and services of libraries are likely to reflect this value. This might include strong print collections and considerable emphasis on children's reading programs, adult literacy programs, and support for school reading programs. If reading is undervalued, or other values are placed above it (e.g., the value of visual entertainment), then emphasis might be placed on different services such as audiovisual services, materials, and programming. Of course, this is not to say that audiovisual materials in and of themselves are incompatible with reading, only that what is emphasized in terms of how resources will be allocated will differ depending on the value placed on reading itself. If, in fact, we are moving to a more visual society, and we presume that libraries are extensions of the values of our society, then we would expect changes in our library collections and services.

Throughout history, libraries have been seen as archives of the great literature of the world. Yet, today, many libraries appear to offer more popular materials and less literature. One might well argue that this is because most people neither value fine literature nor desire to read it. The argument is well taken. One study of American reading habits found that less than 1 percent of reading materials read by the public were what one would call "literature" (Zill and Winglee 1989). No matter what one thinks of this situation, a society that does not value literature is not likely to expect its libraries to devote many resources to its collection and preservation, especially, if other types of materials or services are valued more highly.

ATTITUDE TOWARD TECHNOLOGY

There is no doubt that new information technologies are influencing almost every aspect of our lives and specifically altering the way we create, organize, store, and disseminate information. The enthusiasm with which a society accepts these new technologies and the reservations it may have concerning them will undoubtedly affect those insti tutions involved in information transfer in profound ways. That libraries now possess a wide array of these information technologies and are experiencing many pressures regarding their access and control is testimony to the impact that the technological culture has already had on library services.

These attitudes, as well as others, influence the mission of today's library and will, no doubt, significantly affect the future of library services and materials. The dramatic nature of some of these changes has led some to speculate that the new technologies have totally revolutionized our society, so much so that the traditional missions of libraries may be obsolete. Enthusiasts of this view see books and print-on-paper being replaced by the virtual electronic library where information seekers will simply go online from their homes or offices to find what they need. The library without walls will become a reality without libraries (Harris and Hannah 1992). Although such predictions may be hyperbole, it is clearly true that the introduction of new technologies has exacerbated and magnified many of the problems and challenges that libraries face.

## Forces that Shape the Future: Values

As we began this chapter, the library was identified as fundamentally serving a social purpose and reflecting social values. Values are strongly held beliefs that serve to guide our actions. When we think of values we associate them with words such as "convictions" or "principles" more than with words like "opinion". Values structure our experience and provide insight when we make important decisions affecting our future and that of others. Institutions and professions have values just as individuals have them. These values provide for institutional and professional stability and consistency when important issues arise. It has been suggested that the American society and the American library may be entering a new era. Whether that is true or not, it may be instructive to check our compasses before embarking. What then are the values held by librarians and American libraries?

### VALUE 1: THE VALUE OF SERVICE

Perhaps the most distinctive feature of library and information science, in contrast, for example to computer science, is that the purpose of the field is to communicate knowledge to people. This is more than just "meeting an information need," which is the common parlance for the activities of the contemporary library. Underlying this notion of service is not just the betterment of the individual, but the betterment of the community as a whole. This activity, of bringing knowledge to people and the society, is the sine qua non of the profession. It also distinguishes it from business and industry in that, for most libraries, and certainly for publicly funded ones, the generation of profit is not the fundamental purpose; rather it is helping others. Pierce Butler (1951) characterized this notion succinctly several decades ago:

> The cultural motivation of librarianship is the promotion of wisdom in the individual and the community . . . to communicate, so far as possible, the whole of scholarship to the whole community. The librarian undertakes to supply literature on any and every subject to any and every citizen, for any and every purpose . . . [these actions], in the long run, will sharpen the understanding, judgment, and prudence of the readers and thus sustain and advance civilization (pp. 246–247).

Libraries and librarianship are about serving people and the society as a whole. Service to others has been the foundation of American librarianship for more than one hundred years, and this notion of service seems to apply to librarianship no matter what type of library or information service is involved. As Finks (1989) has recently observed:

> Our natural reaction to the approach of a patron is not irritation at being interrupted, but delight at another chance to help someone pick his or her way through our beloved maze. It is, we should admit, a noble urge, this altruism of ours, one that seems both morally and psychologically good (p. 353).

Winter (1988) has pointed out that librarianship emerged as one of the service-oriented professions of the nineteenth century, in contradistinction to the profit-centered, capitalistic enterprises emerging at the same time. Librarianship grew out of the same American well-spring as nursing, social work, teaching, medicine, law, and the clergy. In addition, part of this service orientation may well be related to the fact that American libraries, at least since the latter half of the nineteenth century, have been numerically, as distinguished from bureaucratically, dominated by women. When women entered the workforce of the nineteenth century, their activities were expected to conform to the stereotypes of appropriate behavior for their gender (Garrison 1972). Women occupied professions that distinguished themselves by their nurturing characteristics: teaching, nursing, social work, and librarianship among them. Garrison (1972) refers to nineteenth-century librarians as "tender technicians" (p. 131). Serving others, usually at a sacrificial wage one might add, was part and parcel of librarianship as with other such occupations.

Interestingly, some have suggested more recently that an emerging business model for library service is seriously distorting this service orientation. As fiscal resources dwindle, more and more pressure is exerted on libraries to act as businesses, emphasizing concepts such as increased productivity, pricing information as a commodity, and "repackaging" information services to market as products for sale. This business approach has led to the use of management techniques, technologies, and marketing strategies often borrowed directly, and with mixed success, from the private sector. Estabrook (1982) argues that this rationalization of library practice using a business model could change the very nature of library service, with unhappy results. For example, it could lead to libraries only serving their most successful clients, those who are easiest to serve and satisfy and hence most cost-efficient, and ignoring those difficult to serve or reluctant to use library services.

Despite these misgivings, the preoccupation of many libraries and librarians with quality service is testimony to the persistence of this value in most libraries—whether in the private or public sector. Part of the reason for service's tenaciousness may be that it has played such an explicit role in the stated philosophical values of librarianship for so long. This can be observed directly in the thinking of one of the most notable philosophical figures in the history of librarianship, S.R. Ranganathan. Ranganathan (1892–1972) was a major figure in the development of a variety of theoretical issues in library and information science, most notably in classification theory and in developing basic principles for the field. He conducted much of his work and study in India, beginning the first school of library science there. His contribution is international in scope, and his work has influenced American librarianship as well as librarianship in other countries. Ranganathan examined the most fundamental underpinnings of libraries and librarianship. In 1931, he observed:

> ... the vital principle of the library—which has struggled through all the stages of its evolution, is common to all its different forms and will persist to be its distinguishing feature for all time to come—is that it is an instrument of universal education, and assembles together and freely distributes all the tools of education and disseminates knowledge with their aid (p. 354).

Ranganathan (1931) proposed five laws of library science that have remained a centerpiece of professional values and reflect his deeply held conviction that the library is dedicated to the service of people. A brief review of these laws provides a surprisingly contemporary perspective on the central value of library service.

*Books are for use.* Looking back to earlier historical uses of libraries, Ranganathan observed that books were often chained to prevent their removal and that the emphasis was on storage and preservation rather than use. He did not reject the notion that preservation and storage were important, but he asserted that the purpose of such activities was to promote the use of the item. Without the use of materials, there is little use to libraries. Certainly, this is even more obvious today. In the past, one needed to protect most materials because, before the invention of the printing press, they were rare and difficult to produce. Today, for most library materials there are many copies, often obtainable at reasonable cost. By emphasizing use, Ranganathan refocused the attention of the field to access-related issues, such as the library's location, loan policies, hours and days of operation, such mundanities as library furniture, and the quality of staffing. Ranganathan's law is certainly a contemporary one. Much emphasis is now being placed on quality of "customer" service and developing a "customer" orientation. Given the attitude of society that public institutions need greater accountability, this orientation is both healthy and essential for survival.

*Books are for all.* This law suggests that every member of the community should be able to obtain materials needed. It is an important egalitarian principle that certainly forms the foundation of much public-library ideology. Ranganathan felt that all individuals from all social environments were entitled to library service, and that the basis of library use was education, to which all were entitled. These "entitlements," however, were not without some important obligations for both libraries/librarians and library patrons. Among these were that librarians should have excellent first-hand knowledge of the people to be served, that collections should meet the special interests of the community, and that libraries should promote and advertise their services extensively to attract a wide range of users. In addition, Ranganathan felt that library selectors should emphasize materials that were strong, well written, and well illustrated. On the other hand, library users should be advocates for library service, should follow the rules and regulations of the library, keep the library in good order, and take out only materials that are needed.

Ranganathan understood that to accomplish this purpose, society would have to contribute. For example, he argued that the state is obligated to provide the financial resources through taxation and legislation so that all people could be served by libraries. In addition, the state should create a state-library authority, with a state librarian, whose duty it would be to ensure library service by creating institutions for that purpose. Similarly, the local library authority is obligated to provide service to all individuals in their local areas.

*Every book its reader.* This principle is closely related to the second law but it focuses on the item itself, suggesting that each item in a library has an individual or individuals who would find that item useful. Ranganathan argued that the library could devise many methods to ensure that each item founds its appropriate reader. One method involved the basic rules for access to the collection, most notably the need for open shelving (direct access by patrons to the book collection). Ranganathan saw the system of open shelving as critical because it gave users the chance to examine the collection freely, much the same way they could examine their own collections at home. As Ranganathan noted: "In an open access library, the reader is permitted to wander among the books and lay his hands on any of them at his will and pleasure" (p. 259). Another aspect of the library that improved the chances for a match of reader with book involved collection arrangement. Ranganathan suggested that the collection arrangement should be by subject if the most effective access was to result. He was not dogmatic, however, about the uniformity of this arrangement, and he possessed a very modern sense of the need for marketing library materials. Evidence of this is his suggestion that the library set up displays of selected materials that singled out collections of books, such as a section for newly acquired materials. He also suggested special reading areas for popular materials. Another aspect of library service that would improve matching books with readers is the use of trained professional staff who could evaluate library collections through surveys, provide reader's advisory services, conduct programs such as story hours, provide extension services, and select good books. Finally, the library could promote and market its services to readers through publicity, library displays, library publications, and public activities such as festivals.

*Save the time of the reader.* This law is a recognition that part of the excellence of library service is its ability to meet the needs of the library user efficiently. To this end, Ranganathan recommended the use of appropriate business methods to improve library management. He observed that centralizing the library collection in one location provided distinct advantages. He also noted that excellent staff would not only include those who possess strong reference skills, but also strong technical skills in cataloging, cross-referencing, ordering, accessioning, and the circulation of materials. All of these functions would contribute to timely service to the user. In a way he anticipated, although not necessarily predicted, the more competitive information marketplace of today in which the information seeker has more than one option available for finding material and information traditionally provided by libraries.

*The library is a growing organism.* Perhaps one of the most sagacious observations made by Ranganathan is this principle. Ranganathan de-

scribed this as the "fundamental principle" that governs library organization (p. 326). Remarkably, it anticipates the management theorists of
the 1960s, who argued that organizations are not self-sufficient; they do
not exist autonomously. Rather, they exist, like living organisms do,
within an environment in which the primary challenge is to survive.
Ranganathan said it this way: "It is an accepted biological fact that a
growing organism alone will survive. An organism which ceases to grow
will petrify and perish" (p. 326). Clearly, the notion expressed by
Ranganathan is kindred to the later theorists who perceived the library
as a dynamic institution constantly subject to changes. Ranganathan's
perspective however focused more on the need for internal change than
on changes in the environment itself. He argued that library organizations must accommodate growth in staff, the physical collection, and
patron use. This involved growth in the physical building, reading areas, shelving, and in space for the catalog. Because of the inevitable
growth in the collections, he anticipated increased need for security
against theft, book lifts anticipating increased demand, and a need to
design traffic flow to permit easy movement around the floors.
Ranganathan also recognized that personnel structure and
decision-making would also be affected by this growth. He anticipated
the increased division of labor among administrative, technical, and reference staff and recommended that an administrative staff council be
created to assist in the operations and organization of the library. This
clearly anticipated the participatory decision-making movements of the
1960s and beyond.

These laws represent the quintessential principles of library service
and reflect the continuing and persistent value of service to those the
profession serves. These laws are also an explicit recognition that the
principles that we accept for our discipline are not merely theoretical
niceties; on the contrary, they are the driving forces, or should be the
driving forces, for structuring library collections, services, and staff.

These values are clearly important both in terms of historical and
contemporary library service. Interestingly, they have been recently revisited by Gorman (1995), who advanced five "new laws" as updates to
Ranganathan's. Gorman asserts the following five laws:

*Libraries serve humanity:* This is a restatement of the service ethic that
permeates librarianship, recognizing that the "dominant ethic of
librarianship is service to the individual, community, and society as a
whole" (p. 784).

*Respect all forms by which knowledge is communicated:* In Ranganathan's time, print materials dominated library materials. For this reason, his principles talk of books and readers. But today, there are many more ways in which knowledge is packaged in libraries. According to Gorman, "each new means of communication enhances and supplements the strengths of all previous means" (p. 784). It is certainly true that most of the time new means of communication merely add to the repertoire of communication techniques provided by the society. This new principle suggests that library workers should not fear that new forms of communication will replace print; rather, librarians should exploit all media to advance library service.

*Use technology intelligently to enhance service:* The obligation of librarians is neither to resist new technologies nor to use technology uncritically. Rather, it is to recognize the potential of some technologies in accomplishing the missions of libraries. To the extent that new technologies can offer tremendous advantages to library service, they should be applied in a constructive and intelligent manner.

*Protect free access to knowledge:* The historical concept of the library as one of the foundations of democratic institutions remains as important today as ever. The controls and centralization that new technologies can produce have exacerbated many of the problems involved in protecting the intellectual freedom of patrons. The legacy of our culture and other cultures must be freely transmitted to all; otherwise freedom is threatened and tyranny promoted.

*Honor the past and create the future:* A central value of librarianship is the recognition that the past serves as a guide for the future. The library has been a central institution for archiving our cultural record and the cultural records of other societies. To this end the library must not only focus on the new information that is constantly being produced but protect the historical record as well.

VALUE 2: READING AND THE BOOK ARE IMPORTANT.

A central value of libraries and library workers has been and continues to be a deep and abiding respect for both reading and the book. Consider some of the advantages that books possess:

*Books . . .*

- are generally lightweight and very portable; they're easy to take to the beach or to bed;
- require no electricity (except when it's dark);
- require no additional equipment such as video display terminals, printers etc.;
- require little maintenance and repair, and when repair is needed it is usually quite inexpensive and can be accomplished by an individual with minimal training; no service contract is needed;
- require no diagrams or documentation to use;
- can get pretty damp and dusty and still function;
- can be dropped on the floor with little damage;
- are comparatively cheap;
- can be browsed easily and contain relatively easy-to-use finding aids such as an index (compared with using Boolean logic);
- provide a large number of thoughtful and interconnected ideas in one place that can be read from start to finish or scanned in sections;
- are an excellent source for stimulating the imagination;
- store easily;
- can be written in and text can be easily underlined for emphasis during later reading and study;
- require little knowledge to operate;
- can last a very long time, especially when printed on acid-free paper.

This is not to say that each of these features is unique to books, but in combination they represent a very impressive technology. It is highly unlikely that any electronic technology, although each has its own distinct advantages, will possess the combination of advantages available in the book in the near future.

But the book has many advantages quite aside from its technical character. Neill (1992) argues, for example, that books stimulate more active involvement and diminish the passivity common when viewing television or movies; they are able to convey more complex concepts and psychological conditions than television and movies and more closely approximate real life; they stimulate intellectual activity; and exposure to books often leads to improved understanding, discovery, and growth in our personal lives.

The fact that librarianship values reading greatly is also seen in the library's concern for those who cannot read. The sad truth is that in this ever more complex information environment, there are many who are unable to read. It is especially regrettable to know that the U.S. is far from immune from this problem. The U.S. ranks forty-ninth in literacy among 156 United Nation member countries. This is a decline of eighteen places since 1950. Millions of U.S. adults are unable to read an eighth grade level book, many of these individuals are unable to read simple but essential items such as bus schedules, newspapers, and maps. For such individuals, the world of information is dramatically inaccessible.

In addition, although book reading overall has been on the increase since 1955, there has been a decline in reading among young people. The proportion of book readers among young adults has dropped 13 percent, from 75 percent to 62 percent. In addition, although it is estimated that 86 percent of the U.S. population (146 million) have read some kind of book or magazine in the last twelve months, most of the literature purchased consists of romances, thrillers, science fiction, and other popular fiction. Contemporary or classic literature consists of less that 1 percent of sales (Zill and Winglee 1989). A *Consumer Research Study on Book Buying* found that among 16,000 single and family households, 60 percent of them had not bought a single book in the preceding twelve months and two-thirds of all books purchased were popular fiction (*Library Hotline* 1992). The causes of illiteracy are many and varied and include the deterioration of schools and school curricula; increased competition with other entertainment media such as television, movies, and compact discs; the deterioration of the value of reading within the family; and exposure to media that encourages a short attention span, which is a hindrance when reading books.

It is no surprise then, that libraries, with their strong history of the book as their primary material, would continue to emphasize books and reading, even while images continue to dominate the popular media. It is no doubt a reason why many library professionals feel a sense of ambivalence when they see more and more library-collection expenditures for audiovisual materials and electronic technologies.

VALUE 3: RESPECT FOR TRUTH AND THE SEARCH FOR TRUTH:

When individuals seek answers to questions, they expect the library to provide timely and accurate information, and library professionals would consider themselves remiss if they provided inaccurate information. Certainly, the provision of accurate information is a duty of the information provider. This respect for truth should, however, be separated from the search for truth that must also be promoted. Often library users are in the process of investigating issues for themselves that are much more complex than simply asking for an answer to a single question.

Libraries are intended to assist individuals in this investigatory process. The consequence of assisting in this process may require the library to collect materials that contain information which is false as well as true. Swan (1986) has noted that the librarian must have the untrue on their library shelves as well as the true, because sometimes these sources prove quite revealing to those exploring complex issues. One may, for example, know that the ideas in Hitler's *Mein Kampf* are outrageous and false, but the historical analysis of such ideas may prove quite useful in teaching individuals about the truth of our past and the dangers that may still lie in the future. So making such material unavailable may impede one's understanding of the truth. Similarly, respecting the search for truth requires that the librarian reduce barriers in this search. This may mean protecting the privacy rights of patrons by refusing to supply information concerning circulation records to others; it may mean not restricting library materials by practices that place a barrier between the patron and the information. Protecting the search for truth means collecting and defending the many points-of-view of authors and creators and respecting each individual's search for knowledge.

VALUE 4: TOLERANCE

A complementary value to the search for truth is that of tolerance. Tolerance has played a critical role in the finer moments of American history, as has intolerance in some of our most ignominious times. Tolerance has a special relationship to truth; tolerance admits of the possibility that our ability to judge the truth is flawed, and that there may be many "truths," or that the truth in some cases may not be known. It presumes that more than one perspective on a subject may be reasonable and that exposure to many ideas may help us understand and approach the truth. The value of tolerance thus suggests that library collections possess a variety of perspectives on a wide array of topics. It suggests that information professionals try to be nonjudgmental in terms of the value or direction of a library user's inquiry. Without such a value, library collections would be little more than the dogmatic assertions of the majority.

VALUE 5: THE PUBLIC GOOD

The notion of the public good is fundamental to library service and has at least three implications for the library. First, it implies that people and society as a whole are changed, and, in the long run, improved by ideas, no matter what format of these ideas. It implies that ideas improve the quality of a person's life and the life of the community. There is little reason for libraries to exist if one does not believe that people can be improved by using them. Improvement may not be the only reason for libraries, but it is an essential function. Examples include stimulating an interest in reading among young children; helping children in their school work; providing training information to adults; providing programming for mothers or the elderly, and providing information to clients to advance their knowledge and careers.

Second, the notion of the public good implies that the citizen has a right to good entertainment, that people have a right to enjoy life, and that the library has a role in promoting pleasure. Certainly the presence of copious fiction, romance, travel, and popularized science and history attests to the strong feelings that librarians have about this dimension of library service. The notion of "healthy entertainment" has been carried over into modern library service from the nineteenth-century concern that the provision of healthy entertainment would deter citizens from embarking on unhealthy ones.

It is interesting that the value of the public good is sufficiently ambiguous to accommodate both the "improvement" function and the "entertainment" one. As noted earlier regarding the historical mission of the public library, the attempt to accommodate this dual mission has accounted for considerable debate in librarianship, especially when it comes to allocation of resources for the library collection. This debate, sometimes characterized as the "quality versus demand" debate, centers on defining the library's primary purpose: Is it to educate or to entertain? Nelson (1990) has suggested that the public library has become too laden with trivialities and entertainment to truly respond to the needs of its citizenry, that its emphasis on meeting immediate entertainment needs has led it to forget its more important social responsibilities. She argues that the library should serve as a community information center rather than an entertainment center.

Perhaps part of the tension can be elucidated by examining the third implication of seeking the "public good." The public good implies that librarians perform their tasks in a selfless manner, placing service to the community above personal interest. An especially thorny problem relates to identifying who or what is the community that the librarian serves. This struggle is perhaps best seen when discussing the public library and the extent to which public libraries should serve the middle-class, better-educated, and wealthier members of the public who historically have used it, and the extent to which seeking the public good requires that the librarian actively seek out those who could benefit from library services but for whom the library has been an unwelcome and unresponsive institution, i.e. the poor, members of minorities, and the undereducated.

Blanke (1989) has suggested that the librarian's quest for political neutrality has led it to serve the more powerful by default. That librarianship's lack of activism or advocacy for the information "have-nots" have led libraries to "uncritically accommodate . . . society's dominant political and economic powers" (p. 39). This has led libraries to adopt a business ethic with marketing attitudes that promote the charging of fees and the privatization of information sources. Accepting an active political role in defense of the information-needy in contrast to focusing on the interests of the wealthy and powerful places in relief the question of our valuing the public good and the ethical duty implied by that value.

### VALUE 6: JUSTICE

This value pertains both to the public and to staff. It implies that each individual has equal access to library and information services. It also implies that every person should be respected as an individual, and the delivery of inadequate service is a violation of such a value. The concept of justice is very complex and a distinction, noted by the philosopher John Rawls (1958), is especially appropriate in the library context. Rawls has noted that justice cannot be understood merely as equality; it must include fairness. Equality implies an equal amount; fairness implies the amount that is needed or deserved. This is an important distinction for librarianship, because in some circumstances it implies that ethical action requires fair rather than equal service or treatment. Unequal service might be an ethical obligation if the needs of individuals differ. This recognizes, for example, that children may receive unequal service, because their needs are different than that of adults. The value of justice implies that we do not provide equal service, but that we provide service that recognizes extenuating or special circumstances. This does not imply that equality is absent in the concept of justice or library ethics; equality of access to library services is basic to the concept of library and information service. Part of the challenge to the librarian is knowing when to apply principles of fairness and when ensuring equality is the appropriate response.

VALUE 7: AESTHETICS

Among all the informational and entertainment materials that are part of library collections there exists a core of materials that are collected because they possess the elements of extraordinary creativity—they are the works of genius that live on. Although librarians value great diversity in materials, there is a special respect for humankind's greatest creations, those that make a special contribution to the society and civilization. The great music, art, literature, and philosophy of the past, as well as those modern works that appear to have like potential are often prized by libraries, even when their circulation levels are low. These works occupy a special place for librarians and often receive special consideration for preservation.

SUMMARY

One could quarrel with one value or another or argue that among some libraries some of these values are less important, or not important at all. Surely, the diversity of libraries makes attempts to generalize extremely difficult. Nonetheless, the values discussed above account for much of the direction libraries take and for their misgivings and resistance when these values are threatened. Libraries have occupied important places, if not central roles, in many societies throughout history. Shera (1965) characterized libraries as "social agencies," rather than social institutions, because he saw them as instrumentalities designed to support a social institution. That is, he argued that social institutions were essential foundations of a society; while social agencies provided important support for those institutions. In this sense, Shera saw American libraries as important supports for institutions such as education. This would fit the picture of libraries throughout history; their mission has primarily supported other more fundamental institutions: religion, government and education. This support function is a particularly important aspect of the library's mission, which is a mission with a special relationship to the people it serves. Shera (1984) described it in this manner:

> That purpose is to make accessible the graphic records of human culture, so that people may understand the totality of the environment in which they find themselves and their own place in it (p. 387).

There are many environments in which we find ourselves; and there are many cultures that must be understood. The library helps orient us economically, educationally, religiously, politically, and aesthetically to those cultures and environments.

## ENDNOTE

1. I am indebted to Professor Donald Krummel whose example in teaching library at the University of Illinois first suggested to me addressing issues in library history from the perspective of the missions of libraries.

## REFERENCES

American Libraries. "REFORMA's Rite of Passage: Coming of Age in Austin." *American Libraries* 27 (October 1996): 20–23.

American Library Association. *ALA Handbook of Organization, 1997–98*. Chicago: ALA, 1997.

Berelson, Bernard. *The Library's Public: A Report of the Public Library Inquiry*. New York: Columbia University, 1949.

Black Caucus of the American Library Association. Mission and Purposes of the Black Caucus of the American Library Association. [Online] Available at *http//www.bcala.org/mission.htm* (December 26, 1997).

Blanke, Henry T. "Librarianship and Political Values: Neutrality or Commitment?" *Library Journal* 114 (July 1989): 39–43.

Boyd, Clarence Eugene. *Public Libraries and Literary Culture in Ancient Rome*. Chicago: University of Chicago Press, 1915.

Butler, Pierce. "Librarianship as a Profession." *Library Quarterly* 21 (October 1951): 235–247.

Carnegie, Andrew. "The Gospel of Wealth." In *The Gospel of Wealth and Other Timely Essays*. Edited by Edward C. Kirkland. Cambridge: Harvard University Press, 1962. Originally published in the *North American Review* 148 (June 1889): 653–664.

Cecil, Henry L., and Willard A. Heaps. *School Library Service in the United States. An Interpretive Survey*. New York: H.W. Wilson, 1940.

Certain, Charles C. *Elementary School Library Standards*. n.p.: National Education Association, 1925.

———. *Standard Library Organization and Equipment for Secondary Schools of Different Sizes*. Chicago: ALA, 1920.

Childe, V. Gordon. *Man Makes Himself*. London: Watts, 1965.

Clanchy, Michael. *From Memory to Written Record*. Cambridge: Harvard University Press, 1979.

———. "Looking Back from the Invention of Printing." In *Literacy in Historical Perspective*. Edited by D. P. Resnick. Washington D.C.: Library of Congress, 1983.

Cresswell, Stephen. "The Last Days of Jim Crow in Southern Libraries." *Libraries and Culture* 31 (summer/fall 1996): 557–573.

Dain, Phyllis. "Ambivalence and Paradox: The Social Bonds of the Public Library." *Library Journal* 100 (February 1, 1975): 261–266.

Dewey, Melvil. "Libraries as Related to the Educational Work of the State." *Melvil Dewey: His Enduring Presence in Librarianship.* Edited by Sarah K. Vann. Littleton, Colo.: Libraries Unlimited, 1978, 136.

————. "The Profession." *Library Journal* 114 (June 15, 1989): 5. Reprinted from *American Library Journal* 1 (1876).

Ditzion, Sydney H. *Arsenals of a Democratic Culture.* Chicago: ALA, 1947.

Dix, T. Keith. "'Public Libraries' in Ancient Rome: Ideology and Reality." *Libraries & Culture* 29 (summer 1994): 282–296.

Du Mont, Rosemary Ruhig, Lois, Buttlar, and William Caynon. *Multiculturalism in Libraries.* Westport, Conn.: Greenwood, 1994.

Dunlap, Leslie W. *Readings in Library History.* New York: R.R. Bowker, 1972.

Eisenstein, Elizabeth L. *The Printing Press as an Agent of Change: Communications and Cultural Transformations in Early Modern Europe.* Cambridge, Eng.: Cambridge University Press, 1979.

Estabrook, Leigh. "The Library as a Socialist Institution in a Capitalist Environment." In *The Economics of Information.* Edited by Jana Varlys. Jefferson, N.C.: McFarland, 1982, 3–16.

Fargo, Lucile F. *The Program for Elementary Library Service.* Chicago: ALA, 1930.

Finks, Lee W. "Values Without Shame." *American Libraries* 20 (April 1989): 352–356.

Franklin, John Hope. "Libraries in a Pluralistic Society." In *Libraries and the Life of the Mind in America.* Chicago: ALA, 1977.

Garrison, Dee. "The Tender Technicians: The Feminization of Public Librarianship." *Journal of Social History* 6 (winter 1972–1973): 131–156.

Gates, Jean Key. *Introduction to Librarianship.* New York: McGraw-Hill, 1976.

Gillespie, John T. and Diana L. Spirt. "School Library to Media Center." In *Administering the School Library Media Center.* New York: Bowker, 1983.

Gleason, Eliza Atkins. *The Southern Negro and the Public Library.* Chicago: University of Chicago Press, 1941.

Gorman, Michael. "Five New Laws of Librarianship." *American Libraries* 26 (September 1995):784–785.

Hamlin, Arthur T. *The University Library in the United States: Its Origins and Development.* Philadelphia: University of Pennsylvania Press, 1981.

Hanson, Eugene R. "College Libraries: The Colonial Period to the Twentieth Century." In *Advances in Library Administration and Organization.* Vol. 8. Greenwich, Conn.: JAI, 1989, 171–199.

Haro, Roberto P. *Developing Library and Information Services for Americans of Hispanic Origin.* Metuchen, N.J.: Scarecrow, 1981.

Harris, Michael. "The Purpose of the American Public Library." *Library Journal* 98 (September 15, 1973): 2509–2514.

Harris, Michael and Elmer D. Johnson. *History of Libraries in the Western World.* Metuchen, N.J.: Scarecrow, 1984.

Harris, Michael H. and Stanley Hannah. "Why Do We Study the History of Libraries?: A Meditation on the Perils of Ahistoricism in the Information Era." *LISR* 14 (1992): 123–130.

Harris, William V. *Ancient Literacy*. Cambridge, Mass.: Harvard, 1989.

Harwell, Richard. "College Libraries." In *Encyclopedia of Library and Information Science*. Edited by Allen Kent, Harold Lancour, and William Z. Nasri. New York: Marcel Dekker, 1968, 269–281.

Hessel, Alfred. *A History of Libraries*. New Brunswick, N.J.: Scarecrow, 1955.

Jackson, Sydney L. *Libraries and Librarianship in the West: A Brief History*. New York: McGraw-Hill, 1974.

Jones, Plummer Alston Jr. "The History and Development of Libraries in American Higher Education." *College and Research Libraries News* (July/August 1989): 561–565.

Josey, E.J. *The Black Librarian in America*. Metuchen, N.J.: Scarecrow, 1970.

———. "Race Issues in Library History." *Encyclopedia of Library History*. Edited by Wayne A. Wiegand and Donald G. Davis Jr. New York: Garland, 1994, pp. 533–537.

Kaser, David. *A Book for A Sixpence: The Circulating Library in America*. Pittsburgh: Beta Phi Mu, 1980.

Knight, Douglas M. and E. Shepley Nourse. "The Functions of Elementary and Secondary School Libraries." In *Libraries at Large*. New York: R.R. Bowker, 1969, 89f.

Kramer, Samual Noah. *Sumerian Mythology, A Study of Spiritual and Literary Achievement in the Third Millennium B.C.* New York: Harper, 1961.

Kruzas, Anthony Thomas. *Business and Industrial Libraries in the United States, 1820–1940*. New York: SLA, 1965.

*Library Hotline* 21 (February 3, 1992): 2.

Neill, Sam D. "Why Books?" *Public Library Quarterly* 12 (1992): 19–28.

Nelson, Anne. "How My Hometown Library Failed Me." *Library Journal* 115 (June 15, 1990): 82–85.

Nichols, Charles L. *The Library of Ramses the Great*. Berkeley, Calif.: Peacock, 1964.

Nielson, Brian. "The Role of the Public Services Librarian: The New Revolution." In *Rethinking the Library in the Information Age*. Washington, D.C.: GPO, 1989, pp. 179–200.

Parsons, Edward A. *The Alexandrian Library*. Amsterdam, N.Y.: Elsevier, 1952.

Ranganathan, S.R. *The Five Laws of Library Science*. New York: Asia, 1963. First published 1931.

Rawls, John. "Justice as Fairness." *Philosophical Review* 67 (1958): 164–194.

REFORMA. The National Association to Promote Library Services to the Spanish Speaking. [Online] Available at *http://clnet.ucr.edu/l . . . y/reforma/refointr.htm* (December 26, 1997).

Roberts, F.B. "The Library and the Foreign Citizen." *Public Libraries* 17 (1912): 166–169.

Shera, Jesse. *Foundations of the Public Library*. Chicago: Shoestring, 1965.

———. *Introduction to Library Science: Basic Elements of Library Service*. Littleton, Colo.: Libraries Unlimited, 1976.

———. "Librarianship and Information Science." In *The Study of Information: Interdisciplinary Messages*. Edited by Fritz Machlup and Una Mansfield. New York, Wiley, 1984.

Shiflett, O. Lee. "Academic Libraries." In *Encyclopedia of Library History*. Edited by Wayne A. Wiegand, and Donald G. Davis Jr. New York: Garland, 1994, 5–15.

Stern, Stephen. "Ethnic Libraries and Librarianship in the United States: Models and Prospects." In Vol. 15 of *Advances in Librarianship*. Edited by Irene P. Godden. San Diego: Academic Press, 1991, 77–102.

Swan, John. "Untruth or Consequences." *Library Journal* 111 (July 1, 1986): 44–52.

Thompson, James Westfall. *Ancient Libraries*. Hamden, Conn.: Archon, 1957.

Trujillo, Roberto G. and Yolanda J. Cuesta. "Service to Diverse Populations." In Vol. 14 of *ALA Yearbook of Library and Information Science*. Chicago: ALA, 1989, 7–11.

Watson, Paula. "Founding Mothers: The Contribution of Women's Organizations to Public Library Development in the United States." *The Library Quarterly* 64 (July 1994): 233–269.

West, Jessamyn. "Social Responsibilities Round Table." [Online] Available at *http://www.jessamyn.com/srrt* (November 20, 1997).

White House Conference on Library and Information Services. *Information 2000: Library and Information Services for the 21st Century*. Washington, D.C.: Superintendent of Documents, 1991.

Wiegand, Wayne A. "The Development of Librarianship in the United States." *Libraries and Culture* 24 (winter 1989): 99–109.

Winter, Michael F. *The Culture and Control of Expertise: Toward a Sociological Understanding of Librarianship*. Westport, Conn: Greenwood, 1988.

Zill, Nicholas and Winglee, Marianne. "Literature Reading in the United States: Data from National Surveys and Their Policy Implications." *Book Research Quarterly* 5 (fall 1989): 24–58.

# 8

# Ethics and Standards: Professional Practices in Library and Information Science

*"...but if indeed we have no philosophy, then we are depriving ourselves of the guiding light of reason, and we live only a day-to-day existence, lurching from crisis to crisis, and lacking the driving force of an inner conviction of the value of our work."*

—D. J. Foskett, 1962

*"The essence of the librarian's obligation can best be expressed in terms of function and purpose, and these should be explicitly stated. Librarians are behaving properly (or ethically) when they act in such a way that they fulfill their function, thereby fulfilling the function of the library."*

—Lee W. Finks, 1991

*"As professionals, we are responsible to those we serve and to each other. As citizens, we are committed to using our special knowledge for the good of society. And as members of the worldwide human family, we take responsibility to preserve and protect human dignity."*

—Martha M. Smith, Editorial, 1993

In previous chapters, we looked at the mission and values of libraries. Although it may not constitute a "philosophy of librarianship," as Foskett refers to it above, it is clear that libraries play important roles and that the values that underlie them are basic to democratic processes. There are many ways that libraries accomplish their missions and thus support their values; one of these ways is through ethical conduct. Through such conduct we recognize that librarians and information professionals are moral agents, responsible to themselves, others, and the society as a whole. The ethical conduct of information professionals is an affirmation of the critical values of service, respect for others, and the need to improve society. Ethics provide a framework for conducting essential information functions, instituting policies, and developing strategies for service. Without them, we are, as Foskett observes above, merely "lurching" about—stumbling in the dark.

Ethical deliberations are extremely complex for at their base they deal with the fundamental questions of "right" and "wrong." Ethics is mostly about how people should be treated and how one should act, if one wishes to act rightly. The discussion of ethics has deep philosophical, religious, and legal roots, and the divergent points-of-view of many disciplines make much fodder for debate and disagreement. These debates will not be explicated here; this chapter is not intended to determine once and for all what is "right" or "wrong" in a given instance. Rather, it will identify some of the major principles, codes, obligations, and situations that are part of our professional environment. In this way, a clearer picture of the many ethical issues that information professionals face may emerge.

Historically, what the field has identified as the focus of ethical concern has varied. Du Mont (1991) has suggested three periods, each with different ethical orientations. The earliest period includes the years prior to 1930. During this time, American librarianship focused attention on its responsibility to the library collections themselves. It was a formative time for libraries, and much attention was directed to collection creation and maintenance. The issues included explicitly moral concerns with the potentially corrupting influence of library materials. The second period occurred between 1930 and 1950. During this time, ethical attention focused on the human aspects of library service, on staff and patrons. This focus was a recognition that staff members, for example, were not simply cogs in the library's wheel, but individuals with human needs. Issues such as job security, working conditions, education, and training arose. The focus on human needs was a recognition that patrons were people whose treatment and needs should be understood. Emphasis was directed toward the obligation to deliver quality service and maintain good relations with the public. This period also focused on the issue of the ethical obligation to provide free access to information. This attention may, in part, have been produced by the rise of fascism in Nazi Germany (Harris 1973) and resulted in the adoption of major intellectual freedom documents such as the ALA Library Bill of Rights and the ALA Code of Ethics (Figure 8–2). In the final period, since 1960, the ethical attention has been drawn to the broader needs of society as a whole. Emphasis has been on improving the public good, promoting social justice, and taking socially progressive political positions. The more general concept of social responsibility extends beyond the current employees of the library or the individuals who were current users of the library, to the society beyond. Issues such as affirmative action and the needs of the underserved have become important ethical issues. In addition, the ethical responsibilities of the reference librarian in answering questions have been questioned. For example, Hauptman (1976) queried whether reference librarians would provide information on building a car bomb, and Dowd (1989) questioned whether reference librarians would or should provide information on freebasing cocaine. The underlying question was whether reference librarians can be totally neutral in the performance of their duties, or whether social consequences of the information should be considered.

Currently, there is continuing and growing interest in professional ethics. Several conferences have focused on this issue, and a new publication, the *Journal of Information Ethics* has been launched. Nonetheless, despite this increasing attention, today's work world allows very little time for reflection. Realistically, practitioners seldom have time to consider the broader ethical implications of their work. It is not that these are considered unimportant considerations, but often they can only be properly considered and evaluated when there is time to deliberate. One study of Management Information System (MIS) professionals found that there was a strong perception among a significant number of them that there were many opportunities for MIS professionals to act unethically. This perception was further substantiated when the respondents were asked about their knowledge of unethical conduct. In fact, a fifth of the respondents indicated that they were aware of incidents in which MIS managers had acted improperly. This does not mean, however, that the information professionals condoned the unethical conduct. To the contrary, 70% stated that the interests of the employer do not always come first; that the interests of the society may rise above the interest of the employer. In fact, nearly all the respondents made it clear that there are broader social responsibilities that MIS professionals must uphold over and above the professional responsibility to the employer and that one's general ethical obligations do not end when one enters the workplace (Vitell and Davis 1990).

The issue of ethics in a professional context is about our dealings with and treatment of people and involves a complex relationship between information producers, intermediaries, and consumers. Froehlich (1992) has identified at least seven stakeholders in the information dissemination process who are affected by our actions. These stakeholders include authors, publishers, database producers, database vendors or networks, information professionals, the organization and managers, and the end users or consumers. The actions of information professionals affect and are affected by these various stakeholders, and the ethical ramifications are complex.

Froehlich proposes a simplified ethical model that reveals three basic elements in professional ethics: self, organization, and environment. The self is the moral agent, the person who must act or suffer the consequences of the actions of others; the organization is the institution that is also a moral agent that acts in an autonomous manner and directs the actions of others; the environment includes the standards of the community or professional societies that create an ethical context in which the self and organization operate. Ethical stresses can often be characterized by the interactions and imperatives that arise for each of these elements. These interactions and imperatives may not be easily or consistently balanced, and as a result, ethical frictions and dilemmas arise. Hence, there may be a conflict between the self as a person and the self as a member of an organization or employee. For example, the librarian may have a personal belief that certain material contains morally offensive content. As an individual moral agent, the librarian may believe that such material is inappropriate for dissemination; at the same time, as a librarian, there are organizational and professional standards of conduct that may dictate that the material be freely disseminated. Such conflicts may be infrequent for some and commonplace for others, but they are inevitable for most.

The need for discussion of ethical concerns is highlighted by the fact that librarianship is a service-oriented profession; our most important stakeholder is our user. As Finks (1991) has observed, "the basic function of the library is to optimize the value of recorded information for humankind" (p. 86). The decisions made by librarians and other information workers may determine who receives information and who does not. Failure to perform this function is a violation of professional ethics. Accomplishing this function, however, requires a careful balancing of interests, realizing that often, even when the interests are balanced, both benefits and harms may arise.

## FACTORS IN ETHICAL DELIBERATIONS

Most of the time, librarians do not think consciously about the ethical ramifications of what they do. As with ethical conduct generally, our behavior follows from habit. It is only when a special situation arises that ethical dissonance arises. In these situations we may feel qualms about what to do, and there is general agreement that there should be standards of conduct to limit unethical actions. In addition, ethical constraints apply not only to individuals but to organizations. Libraries and other information organizations are not value-neutral; they act, make choices, affect human beings, and receive, allocate, and disseminate resources in ways analogous to individuals. They too have ethical obligations.

When one considers ethics for a given discipline or for the practitioners in that discipline, it is not necessarily to suggest that ethics are different for that discipline than for others. On the contrary, there are very few disciplines in which normal ethical practices do not apply. Rather, it is to say that there may be special situations that arise within a particular professional context to which ethics must be applied. Understanding these situations, being familiar with the ethical prescriptions of the field, and reflecting on the factors that must be considered when making ethical deliberations is important if informed and appropriate actions are to be taken. Certainly such issues arise in library and information science, and practitioners must become aware and sensitive to these issues.

Part of the complexity of dealing with ethics in library and information science is that it has at least two focuses. One focus might be called *information ethics*. Information ethics among other things is an area of applied ethics concerned with the use and misuse of information. This would include such areas as the ownership of information, intellectual-property rights, free or restricted access to information, use of government information, assuring privacy and confidentiality, data integrity and the international flow of information. A second focus deals with professional behavior specifically. This is referred to as *professional ethics*. Professional ethics deals with how we apply ethical principles to our decisions and actions as information professionals (Smith 1993a).

Fortunately, for discussion purposes, information ethics and professional ethics are closely related and often overlap. It is more a matter of emphasis rather than unique content, and often discussion of one cannot proceed satisfactorily without discussion of the other.

Regardless of focus, when attempting to make ethical judgments, those who make decisions often find themselves with a residue of dissatisfaction, even when they think they have made the best decision. Part of this ambivalence may be the result of the organizations and practitioners being subject to competing demands from a variety of sources, including the public, clients, board members, administrators, and staff. Attempts to satisfy so many parties require a very careful balancing of interests and frequently produce ethical tensions. When ethical decisions are being considered, there are at least four factors that affect the deliberative process: social utility, survival, social responsibility, and respect for the individual. These factors may not be explicitly considered by the individuals making the decision; often they are obscured. But they are often implicit and underlie the decision-making process. These factors are not in themselves ethical principles, but they are critical considerations. In fact, it is the constant attempt to balance these factors that often make decisions so difficult from an ethical perspective.[1]

*Factor 1: Social Utility*

Organizations, especially public ones, are intended to serve important social ends. Libraries are certainly among those institutions that have a socially desirable purpose. For example, academic libraries are intended to advance society by educating students and producing research that will improve society; public libraries are created to meet the educational, informational, and recreational needs of the general public, and school libraries are expected to prepare students to enter the job market and to provide them with the general life skills to function effectively in society. The extent to which the purpose of an organization can accomplish its social purpose is its social utility. Because this is a desired end, decisions and actions taken that would aid an organization in accomplishing its social purpose can be seen as ethically desirable.

However, sometimes ethical conflicts can arise when attempting to meet the goals of the organization, and sometimes, albeit unintentionally, helping the library may have a negative effect on other institutions. For example, the library may compete with other worthy public institutions for a limited amount of public monies. Hence city parks, law enforcement, or schools, all of which need funds, might suffer from the political successes of the library. Similarly, ethical qualms may arise when the library develops collections that might have a detrimental effect on local businesses. For example, the development of entertainment-videocassette collections might pose a threat to some video stores. From a staffing perspective, ethical concerns may arise if a library director or supervisor needs to release an employee who is unable to perform his or her library-service duties effectively. The employee may be a likeable individual who is making an earnest effort. The decision to terminate may, therefore, produce considerable ethical discomfort despite the fact that keeping the employee will impair the library's function.

*Factor 2: Survival*

A key requirement for an organization is that it survive. This is no different from individuals. It is generally presumed that individuals are acting correctly when they act to preserve their own lives. Without survival, organizations would not exist to perform the functions for which they were created. As such, it is reasonable to assume that insofar as an organization performs a worthy purpose, that it would have an ethical obligation to maintain itself.

Libraries confront issues related to their survival regularly. Perhaps the most obvious is when some members of the community object to a particular item or items held in the library collection. When censorship attempts arise, the protests are often linked to threats to the library's funding sources. Unhappy citizens may threaten to campaign against a levy or lobby political bodies to reduce funding. Under these circumstances, the library's leadership may consider bowing to pressure because the continued existence of the library is considered more important than the retention of a few items in the library collection. Such an example highlights how the various factors can come into conflict. For example, in a censorship case, the factor of survival may conflict with the factor of social utility: by protecting the library's fiscal survival, one may be sacrificing the purpose for which the library was established— free access to all types of ideas, even objectionable ones.

*Factor 3: Social Responsibility*

Not only do organizations have an ethical obligation to fulfill the specific purposes for which they were created. They also function in the society-at-large, and it is generally recognized that organizations have an obligation to serve the larger society. It seems reasonable that public organizations have a particular obligation to act on behalf of the society because they receive their fiscal support from that society. Librarians and administrators recognize that they have social responsibilities as well as responsibilities to survive and perform their particular functions. There are a variety of actions and decisions that are taken in libraries that indicate that social responsibilities are important to them. For example, there may be a policy to order as many items as possible on acid-free paper to minimize pollution and the need for replacement copies. Alternatively, library policy may actively promote equal-employment opportunity to ensure that all members of the society have an equal opportunity for library positions. Of course, in attempting to meet social responsibilities, there may be conflicts with other factors. For example, purchasing materials on acid-free paper may be more costly to the organization, which in turn may have a negative impact on the survival of the organization.

*Factor 4: Respect for the Individual*

A fundamental factor in ethical deliberations concerns how individuals are treated. This factor implies that individuals must be treated with dignity and respect, and that employees and patrons have a right to act as they see fit, insofar as they do not violate the dignity and respect of others.

Libraries and other information organizations strive to accommodate this factor in many ways. For example, libraries are open to all persons. In the area of collection development, librarians develop the collections tailored to individual interests as well as for "the masses." Librarians pay special attention to building collections that represent a wide range of materials, reflecting diverse perspectives and in a variety of formats. Respect for the individual is also recognized when libraries protect the privacy of patrons, for example, when protecting the privacy of their circulation records. Respect for the individual is also reflected in the managerial and administrative practices of the organizations. This is a factor when the rules and policies are developed so that individuals are treated fairly and employee privacy is respected.

Of course, as with the other factors, conflicts can occur. For example, in terms of collection development, a library director may feel that appealing to the broader mass tastes, rather than to individual tastes, improves the prospects of the library's survival because then the public will be more inclined to support the library, and there is less possibility of public dissatisfaction with controversial selections. By appealing to popular taste, the director puts greater emphasis on the factor of survival and less on respect for the individual. Conflicts with the factors may also occur when dealing with respecting an individual's privacy. For example, the staff may comply with law-enforcement authorities who request the circulation record of a patron who may have committed a serious crime. In this circumstance, one may feel that the factor of social responsibility, i.e., aiding society in the apprehension of criminals, outweighs the factor of respect for the individual.

All of the factors mentioned above are important to librarians. Balancing them is a complex and challenging task. Although experience and professional codes and guidelines may provide some assistance, each situation has its own unique circumstances. There is no simple formula for determining which factor weighs more heavily in a given situation. Rubin and Froehlich (1996, p. 41) suggest that the concerns of libraries involved in ethical deliberations are reflected in four questions:

1. To what extent is the survival of the organization threatened?
2. To what extent will the purpose of the organization be benefitted or harmed?
3. To what extent is the organization or employee socially responsible or irresponsible when acting in a particular manner?
4. To what extent are the actions of the organization or individuals acting in its behalf harming or benefitting other individuals, organizations, or the profession?

## CATEGORIES OF ETHICAL CONCERN

Consider some of the many categories of ethical concern within the library and information context:

### Free Access to Information/Effects of Information

The ethical ramifications of information dissemination are considerable and touch virtually all activities and policies of libraries. In general, however, much of the energy and ethical attention in this area have focused on the responsibility to maintain intellectual freedom. The ALA Code of Ethics explicitly refers to intellectual freedom as a central ethical doctrine (Section 2), and the American Society for Information Science's ASIS

Professional Guidelines refer to "free and equal access" (ALA 1995; ASIS, 1994). This is no doubt a correct emphasis, and the profession has created numerous additional information policies to protect this freedom (see detailed discussion in Chapter 5). Nevertheless, one must be careful not to exclude other potentially pertinent considerations that fall into the ethical domain. Most notable has been an ongoing debate in our profession about our social responsibilities. That is, to what extent do libraries serve to improve and protect society? In this regard, what is a library's obligation to limit access to materials that might be socially unhealthy or promote materials that are considered beneficial to the health of the society? This duality between protecting individual rights and the imperatives of acting in a socially responsible matter creates a critical tension for ethical decision-making. Smith (1993b) characterized this tension as a dynamic relationship between three components: (1) Freedom, meaning intellectual freedom; (2) Information democracy, i.e., promoting the need for social equity in information; and (3) Responsibility: the obligation to promote the social good.

Such considerations can complicate discussion of ethical issues in information dissemination and may account for the ambivalence librarians feel about providing all types of information to anyone. Baker (1992) articulated this consideration as "Do no harm." Baker was referring specifically to the activities of library administrators, not to intellectual-freedom issues, but the underlying notion applies to library users as well. It suggests that library activities should minimize harm to others and reminds us that ethics deal not only with protecting the rights of others, but also their welfare. For example, there is debate over whether librarians should freely disseminate materials about suicide to minors. Similarly, there is some evidence that exposure to violent materials may lead to levels of increased aggressive behavior; as a consequence, some librarians are concerned about the dissemination of violent materials to minors (Green and Thomas 1986). It is not being suggested here that librarians should act as censors, but it is to say that considering the effects of information on the patron lies well within the domain of ethical deliberations, and that intellectual freedom issues, although clearly intimately related, do not exhaust the important considerations when making ethical decisions.

*Selection Decisions*

Selection decisions are extremely important for libraries because they determine the nature of the library collection. At the most basic level, there is an ethical obligation to use appropriate selection criteria, to hire qualified selectors, and to develop an efficient system for the procurement of selected items. The mission of libraries is to meet the needs of users, thus decisions should generally be made for the benefit of users. This seems obvious, but ethical issues may arise. For example, selectors may select items that are of particular interest to them, rather than their patrons. Selectors might acquire items simply because they are popular and increase the chance for improved funding. They may select items that fail to meet their selection criteria because of pressure from administrators or powerful members of the community. Perhaps even more common, sometimes selectors fear that a particular selection will be both popular and controversial and fail to select it. It could be a well-known and heavily promoted, sexually explicit or violent book, video, or compact disk. In each of these cases, ethics are a factor.

*Privacy*

Respect for privacy is a fundamental concept in a democratic society, and with the increasing computerization and networking of information, the problems are magnified further. Not only library records, but medical, financial, and credit records, and consumer information are now part of national and international networks. Information professionals are rapidly developing the skills to access this type of information, and the potential to invade the privacy of these records is considerable. In terms of libraries, one can conceive that without privacy protections individuals may decide not to seek out information because they feel that subsequent public exposure may subject them to censure or intimidation. Librarians, therefore, try to protect user privacy as much as possible. The issue becomes especially sensitive in the area of circulation records. In the broader information environment, there are privacy issues regarding proprietary information. For example, competitors may attempt to access information that is the property of another organization through deception or other inappropriate means, violating the privacy rights of these organizations.

*Copyright*

Although copyright is fundamentally defined and treated as a legal concept subsumed under the broader notion of intellectual property, it is also an ethical issue. At its heart is the question of whether individuals should copy the intellectual work of others without asking the originator's permission. Librarians often make copies of materials or encourage others to do so without seeking copyright permission. This encouragement is not done with the intention of depriving copyright owners of their rights, but in fulfillment of the library's mission to provide information to their citizenry. This situation highlights the fundamental question: To what extent does the creator of a work have the right to control its dissemination following publication? Interestingly, there are competing ethical considerations here. If the library's mission is to promote the dissemination of information to all users to fulfill its democratic mission, then is it not ethically bound to disseminate as much information as possible? Essentially, are not librarians ethically obligated to test the bounds of others' control over the dissemination of information. Librarians feel an ethical tension to respect and protect the rights of both authors and patrons. They want authors to profit, but not to permit authors and publishers to unnecessarily restrict and control the flow of information. As more and more information becomes available electronically, the ethical debate will no doubt flourish.

*Information Organization*

The challenge of organizing information (e.g. through classification, controlled vocabulary, and bibliography) has been central to American librarianship since its early development. Usually, this task is considered strictly a conceptual and procedural one. It is largely a question of techniques: which ones are best, which ones are the easiest to understand and use? From time to time, however, there are ethical issues that confront us, because how information is organized directly affects the effectiveness of our services. Some types of information organization may reflect prejudices and biases of the organizer. For example, a cataloger may classify some materials as adult that are really aimed at young people, because the cataloger believes the material is inappropriate for children. These biases, whether intentionally applied or not, may deprive or inhibit access to information, inappropriately silencing the voices of authors or producers who have a right to be heard. Such actions violate a fundamental value of librarianship: excellence in service.

How knowledge is organized may also be a broader reflection of the society's attitudes. The Dewey Decimal System has been criticized for diminishing the importance of writings from non-Western cultures. The library's primary mission is to organize materials for access—as we organize them we must consider what values, prejudices, or preconceptions affect this access.

The ethical ramifications of organizing knowledge suggest that there is a substantial ethical contribution that is made by an often overlooked department in this regard—technical services. Perhaps this oversight results from the fact that technical services is perceived as having only an oblique relationship to the patron. But the purpose of technical services is the same as all other library functions: to provide the highest quality of service to the user. In fact, the relationship between the patron and technical services is direct, because it is technical services that often determines how access will be provided and the ease with which information and materials can be obtained. As Bierbaum (1994) notes: "The mission of technical services is to provide bibliographical and physical access to collections and information...." (p. 13) Among other things, this entails that the technical services professionals have the ethical obligation to maintain high bibliographic standards, to process materials efficiently and effectively, to reduce barriers to information, to keep up with technical and professional issues in technical services, and to resist censorship.

*Information Policy*

The information policies of nations, communities, libraries, and other information organizations may have a profound effect on access to information in society. Information policies of ethical import include the economic, social, and cultural impact of laws and regulations governing information technologies, national and international policies affecting the ability of citizens to access information, and the effects of organizational policies and practices on information access.

In the latter case, there is no doubt that libraries are replete with policies that affect the organization and dissemination of information. Among them are reference service policies, intellectual freedom policies, circulation and registration policies, and policies on access to meeting rooms. Obviously, these policies could have profound effects on how patrons are treated and hence have serious ethical ramifications. Consider just a few such examples: restricting materials to those over eighteen; failing to develop policies or practices that attract users who are poor, disabled, or members of minority groups; revealing circulation records to others. All these raise important ethical questions.

*Information Quality*

The ethical obligations inherent in the value of service also extend to practices that affect the quality of information. To the extent that a library can, within the scope of its activities, ensure that the information it provides is timely and accurate, it preserves its service values. When libraries cannot ensure quality, they may well have the obligation to indicate to a user that there may be deficiencies, limitations, or biases to the information system being used. This has become especially problematic in any information environment in which the searcher is using automated databases. There may be a temptation to let consumers believe that these information systems are perfect systems that access all relevant information. We know that all databases have their limitations, biases, and deficiencies. Information professionals have ethical duties, if not legal ones, to ensure that such systems are not misrepresented.

The notion of information quality suggests also its opposite—information malpractice. If one assumes that information professionals are just that—professionals, then they have an ethical obligation to maintain high professional standards in their work. One assumes that a doctor's recommendations are based on the most current thinking; the same can be said for the work of attorneys. When they fail to meet the standards of practice in their fields, then they are subject to charges of malpractice. Librarians and other information professionals may not have the same legal obligations, but the field recognizes that the ethical obligations to maintain the highest standards of service are similar to that of any profession. Hence, information professionals that produce inferior products, or misrepresent their capabilities to produce a quality product may well be guilty, at least ethically, of malpractice.

*Administration*

Libraries and other information organizations inevitably have administrative and managerial components. The subject of business ethics is now commonplace in the management literature, and the concerns raised in this literature are no strangers to the library environment. Among the ethical issues facing both the employer and the employee are (1) the ethical use of consultants; (2) the ethical obligations that arise when dealing with vendors or others engaged in business with the library; (3) and ethical aspects regarding the treatment of personnel. The last category is a common and critical area of ethical concern and debate. Consider the following areas of potential ethical breaches when dealing with library personnel (Rubin 1990):

VIOLATIONS OF PRIVACY

Revealing information about employees to individuals who do not need to know such information, or revealing information that may unnecessarily damage the individual's personal or professional reputation. Misusing personnel records or files, including inappropriate access to computer files. Collecting any personal information about employees that is not related to the necessary functions of the organization. Conducting inappropriate investigations of an individual's personal history or using irrelevant personal information to make a personnel decision. Conducting drug, alcohol, HIV, or other testing unless it is essential to the safe operation of the job or is directly related to the safety of others. Monitoring employees with video cameras or tape recorders without their knowledge or consent, unless significant and specific job-related reasons make such monitoring necessary. Using a polygraph unless there is clear and substantial reason for its use, e.g., in cases of suspected theft. Attempting to censor the writing or speech of employees unless such speech or writing would significantly damage the institution's ability to perform its essential function.

MISUSES OF AUTHORITY

Showing favoritism to friends or relatives. Making personnel decisions out of anger or spite. Writing inaccurate job references for employees to prevent them from gaining other employment or to encourage their departure. Collecting job-related information from employees, without informing them of the potential consequences—for example, for disciplinary action. Retaliating against employees who are outspoken or who have merely exercised their legal rights. Withholding information from an individual to ensure or promote job failure.

ORGANIZATIONAL INADEQUACIES

Designing a system of rewards that fosters cheating, sabotaging the work of others, or withholding important information, or that places emphasis only on quantity rather than quality (e.g., providing substantial financial rewards for higher library circulation). Paying wages and benefits that do not give minimal protection and security to employees.

Creating a personnel system that discriminates or is unfair in administering essential personnel functions. Permitting the hiring and placement of individuals with a Master of Library Science degree in support-staff positions. Misusing behavior modification techniques to manipulate employees. Knowingly allowing employees to work in unsafe or unhealthy working conditions, especially without their knowledge or consent (pp. 34–35).

*Archival Issues*

An area often unrecognized as raising ethical issues involves materials stored in archives. Such records play a critical role in the preservation of materials through which history is written. Although some of the issues confronted by archivists overlap with issues noted above, the special function of archives—the storage and dissemination of usually unique records of long-term value—places special ethical burdens on the archivist.

The members of the Society of American Archivists (SAA) recognized this in their promulgation of their own Code of Ethics, most recently revised in 1992 and reprinted in Figure 8–1 (Society of American Archivists, Council 1992). This code deals with many issues, including ethical issues, in the acquisition of and access to archival collections, as well as defining business and research conduct. Overall, there is a critical tension concerning the function of archival services that can generate considerable ethical friction. One aspect of this tension arises from the need first and foremost to preserve the archival records. This is recognized in the code as the critical purpose of the archivist—to provide for the safety and protection of records of long-term value. Obviously this means that adequate safeguards and preservation techniques are applied to preserve the integrity of the collections. The second aspect that generates the tension concerns itself with the concomitant responsibility to promote access to these records by ensuring that only reasonable restrictions be placed on their use. It is a natural temptation for an archivist to do everything possible to preserve records, but records are of little value if they cannot be consulted relatively easily. Hence, the archivist is ethically bound to minimize such restrictions and to create the necessary finding aids so that the collection can be used. This tension is certainly a part of much library and information-science work, but it is especially prevalent in archival records where the works are likely to be rare and fragile.

---

## Figure 8–1
## Code of Ethics for Archivists

Archivists select, preserve, and make available documentary materials of long-term value that have lasting value to the organization or public that the archivist serves. Archivists perform their responsibilities in accordance with statutory authorization or institutional policy. They subscribe to a code of ethics based on sound archival principles and promote institutional and professional observance of these ethical and archival standards.

Archivists arrange transfers of records and acquire documentary materials of long-term value in accordance with their institution's purposes, stated policies, and resources. They do not compete for acquisitions when competition would endanger the integrity or safety of documentary materials of long-term value, or solicit the records of an institution that has an established archives. They cooperate to ensure the preservation of materials in repositories where they will be adequately processed and effectively utilized.

Archivists negotiating with transferring officials or owners of documentary materials of long-term value seek fair decisions based on full consideration of authority to transfer, donate, or sell; financial arrangements and benefits; copyright; plans for processing; and conditions of access. Archivists discourage unreasonable restrictions on access or use, but may accept as a condition of acquisition clearly stated restrictions of limited duration and may occasionally suggest such restrictions to protect privacy. Archivists observe faithfully all agreements made at the time of transfer or acquisition.

Archivists establish intellectual control over their holdings by describing them in finding aids and guides to facilitate internal controls and access by users of the archives.

Archivists appraise documentary materials of long-term value with impartial judgment based on thorough knowledge of their institutions' administrative requirements or acquisitions policies. They maintain and protect the arrangement of documents and information transferred to their custody to protect its authenticity. Archivists protect the integrity of documentary materials of long-term value in their custody, guarding them against defacement, alteration, theft, and physical damage, and ensure that their evidentiary value is not impaired in the archival work of arrangement, description, preservation, and use. They cooperate with other archivists and law enforcement agencies in the apprehension and prosecution of thieves.

Archivists respect the privacy of individuals who created, or are the subjects of, documentary materials of long-term value, especially those

---

**Figure 8–1 (cont.)**

who had no voice in the disposition of the materials. They neither reveal nor profit from information gained through work with restricted holdings.

Archivists answer courteously and with a spirit of helpfulness all reasonable inquiries about their holdings, and encourage use of them to the greatest extent compatible with institutional policies, preservation of holdings, legal considerations, individual rights, donor agreements, and judicious use of archival resources. They explain pertinent restrictions to potential users, and apply them equitably.

Archivists endeavor to inform users of parallel research by others using the same materials, and, if the individuals concerned agree, supply each name to the other party.

As members of a community of scholars, archivists may engage in research, publication, and review of the writings of other scholars. If archivists use their institutions' holdings for personal research and publication, such practices should be approved by their employers and made known to others using the same holdings. Archivists who buy and sell manuscripts personally should not compete for acquisitions with their own repositories, should inform their employers of their collecting activities, and should preserve complete records of personal acquisitions and sales.

Archivists avoid irresponsible criticism of other archivists or institutions and address complaints about professional or ethical conduct to the individual or institution concerned, or to a professional archival organization.

Archivists share knowledge and experience with other archivists through professional associations and cooperative activities and assist the professional growth of others with less training or experience. They are obligated by professional ethics to keep informed about standards of good practice and to follow the highest level possible in the administration of their institutions and collections. They have a professional responsibility to recognize the need for cooperative efforts and support the development and dissemination of professional standards and practices.

Archivists work for the best interest of their institutions and their profession and endeavor to reconcile any conflicts by encouraging adherence to archival standards and ethics.

---

Of special ethical interest is the issue of privacy. One can imagine many instances in which a collection of letters and correspondence is given to an archive by an individual, but those who wrote the correspondence, or who are the subject of the correspondence may not know that this material has been donated. Archivists are exhorted to protect the privacy of such individuals, especially if they had no control over the provision of such records to the archives. This highlights the careful balancing of interests required of archivists who must consider both the rights of access to information and the protection of the privacy interests of others.

Finally, archives may often find themselves in competition with other archives to obtain certain materials from donors. Archivists are expected to act ethically in the procurement of such materials, accurately representing the capacity of the archive to store and maintain such materials. Similarly, archivists must avoid competition that would work to the detriment of the preservation of such records, and they should not attempt to appropriate records already archived in other organizations.

## PROFESSIONAL CONSIDERATIONS IN ETHICAL DELIBERATIONS

When considering professional ethics, the focus is on the ethical obligations and principles that arise when an individual is acting as an information provider. As noted earlier, most of our ethical actions are the result of our ethical education and training which we received as children. Consequently, as situations arise, we act almost automatically in most instances without taking much time to reflect on the ethical implications or bases of our acts. The fact that we often act out of habit highlights the power of our early ethical socialization. It also suggests that this same type of socialization is needed if the ethics of the profession are to be followed. Once the ethics of one's profession are inculcated, acting in accordance with them should also follow normally as part of our everyday behavior. This is not to say that one's personal ethics are necessarily in conflict or wholly distinct from one's professional ethics. In most cases, in fact, professional ethics can be seen as a specialized example of our normal ethical practices. From time to time, however, they may conflict.

Regrettably, it is not clear how the socialization process of inculcating professional ethics in information professionals takes place. The basic ethical principles are often reviewed in schools of library and information science, but such training is usually superficial and seldom systematic. The primary means of communicating ethical principles in the professions are through the codes of ethics mentioned earlier: ALA's Code of Ethics (Figure 8–2), the ASIS Professional Guidelines (Figure 8–3), and SAA's Code of Ethics for Archivists (Figure 8–1).

Professional codes are important for at least four reasons: (1) they represent a statement of the fundamental values of the profession; (2) they are useful in teaching new librarians about the fundamental values of the profession; (3) reading (and rereading) them and listening to other professionals discuss and apply provisions of a code promotes the assimilation of important professional values; and (4) when particularly knotty ethical issues arise and important ethical concerns may be ignored, the professional code can serve as a decision-making guide and as a jog for one's conscience.

Codes, however, are not magic formulas. Unfortunately, because most of the individuals in a profession did not participate in the discussions that created the code, the rationale for each provision of the codes is generally obscured. As a result, the code may appear to be unnecessarily arbitrary. This is especially problematic when a professional must justify acting in a manner consistent with the code. Unless there is a solid understanding of the code's rationale, the explanation is likely to sound dogmatic rather than a thoughtful justification of professional conduct.

## ALA Code of Ethics

Discussions of a need for an ethical code for librarians was sparse or non-existent before the twentieth century. An early version, although not official, was discussed between 1903 and 1909. Two individuals contributed most to these early discussions: Mary Wright Plummer, director of the Pratt Institute Library School, and Charles Knowles Bolton, librarian of the Boston Athenaeum. The ALA actively considered adopting a code by 1928, but it was not formally adopted until 1938 (Lindsey and Prentice 1985). Interestingly, the ALA Library Bill of Rights was adopted just a year later. Together, these two documents form an important ethical foundation for librarianship. Revisions of the ethics code have been adopted over the years, in 1975 and 1981, and most recently in 1995.

The current ALA Code explicitly recognizes the potential conflicts in values that are inherent in library work and establishes one over-

## Figure 8–2
## American Library Association Code of Ethics

As members of the American Library Association, we recognize the importance of codifying and making known to the profession and to the general public the ethical principles that guide the work of librarians, other professionals providing information services, library trustees, and library staff.

Ethical dilemmas occur when values are in conflict. The American Library Association Code of Ethics states the values to which we are committed, and embodies the ethical responsibilities of the profession in this changing information environment.

We significantly influence or control the selection, organization, preservation, and dissemination of information. In a political system grounded in an informed citizenry, we are members of a profession explicitly committed to intellectual freedom and the freedom of access to information. We have a special obligation to ensure the free flow of information and ideas to present and future generations.

The principles of this Code are expressed in broad statements to guide ethical decision making. These statements provide a framework; they cannot and do not dictate conduct to cover particular situations.

I. We provide the highest level of service to all library users through appropriate and usefully organized resources; equitable service policies; equitable access; and accurate, unbiased, and courteous responses to all requests.

II. We uphold the principles of intellectual freedom and resist all efforts to censor library resources.

III. We protect each library user's right to privacy and confidentiality with respect to information sought or received and resources consulted, borrowed, acquired, or transmitted.

IV. We recognize and respect intellectual property rights.

V. We treat co-workers and other colleagues with respect, fairness, and good faith, and advocate conditions of employment that safeguard the rights and welfare of all employees of our institutions.

VI. We do not advance private interests at the expense of library users, colleagues, or our employing institutions.

VII. We distinguish between our personal convictions and professional duties and do not allow our personal beliefs to interfere with fair representation of the aims of our institutions or the provision of access to their information resources.

VIII. We strive for excellence in the profession by maintaining and enhancing our own knowledge and skills, by encouraging the professional development of co-workers, and by fostering the aspirations of potential members of the profession.

—Adopted by *ALA Council*, July 28, 1995
Reprinted with permission. American Library Association.

riding value: "commitment to intellectual freedom and freedom of access to information" (ALA 1995). Although not formally subdivided, the eight provisions of the code focus on three general areas: access issues, rights of authors and creators, and employment issues.

### ACCESS ISSUES

Consistent with the overriding value cited in the preamble, three of the eight principles of the code deal directly with the issue of access to the library by patrons. The first section emphasizes the obligation to treat all equally, emphasizing the principle of equal treatment and access. The second section suggests that there is a positive obligation to promote intellectual freedom and to resist attempts to censor library materials. The third section is a recognition of the individual and the special nature of librarian-patron interactions. It highlights the "privileged" character, albeit not necessarily in the legal sense, of library use. To this end, the librarian is exhorted to protect the privacy of all patrons and to ensure that their interactions remain confidential.

### RIGHTS OF AUTHORS AND CREATORS

Although the code of ethics places great emphasis on service to patrons, one section recognizes that the producers or creators of information are critical participants in this service process; they also deserve ethical treatment. Obviously, failure to recognize this aspect of information transfer and dissemination could seriously restrict the distribution of information products to libraries, with unhappy consequences for library service. To this end, Section IV of the code recognizes that authors and creators of works have the right to benefit from their creativity through their intellectual property rights. This is a clear reference to librarians' need to respect copyright protections.

### EMPLOYMENT ISSUES

Employment issues actually comprise more provisions of the code than any other issue. One section deals with the interrelationships between employees and the need to create a sense of mutuality and community. These sections explore the treatment of fellow employees, the promotion of self-interest, the clash between personal and professional values, and the obligation to pursue and promote continuing education. Section V suggests that treating fellow employees in an ethical manner is itself an ethical obligation and part of the obligation to respect the rights and welfare of all employees. Section VI recognizes the essentially altruistic nature of the professional obligation. It admits to the fact that in some circumstances librarians could personally benefit from their employment relationship and reminds professionals that one's personal or private interests are not to be served above the interests of patrons, the employer, or other employees. Section VII focuses on a very delicate aspect of professional work. Each of us brings to the workplace a set of values, beliefs, and moral perspectives that govern our everyday behavior, but sometimes, acting in our professional capacity, we should act in the best interests of our clients. For example, what if a patron asks for a book that supports the concept of abortion, but we personally abhor it. Section VII suggests that we act to serve the patron, even if the material provided may violate our own values. Finally, Section VIII emphasizes the professional obligation to improve one's skills continually. In an increasingly complex information and technological environment, this is certainly a vital obligation. Interestingly, the obligation as set forth in this provision is broader than just self-improvement; it suggests that the obligation extends to the development of others. As such, it is especially pertinent to library decision-makers and managers who have the capacity to create opportunities for training and development for their staffs.

*ASIS Guidelines for Professional Conduct*

The ethical guidelines from ASIS, as might be expected, are more broadly written, because they are aimed at information workers in all types of occupations, not just librarianship. These guidelines also recognize that some information services are part of private organizations and that the proprietary interests of such employers must be taken into account when making decisions concerning the dissemination of information.

Nonetheless, many of the underlying principles are similar to the ALA Code of Ethics. ASIS's code identifies three basic areas of ethical responsibility: (a) responsibilities to employers, clients and systems users; (b) responsibilities to the profession, and (c) responsibilities to society. Like the ALA code, these guidelines consider the right to privacy, confidentiality, and fair treatment rights of clients, users, and employers. The ASIS Professional Guidelines, under the more general notion of protecting privacy and confidentiality, also highlight a critical obligation of those who design and administer information systems—to pro-

---

### Figure 8–3
### ASIS Professional Guidelines

*Dedicated to the Memory of Diana Woodward*

ASIS recognizes the plurality of uses and users of information technologies, services, systems and products as well as the diversity of goals or objectives, sometimes conflicting, among producers, vendors, mediators, and users of information systems.

ASIS urges its members to be ever aware of the social, economic, cultural, and political impacts of their actions or inaction.

ASIS members have obligations to employers, clients, and system users, to the profession, and to society, to use judgement and discretion in making choices, providing equitable service, and in defending the rights of open inquiry.

*Responsibility to Employers/Clients/System Users*

**To act faithfully for their employers or clients in professional matters.**

**To uphold each user's, provider's or employer's right to privacy and confidentiality and to respect whatever proprietary rights belong to them, by**

- limiting access to, providing proper security for and ensuring proper disposal of data about clients, patrons or users.

**To treat all persons fairly.**

*Responsibility to the Profession*

**To truthfully represent themselves and the information systems which they utilize or which they represent, by**

- not knowingly making false statements or providing erroneous or misleading information
- informing their employers, clients or sponsors of any circumstances that create a conflict of interest
- not using their position beyond their authorized limits or by not using their credential to misrepresent themselves
- following and promoting standards of conduct in accord with the best current practices
- undertaking their research conscientiously, in gathering, tabulating or interpreting data; in following proper approval procedures for subjects; and in producing or disseminating their research results

## Figure 8–3 (cont.)

- pursuing ongoing professional development and encouraging and assisting colleagues and others to do the same
- adhering to principles of due process and equality of opportunity.

*Responsibility to Society*

**To improve the information systems with which they work or which they represent, to the best of their means and abilities by**

- providing the most reliable and accurate information and acknowledging the credibility of the sources as known or unknown
- resisting all forms of censorship, inappropriate selection and acquisitions policies, and biases in information selection, provision and dissemination
- making known any biases, errors and inaccuracies found to exist and striving to correct those which can be remedied.

**To promote open and equal access to information, within the scope permitted by their organizations or work, and to resist procedures that promote unlawful discriminatory practices in access to and provision of information, by**

- seeking to extend public awareness and appreciation of information availability and provision as well as the role of information professionals in providing such information
- freely reporting, publishing or disseminating information, subject to legal and proprietary restraints of producers, vendors and employers and the best interests of their employers or clients.

*Information professionals shall engage in principled conduct whether on their own behalf or at the request of employers, colleagues, clients, agencies or the profession.*

**(Adopted May 1992)**

vide security for these systems. In addition, as in the ALA code, the responsibility to the profession includes the promotion of continuing education. The guidelines add, however, the responsibility not to misrepresent one's qualifications or the information system that is being used. The responsibility to the society also echoes that of the ALA code in the emphasis on free and equal access to information.

Professional ethical codes can be useful in setting an ethical context for employees who work within a given profession, but they are seldom sufficiently elaborate to be of great help. Such codes tend to be wooden documents that prescribe and proscribe general conduct, but because of their dogmatic character, seldom do they provide a deep understanding of the ethical issues that need to be addressed and resolved. This has not deterred the creation of codes, and additional codes have been suggested in librarianship. For example, Bierbaum (1994) has suggested a code of ethics for technical services, and Baker (1992) has suggested an ethical code for library administrators. Finks (1991) has suggested an entirely new general code of ethics for librarians.

## SPECIAL ETHICAL PROBLEMS WITH INFORMATION TECHNOLOGIES

The deficiencies of ethical codes become more apparent when they are applied in today's technological environment. There is some reason to believe that these technologies may encourage or even promote unethical conduct. If so, then depending on formal ethical codes may be even less desirable and the need for careful ethical reflection more important. This is not to renounce traditional ethical concerns, but new information technologies can create new ethical dilemmas. It is worthwhile to consider some qualities of these new technologies that might promote unethical actions.

### Computers Are Extremely Fast

The speed of computers is one of their greatest attractions. Indeed, they are often promoted and advertised based on how fast the latest versions can perform their functions. However, the speed of computers also increases the temptation to act unethically because it suggests that one might be able to escape detection more easily. Stealing a file, for example, was much more difficult in the past. One had to enter a building or an office unobserved, locate a file drawer, locate a file, and either hide the file on one's person or make copies of the material. At each step, there was always the possibility of being detected. In contrast, the appropriation of a computer file by another computer is nearly instantaneous and chances of being caught severely limited.

### Computer Use Is Often Private and Anonymous

Although some computer use is performed in public areas, most personal computer use is performed either in an office or at home. Generally, if one wants to work unobserved, the opportunities are available. Even if people are in the same room, it is relatively difficult for them to observe computer use without being noticed. Such privacy is very attractive to an individual who wishes to commit unethical acts. Similarly, the fact that the computer user is free from detection provides a sense of anonymity. The feeling that one can not be "found out" tends to increase one's propensity to commit unethical acts.

### Computer Access Can Be Accomplished from Great Distances

In general, committing acts such as theft require that the thief be present when the item is stolen. Computers, on the other hand, permit the accessing of the item through telephone or cable lines. The result is that a computer file may be stolen by an individual in another city, state, or country. It is likely that individuals would not feel the same vulnerability in these circumstances, nor does the act require nearly the same physical effort and stealth.

### The Electronic Medium Is Easily Copied

The electronic medium is highly flexible. It is usually quite simple to download or make a physical copy of an electronic file while leaving the original unchanged. Under these circumstances, it is tempting to rationalize that nothing has actually been taken. Electronic theft is essentially an intellectual rather than artifactual act; electronic impulses are not nearly as tangible as paper or objects. Perhaps this is why individuals seem to have fewer misgivings about copying software than about copying a print edition of a work.

*Large Numbers of People Are Easily Reached*

Because of the presence of the National Information Infrastructure and Global Information Infrastructure messages can now be sent quite easily to millions of individuals simultaneously— without the traditionally burdensome costs of postage, supplies, or long-distance tolls. Although this is a wonderful opportunity for communication, it also presents an opportunity for the unscrupulous to exploit large numbers of unwitting victims. In fact, there is a new term to describe sending uninvited electronic messages, usually for business or commercial purposes. It is called "Spamming". Because the available audience is so large, and the ease of communicating with them so great, the temptation to act unethically increases.

*A Code of Ethics for Computer Use*

It is interesting that there has been an explicit recognition of the ethical issues raised by computers through the development of a "Ten Commandments" of computer ethics developed by the Computer Ethics Institute (Figure 8–4).

---

### Figure 8–4
### Ten Commandments of Computer Ethics

1. Thou shalt not use a computer to harm other people.
2. Thou shalt not interfere with other people's computer work.
3. Thou shalt not snoop around in other people's computer files.
4. Thou shalt not use a computer to steal.
5. Thou shalt not use a computer to bear false witness.
6. Thou shalt not copy or use proprietary software for which you have not paid.
7. Thou shalt not use other people's computer resources without authorization or proper compensation.
8. Thou shalt not appropriate other people's intellectual output.
9. Thou shalt think about the social consequences of the program you are writing or the system you are designing.
10. Thou shalt always use a computer in ways that insure consideration and respect for your fellow humans.

---

Reprinted with permission: Computer Ethics Institute, P.O. Box 42672, Washington, D.C. 20015 (301) 469–0615. psullivan@brook.edu (www.brook.edu/sscc/cei/cei_hp.htm)

These commandments direct those who use computers to resist harming others or interfering with their work and to refrain from stealing or deceiving others with computers, violating copyright, or plagiarizing. They also recognize the need to respect others. As librarians increase their use of computers, it would be well for them to heed this code as well as their own profession's.

## ETHICAL APPROACHES

When one sees how complex the ethical situation is for an information professional, it is tempting to try to create basic principles for ethical action. In large part, these principles are embodied in the ethical codes of the profession, and generally, they do a pretty good job, although sometimes they do fail us with their inevitable generality. Others have tried to restate or supplement these codes with additional principles, although none argue that their particular suggestions represent absolutes or a definitive list (Baker 1992; Rubin and Froehlich 1996). Froehlich summarized five of these principles as the obligations to minimize harm, to respect the autonomy of others, to act justly and fairly, to seek social harmony, and to comport with organizational, professional, and public trust (Froehlich 1992).

Another approach to examining the desired ethical behaviors has been to subdivide the discipline, identifying three venues for ethical actions: the organizational, the professional, and the individual (Rubin and Froehlich 1996).

On the organizational level, there is little evidence that information organizations or agencies attempt to address ethical issues systematically. It is likely that concern for ethics most often arises, not because the actions themselves may be unethical, but because of an undesired result or diminished productivity. Nonetheless, among the approaches that have been taken to promote ethical conduct are (1) establishing rules and regulations that clearly identify the ethical obligations of employee and management and clearly stating the penalties for ethical violations; (2) developing training and education programs that sensitize information professionals to ethical issues; (3) punishing individuals for ethical violations; (4) establishing an ethics code with the organization; (5) hiring and promoting individuals who demonstrate ethical behavior and understanding; and (6) developing a system of rewards that provides an incentive for ethical actions and a disincentive for unethical ones.

On the professional level, librarians and related information professionals have promulgated ethics guidelines and codes, as noted above. Professional associations also attempt to reinforce these codes through programs and speeches at association meetings and articles in professional publications. Some associations actually have the power of sanctions for unethical conduct. For example, the American Medical Association can withdraw a physician's power to practice, and the American Bar Association can prevent an attorney from practicing law. Such a sanctioning power, however, is not part of the arsenal of ALA or ASIS. It is through professional discussion and persuasion that the information professions attempt to promote ethical conduct.

Preventing unethical acts rests first and foremost on the individual level. Each of us is an individual moral agent and we do not give up our ethical obligations merely because we become employees. It seems clear that certain duties form a foundation for ethical conduct in the information profession. Some of the more obvious ones are that individuals should (1) promote open, unbiased access to information; (2) maintain professional skills and knowledge; (3) act honestly with colleagues and consumers of information; (4) respect the privacy and confidentiality of others; and (5) provide the best service possible.

## SUMMARY

No matter which principles or codes are used, it is clear that these statements reflect a consensus that the duties of information professionals are far greater than simply "doing their job." Their obligations follow from the more fundamental notions of respect for the individual and the desire to benefit the organization and the society. These are not new notions, on the contrary, they are quite old and seek expression in professional contexts. Ethical situations arise in many contexts for the information provider, and the ethical deliberations that ensue are complex. These deliberations often require a balancing of many interests and considerations: individual, organizational, and societal. If librarians and information specialists abide by fundamental ethical notions expressed in a professional context, the mission and values that underlie institutions like libraries can be preserved and sustained.

## ENDNOTE

1. I am indebted to Dr. Thomas Froehlich, Kent State University, for many discussions on the ethical factors that affect deliberations in library and information science. The factors presented are a product of these discussions.

## REFERENCES

[ALA] American Library Association. "Code of Ethics." *American Libraries* 26 (July/August 1995): 673.

[ASIS] American Society for Information Science. "ASIS Professional Guidelines." *Bulletin of the American Society for Information Science* 20 (1994): 4.

Baker, Sharon L. "Needed: An Ethical Code for Library Administrators." *Journal of Library Administration* 16 (1992): 1–17.

Bierbaum, Esther Green. "Searching for the Human Good: Some Suggestions for a Code of Ethics for Technical Services." *Technical Services Quarterly* 11 (1994): 1–18.

Dowd, Robert. "I Want to Find Out How to Freebase Cocaine; or Yet Another Unobtrusive Test of Reference Performance." *The Reference Librarian* 25–26 (1989): 483–493.

DuMont, Rosemary. "Ethics in Librarianship: A Management Model." *Library Trends* 40 (fall 1991): 201–215.

Finks, Lee W. "Librarianship Needs a New Code of Professional Ethics." *American Libraries* 22 (January 1991): 84–92.

Foskett, D. J. "The Creed of a Librarian: No Politics, No Religion, No Morals." Paper given at North Western Group, Reference, Special, and Information Section, Manchester Literary and Philosophical Society House, Manchester, England (March 27, 1962).

Froehlich, Thomas J. "Ethical Considerations of Information Professionals." *Annual Review of Information Science and Technology (ARIST)* 27 (1992): 292. Medford, N.J.: Learned Information for ASIS, 1992.

Green, Russell G. and Susan L. Thomas. "The Immediate Effects of Media Violence on Behavior." 42 (1986): 7–27.

Harris, Michael. "The Purpose of the American Public Library." *Library Journal* 98 (September 15, 1973): 2509–2514.

Hauptman, Robert. "Professionalism or Culpability? An Experiment in Ethics." *Wilson Library Bulletin* 50 (1976): 626–627

Lindsey, Jonathan A. and Ann E. Prentice. *Professional Ethics and Librarians.* Phoenix: Oryx, 1985.

Rubin, Richard. *Human Resources Management in Libraries: Theory and Practice.* New York: Neal-Schuman, 1990.

Rubin, Richard E. and Thomas J. Froehlich. "Ethical Aspects of Library and Information Science." *Encyclopedia of Library and Information Science.* Vol. 58 (Supplement). New York: Marcel Dekker, 1996, 33–52.

Smith, Martha M. "Editorial," *North Carolina Libraries* (spring 1993): 4.

————. "Information Ethics: Freedom, Democracy, Responsibility." *North Carolina Libraries* (spring 1993): 6–8.

Society of American Archivists Council. "Code of Ethics for Archivists." 1992.

Vitell, Scott and Donald L. Davis. "Ethical Beliefs of MIS Professionals: The Frequency and Opportunity for Unethical Behavior." *Journal of Business Ethics* 9 (1990): 63–70.

# 9

# The Library as Institution: An Organizational View

Institutions, including libraries, cannot be conceived as independent and self-sufficient entities whose survival relies solely on the efficient internal operation of the organization. Libraries must be thought of as organisms whose purpose is to adapt, as all organisms do, to a constantly changing environment. As organizational theorists have noted, simply surviving is an essential purpose and focus of an organization, and in this complex social, political, and economic climate, this task is no less an issue for libraries. Among the many environmental factors threatening the library's survival are the rapidly increasing costs of library materials and human resources, the reluctance of the public to provide continued and increased support for libraries, the increase in the diversity and quantity of published materials, the pressure to acquire computerized systems and resources, and the increasing power of publishers to control access to the information they produce and hence to control the costs of such information (Young 1994).

Libraries, as Wilson (1984) has noted, are part of the *bibliographic sector* in our society. This sector is "the assemblage of institutions and organizations that collectively take the output of the publishing industry and try to make it accessible for public use" (p. 389). Members of this assemblage include not only libraries, but publishers, materials retailers and wholesalers, networks, and indexing and abstracting services. The purposes of this sector are to provide both intellectual and physical access to information (Wilson 1984). Libraries, of course, provide both services, but there are other organizations that compete with them, and the competition is becoming keener all the time. Libraries are under threat from many quarters. There is lack of money, lack of political support, social controversy arising from the materials and services that libraries provide, information competitors, changes in how information is produced and supplied, legal threats and constraints, personnel issues, demanding publics insisting on traditional and nontraditional materials and services, and technological changes that are altering the very function and structure of libraries themselves. It is crucial, then, to understand the many ways in which libraries are organized and to identify some of the major issues confronting them as organizations.

There are many ways in which contemporary libraries are organized, but no matter what form the organization takes, libraries are designed to perform certain basic functions. These include (1) selecting materials and developing collections, (2) ordering and acquiring materials, (3) making information available through document delivery, electronic delivery of information, and the provision of information-access mechanisms, (4) conserving and preserving materials, and (5) programming, including bibliographic and other forms of instruction in information access. Some libraries will place greater emphasis on some of these functions, and their organization may reflect these differences in emphasis.

In order to provide a general overview, the following discussion will emphasize a functional view of libraries as organizations. That is, it will attempt to identify the major functions that a library performs and the units that are traditionally responsible for those functions. Suffice it to say that other forms of organization such as matrix organizations have evolved. Their influence may increase in years to come.

## THE FUNCTIONAL ORGANIZATION OF LIBRARIES

For libraries to perform their essential functions, they are commonly divided into various units, with the number and types of units varying depending on the size and type of library. The units noted below are generally associated with those of a larger public library, although many other types of libraries also have them. Smaller libraries or libraries of different types may combine many functions within one unit. School library media centers, for example, tend to be very simple organizationally with few separate units; large university or public libraries are quite complex organizations and have many individual units.

Typically, the units in a library consist of boards of trustees, library administration, public-service units, and support-service units.

*Boards (of Trustees)*

In one fashion or another, most libraries are ultimately controlled by a board. Most direct board control is exercised directly in a public library where the chief administrator reports to an elected or appointed board of trustees. Boards generally possess the statutory authority to operate the library, as well as other organizational functions, as in the case of schools, academic institutions, and special libraries. The primary purpose of boards is to establish policies, strategic plans, goals, and directions for the library. In academic libraries, school library media centers, and special libraries, the control by the board is less direct in that the directors of these libraries generally report to other administrators, such as an academic dean, principal, or department head.

*Library Administration*

The administration includes the director and other individuals such as the treasurer, assistant or associate directors, and heads of administrative departments such as personnel, planning, and information systems. These individuals are responsible for the overall operation of the library. They contribute to policy creation, enforce those policies, administer personnel practices, conduct fiscal operations, and carry out planning functions.

*Public Service Units*

Many of the library departments are responsible for providing services and materials directly to the users. In addition, these departments often have direct responsibility for the selection of materials in their units. Each unit usually has at least one individual at the management level. The purpose of management levels in libraries is usually to oversee units that perform specific service functions either directly or indirectly. Supervision of staff, participation in budgeting, and planning are often involved, as well as providing direct public service in many instances. Examples of management levels include heads of individual branches, departments, or divisions. There are several public service units:

*Reference Department*: This department's primary purpose is to meet the information needs of users. As a rule, the reference staff deal with user-initiated inquiries. Today, the department might be called an "Information Division," "Information Center," or like term. Depending on the size of the library and its service philosophy, a library may have a single department responsible for giving information service to patrons or there may be many such departments. Reference departments are usually subdivided by subject (history, science, business), although they also are organized by age or other characteristics of the user (children, adults, young adult [YA], blind or visually impaired), or by geography (branches or decentralized libraries). The services they provide might include, but are not limited to, answering information questions from manual or automated sources, reader's advisory, assistance in locating materials, interpreting materials, preparing guides, instruction on how to use materials and services in the library (bibliographic instruction), maintenance of reference files, and conducting tours and programs. Reference staff may also select materials for the department and the library. In addition to these functions, reference librarians in school library media centers may offer story times for children either in the library or in classrooms.

*Circulation Department (Access Services)*: The term circulation implies the activity of dispensing or receiving library materials. The term coming into more popular use is "access services". No matter what it is called, its concern is the flow of materials and control over the conditions under which materials are used. The most common activities are checking materials out, receiving returned materials, and administering fines and procedures for late or lost materials. Circulation staff may also have control over periodicals, interlibrary loans, and materials held for restricted use (e.g., reserve files in an academic library).

*Audiovisual (AV) Department*: With the growth in the popularity and variety of audiovisual materials, many libraries have separate AV departments. These departments include both materials and AV equipment and sometimes advice on AV programming. Organizationally, not all AV materials are necessarily included in this division. For example, music compact disks might still be found in a music or fine arts department, while videocassettes and 16mm films might be found in an AV department.

*Archives and Special Collections*: This department deals with records that are of local or general historical importance. In addition, it often deals with materials that are considered rare or especially fragile. The size and scope of special collections departments vary tremendously. Research libraries (special, public, or academic) with special collections in specific areas are more likely to have actual departments that house, manage, and preserve the collection.

*Special Services*: Some libraries have departments that are designed to serve special clientele. For example, there may be departments for the blind or visually impaired. Other departments may be designed for those who are physically unable to come to the library, such as services to prisons or jails, service to nursing homes, or home visits. Bookmobile service could also be considered in this category.

*Support*

There are also units in libraries that perform essential functions that are not, in themselves, providing direct service to the users. These support services, however, are needed if the library is to perform its service function. These units include the following:

*Technical Services*: Technical services staff perform the task of receiving and preparing materials so that they can be effectively accessed. This unit is responsible for maintaining publishers' and vendors' catalogs, acquiring materials, monitoring acquisition expenditures, preparing materials for use, e.g., cataloging, classification, bar coding. It may also perform managerial functions such as assisting in negotiations with vendors and publishers. Technical services staff may also be responsible for conservation and preservation of library materials. The level of sophistication for preservation and conservation vary considerably. Most public or school libraries have only rudimentary means for repair of materials. In constrast, the preservation and conservation units in major university libraries may be quite elaborate with means for deacidification or encapsulation of rare or otherwise special materials.

*Maintenance*: Probably the least-visible and least-appreciated unit of a library is that of maintenance. This department ensures that the physical facilities operate smoothly and are appealing. The functions may vary considerably but generally include cleaning and housekeeping, maintaining and landscaping of grounds, heating, plumbing and electrical repair, and constructing displays. In small libraries, the maintenance department may perform some security functions as well.

*Public Relations*: Public-relations units are intended to provide an important conduit for communication to the public and to listen to the public about the library. Among its functions are the preparation of promotional materials for library programs and agencies; systemwide programming activities; grant-writing; and the managing of communication with the public; media; political, civic, and religious leaders; and taking on crisis management when controversies arise.

*Security*: The need for a specific unit on security varies with the environment and nature of the community. Security problems can arise on a continuum from minor nuisances to major felonies. Security maintains a reasonably safe environment for users and staff. Its functions extend to patrolling the premises; protecting library property by monitoring users on the premises and when they exit; dealing with difficult or problem users; and contacting additional safety forces needed.

*Integrated Systems*: A relatively new unit has emerged in some libraries with the increasing integration of technologies into all aspects of library service. Given the fiscal and human resources now devoted to information technologies, it has become clear that the need to coordinate the acquisition and use of such technologies is vital. For this reason, some libraries have created a separate department or appointed a specific individual to be responsible for these technologies. Generally, this unit deals with such activities as participating in the evaluation and selection of information technologies, training staff, and trouble-shooting technological problems.

## THE ORGANIZATION OF AUTHORITY IN LIBRARIES

The structure of organizations can also be understood in terms of sources of authority. Authority is the power to command or influence others. In most organizations, including libraries, there are usually three types of authority: bureaucratic, professional, and informal.

## Bureaucratic Authority

The primary organizational structure of most libraries is bureaucratic. In a bureaucracy, one conceives of an organization as a group of formal positions that exist independently from the individuals who fill them. Different people may occupy these positions, but the positions themselves exist to fulfill basic organizational functions. Each bureaucratic position has at least three elements: (1) a set of clearly defined responsibilities; (2) an appropriate level of authority to meet these responsibilities; and (3) a set of clearly defined qualifications required for the individual to properly fill the position. In a bureaucracy, it is the responsibility of organizational leaders to rationally and objectively locate individuals who can satisfy the needs of the specific position. Personal considerations or any considerations unrelated to the required skills are to be ignored.

Within the bureaucratic structure, positions are arranged so their relationship to each other is clear. The most common arrangement is pyramidal and hierarchical. In such arrangements, a set of positions of similar character and authority report to a smaller number of positions of higher authority. For example, a group of reference librarians may report to the "head" of the reference department, the heads of various departments report to a "director." This hierarchical relationship is sometimes referred to as a "scalar chain of command." As the positions occupy a higher level in the hierarchy, the number of positions diminishes until there is a single position at the top (the director). In smaller organizations, the pyramid has far fewer levels and is therefore "flatter."

Bureaucratic authority rests on position rather than on the technical skills of the individual, and a bureaucracy relies on the authority to impose sanctions to get subordinates to obey (Lynch 1978). Individuals who leave a particular position no longer have the authority that is derived from it.

## Professional Authority

Examining authority purely from a bureaucratic perspective provides an incomplete picture. Within the library bureaucracy is a professional activity—librarianship. Librarians derive professional authority by virtue of their expertise. Professional authority has evolved, in part, as a counterbalance to the profit-oriented traditions spawned in the factory system of the nineteenth century (Winter 1988). As Winter has observed,

... professionalization is a way of dealing with the more immediate challenges of bureaucratic authority, in the everyday sense of fighting off the attempts of business to invade spheres of professional practice ... (p. 13).

Similarly, Lynch (1978) characterizes this to some extent as a clash of ends: the purpose of bureaucracies is to increase organizational efficiency; the purpose of professionals is the provision of superior service, i.e., effectiveness. This inevitably leads to internal frictions as librarians clamor for more services and materials, and bureaucrats resist on the basis of lack of resources. Bureaucratic authority clashes with professional authority when administrators make decisions that actually require professional, as well as administrative, expertise. Staff may, in fact, reject, sabotage, or otherwise make the work situation difficult if they believe that formal authority is being used by individuals to make decisions that lie outside their intellectual and professional ken. This is not, however, to suggest that all bureaucrats lack professional knowledge or care less about service. It does suggest, however, that the bureaucratic character of managerial or administrative positions themselves involve different perspectives and concerns that lead to inevitable frictions with professional positions designed to deliver services.

*Informal Authority*

The third type of authority arises from the informal, social relationships among staff. It is defined by the persuasiveness of the individual or group or the personal relationship of that individual or group to those who are more powerful. These informal relationships are referred to as the "informal organization." Sometimes individuals or groups can be more powerful than the formal authority structures or than their expertise would warrant. Because libraries are labor intensive there is a relatively complex set of social relationships that define which individuals or groups are influential and which are less so. There is no reason to presume, however, that informal authority always works against the interests of those with formal authority.

*Is Bureaucracy the Best Way to Organize Libraries?*

One of the most common issues for discussion regarding the organization of libraries is whether a bureaucratic structure is best for library service. Hierarchical structures persist primarily for three reasons: (a) administrators believe that changes in traditional decision-making structure can lead to chaos; (b) they believe that participatory decision-making produces mediocre choices, and (c) participation is seen by administrators as an abdication of their responsibility (Euster 1990). Although these reasons are not entirely without sense, do they represent convincing reasons for preserving a structure that may be unresponsive to the organizational needs of the future?

Some theorists suggest that bureaucratic structures are only best in organizations that exist in stable and predictable environments. In such an environment, where the dangers of and demands on the organization are predictable, features such as written rules and standardized procedures and practices are appropriate. In these settings, a methodical, deliberate, and centralized decision-making process is also appropriate. However, if the environment is unstable and the threats less predictable, it is necessary to be much more sensitive to environmental changes and to react to these changes quickly and effectively. To do this, more power has to be invested in those parts of the organization that are in close contact with the environment itself; this would generally be units that deal directly with "customers" (users) and that are constantly on the watch for new developments, such as new technologies or competitors. In such environments, decentralized authority seems more appropriate.

Euster (1990) argues that the increasing complexity of librarianship makes the traditional hierarchical structure obsolete, that "leadership and expertise must reside at all levels of the organization not just among designated leaders" (p. 41). No longer can one individual be expected to be sufficiently knowledgeable to make the necessary decisions. There is a need for the effective exchange of information among all individuals. The system must be designed to coordinate and share information so that decision-making can be a joint process. Euster refers to the sharing of information for decision-making, usually via automated systems, as "informating" the organization. Such systems convey critical information to the relevant parts of the organization so that decisions are made by whoever has the most information (p. 43).

Alternative organizational structures have been proposed that tend to decentralize decision-making. Most notably, Martell (1983) has proposed a "client-centered" organization for academic libraries that tailors the structure directly to the needs of the users rather than to the needs of the bureaucracy. We must begin to think anew about how libraries are organized. How well a library functions should be assessed by its ability to adapt to the changing and increasing demands of the environment in which it operates. Given the remarkable technological transformation occurring, it is likely that only structures that can respond rapidly and sensitively will survive and prosper in the years to come.

## ORGANIZATION OF LIBRARIES BY TYPE

Another approach to library organization is to examine the various types: public, academic, school, and special. Although it is a convenient way of looking at libraries, it must be noted that within a given type there may be tremendous variation. The *American Library Directory* (1999) breaks down the number of libraries as seen in Figure 9–1.

### Public Libraries

The public library in the United States represents a unique contribution to the dissemination of knowledge to citizens. There are few countries that can boast of a tradition comparable to the historical contribution that this institution has made to create an informed citizenry. Public libraries have been part of American life for nearly 150 years, with the first large public library established in Boston in the 1850s (see Chapter 7). Today there are more than 9,000 public libraries in the United States, and more than 16,000 outlets when branch libraries are included. Total library collections exceed more than 711 million books and serial volumes, and more than 30 million audio and visual materials. Total oper-

---

**Figure 9–1**
**Number of Libraries in the United States**

| | |
|---|---|
| Public libraries | 16,213 |
| Public libraries excluding branches | 9,837 |
| Public library branches | 6,376 |
| Academic libraries | 4,723 |
| Junior college libraries | 1,274 |
| University and college libraries | 3,449 |
| Special libraries including law, medical, and religious libraries | 13,734 |
| School and media center libraries | 91,587 |

ating income exceeds $5.8 billion, 78 percent of which comes from local funding, and only 1 percent from federal sources (*Digest of Education Statistics* 1998; NCES 1996).

Public libraries, almost since their inception, have possessed certain characteristics as organizations. Although these characteristics in and of themselves are not unique, taken as a whole, they define this particular organizational nature. Public libraries

1. are created by public law through enabling legislation and local statutes;
2. tend to be independent of other governmental bodies and run by boards appointed or elected to serve the entire community;
3. are voluntary institutions;
4. are open to all;
5. are supported by public funding, usually property or income taxes. Today, the largest percentage comes from local taxes (about 80 percent), with much smaller amounts coming from the state (15 percent), and even smaller amounts from the federal government. There are exceptions, such as Ohio, where the vast proportion of funding comes from the state income tax, but this is a rarity; and public libraries
6. focus on service to the individual.

The broad-based public support that public libraries receive is not surprising. Americans are heavy users of their libraries. Despite the fact that public libraries are not used by all cross-sections of the American population in equal proportion, there are millions of library users circulating millions of items and asking millions of reference questions each year. The National Center for Educational Statistics (1996) reported more than one billion public library visits in 1996, with patrons circulating more than 1.6 billion items. A Louis Harris national survey of 2,254 adults conducted in 1990 showed just how heavy public library use is in the United States. Two out of three of those interviewed (66 percent) indicated that they had used the services of a public library in the past year, and 42 percent of these had used the service twelve or more times a year (Westin and Finger 1991). Some studies have demonstrated somewhat less use. In 1996, the National Center for Education Statistics (1997) reported on the 1996 National Household Education Survey, which is an annual survey on educational issues. The 1996 survey included specific questions on public library use. The study revealed that 44 percent of U.S. households had at least one individual who had used the public library in the previous month. It also reported that 65 percent of the households had used the public library in the last year. Again, there are other studies that have reported somewhat less use, but it is clear that annual library use is well above use in the past, which was closer to 10 percent. As a rule, the more frequent users are under fifty years of age, with at least a high school education and, more commonly, some college education. Generally, as income levels increase, so does library use; and whites are more likely to use libraries than African Americans or Hispanics. Nonetheless, the Harris data suggest that library use is considerable among minorities, with 58 percent of African Americans and 62 percent of the Hispanics indicating library use in the previous year (Westin and Finger 1991). Public library use also tends to increase in families with children (NCES 1997).

The National Household Education Survey also revealed that the most common use of the library was for enjoyment or hobbies (32 percent); followed by getting information for personal use, such as health or consumer material (20 percent); or using the library for school assignments (19 percent) (NCES 1997).

The organizational goal of the public library is broad—perhaps overly broad. This goal can be stated simply: to meet the informational, recreational, educational, and cultural needs of the community it serves. Although the goal can be stated simply, it is another matter to try to satisfy it. Its comprehensiveness taxes library resources and can lead to an unfocused use of these resources. The Public Library Association (PLA) has made attempts to help public libraries focus their goals through its public-library planning process. PLA has recommended that libraries select only a few basic roles from eight possibilities, and in this way they have a means of focusing their resources and energies (Palmour 1980). These roles include the following:

> *Community-Activities Center*: The library is a central focus point for community activities, meetings, and services.
>
> *Community-Information Center*: The library is a clearinghouse for current information on community organizations, issues, and services.
>
> *Formal Education-Support Center*: The library assists students of all ages in meeting educational objectives established during their formal courses of study.
>
> *Independent-Learning Center*: The library supports individuals of all ages who are pursuing a sustained program of learning on an independent basis.
>
> *Popular-Materials Library*: The library features current, high-demand, high-interest materials in a variety of formats for persons of all ages.

*Preschoolers' Door to Learning*: The library encourages young children to develop an interest in reading and learning through services for children and for children with their parents or caregivers.

*Reference Library*: The library actively provides timely, accurate, and useful information for community residents.

*Research Center*: The library assists scholars and researchers who conduct in-depth studies, investigate specific areas of knowledge, and create new knowledge (Palmour 1980, p. 28).

Obviously, the missions or groups of missions a library chooses may reflect the type of community that it serves. For this reason, one is likely to find a research mission selected by only the largest of public libraries where there is a business, technological, academic, and scientific infrastructure that would use these types of resources regularly. Suburban libraries or libraries located in small cities and towns are more likely to emphasize popular materials for the community and materials that support the education of the young. However, these generalities are not hard and fast, and certainly libraries can and do maintain multiple missions.

MAJOR ISSUES CONFRONTING PUBLIC LIBRARIES

*The political climate.* The inherently political nature of public librarianship is often overlooked and greatly underestimated, but it is a vital part of a public library's survival. The political considerations are not necessarily partisan—often they are quite the opposite as public library administrators attempt to preserve a nonpartisan and effective working relationship with the various political groups. The political character of public librarianship is further reinforced, in that public libraries rely almost entirely on public monies to finance their operations, and library board members are often appointed by local political powers. Balancing the various political interests is a complex and challenging task. Consider the various interests that are concerned with public library resources: the business community, governmental agencies and legislative bodies, schools and other educational institutions, religious groups, clubs and civic organizations, and parents. The expectations of each of these groups vary. These factors, coupled with increasing financial strains and a social climate that is often antagonistic to public institutions in general make the political complexities of running the public library considerable.

*Financial stresses.* There are a variety of factors combining to make life difficult for the public library. Decreasing public support for most public institutions is an obvious problem. Projections by the federal government suggest that public funding on the local and state level is expected to remain static or even decline in the near future. There have been many states, including major ones like California and New York, that have suffered serious drops in public support for libraries, leading to reduction in hours and staffing. Other sources of financial stress include the increasing prices of traditional library materials, especially periodicals, and additional costs incurred by use of the new information technologies. The costs of CD-ROM subscriptions and computer software and hardware are considerable. These costs, coupled with static budgets, make the burden on public library service tremendous. Attempts to save money and improve operational efficiency has led to the first example of "outsourcing" a public library to a private vendor. In 1997, Library Systems and Services, Inc., located in Maryland, took over the operations of the Riverside County Public Library System in California ("Riverside County . . . ", 1997). Whether this will become a more common practice is yet to be seen.

*The introduction of new information technologies.* The introduction of new information technologies creates more than financial challenges. Public library services, physical structures, and organizational charts are all being redesigned as information technologies permit an entirely new way of accessing information on a local, regional, national, and global scale. CD-ROMs have transformed traditional index-searching into a far more comprehensive activity, including access to the full text of materials. Not only do such technologies cost a great deal, they require staff and patron training and may result in significantly increased demands for materials. No less important, the development of the national information infrastructure (NII), as well as local, state, and regional networks, opens vast amounts of information to libraries through cooperative agreements. How this will affect collection development, materials selection, fee structures, and access issues is yet to be determined. There is mounting evidence that the citizenry expect their public libraries to integrate electronic technologies into their services. A survey by the Benton Foundation (1996) found that 60 percent of the respondents considered it very important for the public library to provide computers and online services, especially to those who do not have their own computers. Nearly the same percentage (58 percent) felt the librarians should have access to such services so that they can assist library patrons.

There is little doubt that the costs of both equipment and technical expertise will be considerable for public libraries. To this end the Microsoft Corporation, in cooperation with the ALA, has taken steps to assist public libraries in providing access to the Internet. As early as 1995, Microsoft began a pilot program known as Libraries Online, which was intended to help public libraries gain access to digital information. This was accomplished by donating the funds to obtain the necessary information technologies, as well as providing technical training. This program reached more than 200 libraries thoughout the United States. In 1997 this concept was expanded by Bill Gates, the founder of Microsoft, and his wife, Melinda French Gates. They established the Gates Library Foundation, which was intended to promote the public library as a key access point for all citizens of the United States and Canada. A five-year mission with two initiatives has been established for the foundation: "(1) Work with underserved public libraries in low-income areas to provide the hardware and software required for community access to digital information; (2) Support and train library staffs to access and manage digital information and to maintain and expand their systems as their patrons and communities require (Gates Library Foundation 1997, p. 1). The foundation intends to distribute approximately $200 million in cash and an additional $200 million in equipment over the next five years ("Gates Foundation to Invest . . . " 1997). The grants will be awarded to statewide partnerships, libraries in urban areas serving low-income residents, and individual libraries.

The new technologies may also create new libraries that serve as public libraries but are not physical structures in the traditional sense. For example, based originally on a classroom project at the University of Michigan School of Information, the Internet Public Library (IPL) was created. The IPL subsequently received funding from the W.K. Kellogg Foundation and the Andrew W. Mellon Foundation ("Internet Public Library: Same Metaphors . . . " 1997). The mission of IPL was to provide free services to the Internet community including both adults and children, and to teach librarians how the digital environment can be exploited (Internet Public Library 1997). It is a twenty-four-hour online service with text files organized by Dewey classification with subject access as well as links to other services and libraries. IPL offers special services to teens and children. More than 3,700 text items were available by February 1997. A small number of reference questions are also answered. The objective of IPL is not to replace local libraries, but to serve as a traditional library model enhanced by the capacities of the Internet ("Internet Public Library: Same Metaphors . . . " 1997).

*Censorship issues.* Attempts to restrict access to materials or remove them is hardly new to public libraries. But the current social climate suggests that citizens are becoming even more active in monitoring access to materials and services in public libraries. Interestingly, challenges are not only being made to individual items, but to the policies of libraries that permit controversial items to be selected and retained. In particular, there have been specific attacks on ALA, especially the ALA Library Bill of Rights, because it is perceived by some as an organization that is influential in developing individual public-library policy. Censorship attacks on individual libraries are now including concomitant challenges to the authority of ALA. The result is that public librarians are forced not only to defend their own libraries, but also their professional association. Attempts to accommodate those who are unhappy with libraries' intellectual-freedom policies have led some librarians to compromise by restricting access or eliminating materials. The problem is likely to become worse as access to the Internet or NII in public libraries becomes commonplace. Because some of the resources on the Internet contain sexually explicit material, for example, librarians are trying to find ways to deal with access to such material. These issues will be a persistent problem for libraries.

*The quality versus demand problem.* The breadth of a public library's mission makes it difficult to determine exactly how the mission should be implemented. An important area for decision making is selection and collection development, and one issue in particular prompts frequent and sometimes intense discussion. This involves the extent to which libraries purchase high circulation materials of limited and ephemeral value versus their purchase of materials of lasting, educational value, even if these items are only rarely consulted. The most typical example of popular materials is the purchase of popular fiction and romances. This controversy is commonly referred to as the *quality versus demand* debate. It is not simply a black and white issue; public libraries order both highly popular materials and those that may be less popular but of more long-term value. Nonetheless, a great deal of money can be spent on popular or ephemeral materials, and the degree to which libraries emphasize one aspect over the other can substantially affect the allocation of resources.

Some of the fundamental arguments in support of acquiring a large number of highly popular materials are (1) these materials are heavily used, indicating that the library is meeting the demand of its community's needs; (2) these materials provide important diversion and entertainment, which is a valid and valuable purpose of public libraries; (3) high circulation is an important indicator of a library's success; and (4) high circulation assists the library in obtaining popular political support.

Arguments that emphasize the purchase of educational and less ephemeral materials include (1) the library is primarily an educational institution, not an entertainment one, hence collections should emphasize materials of lasting educational value; (2) high demand is artificially created by mass-market publishers, and libraries should not cater to what is basically a marketing campaign of popular publishers; (3) libraries have a duty to serve individual tastes and not cater to mass-market appetites; (4) there is already too much emphasis on circulation statistics, which promote the purchase of ephemeral popular materials. There are other important uses of libraries, such as in-house use of educational or reference materials, that are often ignored, yet support the selection of educational material; (5) mass-market materials have a degrading effect on the public's intellect (Bob 1982; Rawlinson 1981). As public library budgets remain tight, the allocation of scarce resources requires that libraries answer important questions about their primary functions so that they may make these allocations wisely.

*Service to multicultural populations.* As the United States population becomes increasingly heterogeneous ethnically and racially, the public library continues to diversify its library services. It is clear that various ethnic and racial groups have unique information needs and may require special services or approaches tailored to these needs. The history of the public library has been uneven in the service of these groups. Some public libraries have not been welcoming; they have been, as Harris (1973) has described, cold, authoritarian institutions. On the other hand, by the turn of the century, public libraries had developed specific programs for various immigrant, racial, and ethnic groups. The adaptation of public libraries to the needs of minority and ethnic populations faces many barriers. DuMont, Buttlar, and Caynon (1994) have identified a variety of these barriers to multicultural services: shortages of resources, lack of multicultural staff, tensions between staff and members of ethnic and racial groups, lack of understanding of other cultures, competing demands among ethnic and racial groups, staff resentment toward the creation of new programs, lack of patron knowledge of libraries, and lack of time. Resolutions to these barriers require increased attempts to recruit minority librarians, greater staff development and training in services to various racial and ethnic groups, improved needs assessments, promotion and target marketing of library services, more support for research on service to ethnic and racial groups, and consideration of minority and ethnic populations in the design and implementation of library services.

*Children's and Young Adult (YA) Services.* One of the great challenges of public library service is providing services to the young. The public is a great supporter of such public-library services. A recent survey of adults found that 83 percent believed it was very important for the library to provide story hours and other children's programming (Benton Foundation 1996). Generally, services to youth are broken down into those serving children and those for young adults (YA), although the boundary line between them is often hard to distinguish and arbitrarily drawn. Nonetheless, it is clear that at their extremes they represent very different groups. The magnitude of children's and YA services is often underestimated. Approximately half of all public library users are under the age of eighteen, and about 25 percent are between the ages of twelve and eighteen (NCES 1988). A substantial portion, more than one-third, of all public library circulation is that of children's materials (Wright 1996), and children tend to take out more materials than the general population. In addition, more than three-fourths of attendees at library programs are children (Zweizig 1993). Despite this considerable participation, one-fifth of the public libraries serving populations over 1,000 lack a children's librarian, and only 11 percent have designated YA librarians (NCES 1988). In addition, despite the clear benefits of reading and library use for children, youngsters between nine and fourteen spend a little more than 1 percent of their waking hours reading, while they spend nearly 21 percent of their time watching television (Carnegie Corporation 1993).

What then are some of the major trends and challenges facing children's librarians?

> *Demographic changes:* Public libraries serve their communities, and over the years the demographics of these communities have changed. Most notably, they have become more racially and ethnically diverse. In addition, the social and family structure of the American family has changed. Many more children are living in single-parent and intergenerational families. Among adolescents between ages ten and seventeen, 20 percent of the whites, 30 percent of Hispanics, and 50

percent of African Americans live in single-parent families. More than a fifth of these youngsters live in poverty or near poverty. Even in two-parent families, 60 percent of the mothers have jobs in the labor force (U.S. Bureau of the Census 1991). The children from these families sometimes have different experiences from those of children in the "traditional" family, in which the father went to work and the mother stayed home with the children. As a consequence, children's services, collections, and programs are expected to respond sensitively to these changes. In terms of children's services this means that collections and services reflect the racial and ethnic realities with which these children deal or reflect alternative family structures. The effect has not only been in the collections, but in programming. Emphases on programs for latch-key children or "children-at-risk" have become more common.

*Proliferation in the variety of quality of children and YA materials*: Providing an up-to-date children's- and YA-book collection has become a central challenge for public libraries. There is little question that children's book publishing is one of the healthier segments of the publishing marketplace, and the result has been a marked proliferation in the number and variety of children's and YA materials. There are about 3,000–5,000 books published each year for children and YAs in the United States, many of increasingly high production quality. The number of children's authors and illustrators has also climbed correspondingly. Today, market segmentation has become so great that there are retail stores that specialize only in children's and YA materials. Similarly, the breadth and depth of various subject areas has substantially increased. These include works in a variety of formats including "pop-up" books. Many of these works, especially those for young children, are brilliantly illustrated using printing technologies that make the illustrated page a feast for youngsters' eyes. Fiction has grown in subject depth as well, confronting difficult situations including drug-abuse, suicide, and divorce. Surprisingly, these subjects have been prepared not only for older children, but for young ones as well, e.g., *Let's Talk About It: Divorce*, by Fred Rogers (1996).

Nonfiction has also seen growth in size and quality. Many of the new nonfiction works are well-researched, well-written works, prepared by knowledgeable authors reflecting a multicultural perspective. There are, for example, far more biographies of minority individuals and women. Books for children in the sciences have also proliferated and include new or newly adapted illustration techniques (pop-up science books!) and even incorporate computer chips that emulate sounds. Picture books for very young children have been written on a wide range of subjects with exceptional artistic and literary merit. All this is good news, but the growth of these materials has placed significant burdens on collection development budgets. Children's librarians must decide if they are going to purchase multiple copies of materials or try to purchase just one of many titles. As the cost of children's materials rises so does the cost of the current collection.

*Advocacy for children's services*: The needs for children and young adult library services are manifest to librarians, but unfortunately not so obvious to many others. For this reason, the American Library Association (1996) developed the "Library Advocacy Now" program, which advocates a strong proactive stance in support of children's services. Included in the obligations of librarians is providing increased support and library services, educating parents about the benefits of libraries to kids, and ensuring that all libraries are able to access the information superhighway.

*Growth of services to special groups, preschoolers, and home-schoolers*: Libraries are developing special programs for infants (lap-sit programs), toddlers, preschoolers, primary schoolers, and young adults. These programs also extend to alternative educational programs such as programs for homeschoolers who depend heavily on public libraries to act as their "school" library. Homeschooling groups can be quite demanding on public libraries and a careful balance must be struck to ensure that children's collections represent all of the needs of the community. Children's librarians are also providing training and resources to caregivers or parents who then can better employ library resources to the benefit of their children. Ultimately, libraries must devote considerable energy to developing a wide array of programs throughout the year and throughout the day and evening to accommodate the heterogeneous nature of our society. All of these functions are costly and time consuming.

*The growth of electronic materials for children*: In addition to the proliferation of materials, there is a marked increase in the variety of formats being developed for children and YA use. Most notable are developments in electronic-information technologies. Computers have become an everyday part of children's experience. CD-ROM technologies have produced a vast array of information products for young people including electronic encyclopedias and other reference materials and educational and entertainment games often modelled after successful children's books. These works provide interactive capabilities, sound, and motion. Their attractiveness to young people gives the library considerable impetus to purchase and promote their use. Regrettably, they are also very costly. Costs include not only the software, but the computer hardware, other peripherals, and furniture or work stations. Similarly, a growing number of these materials are accessible through the Internet. Librarians are thus confronted with completely new challenges of identifying these Internet sites and making them known and available to children. Public libraries are hard-pressed to find both the fiscal and physical resources to accommodate these new developments, and they are also faced with providing the training to keep their staff members up-to-date.

*Outreach*: The changing family structure has challenged libraries to consider moving outside the four walls of their buildings to provide alternative library services. For example, with the increasing number of families in which both parents work, there has been a proliferation of daycare and preschool programs. This is an opportunity for children's and YA librarians to network with outside agencies: schools, Head Start programs, daycare centers, and other agencies that work with young people. Some public libraries are sending their library professionals into these establishments to provide programs that were traditionally provided only at the library. Similarly, some libraries are preparing predesigned kits of print and AV materials that can be borrowed by various agencies serving children at remote sites. No doubt, this type of outreach is vitally important, but it is also costly in terms of personnel and time. Nonetheless, children's need for library materials is critical. If children cannot come to the library, then librarians have made a commitment to bring materials and services to them.

*Intellectual Freedom*: The issues of censorship and intellectual freedom are always at the forefront of library services to children and young adults, and the problem has been exacerbated by the increasing use of electronic networks, especially the Internet. This issue will be discussed in more detail in the following section on school library media centers. It should be kept in mind, however, that in terms of intellectual freedom, the public library differs fundamentally from school library media centers in at least two important ways:

(1) Public libraries do not serve *in loco parentis*, that is, in the place of the parent. As a consequence, they have more freedom in the dissemination of materials to young people. By the same token, parents and some political groups are putting considerable pressure on public libraries to act as monitors and censors.

(2) Public libraries contain materials primarily published or produced for adults. School library media centers seldom have adult materials, except those for teachers, on their shelves. Given ALA policy on open access to public library materials, there is considerable concern about children's reading, viewing, or hearing material that has been prepared for adults. The intensity of this issue is likely to increase, not only because of the increasingly graphic nature of violence and sexual activity in visual and audio materials, but also because access has been expanded even more through the availability of the Internet in public libraries. The political and legal tensions that are sure to arise will require ever more vigilance on the part of librarians to protect the rights of minors to library materials. To some extent, ALA has tried to accommodate the concerns of parents and other adults by establishing a Web Site that links over 700 educational and recreational sites for parents and their children ("ALA Launches . . . " 1998).

*Public library–school library media center cooperation*: As the challenges of providing library service to diverse communities and family structures continues, cooperation between public libraries and schools becomes even more important. Cooperative programs can include class visits by school librarians, extended loans to teachers, coordination of curricular units with available public-library materials, provision of library instruction and library tours to students by public librarians, and participation of public and school librarians on joint education-related committees. Despite the obvious advantages of school-public library cooperation, there are also factors that tend to inhibit cooperation:

1. Because schools and public libraries are often separate political sub-divisions, a concerted effort must be made to promote coopera-tion.
2. There is little or no administrative or board support for coopera-tion.
3. Schools (classrooms and libraries) and public libraries tend to be understaffed; teachers and librarians focus their time and atten-tion primarily on the duties within their own institutions.
4. Limited fiscal resources reduce the time and staffing available for cooperation.
5. Public librarians are sometimes suspicious that their cooperation is really being used as an inappropriate subsidy of the school budget. That is, the public library budget is being used to support services that should be provided by the school budget.
6. There is insufficient expertise to develop effective cooperation.

## School Library Media Centers

The term "school library media center" can take on many meanings and comes under many additional names such as "school library" or "me-dia center." Organizationally, these terms refer to the same type of orga-nization, which is defined by the American Association of School Li-brarians (AASL, a division of ALA) and the Association of Educational and Communication Technology (AECT) in the following way:

> A school library media center is defined as an organized collection of printed and/or audiovisual and/or computer resources which (a) is administered as a unit, (b) is located in a designed place or places, (c) makes resources and services accessible and available to students, teach-ers, and administrators (Ingersoll and Han 1994, p. 8).

In a general sense, the school library media center has one central function—to support the curriculum of the school. The fiscal and hu-man resources are directed to this end. There are many secondary, albeit important, functions that the school library media center performs as well. It stimulates the imagination of children, it promotes critical think-ing, it exposes children to diverse points of view on important topics, it provides exposure to the cultural differences that exist in the world, and it provides some entertaining diversions as well. The AASL, a leading representative of school library media specialists, has asserted that "the mission of the library media program is to ensure that students and staff are effective users of ideas and information" (ALA 1988, p. 1). This mission is effected in three ways: "by providing intellectual and physcial access to materials in all formats; by providing instruction to foster competence and stimulate interest in reading, viewing, and using information and ideas; [and] by working with other educators to design learning strategies to meet the needs of individual students" (ALA 1988, p. 1).

School library media centers are imbedded in much larger organizations. On one level, although there may be a school librarian who exercises immediate control, ultimate control and supervision of the library is the concern of the school's principal. Alternatively, school library media centers may be governed by a special administrator in charge of curriculum for the entire school system, who may be responsible for selection or approval of materials for all of the schools' library media centers. Finally, because school library media centers exist as part of the entire school system, they are governed by a school board, whose administrative powers are delegated to a school administration. This administration often consists of a superintendent and assistants. Although these individuals seldom get involved in direct supervision or control, they often become involved when there are complaints about materials.

The school library media centers in the United States have nineteenth-century origins, but there were actually very few of them until the twentieth century. Their development was accelerated in the twentieth century by many factors. In the 1920s impetus for school library media centers grew because of the development of regional accrediting agencies, which promoted the need for trained librarians (Woolls 1994). In the 1950s another push was given when the Soviet Union launched Sputnik. The successful placing of a satellite in space by the United States' rival created considerable social and political upheaval as Americans feared they would soon be militarily inferior to their adversary. The space race thus gave a strategic significance to efforts to improve the American educational system. One of the results was substantial increases in federal funding for elementary and secondary education, especially to improve curricula and the training of teachers. It was a logical extension to provide money to expand the library collections of these schools.

Expansion in the number of school library media center collections began in the 1960s. This decade saw the development of standards for elementary schools, support from private foundations to improve school library media centers, and strong political support. This resulted in the passage of the Elementary and Secondary Education Act (ESEA) in 1965, which provided federal support to purchase materials for schools and libraries. The ESEA is discussed in more detail in Chapter 3, but suffice it to say that it resulted in a tremendous expansion of school library media center collections.

The growth of school library media centers can be seen in the following table (NCES 1991):

### Figure 9–2
### Percentage of Schools with Library Media Centers

| Date | Public | Private |
|---|---|---|
| 1958 | 50 | NA |
| 1962 | 59 | 44 |
| 1974 | 85 | NA |
| 1978/79 | 85 | 83 |
| 1985 | 93 | 75 |
| 1990/91 | 96 | 87 |

**Source**: National Center for Education Statistics (NCES). *NCES Schools and Staff Survey, 1991, and Statistics of Public and Private School Library Media Centers. 1985–86.* Washington D.C.: U.S. DOE, 1991

The tremendous expansion in the percentage of schools with school library media centers is testimony to their vitality. Today, it is estimated that there are nearly 74,000 school library and media centers located in 95 percent of public schools and 86 percent of private schools have library/media centers. Nearly 97 percent of the elementary public schools have libraries, and 95 percent of the high schools (WHCLIS 1991; NCES, Schools and Staffing 1991 ). The size of the workforce in these libraries is considerable. There are nearly 59,000 librarians and 41,000 library aides working in public school library media centers alone. The picture is not, however, uniformly bright. For example, a quarter of all schools have no school librarian (ALA 1996). And even where there is a school librarian, the school library media center of today faces many organizational challenges.

ENSURING THAT THE LIBRARY PLAYS AN INTEGRAL ROLE IN THE FUNCTION OF
THE SCHOOL

If school library media centers are to thrive in the future, they must be recognized for their importance to the function of the school. Too often, the library is considered an expensive appendage to the educational process rather than an integral part. This is especially ironic, given the evidence of the relationship of school library media centers to academic achievement. Lance, Welborn, and Hamilton-Pennell (1993) found that students who score higher on norm-referenced tests tend to come from schools with larger library staff and larger collections. In addition, high academic performance of students was also correlated with school library media centers in which librarians served in an instructional and collaborative role. The size of the library staff and the collection were the best predictors of academic performance, with the exception of the presence of at-risk conditions such as poverty. This highlights the fact that school librarians need to communicate clearly and cooperate closely with teachers, principals, and administrators. By demonstrating the importance of the library and its ability to contribute to the school's mission, greater political and fiscal support is more likely to follow.

DEALING WITH THE INCREASES IN TECHNOLOGY

Schools have devoted considerable resources to educational technologies. In many ways they are leaders in this area. They have incorporated television as a part of classroom teaching for years. To this they have added laser discs, videocassettes, CD-ROMs, and computers, including access to the Internet. Computer use among primary and secondary students has increased considerably. For example, in 1997 student use of computers increased to 79 percent for grades 1–8, up from 69 percent in 1989; computer use increased to 70 percent (1993) for grades 9–12, up from 58 percent in 1993 (*Digest of Education Statistics* 1999). As technologies and technological use increase, the school library media center will have to respond in kind, meaning increasing demands in terms of costs, staffing, training, equipment, and physical facilities.

DEALING WITH DECLINING FUNDS IN SCHOOLS

There is little doubt that many citizens have limited confidence in their school systems. This, coupled with a general feeling among tax payers that they have been taxed enough, has led to a resistance to increasing their tax burden for the public schools. The damage to schools from this trend is magnified by the need for additional monies to accommodate the rapid changes in learning technologies and the proliferation of excellent print materials published today for young people. Because schools are undergoing financial strains, there is an understandable temptation to place existing resources directly into teaching along with classroom materials and activities. Such a reallocation merely increases the drain on dwindling school library media center financial resources.

DEALING WITH CENSORSHIP OF LIBRARY MATERIALS

There are few issues in librarianship that generate so much heat and so little light. Schools have traditionally been vulnerable to censorship attempts, especially because they are supposed to serve *in loco parentis*. The general issue of censorship is dealt with in the chapter "Information Policy as Library Policy," but schools represent, in some sense, a unique situation. Among the crucial issues that define school censorship problems are (1) the differing views of the function of schools and school library media centers; and (2) the rights and powers of school boards versus the rights of students and parents. These issues have been battled out in years of court cases, many of which have resulted in unclear or contradictory conclusions. This judicial ambivalence was highlighted in one of the most important school library media center cases, which reached the United States Supreme Court. This case is now referred to as the "Island Trees" case, or "Pico," named after Stephen Pico, the student who filed the complaint (Board of Education 1982). The purpose here is not to review in detail this particular case, or the legal issues *per se*, but to discuss briefly some of the fundamental issues raised by the legal and philosophical arguments found in the various cases.

*The functions of schools and school library media centers.* Defining the functions of schools can have profound consequences on how one perceives the functions of school library media centers. There are at least two fundamentally differing accounts. One can view the schools as a place to inculcate the values of the local community—the majority values. Such a view perceives the school as an instrument of particular values. Children, in this sense, are perceived as highly vulnerable to outside influences and need protection until they are old enough to know that these influences are problematic. Such a view is, in itself, not wholly unreasonable. It seems obvious that children do need protection from physical abuse, and some might argue that this is easily extended to intellectual harm as well. The purpose of schools is to inculcate the students with specific orthodox attitudes as well as basic knowledge. Exposure to unorthodox points of view would be undertaken only under conditions in which substantial control is exercised to ensure that the views are not mistakenly understood as acceptable or reasonable alternatives. From this perspective, the school library media center represents a potential problem. Most obvious is that the school library media center has traditionally been a place of voluntary attendance, where the materials are voluntarily selected by the student. Some guidance may be involved, but as a rule, there is considerably less guidance and control over exposure and interpretation of materials in the library than in the classroom. If the inculcation of values is to be effected, one function of the librarian or library worker would be to monitor each student's selections. In many cases, this is a practical impossibility. The alternative is that the library exercises very careful and restrictive selection of materials and, most likely, restrictive access to materials for some, usually younger, children.

The second perspective is to view the school as a place where students are exposed to a wide variety of points of view. The function of the school is to familiarize students with many perspectives, emphasize critical thinking skills and judgement-making skills. It is not the school's place, however, to assert a particular perspective or attempt to inculcate the specific values of the local or majority community. It attempts to prepare students to discriminate among ideas so they can make future judgements on important issues in which there are many differing opinions. The school library media center in this setting would likely function quite differently. The library collection would likely contain many perspectives, some unorthodox as well as orthodox, and the librarian's function would be less supervisory and controlling. Access would tend to be unrestricted.

These two perspectives have been painted here as polar opposites, although there are certainly many gradations that reflect the realities of school library media centers. All schools inculcate values, and all try to get students to think, more or less. But how one perceives a school's primary purpose is likely to affect one's attitude seriously when one hears that a book on suicide, one by a revolutionary, or books that contain explicit language about sex are part of the library collection. Those who subscribe to the former view are much more likely to restrict or control materials.

Similarly, even in schools in which the inculcation of local or majority values is paramount, a more subtle distinction might be made regarding its school library media center. One can perceive, for example, that the function of the classroom is different from the function of the school library media center. One can argue that the classroom is the place where values are inculcated and still believe that the school library media center's purpose is different, a place for exposure to a wide array of ideas, even those that are unorthodox. In this sense, the concept of the library carries with it the supposition that it is a special forum—a place where many different, even controversial and subversive, ideas may coexist. In this way, a distinction between classroom purposes and library purposes is possible. Obviously, if one perceives the library as a special forum for ideas, the library collection would predictably be more catholic in perspective, no matter what the defined purpose of the classroom.

*The rights of school boards and students (and parents?).* Censorship problems in schools also arise from the friction created by the conflicting authority of the school board and the rights of young people. Traditionally, school boards have exercised considerable legal authority and power in the United States. Generally, education falls primarily within the province of the states. States have delegated the authority to local school boards that have been given broad authority to run their school systems, including the selection of teachers, curricular materials, and materials for the school library media center. There is little doubt that school boards are responsible for school library media centers, but it is seldom their central focus. From time to time, school boards are surprised to discover that some of the materials on the school library media center shelf are not to their liking or the liking of parents. Problems usually arise when parents file objections to materials their children have selected from the school library media center. But objections also arise from principals, teachers, students, and school board members themselves. Sometimes, the school board acts autonomously without provocation. In one major national study, about 30 percent of the responding school librarians reported some type of challenge to their school library media center materials. The most frequent challenger was a parent (Association of American Publishers 1981). When challenges occur there is a tendency in many cases to restrict or withdraw the material, especially when there are no formal policies for selection and reconsideration of these materials.

The actions of school boards to remove or restrict materials may often go unchallenged. Although the rights of young people may be limited, the courts have recognized that students do not give up First Amendment rights and due-process rights just because they are in school. This highlights the delicate balance that must be struck in schools concerning the rights of school boards to run their schools as they see fit and the individual rights of citizens, including young people, to First Amendment and due-process protection. The balance is dynamic. As one court decision noted:

> A library is a storehouse of knowledge. When created for a public school it is an important privilege created by the state for the benefit of the students in the school. That privilege is not subject to being withdrawn by succeeding school boards whose members might desire to 'winnow' the library for books the content of which occasioned their displeasure or disapproval. (*Minarcini v Strongsville City School District*, 1977).

Similarly, in the *Island Trees* case, the Supreme Court noted that the school board members "possess significant discretion to determine the content of their school libraries" (Board of Education 1982, p. B3922). But the court also noted that the school board cannot exercise its discretion in a "narrowly partisan or political manner" (Board of Education, p. 3922). If the school board intended to deprive students of access to ideas just because the board didn't like those ideas, then the board was violating the constitutional rights of the students. Interestingly, the Supreme Court left open the possibility that the school board could remove materials that were "pervasively vulgar" or were educationally unsuitable, especially if the board followed a well-structured procedure to review and evaluate those materials.

The lack of clarity regarding the legal rights of boards, the place of the school library media center, and the rights of students literally ensures that more problems await on the horizon. The problem will be magnified as the library media center collections expand to include resources on the Internet. There is certainly plenty of dissent in our society regarding what is suitable material for young people, and the school library media center will remain a lightning rod of political controversy in this arena.

*Academic Libraries*

The academic library has been extant in the United States since the seventeenth century, beginning with the library at Harvard. There were nine colonial colleges with libraries by 1792, though the collections were quite small (Jones 1989). The model of classical learning in vogue at that time emphasized theology and required little "library" study. Well into the nineteenth century, the collections were too small to have a separate structure for the library, and the library collection was not emphasized in academic instruction. Often, professors, academic departments, and college debating societies maintained their own collections, which were superior to that of the academic library (Jones 1989). It wasn't until the latter half of the nineteenth century that academic libraries as we know them began to prosper. Their emergence was a result of a change in academic orientation, away from the classical model of education that emphasized religion, rhetoric, and the classics, and toward professional, technical and scientific, and social scientific education. This change was heavily influenced by European trends of industrialization and the promotion of the German model of the university, which identified research as a central role of the university. In the United States, its premier exponent was Johns Hopkins University, which set a model for other universities. As American higher education adapted to this model, the role of the library grew in status. It was a logical place to centralize research collections and provide a place for consultation of these materials. Over the years, support for developing academic libraries has come from outside as well as from within academic institutions, including the American Library Association and its division, the Association of College and Research Libraries, the Association of Research Libraries, and the federal government. The result has been the significant growth of academic library collections, the creation of separate library buildings, and increased staffing of these facilities. Today, the academic library plays a vital role in curricular support, teaching, research, publication and self-education on the part of students.

The term "academic" library is a generic one applying to many different varieties of institutions. Overall, a library is an academic one if it serves an educational institution providing a curriculum beyond the primary or secondary level. This would include universities, four-year colleges, and community and junior colleges. As with school library media centers, the academic library is embedded in a larger bureaucracy. Usually, the library is headed by a director or dean who reports directly to a higher level academic administrator. The academic library does not have an independent purpose; its functions are directly related to the function of the larger academic institution. In a general sense, its purpose is to serve the students and faculty of the academic community, and to a lesser extent the administration and staff of the institution and the greater academic community that exists nationally and internationally. In addition, the academic library may provide some service to the local community by way of making materials available to local citizens.

The type and sophistication of materials in the library collection will reflect the mission of the academic institution. Areas of emphasis usually revolve around two aspects: teaching (curriculum support) and research (publication). Various types of academic libraries tend to emphasize different aspects of academic life. Major university libraries, for example, tend to emphasize research and graduate programs. The collections include many current research journals, special collections, rare materials, dissertations and theses as well as general monographs. The general curricula is still supported, but much of the library's financial resources will be devoted to research materials for faculty and graduate work. This may also be true for some four-year liberal arts colleges, but less so. For the most part, the liberal arts college tends to de-emphasize graduate programs and emphasizes a well-rounded education to undergraduates. Hence the collection is primarily for curricular support. Insofar as the college expects research and publication from its faculty, the library will be expected to provide a supporting collection, but focus is likely to fall in the teaching area. Community and junior colleges devote almost all of their energies to teaching and continuing education in the community, and their collections and services reflect this emphasis.

Academic libraries, like school libraries, face a variety of challenges and issues. Among these are the following: preservation, cooperative collection development and resource sharing, competition, autonomy, increasing costs of materials, declining budgets, new information technologies.

### PRESERVATION/CONSERVATION

A far-reaching problem that academic libraries face is the serious deterioration of their library collections and inadequate resources to preserve them. Academic libraries are particularly vulnerable because they retain their collections for long periods of time so that they may be consulted when needed. The problem is really two-fold: preservation and conservation, although some would claim this is a distinction without a difference.

There are many sources of the preservation problem, but the primary one is acid paper. The acidity introduced in the paper-making process is self-destructive. The result is that over a period of years, the acidity in the paper dries the paper until it is brittle. Once brittle, simply touching or turning the pages can lead to the paper's crumbling. Since most books and other print materials have been printed on acid paper since the 1860s, the magnitude of the brittle book problem in research libraries is immense. The Council of Library Resources has estimated that there are more than 75 million brittle books in American research libraries alone, and to preserve just 3 million of them would cost over $200 million dollars (Bynes 1992). The simple fact is that there are few dollars to expend in this area when money must be diverted to collect the ever-expanding amounts of new knowledge available in new formats. The problem is exacerbated by a variety of other factors as well. These include improper use of materials by patrons and staff, improper heating and air conditioning, improper lighting, poor plumbing, fire hazards, insects, poor security to prevent theft and mutilation, and the lack of a disaster plan when and if flood or fire arise.

Information stored in the new electronic formats brings additional changes in the area of preservation that were totally unanticipated only a decade ago. Cloonan (1993) sees at least three issues which can be summarized as follows:

1. There is lack of durability of some electronic formats. There was a time when CD-ROMs were advertised as being almost indestructible, but this is not the case. Hard drives and floppy disks are vulnerable to many problems. Compared to some new media, the print form has been a highly stable format overall. Acid-free paper can last for hundreds of years; even many acid papers can last for decades.
2. Electronic data has a tendency to deteriorate over time. Information stored in electronic formats must, therefore, be monitored and periodically refreshed or transferred onto new storage devices lest the integrity of the data be lost.
3. The equipment involved in electronic formats may become obsolete. Given the fact that there are continuous innovations in information technologies, it is likely that new storage formats will be developed. As the hardware changes, how do we deal with the previous formats? One merely has to think of earlier formats such as the eight-track audiotape and the phonodisc to realize that preserving the information on obsolete formats can represent a formidable challenge for libraries. If CD-ROMs and laser disks are replaced in the years to come, will libraries be able to store and preserve the information contained on them in a format that can be effectively consulted?

As a result of these serious preservation problems major universities have started preservation programs, and the national effort to develop effective preservation strategies has substantially increased. These strategies include an effort to digitize significant collections at the Library of Congress. Emphasis has been on preserving important research collections, but there have also been cooperative preservation efforts among smaller academic libraries.

COOPERATIVE COLLECTION DEVELOPMENT AND RESOURCE SHARING

The fundamental crisis facing academic libraries is the continuing growth of knowledge and the constant reliance of researchers, faculty, and students on obtaining the highest quality and most recent knowledge available. These forces are making significant demands, while at the same time libraries are suffering from diminished resources to meet these needs. One of the seemingly obvious ways to deal with this problem is through cooperative collection development and resource sharing. Although closely related, these are two different activities. Cooperative collection development involves describing and communicating the contents of individual collections, identifying strengths and weaknesses in the different collections, and designating specific libraries to take responsibility for collecting in different areas. Resource sharing is the exchange of materials among designated libraries. Obviously, these functions can exist independently; most common is that resource sharing exists where cooperative collection development does not. In the academic environment, there has been a considerable effort to accomplish both.

In the late 1970s, collection development librarians associated with the Research Libraries Group (RLG) saw a need for "consortium-wide collection development policies, especially because of the scarcity in dollars and the reduction in purchasing power" (Coleman 1992, p. 25). The primary purposes were to avoid unnecessary duplication of research materials and identify weaknesses in various subject areas. Coordination of collections was effected by designating specific libraries to take primary collection responsibilities for certain subject areas to be collected at designated collection levels. This coordination coupled with effective document delivery would significantly benefit research libraries' abilities to deliver information at the lowest costs (Coleman 1992). This led to the formal development of the RLG Conspectus, which both described national collections and helped coordinate the further development of collections.

A conspectus is a "stratified, subject-based description of an area of intellectual inquiry" (Coleman 1992, p. 27). It also includes definitions of levels of collection development. The prospectus addresses two important questions: Which library should collect what materials? In what depth (intensity) should specific subject areas be collected? The subject basis of the RLG Conspectus is the Library of Congress classification system. There might be, for example a "History Conspectus." However, there might also be an area conspectus that overlaps, such as the "East Asian Conspectus" that would include history as well. Despite these difficulties, the Conspectus is important. In essence, it coupled cooperative collection development with resource sharing and can be useful for both local planning and collection development as well as consortium-level planning and collection development. The work of the Conspectus is under the guidance of the Task Force on Conspectus Analysis, created in 1983. Used by the Association of Research Libraries (ARL) as the conspectus for its National Collections Inventory Project (NCIP) since 1983, it is available as the Conspectus Online, an online tool for local and consortium collection development (Coleman 1992). The use of the Conspectus has grown far beyond the RLG libraries and is used by many other consortia today.

Despite the desirability of the RLG Conspectus, there are many barriers to cooperative collection development among academic institutions (Ferguson 1992):

*Competition*: Universities want to attract the best faculty and students; to do this they need the best libraries. Allowing other libraries to collect for them may increase other institutions' resources, making them more attractive, and their libraries more prestigious in terms of size, volumes added, and ranking.

*Autonomy*: Librarians want freedom of action in building their own collections. Building collections for other institutions is not nearly as important as building them internally. The more agreement they have, the less freedom they have to act on behalf of their local constituencies.

*Ownership paradigm*: Libraries operate under the general notion that physically owning the item is the most efficient means of meeting a patron's need.

INCREASING COSTS OF PERIODICALS AND OTHER MATERIALS

Academic libraries rely heavily on periodicals to support their research and teaching. Journals often provide some of the most current information on a topic, especially when compared to books. Researchers rely heavily on periodicals in their field to maintain their currency in their areas of expertise. The Association of Research Libraries estimates that research libraries now serve 10 percent more students and 16 percent more faculty than they did in 1986, yet they are buying fewer serials and monographs. In addition, approximately twice as many items are being borrowed by students and faculty than in 1986 (ARL 1995).

It is estimated that in some academic libraries, periodicals budgets account for as much as 70–80 percent of the collection budget. Unfortunately, the cost of periodicals has risen significantly in the last decade, and, generally much faster than the cost of books. For example, periodicals averaged a 10 percent increase in price in 1996, while academic books rose at 3.6 percent (*Bowker Annual* 1999). The Association of Research Libraries reports that serial costs have risen on average more than 10 percent a year since 1986. The situation is exacerbated because academic institutions often have substantial science and technology programs, and it is in this area that inflation has been the worst. Medical periodicals, for example, have increased 29 percent since 1997 (*Bowker Annual* 1999). Foreign publications are also a special problem. Unlike most public and school library media centers, academic libraries often require a substantial collection of materials published from foreign countries. Foreign currency fluctuations alone can create substantial fluctuations in the costs of materials. The effect of the increased costs of the item is thereby magnified. During the 1980s and early 1990s this posed serious problems and constant vigilance concerning foreign publishers was required.

The effects of these financial pressures are troubling. Research libraries report a decline of 4 percent in serials purchases since 1986. Given the expansion of knowledge, one would expect a significant increase rather than a decrease. Although not as severe, prices of monographs have also increased significantly. The Association of Research Libraries reports that the prices for monographs have increased on average 5.7 percent per year since 1986, while expenditures for monographs have increased only 2 percent per year. Inflation for monographs for research libraries increased substantially in 1994, increasing 6.5 percent. In fact, research libraries have acquired 32 percent fewer monographs and 10 percent fewer serials than in 1986 (ARL 1995). Although some of these dismal figures are mitigated by the fact that online databases and CD-ROMs provide access to some of these materials, it is clear that there are considerable pressures on academic institutions to reduce the number of periodicals—a form of knowledge that remains quite popular and useful to scholars and students alike.

DECLINING BUDGETS

Most academic institutions are constantly struggling for fiscal security. These struggles are acute in public institutions where the political climate for taxation is generally negative. Given the inflationary pressures and increasing costs of operation of academic institutions, the decline in fiscal support often leads to cuts in expenditures. In this climate, academic institutions compete with other public agencies such as schools and social service organizations for these dwindling resources. This problem is similarly acute in private institutions that rely on tuition, donations, and investments to stay financially stable. Regardless of whether the institution is private or public, the academic library must compete with other academic departments and agencies for the few dollars that remain. This comes at an especially unfortunate time because academic libraries are experiencing a need for increased dollars for traditional library resources and for developing information technologies, including the accompanying peripherals for effective operation, e.g., ergonomically designed furniture. These many and varied costs place considerable responsibility on the academic library to make the most of its resources.

PROLIFERATION OF NEW INFORMATION TECHNOLOGIES

Although the growth of information technologies obviously affects all types of libraries, academic institutions are especially vulnerable because of the immense variety of subjects that are taught within them, the academic depth at which they are taught, and the resulting demands of students and the need for complete access to the latest knowledge for researchers. These conditions make information technologies extremely attractive. The result is that the academic library must try to accommodate efficient access to the latest information for as many departments as expect it. Tenopir (1995) in a study of ninety-six ARL libraries reported that all of these libraries used CD-ROM databases, with nearly one-third possessing more than a hundred CD-ROM titles. In addition, 98 percent had mediated online searching, two-thirds had locally mounted online databases, and three-fourths permitted patron access to the Internet. As the number of CD-ROMs in the various disciplines continue to grow, libraries will need to increase their expenditures in these areas. But the cost of CD-ROMs is hardly slight. In 1998, a typical CD-ROM in the field of business costs more than $3,700, in the social sciences more than $2,700, and in the sciences more than $2,200 (*Bowker Annual* 1999). Other issues besides cost must also be addressed in acquiring and using such technologies. These include determining the selection criteria for acquiring CD-ROMs, staffing CD-ROM work stations, training staff as new information resources are developed, developing rules and regulations for the use of information technologies, considering fees, arranging the physical placement of electronic technologies, providing security, and overseeing copyright issues.

### Special Libraries and Information Centers

School and academic libraries are relatively easy to identify and define. Special libraries and information centers are somewhat more difficult, because of their immense variety. There is no one definition that can aptly accommodate the variety of special libraries and information centers, and usually a distinction is made between the two. Mount (1995) defines special libraries as "information organizations sponsored by private companies, government agencies, not-for-profit organizations or professional associations" (p. 2). The definition would also include special subject units in public and academic departments. Information centers are seen as "special libraries with a very narrow scope" (Mount 1995, p. 3). One example might be a library devoted to a special metal, e.g. aluminum library. Under this view, then, an information center is subsumed under the broader notion of special library.

The "roots" of special libraries and information centers can be traced to the ancient and medieval periods since these libraries tended to focus on a particular mission (Wiegand and Davis 1994). The archival functions of Sumerian libraries might fit the special library pattern, or the monastic libraries might be considered special religious libraries. Nonetheless, the special library, as we know it, is probably better located in the eighteenth and nineteenth century. Mount (1995) places the date at 1777 with the founding of the army library at the Military Academy. White (1984) suggests that the earliest special libraries were associated with scientific and historical societies. Early legal and medical collections provided training in law and medicine. The development of social libraries that focused on the specific and often professional or technical interests of their clientele also serve as early models of special libraries and information centers of which mercantile and mechanics libraries represent examples. Libraries associated with commercial firms were found as early as the 1880s. Reflecting the growth of science, technology, and industrial development, there was considerable growth in the special library entering the twentieth century. This development was sufficient to generate an interest in an association specifically designed to serve special libraries and information centers, hence the creation of the Special Library Association (SLA) in 1909. By 1910, there were probably about a hundred special libraries and information centers. This number grew rapidly to about one thousand by 1920. The major growth occurred after World War II, exceeding ten thousand in the 1960s. Information centers, as defined above, arose in this latter period and started primarily in scientific and technical laboratories (Mount 1995).

As society recognized that quick access to up-to-date information is the cornerstone of a competitive intellectual and economic climate, the role of special libraries and information centers became obvious. Recognition of the importance of quick access accounts for White's projection that special libraries and information centers will grow in number about 5 percent per year—a significant contrast to traditional public and academic libraries (White 1984). The continuing growth in the number of special libraries and information centers is attributable to at least three forces: the rapid increase in the amount of information; continuing development in information technologies; and the recognition of how important information has become as an essential resource for organizational survival (Christianson, King and Ahrensfeld 1991). From an organizational perspective, the importance of special libraries and information centers is likely to increase. As more and more information is stored in electronic formats and the importance of the written document or monograph declines, especially in the areas of science, technology, and business, the function of special libraries and information centers appears more and more relevant and vital.

Although it may be difficult to define today's special library or information center, it may be useful to highlight some of their most important characteristics. White (1984) has attempted to identify these. These can be summarized as follows:

*Special libraries and information centers . . .*

- tend to emphasize the provision of information for practical purposes rather than instruction on how to find the information or a physical document.
- generally involve the librarian researching and finding the answer for the client, rather than the client expecting to locate the answer with the librarian's assistance.
- tend to give librarians a great deal of autonomy because those requesting the information are unfamiliar with the function of information centers.
- tend to have a relatively small number of users, and restricted access to relatively small, but highly specialized collections.
- are directly and narrowly related to the mission of the organization in which they are located, and must regularly demonstrate their usefulness in order to survive.
- tend to work for organizations with managements that are not library-oriented; rather management is oriented to the goals of the larger organization, and the library staff itself represents only a small fraction of the total organizational workforce.

The list above suggests that special libraries and information centers tend to operate in a more entrepreneurial environment, often within private, profit-oriented organizations—quite different than most other types of libraries. Generally, special libraries and information centers serve their special clients or sponsors, in contrast to public libraries and institutions that tend to serve anyone.

There are probably between 14,000 and 21,000 special libraries and information centers in the United States, depending on how they are defined. (There are approximately 35,000 special libraries and information centers worldwide.) These libraries vary greatly in size. The *Directory of Special Libraries and Information Centers*, 17th edition (1994) has created five basic categories into which special libraries and information centers fall: (1) subject division, e.g., departmental collections and professional libraries of colleges and universities; (2) branches division, e.g., departments, and special collections in large public library systems that focus on a particular subject or group of subjects; (3) company libraries located in a business or industry; (4) governmental libraries; and (5) libraries of nonprofit organizations, associations, and institutions. It is obvious that many of these libraries are nonprofit and public in character. The heterogeneous character of special libraries and information centers is further highlighted by noting the twenty-eight subdivisions (Figure 9–3) of the Special Library Association (SLA), an association specifically created to serve these libraries (SLA 1995).

## Figure 9–3
## Types of Special Libraries Based on Special
## Libraries Association Divisions

**Business and Industrial**

Advertising and Marketing
Business and Finance
Insurance and Employee Benefits
Legal
News
Public Utilities
Transportation
Telecommunications

**Humanities**

Museums, Arts, and Humanities

**Science and Technology**

Aerospace
Biological Sciences
Chemistry
Engineering
Environment and Resource Management
Food, Agricultural, and Nutrition
Metal/Materials
Nuclear Science
Petroleum and Energy Resources
Pharmaceutical
Physics-Astronomy-Mathematics
Science-Technology
Information Technology

**Social Science**

Education
Geography and Map
Library Management
Military Libraries
Social Science
Solo Librarian

Today, special libraries and information centers are confronting many important issues: scarce resources, defining and promoting their roles, keeping up with how information is stored and located, copyright issues, and the demands of individualized service.

### THE BURDEN OF SCARCE RESOURCES

Few special libraries and information centers are publicly funded. Their existence depends on keeping their labor costs low and their productivity high. This creates a considerable burden for information managers because the organizations expect high performance with a minimum of expenditures. As a consequence, library staffs tend to be quite small. Mount (1995) reports, for example, that nearly one-third of special libraries and information centers have three or fewer people, and only 1 percent have more than twenty people. The profitability of the organization may well depend on the timeliness and accuracy of information provided by the library staff—the challenge is tremendous.

### NEED TO DEFINE AND PROMOTE ONE'S ROLE INSIDE THE ORGANIZATION

Even if a library is functioning well, within the corporate environment especially, each department is often in competition for scarce resources. Because a library seldom produces a product of its own for sale, it is often viewed as a "cost center" rather than a "profit center." This means that the library and librarians must justify their existence in other ways or be trimmed from the budget. Attempts to tighten budgets or changes in administration can seriously jeopardize a special library or information center's survival. Therefore special libraries must actively promote their product—information—as something that improves the performance of others and the organization as a whole. This means that the librarians or information managers must be able to measure and evaluate their effectiveness and be able to communicate the value of their libraries in a measurable, clear, and businesslike manner.

### NEED TO KEEP UP WITH HOW INFORMATION IS BEING STORED AND LOCATED WITHIN THE FIELD

Because there is less emphasis on the package in which information comes and more on the information itself, it is necessary that the information be provided, in whatever form, quickly and accurately. Given that a large proportion of special libraries and information centers deal with technical, scientific, and economic information, it is crucial that the most timely information be procured. Meeting this responsibility entails increased reliance on information technologies. Special librarians must, therefore, be on the cutting edge of innovation, constantly updating their knowledge.

### DEALING WITH COPYRIGHT ISSUES

The ability to make copies is an extremely important method of disseminating current information. This is especially important in research-related contexts. The application of copyright restrictions to special libraries and information centers has raised considerable concern. The issue was highlighted in a 1992 case called *American Geophysical Union v Texaco*. A research scientist at Texaco, a for-profit company, made copies of eight articles from various journals from the company library for future research purposes. Although the copying of materials for research purposes generally meets the "fair use" criteria, the court found that the purpose was commercial rather than research, that the researcher copied the entire article rather than just small parts, and that Texaco's action had a deleterious effect on the market of journal publishers. That is, the company could have taken alternative actions that would have accomplished the same research purpose while respecting the copyright privilege of the journal, for example, ordering more journal subscriptions, ordering copies from a document delivery service, or paying additional royalties to the Copyright Clearance Center (designed to reimburse publishers). These arguments led the court to find in favor of the publisher. This is a very disturbing ruling for special libraries and information centers. The activity of copying articles is an extremely common and important method of keeping current in a researcher's area of interest. This case was upheld on appeal to the Second Circuit court and Texaco ultimately settled the suit at considerable expense ("Court Upholds Ruling . . . " 1994; "Texaco settles . . . " 1995). This decision is likely to have a substantial impact on academic as well as special libraries and information centers, and it might require librarians to inquire of patrons the purpose of making the copies. Such an action would be unparalleled and raise serious privacy and intellectual freedom issues.

THE DEMANDS OF INDIVIDUALIZED SERVICE

A major challenge of special library service is to deliver the information on request as quickly as possible. The services are specifically tailored to the needs of the organization and the people making the query. This requires highly flexible library service and the ability of the special librarian to work under considerable time pressure as the information may be vitally important but lose its utility after a short period of time.

## HUMAN RESOURCES IN THE LIBRARY AND INFORMATION WORKFORCE

No discussion of libraries as organizations is complete without some discussion of the nature of the library and information workforce. Library organizations are generally labor-intensive; they rely heavily on people in order to accomplish their ends. As might be expected, the information labor market is quite diverse. Debons, Horne, and Croneweth 1988) have identified at least six types of information workers:

1. **Information Scientists/Theorists**: Individuals concerned with the laws, theories, philosophy, and sociology of the generation, use, and dissemination of knowledge.
2. **Information System Specialists**: Individuals who analyze information problems and design systems or networks for their solution.
3. **Information Intermediaries**: Individuals who assist those in need of information by facilitating access to the body of knowledge consulted.
4. **Information Technologists**: Individuals who operate, maintain, and control information systems, equipment, and processes.
5. **Managers of Information**: Individuals who plan, develop, coordinate, and control information programs and resources.
6. **Educators and Trainers of Information Workers**: Individuals who provide the knowledge and training required of information professionals, paraprofessionals, and nonprofessional information workers.

Most librarians fall into the category of information intermediaries. But the labor market, even among intermediaries, contains many more job titles than that of "librarian." Debons (1988) estimates that the total work force of information professionals is approximately 1.6 million, of which about 19 percent work in libraries. Most of these workers are employed in the private sector, with only 27 percent employed in federal, state, or local government.

A more complete view of the labor force can be determined from U.S. Bureau of Labor Statistics data.

### Figure 9–4
### Occupational Outlook Projections for Selected Professions
### 1998–2008

| Occupation | Employment 1998 | Projected Increase (Numerical change) in employment 2008 | Percent increase 1998–2008 |
|---|---|---|---|
| Library assts. and bookmobile drivers | 127,000 | 21,000 | 17% |
| Library technicians | 72,000 | 13,000 | 18% |
| Librarians | 152,000 | 7,000 | 5% |
| Information clerks | 1,293,000 | 305,000 | 24% |
| Retail sales workers | 4,056,000 | 560,000 | 14% |
| School teachers secondary | 1,426,000 | 322,000 | 23% |
| Computer scientists, computer engineers, and systems analysts | 1,013,000 | 1,015,000 | 100% |
| Social workers | 604,000 | 218,000 | 36% |
| Archivists and curators | 23,000 | 3,000 | 13% |

Source: Bureau of Labor Statistics. "Occupational Employment, Training, and Earnings." (Online) Available at: *http://stats.bls.gov/asp/oep/* (Noted: November 30, 1999.)

### Figure 9–5
### Racial and Gender Characteristics of Selected Occupations

| Occupation | Percent Female | Percent African American | Percent Hispanic |
|---|---|---|---|
| Librarians | 84 | 7.7 | 4.8 |
| Social workers | 71.4 | 24.2 | 7.4 |
| Library clerks | 74.4 | 9.8 | 11.1 |
| Teachers, except college | 74.9 | 9.9 | 5.4 |
| Computer systems analysts | 28.5 | 7.4 | 3.4 |

**Source:** U.S. Department of Labor, Bureau of Labor Statistics. "Employed Persons By Detailed Occupation, Sex, Race, and Hispanic Origin." (Online) Available at *http://ftp.bls.gov/pub/special.requests/if/aat11.txt*

Estimates of the librarian work force vary, but they usually approach 150,000 (Figure 9–4). Compared to the work force of computer scientists, analysts, and engineers, with more than one million workers, librarians are but a small fraction of the information professionals. A similar proportion is found when comparing the number of librarians to school teachers.

Support staff in libraries (library assistants, library technical assistants, and bookmobile drivers) comprise approximately 200,000 workers. This also represents a small percentage when compared to 1.3 million information clerks. This is not to say that the size of the total library work force is trivial, as it is more than 350,000.

The racial and gender characteristics of the labor force are also revealing when compared to other occupations (Figure 9–5). It comes as no surprise that librarianship is comprised primarily of women. About 88 percent of all librarians are female. The profession is primarily white: only 7 percent of librarians are Black, and 3.5 percent Hispanic. The representation of Blacks and Hispanics is even lower in academic libraries. The *1996–97 ARL Annual Salary Survey* (1996) reports that in research libraries Blacks comprise 3.7 percent of the professional work force, and Hispanics 2.2 percent (*ARL Annual* 1996). The proportion of library clerks is similar.

Comparisons to other information professions suggest that librarianship may be quite different. For example, the proportion of women to men is reversed when dealing with computer systems analysts and scientists. Only 30 percent of this work force is female. The percent of African Americans and Hispanics is similar to that of librarianship.

It is also interesting to examine the projected growth of the work force to the year 2008 (Figure 9–4). The growth of the library work force is expected to be slow. A 5 percent gain among librarians is expected over the eleven-year period beginning in 1998 with more rapid, but still very modest, growth for library assistants. The Bureau of Labor Statistics (1996) speculates that the slow growth of librarians is due to lack of fiscal resources in school, public, and college libraries and competition from computerized information resources. Greatest growth is projected for nontraditional library positions such as those in private corporations, consulting firms, and information brokers. Average growth is expected for library technicians, around 28 percent. Interestingly, the Bureau of Labor Statistics projects this larger growth rate because new technologies have made some tasks that were considered professional, such as cataloging, accessible to technicians (BLS 1996). This situation is bound to tempt employers to replace librarians with library technicians, thus increasing technicians' job opportunities at the cost of librarians.

Overall, on an annualized basis, library labor force growth will be minimal, especially when it is compared to the projected growth among computer occupations. Systems analysts, computer engineers, and computer scientists are expected to experience a growth of 100 percent. This is due to the technological advances in office and factory automation, telecommunications, and research (BLS 1999).

It is difficult to predict the shape of the library work force in the future. But some significant labor force issues have arisen that have a significant effect on library organizations.

### The Persistently Low Numbers of Minority Librarians

As a profession, librarianship has not attracted a large number of individuals from ethnic and racial groups, especially African Americans and Hispanics. The profession needs to determine if there are structural aspects of the educational and employing institutions that tend to discourage minorities from applying. For example, it may be that schools of library and information studies and employers are not devoting enough energies to recruitment. Effective recruitment strategies might increase the number of candidates from minority groups. Similarly, library schools may need to assess whether their schools are providing the necessary academic and financial support for minority students so that once admitted they can remain in the academic programs. There may, of course, be other external factors as well. The master's degree requirement may disproportionately screen out minorities, who, for a variety of reasons including discrimination, have been unable to obtain higher academic degrees at the same rate as others. Additionally, members of some ethnic and racial groups may not be considering librarianship as a career because they may not have been introduced to it as a career option, their experiences with libraries may have been more negative, and hence, working in a library may appear less desirable, or they may have access to more highly paid career options. Demographically, the United States is increasing in its heterogeneity and the field must constantly evaluate its practices so that the library work force reflects this heterogeneity.

*Sex Discrimination*

Analysis of gender-based data in the library labor force suggests differences in the wages and placement of women. One report on library school graduates in 1995 suggests that men entering the profession are paid on average 5.3 percent more than women. This is an increase over previous years when the difference was closer to 1–2 percent. Although the percentage of difference may vary by region, women entering the profession are paid less than men in all regions of the country (Carson 1996). Perhaps more significant, women occupy a disproportionately low number of management and administrative positions compared to their general representation in the librarian work force. For example, although women occupy approximately 65 percent of academic librarian positions, they hold only about 48 percent of the directorships, deputy directorships, or assistant directorships (American Library Association 1986). Recent data from the Association of Research Libraries indicate that 59 percent of the ARL library directorships are held by men (Kyrillidou 1996). This problem appears to be true in public libraries as well, where about 75 percent of the librarians are female, but hold only 59 percent of the directorships, assistant directorships, or deputy directorships (ALA 1986).

Explanations have ranged widely regarding this disparity, including the assertion that men have a higher motivation to manage, which would incline them to apply for managerial or administrative positions. However, when research has been conducted on the difference in the motivation to manage between male and female librarians, no differences in motivation have been detected (Swisher, DuMont, and Boyer 1985). Men, on average, may have more years of managerial or library experience or more formal education, but research suggests that even when these factors are taken into consideration, there is a disparity in the representation of women in higher-level positions (Heim and Estabrook 1983). Certainly, the appearance of discrimination against women in management positions is hardly unique to librarianship, but its presence in a field numerically dominated by women makes it doubly regrettable and ironic. The abolition of discrimination is essential for a healthy labor force.

## The Creation of New Technology-oriented Positions

With the proliferation of new information technologies, special competencies have entered our field that were not there a couple of decades ago. Knowledge of computer systems, including their evaluation, operation, maintenance, and replacement has become essential for at least some library staff. Library positions requiring these skills have led to the creation of new job categories. Some of these categories may require levels of skill equivalent to or exceeding those of librarians, and their place in the organizational hierarchy in terms of pay, responsibility, and authority have been problematic.

## Support/Professional Strains

Support staff play a vital role inside libraries and these roles are quite various. A support staff worker can be a clerical employee, paraprofessional, bookkeeper or accountant, public relations officer, business manager, computer programmer, or systems analyst. The organizational, political, and pay relationships within libraries are becoming more and more complex. These complexities become especially problematic with the new information technologies. New information technologies have given new impetus to some support staff to increase their authority and responsibilities. Traditional clerical workers are becoming "desk-top publishers" or "database managers." How library administrators deal with this issue could have serious implications for the morale and productivity of their staffs.

## SUMMARY

The complex and various functions of libraries are reflected in their organization. It is not surprising that libraries are often organized in conventional bureaucratic and hierarchical fashion: they have prospered quite nicely over the years employing these organizational patterns. However, today's environment is constantly presenting challenges that require rapid and effective responses. Many of the difficult issues that librarians face are caused by situations and events that lie outside their direct control. Common environmental influences in libraries are decreasing budgets and increasing inflation, the rapid expansion of knowledge, the obsolescence of knowledge, and the growth of new technologies. Other challenges are unique to various types of libraries. No matter what the source of these challenges, libraries, as organizations, will need to maintain clarity of mission, design their functions, and harness their human resources to ensure that the library users' needs are effectively satisfied.

## REFERENCES

"ALA Launches Web Site with Links for Kids." *American Libraries* 29 (January 1998): 11.

ALA (American Library Association). *Academic and Public Librarians: Data by Race, Ethnicity and Sex.* Chicago: ALA, 1986.

———. *Information Power: Guidelines for School Library Media Programs.* Chicago: ALA, 1988.

———. *Library Advocacy Now!: Kids Can't Wait.* Chicago: ALA, 1996.

*American Library Directory 1999–2000.* New York: R. R. Bowker, 1996.

*ARL Annual Salary Survey 1996–97.* Edited by Martha Kyrillidou and Kimberly A. Maxwell. Washington, D.C.: ARL, 1996.

ARL (Association of Research Libraries). *ARL Statistics 1993–1994.* Washington, D.C.: ARL, 1995.

Association of American Publishers, American Library Association, and Association for Supervision and Curriculum Development. *Limiting What Students Shall Read.* Washington, D.C.: Association of American Publishers, 1981.

Benton Foundation. *Buildings, Books, and Bytes.* Washington, D.C.: Benton Foundation, 1996.

*Board of Education, Island Trees Union Free School District v. Pico* [42 CCH S. Ct. Bull. (1982).

Bob, Murray C. "The Case for Quality Book Selection." *Library Journal* 107 (September 15, 1982): 1707–1710.

*The Bowker Annual: Library and Book Trade Almanac.* New Providence, N.J.: Bowker, 1996, 1999.

Bureau of Labor Statistics. "The Job Outlook in Brief." *Occupational Outlook Quarterly* 40 (spring 1996): 3–43.

Bynes, Margaret M. "Preservation and Collection Management: Some Common Concerns." In *The Collection Building Reader*. Edited by Betty-Carol Sellen and Arthur Curley. New York: Neal-Schuman, 1992, 57–63.

Carnegie Corporation of New York. *A Matter of Time: Risk and Opportunity in the Nonschool Hours: Executive Summary*. New York: Carnegie, 1993.

Carson, C. Herbert. "Beginner's Luck: A Growing Job Market." *Library Journal* 121 (October 15, 1996): 29–35.

Christianson, Elin B., David E. King, and Janet L. Ahrensfeld. *Special Libraries: A Guide for Management*, 3rd ed. Washington, D.C.: SLA, 1991.

Cloonan, Michele Valerie. "The Preservation of Knowledge," *Library Trends* 41 (spring 1993): 594–605.

Coleman, Jim. "The RLG Conspectus: A History of Its Development and Influence and a Prognosis for Its Future." In *Collection Assessment: A Look at the RLG Conspectus*. Edited by Richard J. Wood and Katina Strauch. Binghamton, N.Y.: Haworth, 1992, 25–43.

"Court Upholds Ruling that Texaco Violated Copyright." *American Libraries* 25 (December 1994): 974.

Debons, Anthony, Esther Horne, and Scott Croneweth. *Information Science: An Integrated View*. Boston: G. H. Hall, 1988.

*Digest of Education Statistics 1998*. Washington, D.C.: NCES, U.S. DOE, Office of Educational Research and Improvement, October 1995.

*Directory of Special Libraries and Information Centers*. 17th ed. Edited by Joanna M. Zakalik. Detroit: Gale, 1994.

DuMont, Rosemary Ruhig, Lois Buttlar, and William Caynon. "Multiculturalism in Public Libraries." In *Multiculturalism in Libraries*. Westport, Conn.: Greenwood, 1994, 37–51.

Euster, Joanne R. "The New Hierarchy: Where's the Boss?" *Library Journal* 115 (May 1, 1990): 41–44.

Ferguson, A.W. "The Conspectus and Cooperative Collection Development: What It Can and Cannot Do." In *Collection Assessment: A Look at the RLG Conspectus*. Edited by Richard J. Wood, and Katina Strauch. Binghamton, N.Y.: Haworth, 1992, pp. 105–114.

"Gates Foundation to Invest $400 Million in Libraries." *American Libraries* 28 (August 1997): 14.

Gates Library Foundation. Gates Library Foundation Background. [Online] Available at *http://www.glf.org/background.html* (December 17, 1997).

Harris, Michael. "The Purpose of the American Public Library." *Library Journal* 98 (September 15, 1973): 2509–2514.

Heim, Kathleen and Leigh S. Estabrook. *Career Profiles and Sex Discrimination in the Library Profession*. Chicago: ALA, 1983.

Ingersoll, Richard M. and Mei Han. *School Library Media Centers in the United States: 1990–91. Survey Report*. Washington, D.C.: GPO, 1994.

Internet Public Library. The Internet Public Library Mission Statement. [Online]. Available at *http://www.ipl.org/newmission.html* (December 17, 1997).

"Internet Public Library: Same Metaphors, New Service." *American Libraries* 28 (February 1997): 56–57.

Jones, Plummer Alston Jr. "The History and Development of Libraries in American Higher Education." *College and Research Libraries News* 50 (July/August 1989): 561–564.

Kyrillidou, Martha. "Librarians' Salaries Continued to Increase." *ARL News Release*. March 29, 1996.

Lance, Keith Curry, Lynda Welborn, and Christine Hamilton-Pennell. *The Impact of School Library Media Centers on Academic Achievement*. Castle Rock, Colo.: Hi Willo Research and Publishing, 1993.

Lynch, Beverly P. "Libraries as Bureaucracies." *Library Trends* (winter 1978): 259–267.

Martell, Charles R. *The Client-Gentered Academic Library: An Organizational* Model. Westport, Conn.: Greenwood, 1983.

McKimmie, T. "Budgeting for CD-ROM in Academic Libraries: Sources and Impacts." *Library Acquisitions: Practice and Theory* 16 (1992): 221–227.

*Minarcini v Strongsville City School District.* 541 F 2d 577 (1977).

Mount, Ellis. *Special Libraries and Information Centers: An Introductory Text.* 3rd Ed. Washington, D.C.: SLA, 1995.

NCES (National Center for Education Statistics). *CES Schools and Staff Survey, 1991, and Statistics of Public and Private School Library Media Centers. 1985–86.* Washington D.C.: U.S. DOE, 1991.

———. *Public Libraries in the United States: 1993.* Washington, D.C.: U.S. DOE, 1996.

———. *Report on Public Libraries, 1992.* Washington D.C.: U.S. DOE, 1994.

———. *School and Staffing Survey 1990–91.* Washington, D.C.: U.S. DOE, 1991. In *School Library Media Centers in the United States: 1990–91. Survey Report* by Richard M. Ingersoll, and Mei Han. Washington, D.C. American Institutes for Research in the Behavioral Sciences, 1994.

———. *Services and Resources for Young Adults in Public Libraries.* Washington, D.C.: GPO, July 1988.

———. *Use of Public Library Services by Households in the United States: 1996.* Washington D.C.: U.u. DOE, March 1997.

Palmour, Vernon E. et al. *A Planning Process for Public Libraries.* Chicago: ALA, 1980.

Rawlinson, Nora. "Give 'Em What They Want!" *Library Journal* (November 15, 1981): 77–79.

"Riverside County Outsources Library—Again." *American Libraries* 28 (August 1997): 19.

Rogers, Fred. *Let's Talk About It: Divorce.* New York: Putnam, 1996.

SLA (Special Libraries Association). *Who's Who in Special Libraries 1995–1996.* Washington, D.C.: SLA, 1995.

Swisher, Robert, Rosemary Ruhig DuMont, and Calvin J. Boyer. "The Motivation to Manage: A Study of Academic Librarians and Library Science Students." *Library Trends* 34 (fall 1985): 219–234.

Tenopir, Carol. "Electronic Reference in Academic Libraries in the 1990s." In *Annual Review of OCLC Research.* Dublin, Ohio: OCLC, 1995, pp. 66–68.

"Texaco Settles Copyright Case." *American Libraries* 26 (July/August 1995): 632–634.

U.S. Bureau of the Census. *Current Population Reports, Series P-20, No. 450: Marital Status and Living Arrangements: March 1990.* Washington, D.C.: GPO, 1991.

Westin, Alan F. and Anne L. Finger, *Using the Public Library in the Computer Age.* Chicago: ALA, 1991.

White, Herbert S. *Managing the Special Library.* White Plains, NY: Knowledge Industry, 1984.

WHCLIS (White House Conference on Library and Information Science). *Information 2000: Library and Information Services for the 21st Century.* Washington, D.C.: GPO 1991.

Wiegand, Wayne and Donald G. Davis ed. "Special Libraries." In *Encyclopedia of Library History.* New York: Garland, 1994, 597–599.

Wilson, Patrick. "Bibliographical R&D." In *The Study of Information: Interdisciplinary Messages.* Edited by Fritz Machlup and Una Mansfield. New York: Wiley, 1984, 389–397.

Winter, Michael F. *The Culture and Control of Expertise: Toward a Sociological Understanding of Librarianship.* Westport, Conn: Greenwood, 1988.

Woolls, Blanche. *The School Library Media Manager.* Englewood, Colo.: Libraries Unlimited, 1994.

Wright, Lisa A. "Public Library Circulation Rises Along with Spending." *American Libraries* 27 (October 1996): 57–58.

Young, Peter R. "Changing Information Access Economics: New Roles for Libraries and Librarians." *Information Technology and Libraries* 13 (June 1994): 103–114.

Zweizig, Douglas, L. "The Children's Services Story." *Public Libraries* (January/February 1993): 26–28.

# 10

# Librarianship:
# An Evolving Profession

Librarianship is in the midst of a great change. It is a traumatic one for many, in part because rapid change has not been an aspect that librarianship has generally had to deal with; the field has remained stable for many years. Since the late nineteenth century, whatever changes have occurred have been slow and evolutionary, not revolutionary, and the role of the librarian has remained relatively constant for more than a hundred years. Not that the field has been stagnant, but the demands that have been placed on it and the expectations of library users have been relatively constant. If changes have occurred, they have been incremental. In many ways, the slowness of change in librarianship has been good. It has created a solid historical identity and important precedents for its actions and goals. From these traditions emerged the central values and duties of librarianship on which the changes in contemporary librarianship may be squarely built.

Historically, the librarian has been closely tied with the physical institution of the library. One does not usually think of librarians without also thinking of the library in which they ply their trade. Is the entire identity of the librarian inextricably linked to this physical entity? If the new world of information transfer can be accomplished without such a physical institution, will the librarian also disappear? Are librarians capable of thinking of performing their tasks without a physical library, and is the rest of the world capable of thinking of them in this way as well? Will there be librarians without libraries? Will we be calling them something different, as some are being called today—"information consultant," "information specialist," or "information manager"?

Such a concern may be more an exercise in hysteria than reality. There is no evidence that libraries are or will be vanishing in the near future. However, it is quite possible that a substantial number of librarians (or whatever we will call them in the future) will be working outside the traditional library building. The librarian of tomorrow may be quite different. The library may have its quiet places for contemplation and study, but it is not a sedate place, it is dynamic, and those who choose librarianship will need to be adaptable, patient, able to withstand uncertainty, and amenable to learning new things. The stable environment of the past is being replaced by a dynamic environment in which the content and function of the institution is constantly being revised and modified by technological, political, and economic change. How the profession comes to be defined will be the result of a dynamic interaction between the qualities of the profession and the demands placed upon it by society-at-large.

Libraries and the profession of librarianship are closely linked; what happens to one is likely also to affect the other. This chapter will focus on three aspects of the profession: the forces that shaped education for librarianship, the current struggle for professional identity, and the characteristics of the contemporary information labor force.


## AN HISTORICAL OVERVIEW OF PROFESSIONAL EDUCATION

The education and training of American librarians has been closely related to developments in professional education and to economic developments as well. As noted in the chapter on the mission and values of libraries (Chapter 7), early American libraries were small and relatively unsophisticated. In most libraries, if staff existed they were very small in number and often functioned in a custodial capacity. Scholarly librarians did exist in the mid-nineteenth century. They were usually found in more sophisticated academic institutions and were invariably male. These individuals were described as "Bookmen" by Pierce Butler (1951) in his history of the profession, because they were scholars, not technicians. Their numbers, nonetheless, were generally small.

Until 1850 there was no training to speak of for those who worked in the library except trial and error. One simply learned on one's own and followed the example of others. Sometimes a novice librarian would contact other experienced librarians for advice and counsel. The earliest type of training, apprenticeship, probably emerged between 1850 and 1875. Apprenticeship involved learning a trade through practical experience under the tutelage of another more experienced individual. A librarian would find an individual who was interested in librarianship and have that person work in the library under close observation.

Another route of professional development consisted of informative publications from private publishers, the United States government, or the American Library Association. *Publishers Weekly*, still a mainstay of the library world, began during this time, 1872. Although it focused on the publishing industry, there were small sections devoted to librarians. The major publication that provided tremendous support for library training was the *American Library Journal*. Created in 1876 as the official organ of the newly created ALA, this journal (which was soon renamed *Library Journal*) was the first to devote itself to the interests of librarians and published articles, summaries of ALA conference proceedings, and a section titled "Notes and Queries," which printed responses to questions and comments from librarians. Many of these questions were queries about cataloging and classification, circulation, library buildings, library equipment, and funds. *Library Journal (LJ)* was filled with advice to novitiates. In the very first issue, Justin Windsor, associate editor and director of the Boston Public Library, wrote an article in which he advised new librarians on learning about the management of libraries. To this end he recommended that the notiviate (1) locate whatever printed materials on librarianship are available; (2) locate similar libraries and ask for their rules and reports; (3) study the materials received, (4) evaluate the extent to which other libraries are good comparisons to the library in question, (5) contact an experienced librarian, and (6) do what seems to come naturally (Windsor 1876). He also warned the novitiate that if he did not have time to do this research and analysis, then he should "resign your trust to some on who has . . . " (Windsor 1876, p. 2).

Another significant source of publications for the librarian were those published by the U.S. Bureau of Education, which produced publications for educators. The most significant publication affecting library education was the bureau's landmark study issued in 1876, *Public Libraries in the United States of America: Their History, Condition, and Management*. A substantial body of statistical data was presented on more than 3,600 public libraries and included data on other types of libraries as well. As part of this work, the bureau issued a manual including articles written by noted authorities on librarianship. The topics included such areas as management, administration, history, cataloging, popular reading, and library buildings. In essence, it was the first authoritative library reader (*Public Libraries* 1876). These early beginnings produced a sparse literature and little formal training for librarianship. The dearth of training reflected both the relatively small number of libraries and little recognition of the potential of libraries and librarians to the society as a whole.

The period from about 1876 to 1923 marks a critical and complex time in the development of library education, and there were a variety of forces at work that created the foundations for the professionalization of librarianship. Among these were the following:

*The Decline of the Classical English and Apprenticeship Models of Education and the Rise of the Model of Technical Education*

American education during the nineteenth century was generally shaped by the dominant immigrant population: the British. This model emphasized study of the classical languages, religion, literature, and grammar. With the rise of the industrial revolution training models needed to change. This change was also needed because it was becoming apparent that training for the factory environment required a more efficient type of training than traditional apprenticeship. In the traditional apprenticeship system, which was designed for training an individual for a craft, only a few individuals could be trained at a time for a specialized, narrowly defined job. With industrialization, many people had to be trained for positions in factories that might be quite similar from factory to factory. Education had to accommodate many people and provide a more generalized approach, employing the general principles and practices the job required. A classical education was inappropriate, and apprenticeship was too inefficient. The rise of technical schools and the vocational emphasis of these educational institutions fit well into the needs of libraries. Exposure to the European technical education model was provided at various International Fairs and Expositions in Europe and the United States, and some library leaders, among others, attended them and found the model attractive (White 1976).

*The Influence of Andrew Carnegie and the Growth of Libraries*

The latter half of the nineteenth century saw a tremendous expansion in the number of libraries. For example, 551 public libraries were established between 1825–1850, but more than 2,200 were established in the ensuing twenty-five years (*Public Libraries* 1876, p. xvi). There were many reasons for this rapid increase, especially at the end of the nineteenth century, including an increased recognition of the important role of libraries in research and teaching. Andrew Carnegie's focus on libraries led to his financing the construction of 3,000 libraries throughout the world, a large proportion of which were public libraries built in the United States. The proliferation of libraries had the inevitable effect of increasing the demand for library workers. Although professionally trained librarians were not required for many of these libraries, especially in the nineteenth century, it was clear that library workers were still needed.

*The Influence of Melvil Dewey and the Professionalization of Librarianship*

There is little dispute that Melvil Dewey was the prime force in the professionalization of librarianship during the latter part of the nineteenth century. Dewey was not alone in promoting the field of librarianship and library education, but he was a central figure whose energy and devotion advanced the profession. It is not possible to discuss all of Dewey's accomplishments, but three will be noted here that were clearly important in establishing the professional foundations for the field.

First, Dewey provided a fundamental context through which materials and disciplines could be understood and organized through his development of his decimal classification system. His earliest experience with libraries came while he was a student working in the library at Amherst College (Massachusetts). After graduation, Dewey remained at Amherst and served as the librarian. It became clear to Dewey that the existing classification system simply did not provide the flexibility and clarity that was desired. The development of a new and more efficient way to organize materials was just the type of project that would have been of interest to Dewey. He was fascinated with labor-saving routines and devices. His fascination was, no doubt, part and parcel of the excitement generated by the possibilities of industrialization. Dewey, for example, was a member of organizations promoting the use of metrics and simplified spelling (hence, *Melvil* rather than *Melville*). The classification system was heavily promoted by Dewey and grew in popularity over the years. In terms of the profession, its use clearly represented a stabilizing force as it provided a fundamental and important theoretical principle by which basic activities of the profession could be organized.

Second, Dewey was an early promoter of professional identity on a national level. Although the need for a professional association had been discussed in the 1850s, the time was not right for its creation. In 1876, Dewey was a guiding force in organizing a national meeting of librarians in Philadelphia. On the final day of the meeting, the American Library Association was founded with Melvil Dewey as its secretary. From the perspective of the sociology of professions, the creation of a national professional association is an important guidepost. It substantially increases professional identity, helps to identify important issues, and establishes standards of service and conduct. The founding of ALA did that for librarianship and, perhaps just as important, it provided librarianship with an identity to those outside the profession. It also provided a common forum for the discussion of ideas and problems. The first conferences, for example, discussed such issues as classification, indexing, and protecting materials from abuse.

Third, Dewey was instrumental in the creation of the first major professional library journal, also in 1876. Dewey's orientation, both in the creation of the association and the journal, was pragmatic. The establishment of the *American Library Journal* was intended to assist librarians in the daily performance of their duties. The emphasis was practical, not theoretical, concentrating on the problems a librarian in the U.S. would face. Dewey served as one of its editors. The attractiveness of such a journal was not lost on the newly created American Library Association. In 1877 it was adopted as the official organ of ALA, and the name was shortened to *Library Journal*.

Although Dewey's work tended to focus on the technical aspects of the profession, he also believed that librarianship was a serious profession with a serious, moralistic, and prescriptive purpose to make people better. The idea of improving people by providing healthy reading would not have been considered a curious notion in those times. Dewey (1876) had some clear notions on this subject, which he directly conveyed in his brief article "The Profession" in *Library Journal*. He argued that individuals are influenced by print materials and that librarians could be quite influential by buying the right materials for their library. Dewey was the consummate social engineer:

He must see that his library contains, as far as possible, the best books on the best subjects, regarding carefully the wants of his special community. Then, having the best books, he must create among his people, his pupils, a desire to read those books. He must put every facility in the way of readers, so that they shall be led on from good to better . . . Such a librarian will find enough who are ready to put themselves under his influence and direction, and, if competent and enthusiastic, he may soon largely shape the reading, and through it the thought, of his whole community (p. 5).

The idea that it is the librarian's duty to shape a community's thinking is strong stuff. At the very least, it implies that books have considerable power. This power could be used for good or evil. The librarian's duty was moral and pedagogical, to provide the "better" books and to improve people so that they could be exposed to even better works in the future.

## The Beginning of Library School Training

At the same time that there was a proliferation of libraries in the latter half of the nineteenth century, and with it an increased need for library workers and trained librarians, there occurred a transition from library work performed by scholars in relatively academic settings to library work focused on routines and practices (Butler 1951). It seems reasonable that if librarianship involved technical manipulations and routines, that training needed to be provided.

Up to this time apprenticeship was generally an informal process. Then in 1879, Dewey tried to promote a system of organized apprenticeship that would provide systematic training under the auspices of various librarians and libraries. The librarians would advise the apprentices on library matters and suggest readings and areas of study. Dewey suggested that the teachers be knowledgeable librarians and that the apprenticeship be associated with a substantial library (Vann 1961). Little interest, however, was generated from this proposal, and it received a cool reception at ALA. Traditional apprenticeship remained one of the typical ways by which a librarian learned his or her trade and was being provided at such notable institutions as the Boston Public Library, Boston Athenaeum, and Harvard. There were also summer schools at Amherst College and library training classes at major public libraries such as those in Los Angeles, Denver, and Cleveland. There were also special classes in library techniques at academic or technical institutes. All of these, however, were usually brief and unsystematic in terms of curricula.

A fortuitous event occurred in 1883. Dewey's reputation for his work at Amherst had grown considerably and quickly, and consequently he was recruited to apply for the head librarian's position at Columbia. His discussion with the president of Columbia, F.A.P. Barnard, and the board of trustees before his hire included the discussion of the need for formal training of librarians. This was met with enthusiastic support on the part of President Barnard and sufficient support from the board, although it is not clear that the board actually understood the full import of Dewey's suggestions. Dewey accepted the appointment in 1884, and the first library school, called the School of Library Economy, opened on January 1, 1887, with a class of twenty students: three men and seventeen women (Vann 1961). As might be expected, the program of instruction at the school was pragmatic, including selection, reader's aids, bibliography, repair of materials, administration, and issues related to the catalog. The program also included practice work so that the students could actually perform the work of their intended profession. The proposed length for the original instructional program was three months, although it was also proposed that students follow their instruction by a substantial period of work experience and then return to the school for several months of further instruction (Vann 1961). The total period was about two years, and some of the students actually followed this course. Unfortunately, Dewey's relations with university officials were tense, and there was a feeling that he had not correctly represented the school to the board, especially in relation to the problematic presence of women as students in the school. By 1888, it was clear that Columbia would close the school. Dewey, anticipating these events, accepted a position as head of the New York State Library in Albany. The state library agreed to have the school transferred there, thus preserving the only formal education program for librarians in the country. Dewey remained the director of the library school, but he was preoccupied with other professional responsibilities at the time. Consequently, the daily operations became the responsibility of Mary Salome Cutler Fairchild, who taught at Albany for sixteen years and served as its vice-director (Maack 1986). Fairchild had worked both as a cataloger and cataloging instructor under Dewey at Columbia. Fairchild's view of library education differed somewhat from Dewey's: hers emphasized more theoretical and cultural aspects of the field while Dewey emphasized the practical aspects, viewing libraries as businesses. For example, Dewey emphasized book selection through the use of standard reviews, while Fairchild emphasized that the librarian should have a broad knowledge of books and an understanding of people's tastes in order to select books (Wiegand 1996). Nonetheless, as Gambee (1978) observes, Fairchild gave "form and substance to the Dewey dream" (p. 168) through her able administration and inspiring pedagogy. She commanded much loyalty from her students and alumnae, and she is credited with establishing and maintaining the high standards of admission and high quality of education that made Albany the standard of library education (Gambee).

The success of the program at Albany led to its imitation in other locations. By 1900, there were four major library schools: Albany, Pratt (1890), Drexel (1892), and the Armour Institute (1893), which became the State Library School at the University of Illinois in 1897 (Vann 1961). Among the directors of these schools were found some of the future women leaders of the library profession; individuals who helped to shape library education and librarianship for years to come.

Pratt was originally established in 1890 to train staff of the Pratt Institute library, and the school experienced a considerable period of growth and development under the leadership of Mary Wright Plummer. Plummer was one of the original members of the first library school class at Columbia and one of its best students. She was an ardent advocate for library school training and became director of the school at Pratt and the Institute library in 1895. Under her leadership, the school broadened its purpose to train librarians for other public library positions (Brand 1996). This involved extending the training program from six months to two years, making it equivalent to the best training provided (Vann 1961). The curriculum underwent considerable enrichment during this period, developing specialized courses in children's work and historical courses in cataloging and bibliography (Brand 1996). In 1896, Plummer experimented with a second year of specialization designed to train librarians to work in more scholarly libraries. Special courses in bibliography, advanced cataloging, and courses on the histories of books, bindings, and engravings were offered. Three years later, Plummer started a second-year specialization in children's librarianship (Karlowich and Sharify 1978; Maack 1986). Despite the difficulties of women acting as leaders and administrators in an era when women were not expected to play such roles, Plummer would eventually become the second woman president of ALA and director of the library school of the New York Public Library (Weibel and Heim 1979).

Drexel's library training program, as well as the library itself, was directed by Alice Kroeger, also a graduate of Dewey's library school after it had moved to Albany. Kroeger's program was deliberately like the one created by Dewey, including course work in cataloging, literature, bibliography, history of books, and library management. The similarities to Dewey's program helped establish this type of curriculum as the model for library education (Vann 1961; Grotzinger, "Kroeger" 1978). In addition to serving as the major instructor at the library school, Kroeger's contributions were many. She was a prolific author and presenter at ALA conferences. At a time when there were few texts for the library-school student, she published the first major text on reference materials as well as a work on book selection.

The Armour Institute, established in 1893 in Chicago, Illinois, was the first library school in the Midwest. It began under the leadership of Katharine Lucinda Sharp, another graduate of Dewey's library school. Sharp's view of library education was heavily influenced by Dewey, especially the idea that librarians could have power because they could influence people's access to print materials (Grotzinger 1966). Sharp's program took one year with the possibility of a second year of advanced work. The advanced training included work in bibliography courses in specialized areas and the history of printing and libraries (Vann 1961). A specialized children's program was also available (Vann 1961). Sharp was not satisfied with the existing admission requirements at Armour and wanted to develop a program comparable to that of Dewey's (Grotzinger 1966). She was especially interested in being able to award a degree, rather than a certificate, for library training. She established such a notable program that two universities became interested in it: the University of Wisconsin and the University of Illinois. As a consequence, she successfully and amicably negotiated a transfer of the program to the University of Illinois, where she would serve as head of the school and head of the university library as well. She also held the title of full professor. This enabled her to use the library as a laboratory for practice work for her students (Grotzinger, "Sharp" 1978; Maack 1986). The program that she developed in terms of academic requirements was comparable to that at Dewey's school in Albany (Vann 1961). Sharp did much to establish the academic respectability of library education and, although she was only able to establish a four-year program leading to a bachelor's degree, she was an early proponent of placing library education on the graduate level. During her tenure, the school was "constantly the center of experimentation and innovation" (Grotzinger 1966, p. 304.) She was an innovative curriculum designer, adding courses on documents, extension work, and research methods to the library school curriculum (Grotzinger, "Sharp" 1978). She also involved students in the life of the community. These students created travelling collections, conducted story hours, and organized collections (Grotzinger 1966). As a consequence, Sharp was highly respected as a library educator and librarian and was twice elected ALA vice-president.

The number of library schools continued to grow in the ensuing decades. There were fifteen such programs by 1919, ten of them founded by women (Maack 1986). They varied in many ways including length of program, type of degree or certificate awarded, and requirements for admission. The M.L.S. was not awarded except at Albany until the 1920s. The master's at Albany was given only after two years of education beyond the baccalaureate (sometimes referred to as the "sixth-year degree"). The Bachelor's of Library Science (B.L.S.) was awarded by most schools, and this was given after one year of library education following the regular baccalaureate degree, sometimes referred to as the "fifth-year degree" (Robbins-Carter and Seavey 1986).

As the number of library schools grew, ALA took a greater interest in their development. The other traditional methods of library training remained and coexisted uneasily with the developing library schools. The library schools wanted ALA to recognize and endorse them as the appropriate forum for library training. Instead, the association created the ALA Committee on Library Training at the end of the nineteenth century. This committee had many transformations, but an important development occurred in 1902 when the committee was asked to make a review of library-training programs. This review resulted in the issuance of standards for library education in 1903. These standards reflected no commitment to any particular type of library education strategy. ALA chose to promulgate standards for the various types of library education rather than identify which type was most desirable. Subsequent standards were issued in 1905 and 1906, again with the same equivocations: a politic choice in an association badly divided over this issue.

The tensions regarding standards for library education became acute in the period between 1910 and 1920. ALA continued to have an interest in library education, including the establishment of a Section on Professional Training. This section conducted some superficial examination of the programs being offered by various organizations, but as far as making a commitment to the library schools was concerned the association continued to keep them at arm's length. The reluctance to endorse the library schools as the only appropriate form of library education led the library schools to create their own organization, the Association of American Library Schools, in 1916. Although it had little influence over ALA activities, it did establish an identity for the library schools that had been lacking. Library-school educators were not simply thinking about the political value of ALA endorsement. Their concerns were both administrative and curricular. Among their issues were establishing consistent standards for admission to library school programs, establishing standards for instructors, determining the length of programs, determining the types of degrees to be awarded, establishing the proper balance between practical and theoretical approaches, and developing a system for transferring credits from one school to another (Vann 1961).

It was neither ALA nor the American Association of Library Schools that had the most effect on the future direction of library education. Rather, it was the Carnegie Corporation, established by Andrew Carnegie to administer his philanthropic activities after his death. The corporation continued to provide funds for public libraries, but had begun to suspect that the libraries, after being built, were often inadequately supported. This, despite the fact that generally Carnegie agreed to provide money for buildings only if the recipient of his largesse would agree to commit 10% of the amount donated each year to maintain the library. This led the corporation to appoint Alvin Saunders Johnson in 1915 to determine the condition of the libraries built with Carnegie funds and to explore the adequacy of library schools. Johnson's report in 1916 suggested that there were serious problems. He observed that those working in libraries were often poorly trained. He criticized the quality of many of the programs and suggested that the corporation assist in the recruitment of better-qualified individuals through scholarships, provide financial assistance to library schools and summer-school programs, and shift the emphasis in the corporation's philanthropy by providing money to improve library service rather than for buildings (Vann 1961).

Johnson's report was met with concern by the Carnegie Corporation. The corporation then subsidized a major study directed solely toward library education, and the library schools in particular. The corporation appointed C.C. Williamson to undertake this study. Williamson had the ideal combination of credentials. He was a political economist, a graduate of Columbia, and a professor of economics at Bryn Mawr. He had served as head of the Economics and Sociology Library at the New York Public Library, and at the time of his appointment was head of the Municipal Reference Library in New York. Williamson (1923) conducted a close examination of fifteen library schools and a final report was issued in 1923. Referred to as the "Williamson Report," its historic importance to library education is unquestioned. A summary of some of his major findings and recommendations are noted below.

1. There is a difference between clerical and professional work. Professional work deals with theory and the application of principles and requires a broad education, including four years of college. Clerical work involves the following of rules and as such requires far less education. Professional, rather than clerical, instruction should be provided by library schools.

2. Library schools do not agree on the subjects that should be taught or the emphasis of subjects. Different schools devote much more time to one subject than to others.

3. The schools' curricula must reflect constant reexamination so that the most current practices can be taught rather than relying on traditional practices.

4. The breadth of content required for adequate library school instruction cannot be realized in only one year of education.

5. There is considerable inconsistency in entrance requirements. Library schools should require a college education (or its equivalent) for entrance.

6. Many current library school instructors are not trained to teach college graduates. Many lack college degrees themselves, few have had training or experience in teaching, and nearly one-third have had no library experience. There is too much reliance on lectures and few good textbooks. Low salaries of teachers need to be corrected, and library schools need to find ways to recruit teachers of better quality. Schools must also provide financial incentives for teachers to produce texts.

7. To recruit students, library schools should maintain high educational standards and provide fellowships and scholarships to make library training more attractive.

8. The library school should be part of an academic department in a university. This conforms with the model that other professional schools have used. Universities are better able to maintain academic standards and increase the status of these programs, and public libraries are unable to devote the resources necessary to maintain these standards.

9. Library programs should consist of two years of schooling. The first year should consist of a general program of study; the second year should be highly specialized. This will involve cooperative efforts with other local educational institutions.

10. There is little incentive for librarians who are currently employed to seek continuing education. Continuing education at this point is centered on subprofessional workers; this needs to be remedied by schools that direct their attention to the enrichment of professional education. Correspondence schools should be considered.

11. There are no fixed standards of training for librarians. The setting of standards should begin with the profession, and once established should eventually be made part of the law. The American Library Association should

      create a system of voluntary certification of librarians regulated by a national certification board.

12.    The national certification board should also serve as an agency for accreditation of library schools (Williamson 1923).

The Williamson Report represents a breakthrough for library education. Although many of the issues raised were not original with Williamson, his report represented a culmination of the historical forces that were working to define library education for this century. Because of the imprimatur of the Carnegie Corporation, the report could not be ignored. It established the essentially theoretical and professional nature of the discipline and appropriately located the focus of the education of librarians at the university. In addition, because Williamson sets forth a college degree as an entrance requirement, it is clear that he considered library education to be on the graduate level (Williamson 1923). Thus the master's degree became the appropriate degree. In a broader sense, the Williamson Report affirmed that a substantial part of librarianship was, or should be, a form of education, rather than simply training. Further, it forced the profession to consider the importance of consistency and high quality in the curricula, administration, and teaching in library schools. Interestingly, some of Williamson's recommendations were not heeded, most notably the certification of librarians. Likewise, only a few library schools have adopted a two-year program of study.

After the issuance of the Williamson Report all other forms of library education did not simply vanish nor did the profession-at-large uncritically accept his recommendations. But its impact was considerable and marked the eventual death knell for all other forms of professional education. ALA responded by creating the Temporary Library Training Board in 1924, which soon became the Board of Education for Librarianship (BEL). The BEL prepared standards for library education in 1925 and 1933, which helped establish master's-level education for one year of education beyond graduate school (Robbins-Carter and Seavey 1986). By the early 1950s, most library schools had adopted the "fifth-year" master's degree for their model.

The Carnegie Corporation's response to the report was even more concrete. Williamson had revealed many weaknesses and inconsistencies in library schools, and there was obviously a considerable need to improve them. In the ensuing fifteen years, the Carnegie Corporation gave nearly $2 million to seventeen library schools to accomplish this. Perhaps the corporation's most notable achievement during this time was the special attention it paid to the lack of research and quality texts for instruction. It was determined that the best way to resolve this problem was to support the creation of a graduate program for librarians—a program that would lead to the Ph.D. The school, called the Graduate Library School, was established at the University of Chicago in 1926, and the doctoral program began in 1928. Rayward (1983) argues that "library science" as opposed to librarianship emerged with the creation of the Graduate Library School because it emphasized theoretical approaches that involved applying the scientific and research tools of other disciplines to library work.

The Graduate Library School at the University of Chicago made special contributions to librarianship. First, its faculty was quite diverse, drawing faculty members with expertise from a variety of fields, including sociology and history. These individuals applied the established methodologies from other academic disciplines to the problems of librarianship. Second, the faculty focused on research. Because the faculty were primarily scholars rather than practitioners, they produced a considerable body of research, which formed the foundation for further research. Finally, the school sponsored many conferences and programs on major issues in the profession. These conferences drew practitioners and other library school faculty together and resulted in numerous publications, which also served as texts.

The Carnegie Corporation during this time also provided funding for the first school specifically designed to train African American librarians. The Hampton Institute Library School was created by a Carnegie grant in 1925. Given the concentration of African Americans in the South at that time, it is notable that before 1925 there was only one accredited library school in the South, Emory in Atlanta, but it did not admit African Americans until 1962 (Campbell 1977; McPheeters 1988). What library training was available was primarily through training programs in libraries or, in very rare instances, attendance at a predominantly white library school. By 1925, there was only one African American graduate of a library school—Edward Williams, librarian of Howard University (Campbell 1977). Obviously, with the growth of colleges for African Americans and the presence of primary and secondary schools that served them, there was a growing need for librarians. The fact that such a school was not founded until this late date is related to the lack of library services for African Americans up to this time. It was only because philanthropic organizations such as the Carnegie Corporation and the Julius Rosenwald Fund focused on library services in the South that the issue of library service to African Americans was highlighted (Campbell 1977). To this end, the founder and first director of the Hampton Institute Library School, Florence Rising Curtis, played a significant role. Rising was a graduate of Dewey's school in Albany. Before coming to Hampton, she had had a distinguished career in the profession. She taught for twelve years at the University of Illinois's library school and had also been vice-director at the Drexel Institute school. She played a major role in the establishment and operation of the Association of American Library Schools, serving as its first secretary (Davis 1978). At Hampton, she was not only largely responsible for the quality of instruction to library school students, but she was devoted to improving library service throughout the South for African Americans. The Hampton Institute produced some notable library graduates during its existence, including Virginia Lacy Jones, who was to become the dean of the Atlanta University School of Library Service, and Wallace Van Jackson, library director at Virginia State College and a teacher at Hampton Institute, who made substantial contributions to academic library service for African Americans (Campbell 1977). Unfortunately, with the decline in the philanthropic resources on which the school depended, the school was closed in 1939. Although the loss of the Hampton Institute Library School was significant, fortunately, it was just two years later that its role was continued by a school established at Atlanta University (Davis 1978) under the urging of its president, John Hope.

The Depression and World War II placed severe burdens both on the development of libraries and on librarianship. Following the war, library educators continued to analyze and reanalyze their methods of education. Many of their concerns echoed those of Williamson. Educators were especially concerned that the curricula of many schools still emphasized routines rather than theory, and there was considerable variation in quality among the schools. In 1951, the Board of Education for Librarianship issued a new set of standards for library education that finally required five years of post-high-school education (in other words, a master's degree) as the standard for professional education. This ended once and for all the alternative forms of library education. In 1956, the ALA Committee on Accreditation (COA) was formed and given the responsibilities of reviewing and accrediting library school programs, a task that it holds to this day.

The decades of the 1950s and 1960s were a fruitful period for libraries and librarians. In particular, the expanding economy, the Baby Boom, the passage of the Library Services Act, and federal legislation supporting the development of elementary, secondary, and higher education institutions and their libraries all led to a significant expansion of libraries and library collections. This concomitantly resulted in an increased need for librarians and provided a fertile market for spawning library schools. By the 1970s there were more than seventy accredited library schools with accredited master's programs in the United States and Canada. This might be considered the "heyday" of library schools, at least judging by the numbers, for the following two decades produced a considerable retreat. This decline included the elimination of library schools with considerable reputations, including those at the University of Chicago and Columbia. By 1999 there were fifty-six ALA-accredited library school programs in the United States and Canada (Appendix E). There may be many reasons for this decline, including economic and social conditions. With the recession of the 1980s, there were deliberate, self-conscious attempts at universities to reduce costs. Tax payers became ever more reluctant to finance higher education, and politicians and board members found the budgets for higher education a tempting arena in which to cut costs. Internally, schools of library and information studies (LIS) are not, as a rule, high profile departments. They are rarely mentioned when speaking of the reputation of an academic institution, nor do they produce many major donors in comparison with law or medical schools. In addition, LIS programs have traditionally not built strong links with other academic departments and have low visibility and prestige within the academic community. Many of these schools failed to develop an energetic alumni network. The result is that higher education administrations have found library schools fairly easy targets for closing, and because of their lack of connections with other academic departments, they find few defenders when closing decisions are made (Paris 1988). Boyce (1994), dean of a school of library and information science, has suggested that such closings may not be all bad. He suggests that library schools try to improve the quality of their academic programs and the profession set higher academic standards. Boyce suspected that an additional one-third to one-half of the remaining library schools might close. It appears, however, that the precipitous decline has ended, and it is hoped that the remaining library schools have learned from the experiences of those less fortunate. In fact, one program that had previously closed at the University of Denver is now establishing a new LIS program.

*Contemporary LIS Education and Training: Background and Challenges*

### LIS STUDENTS

Although concern has been expressed that the overall number of library school graduates has declined (enrollment peaked in 1992), the decline has been minimal. In 1998, 5,024 masters degrees were conferred, in comparison to 5,068 in 1997. In 1998 there were more than 12,800 master's students enrolled in accredited master's programs in the United States and Canada. In the same year, more than 5,000 students received a master's degree, 78 percent of whom were women (ALISE 1999). The largest group of male students are (43 percent) between twenty-five and thirty-four, while more of the females are older. This may be a reflection of many factors. Librarianship is considered a career of "late deciders," because it is not usually considered a first career choice. It is unlikely, for example, that recent college graduates are counseled that librarianship is a good career. It does not have high visibility or status, nor does it offer competitive salaries compared to many other occupations. Recruiters for LIS programs are generally unaggressive. Similarly, given the numerical dominance of women in its labor force, it is often a career that for many is delayed during their early child-bearing years. It is notable that in 1999 approximately 15 percent of the male enrollees and 22 percent of the women enrollees were forty-five or older: overall one in five enrollees were forty-five years or older (ALISE 1999).

### LIS PROGRAMS

Programs in library and information science (LIS) have undergone a substantial evolution over the last decade. This, in turn, has led educators to rethink a substantial part of their curricula. The evolution has in large part been precipitated by the expansion of information technologies and the resulting changes in the way that information is being created, organized, accessed, and disseminated. This can be seen in the name of the schools that were traditionally known as schools of library science. Today, with minor variations, most are known as one of the following:

School of Information Science and Policy
School of Library and Information Studies
School of Library and Information Science

School of Information Studies
School of Information

The introduction of "information studies" is a recognition of at least three factors: (1) information rather than books has become a central focus of many programs; (2) information technologies are significantly influencing the basic functions of libraries; and (3) there is a considerable market for information specialists, who may or may not be associated with libraries, whom schools of library and information science can educate and train. This recognition has been formalized by the American Library Association, which has determined that programs of education for librarianship will be referred to officially as programs in "Library and Information Studies."

### INTEGRATION OF INFORMATION TECHNOLOGIES INTO THE CURRICULUM

Because information technologies play such an important role, LIS curricula have had to make substantial changes. They have had to integrate new information into current courses and add a wide variety of courses, including information storage and retrieval, networking, and programming, to an already full course of study.

### COMPETITION FROM OTHER ACADEMIC DISCIPLINES

As the function of libraries and library education has become more generically related to the broader concept of information access, the content in a variety of disciplines tends to overlap with LIS programs. For this reason, academic disciplines such as computer science, communications studies, and business programs have developed programs that mirror many aspects of LIS. In some cases, this has led to a combining or integration of library science programs with other departments. LIS programs must walk a fine line between broadening their curricula and retaining their unique identities. Failure to do so results in loss of fiscal and human resources, and sometime even more troubling, the loss of departmental identity within the institution.

### FINANCIAL STRESSES

The integration of information technologies into LIS programs has substantially increased the costs of operation. The costs are rather impressive: computer hardware and software, support materials such as books and periodicals, peripherals, maintenance and replacement of computers, network and telecommunication costs, and hiring individuals to support the computer systems. This is in addition to the costs of hiring faculty to instruct in these new and developing areas and the costs of supporting faculty training to use the new technologies.

### CONTINUING EDUCATION

Continuing education involves the improvement of the knowledge, skills, and abilities of individuals in their professional performance. With the rapid changes occurring in the information environment, much of the knowledge conveyed in library and information programs inevitably becomes obsolete quickly. Consequently, many LIS programs have recognized that there is a significant need to continue the education of graduates, as well as to provide training for other library employees. Adding to the pedagogical burdens of LIS faculty can be problematic. Therefore, these programs must develop techniques to identify the specific course content needed by returning students.

### DISTANCE EDUCATION

The economic pressures in higher education have led administrators to search for techniques to increase enrollments while delivering education at minimum costs. With developments in telecommunications, it has now become possible to deliver education at remote sites using television. This technique, as well as other distance learning techniques, are being employed by some LIS programs, such as those at the University of South Carolina and the University of Arizona.

This form of education brings its own set of issues. Among these are (1) how to ensure that the quality of education provided in distance learning is equal to that provided in the traditional classroom; (2) how to create a sense of educational community for students who may have little face-to-face contact with faculty members and other students; (3) how to train faculty to employ new distance learning technologies effectively; (4) how to administer distance learning programs; and (5) how best to assess academic performance in the distance learning environment. Many of these issues are not unique to distance education, but they must be addressed yet again with the development of this new channel for library education.

The American population is becoming increasingly heterogeneous. It is projected that by the year 2000 the four major minority populations—Native Americans, African Americans, Hispanics, and Asians—will comprise approximately one-third of the U.S. population; in the next century, whites are likely to become a minority population (Josey 1989). In many large cities, minorities comprise the majority, or, at least, a very substantial proportion of the urban population. In order to serve these populations it has become increasingly necessary for LIS programs to recruit more minority M.L.S. students and to provide some focus on how to serve ethnic and minority populations.

The problem of minority recruitment has been recognized for decades, especially the small number of African Americans. The small number of African-American librarians and the lack of ALA involvement at the higher levels were among the main reasons for the creation of the Black Caucus of ALA in 1970 under the chairmanship of E. J. Josey. Current minority enrollments in M.L.S. programs remain well below 10 percent. McCook and Geist (1993) have suggested ways to improve the situation, including developing cooperative partnerships between LIS schools and employers, greater monetary support for minority students, more active recruitment activities in undergraduate and secondary education programs, recruitment in nontraditional settings such as military and community colleges, and creation of an educational environment more conducive to minority students. In addition to recruitment, LIS schools need to develop education programs that provide training sensitive to cultural and language differences and to the special information needs of these populations.

IDENTIFICATION OF COMPETENCIES FOR LIBRARY AND INFORMATION PROFESSIONALS

What knowledge and skills are essential for the education of librarians? What constitutes the core of information needed for education and training of LIS professionals? Lynch (1989), for example, in her examination of courses in LIS programs, found there were only a small number of core courses on which there was agreement and little agreement as to what constituted courses for specialization in the field.

As the field of library and information science expands, the potential areas for training and education will expand further. Given the variety of competencies that are possible, LIS programs need to identify those that are essential so that graduating students will have a basic level of knowledge and skill to perform their jobs. This will require a careful understanding of the dynamic library and information job market and tailoring of the curricula to meet the needs of this market. Will this mean a reduction of theoretical material and a significant increase in practical "how-to" material on information technologies? Main (1990) has suggested that this is the desirable course:

> ... there is no longer a need to be concerned with theoretical and philosophical issues. What we must be concerned with is what enables us to survive in a competitive world, namely information technology. And information technology is a practical discipline (p. 228).

Such a view is quite different from that advanced by Williamson in 1923, and other academics would no doubt argue that the challenges and issues raised by these same information technologies make understanding the philosophical issues even more important today. Similarly, it is argued that there is a need to increase librarians' theoretical understanding so that they can perform the planning, evaluation, and decision-making functions that will be so vital in the rapidly evolving information environment. As Lynch (1989) has noted: "The shaping of the future of librarianship rests not on the vocational skills necessary to the time, but on the principles common to all specialization in the field. The professional expects library education to be built on a solid intellectual foundation" (p. 81). No doubt, these different perspectives will generate tensions within LIS programs for years to come.

An underlying aspect of this debate centers on the centrality of the M.L.S. for professional education. As the professional model of education has developed in the latter part of the twentieth century, formal education has become increasingly important. This is based on the notion that within a profession is a substantive body of theoretical knowledge and principles upon which professional practice is based. Obviously, this is a critical point for LIS education. Even today there are some who assert that there is not a sufficient body of theoretical education to require graduate academic training. As Hauptman (1987) has asserted:

> ... there is not even any mandatory *a priori* knowledge necessary to function effectively as a librarian of any persuasion. Any intelligent college graduate can begin working in a special, public, or academic library and quickly learn the skills necessary to catalog, do reference work,

manipulate overrated computer systems, or even administer (pp. 252–253).

Hauptman describes the work of the librarian as "90% clerical" and asserts that librarians create a mystique, regarding their work much like other professions. The patron can often learn to perform some library functions in only a short time. Campbell (1993) takes a different view but raises the same issue. He argues that the computer revolution has created the need for greater and greater technical proficiencies and that the failure to alter library education significantly may lead to its obsolescence. As he notes: " . . . the MLS may no longer be a viable credential given the nature of the technological and practical challenges we face in everyday library work" (p. 560).

On the other hand there are many who would disagree with the diminution of LIS education and the master's degree. Librarianship, like many professions, is a combination of work that appears routine and work that requires theoretical and conceptual knowledge and judgement. Such a view does not see librarianship so much as a set of individual tasks, as it does a field that performs an essential social and political function demanding a broad understanding of the nature of knowledge, information, people, and society. It requires an understanding that permits us to evaluate, make judgements, and set future courses of action. For example, knowing the name of a particular source may be useful for answering a specific query, but understanding people's information needs and how to identify and evaluate them requires a different type of understanding. This latter type of understanding helps librarians design their information systems, choose areas of emphasis, and design methods for encouraging the use of such systems. The same may be said for understanding the principles of selection, the effects of information policy, the uses of technology, the manner by which knowledge is organized, and the principles that guide the operation of information-giving institutions. As White (1986) has noted, the master's degree is not so much a qualification for a particular position, as it is a qualification for entry into the profession.

The American Library Association (1996) has recognized the importance of graduate education among its own policy statements. In part it states:

> The American Library Association supports the provision of library services by professionally qualified personnel who have been educated in

graduate programs within institutions of higher education . . . The American Library Association supports the development and continuance of high quality graduate library/information science educational programs of the quality, scope and availability necessary to prepare individuals in the broad profession of information dissemination.

The American Library Association supports education for the preparation of professionals in the field of library and information studies (LIS) as a university program at the master's level (p. 137).

This supporting statement is strong but not unequivocal. It does not, for example, insist that all professional librarians possess a master's degree from an accredited LIS program.

The importance of the master's degree in library science became quite public when a legal challenge was lodged against its use as a criteria for hiring a librarian at Mississippi State University in the 1980s. Title VII of the Civil Rights Act protects various classes from discrimination by age, race, color, religion, or disability. The act extends to protecting individuals from being discriminated against in the hiring process, especially when an irrelevant characteristic or qualification is considered in that process. In other words, employers are obligated to employ only those criteria that directly relate to the individual's ability to perform the job. Glenda Merwine sued Mississippi State University when she was not hired for a librarian's position at the Veterinary Medicine Library. Although the case, *Glenda Merwine v. Board of Trustees for State Institutions of Higher Education* (Holley 1984) had many complications, one of her arguments was that she was denied employment because she did not possess a master's degree from a program accredited by ALA. Interestingly, ALA did not take a stand on the issue, but several prominent library educators did testify. The court found that no reasonable alternative to the master's degree had been provided and that the master's degree was both relevant and broadly accepted as the professional degree. This case did not permanently resolve the possibility of subsequent challenges, but an adverse decision would have seriously damaged the professional degree's standing. In addition, it put the profession on notice that it must be able to clearly articulate why the professional degree is essential. Nor has it inoculated the profession from attacks from other sources, most notably the Office of Management and Budget of the federal government, which has challenged the need for a master's from an accredited LIS program for some positions that previously required it.

EVALUATION OF LIBRARY EDUCATION

Since the 1950s the ALA Committee on Accreditation has served as the formal professional means of quality control for LIS education. Only LIS programs on the master's level are accredited. The purpose of such accreditation is to assure that LIS programs are of sufficient quality to provide library service. There are no formal bodies assessing LIS education at the doctoral level.

The accreditation standards have changed as the field has evolved and as schools have expressed their dissatisfactions with the evaluation process. In 1992 a new set of standards replaced those created in 1972 (ALA 1992). Each standard is considered to be an essential component of a master's degree LIS program. The standards address six basic areas: Mission, Goals, and Objectives; Curriculum; Faculty; Students; Administration and Financial Support; Physical Resources and Facilities. Contemporary accreditation places strong emphasis on the school's ability to articulate its own mission, to develop planning mechanisms to implement its mission, and to provide effective methods for evaluating the outcomes of its educational program. In addition, reflecting the development of alternative teaching approaches, the standards explicitly recognize that LIS education can be provided through nontraditional mechanisms such as closed-circuit television or satellite transmission. The standards, however, remain the same regardless of the delivery technique.

Although the need for accreditation is strong, not all library educators are satisfied with the current standards and approach. Saracevic (1994) has suggested that allowing schools to set their own missions is illogical and focuses too much attention on setting their own objectives rather than developing a basic curriculum centered on the content and theoretical foundations of the field. Saracevic is concerned that universities in which LIS programs are located perceive them as vocational institutions rather than academic departments. Without the necessary theoretical underpinnings library schools are in jeopardy of closure.

DEVELOPMENT OF ENTIRELY NEW APPROACHES TO PROFESSIONAL EDUCATION

It has been argued that the curriculum of library and information science programs requires more than mere adaptation to new technologies—the curriculum should be revolutionized. This has already occurred at the University of Michigan School of Information. The school, sponsored by a major grant from the W. K. Kellogg Foundation, started the Kellogg Coalition on Reinventing Information Science, Technology, and Library Education (CRISTAL-ED). CRISTAL-ED was created out of concern that current schools of library and information science were not adapting adequately to the rapid changes in information technologies and their uses. Similarly, computer science and management information programs were not taking a sufficiently broad view of the human aspects of information systems (CRISTAL-ED, "Charting," 1997). A need to integrate these disciplines with a new curriculum is asserted. CRISTAL-ED is intended to develop information professionals that will be able to exploit both digital and print technologies and to transform information processes with their new understanding of information systems (CRISTAL-ED, "Objectives" 1997). The stated goals of CRISTAL-ED (1997) are to:

> (1) Build a coalition to reinvent an information and library science learning environment that produces information and library leaders for the digital information world; (2) Conduct joint pilot projects to support research, hands-on learning, creation of "living specification," and continuing education. (3) Apply collaboratory ideas to distance-independent learning—perhaps, create a federated (virtual) school (p. 1).

## THE LIBRARY PROFESSION: THE STRUGGLE FOR PROFESSIONAL IDENTITY AND PURPOSE

Librarianship, for some time, has been occupied, some might say preoccupied, with the question: "Are we a profession?" This self-reflection has created a substantial literature, but leaves the question unresolved. As early as 1876, Melvil Dewey thought he had resolved the issue in his editorial in the first issue of *Library Journal* when he pronounced, "The time has come when a librarian may, without assumption, speak of his occupation as a profession . . . " (p. 5). Few, however, have accepted this pronouncement as final. Underlying the concern over the professional question are some substantial issues, and the stakes are high: recognition as a profession could lead to increases in status and concomitant increases in wages and authority.

*Do Librarians Have a Distinctive Function?*

To a substantial degree, the professional status of librarianship rests on the belief that librarians do special things and possess special expertise. This is sometime referred to as the "asymmetry of expertise," implying that the client or patron places special trust in the knowledge of the professional (Abbott 1988, p. 5). The historical image of the library and librarian and their source of authority was based in part on the fact that the library performed an essentially unique function in a unique way. It was, after all, often the only place in town with a substantial collection of materials that was well-organized and readily available to its users, and it had librarians who had at least some idea how to locate the right materials. This gave the librarian, if not a monopoly, a limited amount of control over some types of knowledge. It was a clearly identified institution where such knowledge could be obtained. Abbott (1988) identifies the type of knowledge over which librarians had control as "qualitative information" (p. 216), in contrast to quantitative information, which would be provided by professionals such as cost accountants, statisticians, and engineers. Librarians "had physical custody of cultural capital" (Abbott 1988, p. 217) which they organized and disseminated for either education or entertainment (Abbott 1988).

But now librarianship is in competition with many other information agencies that may also provide information. In turn, this competition leads to a struggle for professional jurisdiction (Abbott 1988). The effect of this competition may change the internal functions of library work. For example, Nielson (1989) argues that the traditional and classical library model of a reference librarian able to answer any reference question put to him or her is changing significantly. There are several factors involved in this transformation:

> (1) increasing availability of remote and local end-user search systems both in and outside libraries, and artificial intelligence systems with icon-based interfaces for responding to both routine and non-routine questions; (2) a user population increasingly sophisticated in a variety of computing application areas; (3) availability of improved software products that encourage library users to integrate computing applications in their day-to-day work; and (4) pervasive availability of computing power and textual, numeric and graphic data commonly accessible in machine-readable form (p. 190).

Today, anyone with a computer, a modem, and access to the NII has access to a considerable amount of knowledge. It is no accident that the promoters of Internet access—major competitors to libraries—describe their service as access to a "virtual library." So to whatever extent the librarian was perceived as having control over access to knowledge, this control may be deteriorating even further.

Mason (1990) echoes deterioration in the distinctiveness of the library profession, placing it within the broader confines of the information profession. He has identified seven major information professions: accountant, archivist, librarian, records manager, information systems analyst, management scientist, and museum curator. The duty of the information professional according to Mason is "to get the right *information* from the right *source* to the right *client* at the right *time* in the form most suitable for the use to which it is to be put and at a *cost* that is justified by its use" (p.125). The information professional's purpose is to improve a client's knowledge. One could add several other categories, including information entrepreneurs or even teacher. All this suggests that the librarian cannot claim sole jurisdiction to this area as a lawyer might claim such jurisdiction for the law.

On the other hand, Winter (1988) sees a distinctive characteristic to the field. He has identified three basic functions of librarians: classification of knowledge to organize it, indexing recorded knowledge so that that knowledge can be accessed, and understanding the formal and informal organization of various bodies of knowledge. Librarianship is engaged in a metascience that attempts to understand not one body of knowledge, but the organization of many bodies of knowledge and their interrelationship. On the face of it, this seems to provide some convincing substance to the argument that librarianship is indeed a profession, for these functions cannot be accomplished without considerable knowledge, both theoretical and practical. Yet it does not follow that librarianship is the only occupation concerned with these functions; other occupations also perform similar functions.

Winter (1988) argues that "mediating between the user and the public record of knowledge is the special province of the librarian . . . " (p. 6). This special province harkens back to a fundamental value of the field, that of service. Librarianship is quintessentially serving a special *social* function, rather than just a specific activity. It is engaged in a social service, emphasizing the welfare of people over profit. Its model historically reaches back to an age in which professions were meant to improve the society: clergy, lawyers, doctors, teachers, nurses, social workers. These professions were dedicated to the betterment of people, not increases in profit, which were characteristics of positions in business and industry. As Abbott (1988) has observed, the professions "stood outside the new commercial and industrial heart of society" (p. 3). Librarians serve the public good by providing library service, by bringing people in contact with the vast body of public knowledge. In doing so, librarians support fundamental democratic values by emphasizing equality of access to knowledge. This cannot be assumed of other information professionals such as accountants, management scientists, computer scientists, or systems analysts. Underlying the special character of librarianship is not its techniques, but its underlying values. The significance of librarianship lies not in mastery of sources, organizational skills, or technological competence, but in *why* librarians perform the functions they do. The fact that librarianship tends to encompass the vast body of print, audiovisual, and electronic information increases the importance of these underlying values further and differentiates it from other, even kindred, professions such as museum curators or historical society professionals.

*Is Librarianship a Profession?*

The debate over the distinctiveness of librarianship will continue, and this lack of clarity spills over into the question of whether it can rightfully be called a profession at all. Traditionally, the debate has been placed in the broader sociological context of defining professions more generally. The most popular approach, although not necessarily the most intellectually satisfying, is called trait theory. In this theory, professions are accepted or rejected based on whether they possess certain traits. Among these traits are the following:

1. Possesses a substantial body of theoretical knowledge that forms the intellectual foundation of the profession. Practitioners hence possess considerable expertise and knowledge of principles that are based on a systematically organized body of knowledge and usually acquired through a significant amount of formal education.
2. Permits a substantial amount of autonomy. Individuals practicing in the profession generally exercise their own professional judgement and, within the bounds of the canons of their profession, are free to act in accordance with these judgements.
3. Exercises control over the conduct of its practitioners through licensure and a code of ethics. Professions are often recognized by codes established that give the profession the authority to control entrance into the

profession and to sanction practitioners if their conduct falls outside professional bounds. This is sometimes referred to as *structural powers* (Reeves 1980, pp. xix-xx). The power to license practitioners, to regulate their conduct and to withdraw the power to practice the profession is usually vested in the appropriate professional association such as the American Bar Association or the American Medical Association. The enforcement of conduct within a profession is not only established by law; it is also defined by codes of ethics promulgated by the respective professional association. Violations of this code can lead to sanctions including suspension or revocation of the license. In many professions however, the professional association does not have the power to sanction or legally control the activities of its professionals. Nonetheless, these bodies can still influence the nature of the professional work and the standards of work and conduct through education and standard setting. Such bodies exercise normative rather than structural power over its professionals (Reeves 1980).

4. Possesses a dominant altruistic rather than self-interested purpose. That is, professions place as their primary purpose the betterment of others and society-at-large. Professions provide an important service to the society, and their values emphasize the provision of such service over the personal and pecuniary interests of its practitioners. Professions are, in this sense a "calling" rather than an occupation. This is reflected in the origin of professions which arose from the clergy and served as a profession of faith. Professions in their modern sense emerged in considerable numbers in the latter part of the nineteenth century and the early part of the twentieth (law, medicine, nursing, teaching, librarianship), and it is notable that they arose in contrast to the many other factory-oriented occupations of the period. Professions had as their central value service to others rather than production and profit.

5. Possesses a monopoly over the practice of the profession. This can be seen prominently in the areas of law and medicine. These professions, in large measure, possess singular control over their fields. It is, in fact, unlawful for others not certified by their respective associations to practice law or medicine, and usually those who attempt to do so are barred from the basic institutions of the profession, such as the courts or practice in hospitals. Even in these fields the monopoly is not complete, but it is substantial.

6. Possesses professional associations. These associations serve many vital functions including providing a professional identity to its members; defining and enforcing the standards for the education needed and accrediting the institutions that provide that education; enforcing standards of conduct; providing continuing education; providing a centralized forum, e.g., conferences and institutes, for the discussion of issues and research; and producing publications for dissemination of research and professional information.

Librarianship shares some of these traits. It is service-oriented and altruistic rather than profit-making in its orientation. It has professional associations that hold conferences, produce publications, promulgate codes of ethics and, in the case of ALA, provide an accrediting function. Yet, upon reviewing these traits, one could argue that librarianship does not meet these qualifications in some very important areas. Most notably, the power of the professional associations is very limited. They do not control the licensing of practitioners and possess no power to sanction practitioners whose conduct violates its professional codes. In other words, there is no monopoly exercised by librarianship, although the field does possess normative authority, including the standards of conduct and work of librarians. One reason for the lack of strong structural control in the profession may be because many of its functions, such as finding and disseminating information, can be generalized and performed outside the library context. Similarly, arguments are frequently made that the discipline lacks a theoretical basis and that the formal education is primarily training rather than theoretical knowledge or principles. It is further argued that any necessary knowledge probably could be acquired just as well on the job as in the classroom. In addition, the formal graduate training, one year in most cases, is not equal to the extensive training required in other professions.

The trait view of professions, however, has been seriously criticized. For example, the extent to which a profession possesses particular traits is difficult to measure, and setting a criterion for how much of a particular trait is required for an occupation to be considered a profession is problematic. An alternative, and perhaps more appropriate, view of librarianship as a profession has been discussed by Winter (1988), who uses a "control model" based on the work of various sociologists. In this view, the nature of a profession is based on the power of that profession and the nature of the control that it exercises over practitioners. Underlying this view is the notion that an occupation and a profession are actually two related but distinct phenomena: a profession is a set of practices that control an occupation. In many ways, professions are more like unions than they are a particular occupation. Hence where one can speak of "unionized" occupations, e.g., auto workers, one can also speak of "professionalized" occupations, which identifies a certain type of control that is exercised (p. 44). The professional control model emphasizes higher educational degrees and intellectual and theoretical knowledge in contrast to unionized control, which relies on work background and manual skills.

The control model, however, does not assume that all control is centered among the practitioners of the profession. There are, in fact, three types of control that dominate the intellectual activities of the profession. These are "collegial control," "client control," and "mediated control." In collegial control, the occupation is controlled by those who provide the service. For example, doctors and lawyers tend to control their practices in regard to their patients. In a client-controlled profession, the clients who use the services determine their wants, their needs, and the means by which they are satisfied. In the mediated type of control, there is a balance between collegial control and client control. Winter (1988) suggests that almost all professions are moving toward mediated control. Even in medicine, for example, patients are exercising a great deal more control over their medical treatment than in the past. Librarianship seems to fall in the mediated control category. Some clients will seek information and the librarian may have a great deal of autonomy in resolving that need; in other cases, the client may ask for a specific item or set of items. The librarian merely locates the information demanded by the user.

The proliferation of information technologies may also be an important factor that affects professional control or the lack thereof. Birdsall (1982) suggests that these technologies have stimulated a trend toward deprofessionalization or the creation of new professional models. Computerization, it is asserted, tends to make expert knowledge and technique much more widely available than in the past. In Winter's terms, it tends to promote a more client-controlled model. According to Birdsall, the newer professions will not be characterized by a monopoly over special knowledge, but a recognition that the society is moving toward a self-help or self-reliant model of service. The purpose of the new professional is not to control knowledge or prescribe what the client must do, but to teach the client to become more and more self-sufficient. Birdsall suggests that the helping professions such as librarianship, social work, and education fall into this category of professional.

What becomes clear, is that the amount and type of control exercised by librarianship may have great impact on how others perceive the profession. This in turn affects status and influence. The increasing awareness that information is a vital resource in our society and the many economic, technological, and political forces used to control the creation and dissemination of this information, could have tremendous impact on who can have access to information, what type, and how much. Librarians have recognized the importance of influencing policies and practices in this arena and their role and contribution could have a significant influence whether or not librarians will be considered professionals. If librarians are perceived as having unique and expert knowledge of the organization and dissemination of information, and if they are seen as integral to the information dissemination process, then it is likely that they will be heard in the information-access debate. The stakes are high.

*What Is the Image and Personality of Librarians?*

How are librarians perceived, and do the perceptions match the reality? It is commonly believed by librarians that their image is negative: they are aging spinsters, have their hair in a bun, wearing sensible shoes and glasses. In addition, librarians believe that they are perceived as authoritarian and controlling, stern in appearance, ready to say "Shhsh" at the slightest disturbance. Male librarians experience additional concerns. They believe that they are seen as anomalous, part of a "woman's" profession, and therefore as ineffectual or effeminate. This fear is great enough so that men are less likely than their female counterparts to admit that they are librarians. They tend to refer to themselves more in terms that sound less feminine, for example, they are more likely to identify themselves as information scientists rather than librarians (Morrisey and Case 1988). Such stereotypes about men and women in librarianship can have pernicious effects. Not only can they affect the influence of librarians in the information environment, but they also impede recruitment of librarians and affect the status and growth of the profession as a whole.

But how much of librarians' fears are real? It is true that some professions are perceived as feminine and others masculine. For example, in 1988 Beggs and Doolittle (1993) found that among 129 occupation titles, "Head Librarian" was considered the sixth most feminine. The only occupations considered more feminine were manicurist, registered nurse, receptionist, private secretary, and prima ballerina. Interestingly, this study replicated a 1975 study that placed "Head Librarian" as the ninth most feminine, suggesting that the stereotyping has increased. This study also suggested that gender stereotyping of professions is greater among males than females. This does not necessarily mean that the traits portrayed in a "feminine" profession are problematic. Morrisey and Case (1988) specifically studied perceptions of male librarians by college students and found that the perception was often quite positive. They found that the most common terms to describe male librarians were "orga-nized," "approachable," "logical," "friendly," "patient," and "serious" (p. 457). Their conclusion was that male librarians perceived themselves in a much more negative light than others did. Schuman (1990) observed that although there are negative images in the media about librarians, the supposition that all such images are negative is unfounded. She points out that notable writers such as Sinclair Lewis, Sherwood Anderson, Henry James, and Edith Wharton depicted librarians in nonstereotypical manners, and that these nonstereotypical depictions were not uncom-mon in fiction. Furthermore, the media's occasional portrayal of librar-ians in a negative light may well be in line with how the media portray most other professions. What occupation does not receive a negative portrayal in the media? Lawyers and politicians receive their share of media ignominy. Even if current images of librarians are somewhat nega-tive, perhaps the future is brighter. One study of 117 children between the ages of four and fifteen by Duffy (1990) examined whether children had a positive attitude toward librarians. Duffy found that 50 percent responded positively when asked if they would like to become librar-ians. Many of the young people had little idea of what librarianship involves and saw the profession in terms of many of the stereotypes—the quiet of libraries, the apparent ease of the job, and the disciplinary atmosphere. In addition, the power of societal attitudes and socializa-tion still played a role, girls were more likely to respond positively than boys, and the older children were less likely to endorse librarianship as a career. It appears that sex-role stereotyping is still in operation, and as children grow older they seem to receive societal messages that librarianship is a less desirable career than others.

Studies of the personalities of librarians have been conducted for many years and generally have focused on either public or academic librarians. The first major study was conducted by Alice Bryan in 1948. The study was part of a much larger study of public libraries in general called the *Public Library Inquiry*. Bryan (1952) found that librarians were submissive and lacked qualities of leadership. Since then, a variety of studies have provided additional data that have been summarized by Agada (1984, 1987) and suggest that, in general, both male and female librarians exhibit personality traits of deference, passivity, nonassertive-ness, and self-abasement. Other studies have found librarians to be re-sistant to change, lacking initiative, and disinterested in decision-mak-ing. These traits persist regardless of whether the studies were of aca-demic or public librarians. Interestingly, there is little evidence that, despite the stereotype, librarians are authoritarian in character. One should also hasten to add that these traits were not considered to be pathological in character and, generally, librarians' personalities fell well within normal ranges.

Recent studies using the Myers-Briggs Type Indicator (MBTI) suggest that librarians tend to be introverted. In terms of the MBTI typologies, the majority of librarians fall into one of two typologies: Introversion, Sensing, Thinking, Judging (ISTJ) or Introversion, Intuitive, Thinking, Judging (INTJ). Among the characteristics of individuals who fall into this type are determination and perseverance, independence, a drive to work hard, the desire to innovate, and placing of a high value on competence (Scherdin 1994). One should, of course, be very careful about trying to apply these findings to individuals. Fisher (1988), in reviewing many personality studies of librarians, concluded that many of the personality tests applied were flawed, and overall, there was no one distinct personality type for a librarian.

Nonetheless, from a historical perspective, the findings of passivity among librarians might, in part, be attributable to the numerical predominance of women in the library profession. Dee Garrison, in her work, *The Apostles of Culture* (1979) suggests that its legacy has been low status for the profession. This numerical predominance of women has been a part of American librarianship, especially American public librarianship, since the latter half of the nineteenth century. The first woman clerk was hired by the Boston Public Library in 1852; by 1878 two-thirds of the library work force was female, and by 1910 more than 75 percent of library workers were women (Garrison 1972). In these years, women were expected to be passive and deferent. Professions that women were permitted to enter were "service" oriented and would thus reflect these traits. Since that time, the proportion of the work force by gender has varied little.

The entrance of women into the library labor force was an outgrowth of several factors. The rapid growth of public libraries produced a substantial need for library workers. However, these libraries were poorly funded, so there was a need to locate individuals who were willing to work for low pay. Women represented just such a group. Male library leaders and managers openly acknowledged the desirability of hiring women because they would be willing to work for half the pay. Librarianship fit the values of work for women at the time. It was not considered fitting for women to enter the labor force except under special circumstances; women were expected to marry and remain in the home. If this proved unfeasible, there was a narrow range of jobs that would be considered acceptable, mostly related to nurturing or educational activities, such as teaching and nursing. For all intents and purposes, these positions permitted women to bring their home-making and child-raising skills into the workplace. They were, therefore, considered dispositionally suited to librarianship, because the library was seen as a civilizing and nurturing environment (Garrison 1972). This all fit very well into the nineteenth-century value of the possibility of individual moral improvement and the capacity of books and reading to effect moral development. Indeed, librarianship was sometimes described as missionary activity. The fact that the profession still draws at least some individuals to its ranks who share these convictions is, in part, a legacy of these historical forces and confirmation that the service aspect of librarianship is still deeply ingrained.

Garrison (1972) has suggested that the feminization of public librarianship created an inferior image for the profession, an image it may not have had, had it remained the domain of male scholars as in previous decades. In other words, an occupation that had had considerable potential had been depressed in terms of status because it had been appropriated into the sphere of women. This sphere generally did not include leadership: women were not perceived as potential heads of libraries, especially of the larger libraries, but rather as support workers—leadership, after all, was not a characteristic generally located within a woman's character. Further, it was assumed, albeit incorrectly, that her physical nature was more delicate and could not tolerate the rigors of administration. Indeed, administrative responsibilities might even lead to mental illness!

The legacy of this attitude still persists: women librarians comprise 66 percent of the academic library work force, but only 48 percent occupy directorships, assistant or deputy directorships of academic libraries. Similarly, although women librarians occupy 80 percent of the public library positions, they hold only 67 percent of the directorships, assistant or deputy directorships (ALA 1986). There are several possible explanations for this trend. Women tend to have more career breaks due to family and marital responsibilities, and they begin their library careers later than men. They also tend to remain within the same organization longer than men, which reduces the number of promotional opportunities. When they do move to other libraries, they are more likely than their male counterparts to relocate because of spouses' job changes. This often entails accepting the only positions available to them, rather than positions involving promotion. The underrepresentation of women in administrative positions, however, is not fully accounted for by the reasons noted above—*sex discrimination still appears to play a role* (Heim and Estabrook 1983).

Internally, the distribution of positions by gender may also reflect sensitivity to problems with image and status. Women are more likely to serve as children's librarians or in cataloging positions; men are more likely to seek technology-oriented and managerial positions, despite the fact that males have no greater motivation to manage than female librarians (Swisher, Du Mont, and Boyer 1985). The former categories reflect values of nurturance or attention to detail, the latter categories reflect technical competence, leadership, or managerial skills. Male children's librarians are a rarity and no doubt raise eyebrows, no matter how undeservedly, when encountered. The predominance of men in the technical and managerial categories further supports the theory that men are uneasy working in a field whose traditions are perceived as "feminine." In the general labor force, technological and managerial positions are still dominated by males; male librarians may find that occupying such positions within libraries mitigates their occupational ambivalence. In turn, it may further serve to depress the status and pay of women. As Hildenbrand (1989) observes, librarians in children's services and cataloging generally receive lower pay than librarians in other positions despite the fact that these are basic functions in libraries. These inequalities in specialties are another example of the messages sent to women that their work is of less value and status.

The apparent passive nature of the profession has led Garrison (1972) to lament that librarianship has not encouraged or drawn to it those with the necessary leadership or aggressiveness to establish librarianship in the pantheon of professions—precisely because of its passivity. As Garrison observes:

> Specifically lacking in the librarian's professional service code are a sense of commitment, a drive to lead rather than to serve and a clear-cut conception of professional rights and responsibilities. The feminization of library work is a major cause of these deficiencies (pp. 144–145).

Although the facts seem clear—that librarianship appears to have relatively low status, that women predominate numerically, that the profession shows segregation in job by classification by gender, and that there is a disproportionately large number of males in administrative and managerial positions—Garrison's explanations for these conditions have been sharply criticized by some social historians, especially those who focus on gender as a critical aspect of historical analysis (Hildenbrand 1992, 1996). Sometimes described as a "feminist" approach or "gendered history," this approach contends that understanding the status and place of women in librarianship necessitates an understanding of the historical, political, and social relationships between men and women, especially in terms of how power is distributed (Hildenbrand 1996). Hildenbrand (1992) argues that the traditional historical analysis applied to library history is biased. For example, important women in the history of librarianship are largely ignored while the achievements of prominent males are studied in detail. Garrison is criticized for attributing to women the responsibility for their poor status in the profession, rather than attributing it to the pernicious attitudes of the times and for failing to recognize the importance of the historical achievement of women librarians. Hildenbrand (1992) argues that a re-analysis of the history of the role of women in librarianship would reveal that they were responsible for its rapid growth, the increase in the quality of library workers, and the growth of a national purpose to public libraries.

Consistent with Hildenbrand's concerns, Roma Harris (1992) has suggested that librarians' self-consciousness with their image is counterproductive, especially when it leads to a self-deprecation of their profession. Such self-criticism leads to blaming the victim and denigrating worthy "feminine" traits rather than on focusing on why society places such low status on nurturing activities. For Harris, the disparaging of caring attitudes and the lionizing of management, research, and technical expertise (considered male traits) is tantamount to endorsing and perpetuating the suppression of women. That the deprecation of these traits occurs by both men and women in the profession is equally disturbing.

Maack (1997) suggests that striving for the status traditionally associated with male-dominated professions such as law and medicine is misdirected. Rather, she argues that there is a need for a reconceptualization of professions to replace the understanding of professions that focuses only on the traditionally male-oriented factors of control and authority. The new concept would admit of three different types of professions: high authority professions such as law and medicine; indirect or product-oriented professions, such as engineering and architecture; and empowering professions, such as education, social work, and library and information science. In empowering professions, "the professional shares expertise with the goal of enabling clients to use knowledge in order to take control of their own lives or their own learning"

(Maack, p. 284). It is a collaborative, client-centered activity in which sharing and facilitation are fundamental activities of the professional. Such a profession contrasts clearly with high authority professions in which "the professional offers prescriptions, directives, or strategies that the client must follow" (Maack, p. 284). In the client-centered model, it is not power and authority that dominates, but the desire to develop abilities and promote confidence in clients so that they can deal with their own problems and challenges. Accepting the concept of empowering professions eliminates the need to strive to be like law or medicine and recognizes the vitality of a profession that increases the independence and abilities of others.

## What is the Future Role of Librarians

Will librarians be performing the fundamental role of locating information in a chaotic information world? Few groups have as much familiarity with meeting information needs as librarians. In conjunction with information scientists, who explore the information needs not only of library users, but of information seekers more generally, librarians should play a vital role in designing and using information systems in a manner that helps people solve their own information problems.

It is likely that a good part of the librarian's functions will be shaped by the rapidly changing information technologies, especially, the tremendous increase in information found outside the library itself. Will librarians of the future perform more direct evaluation of information for library users in the future? The issue has been raised by Rice (1989), who observed that librarians have never had difficulty in making judgements about what should be included in library collections, but find it very difficult to make judgements advising patrons about the quality and accuracy of information they provide. There are many difficulties in deciding for the patron which information is more valuable but, as Rice points out, "There is seldom a problem in finding information nowadays. The problem is usually in sorting through all of it and deciding which is best" (p. 59). Rice suggests that future librarians will exert much greater effort in consulting, teaching, and advising individuals in their search for information, and such activities will become an essential part of the librarians' function. This role will be advanced as the library "collection" consists increasingly of information available through networks. Many patrons will feel adrift in this sea of information and expect the librarian to provide advice and counsel on the reliability and value of various information sources.

These changes may require a reconceptualizing of the role of the librarian. The librarian of the twenty-first century, according to Debons (1985), will be seen as an "information intermediary," performing at least three basic functions:

- *Diagnosis*: Estimating the information need. The librarian as diagnostician employs analytical interviewing techniques to assess the patron's personal abilities, the level of information required, the appropriate type of information package, appropriate cost, and method of delivery.
- *Prescription*: Organizing the information and processing to meet the patron's needs.
- *Evaluation*: Determining if the diagnosis and prescription was effective (p. 27).

Although the model appears rather "medical" in nature and may be an incomplete picture of all the functions of the future librarian, it provides an important context for the information-giving function that librarians often perform. The focus of the model is to adapt to the users' special needs and problems and to see the library as an information system. Adopting such a model is likely to require a restructuring of library policies and practices to reflect individual constituencies. Information systems are only effective if they meet client needs rather than the needs of the bureaucracy. This will mean that librarians will need to conduct a regular analysis of the information needs of their constituencies and an analysis of organizational barriers to access. Similarly, they will constantly improve access to information through increased networking and exploitation of information technologies.

## SUMMARY

Information does not organize itself, the order must be imposed, and librarians and information scientists perform a valuable service in imposing this order. Although part of this function is accomplished through classification systems and controlled vocabularies, a major part of the task goes to the librarian, who applies organizing systems so that the information needs of patrons will be met. The role of the future librarian will be to anticipate and satisfy the information needs of patrons and to collect or provide access to the information that will be needed. The librarian will meet not only individual needs, but ensure that systems and services are effectively designed so that future needs can be met. The librarian of the future will be an information-needs assessor, information evaluator, information planner, manager of information services, and information instructor. One may well argue that this has been the role of librarians throughout their history, but it is clear that the challenge and breadth of their responsibilities have grown substantially. If they are able to adapt to the new information environment, they may well become important contributors to controlling an ever-expanding information universe.

This is an exciting prospect, but there are pitfalls as well. This shift in emphasis toward accessing information through electronic technologies may have unintended negative consequences to the profession. Information technologies have focused librarians' activities on techniques for information access—emphasis being on locating specific information or citations. It is a role that fits comfortably in a society that sees information as a commodity, a role that can be comfortably exploited by those who know the value of information and can use it profitably. As such, the technical character of the knowledge needed to access information and the value of the knowledge that can be accessed tends to raise the status of the librarian (at least temporarily) insofar as he or she is perceived as possessing the special skills to find the knowledge needed. Yet librarians in a rush to exploit this trend may not be considering all the consequences. Estabrook (1981) has warned that this enthusiasm may be short-lived, as those with greater capital recognize the potential of information control and appropriate the information marketplace for themselves. Her prediction seems to be coming true with the entrance of major telecommunication organizations into the information marketplace.

Perhaps, even more important, will the emphasis on electronic information access lead librarians to neglect other obligations? Finding pieces of information has always been part of the librarian's role, but this role has traditionally been subsumed under larger purposes: the humanistic and democratic values of traditional librarianship, a tradition with the goal of helping people or providing education. Information provision is only one part of this function. The humanistic values in librarianship were referred to as the "cultural motivation" of librarianship by Butler (1951). This motivation was "the promotion of wisdom in the individual and in the community" (p. 246). The librarian was to foster understanding and judgement within the citizenry and society. From this perspective, librarians are educators, individuals who enrich the lives of library users through their advice and guidance. They foster the love of reading, provide intellectual stimulation, bring those not familiar with libraries into their confines, provide instruction so that library users can continue to grow and develop intellectually throughout their lives, and provide entertainment and diversion from an often weary world. It is not technological competence that forms the basis of such a model; it is service to people. What makes the role attractive is not merely satisfying an information need but caring about people, solving human problems and improving lives.

The librarian is thus battered on the rocks of Scylla and Charybdis: needing to respond to rapidly changing modes of information access and the demands of those who require the most technologically intensive services and equipment and, at the same time, trying to satisfy traditional readers and promoting library services among those with poor or nonexistent reading skills. These are not entirely incompatible obligations. Rather, the key question is whether the traditional social values of librarianship should form the context for the exploitation of information technologies by librarians, or whether the new information technologies create a new social context that changes the meaning and significance of libraries and librarians.

# REFERENCES

Abbott, Andrew. *The System of Professions*. Chicago: University of Chicago, 1988.

Agada, John. "Studies of the Personality of Librarians." *Drexel Library Quarterly* 20 (spring 1984): 24–45.

———. "Assertion and the Librarian Personality." In *Encyclopedia of Library and Information Science*. New York: Marcel Dekker, 1987, 128–144.

(ALA) American Library Association. "ALA Policy Manual: Policy 56.1." *ALA Handbook of Organization*, 1995–96. Chicago: ALA, 1996.

———. *Standards for Accreditation of Master's Programs in Library and Information Studies*. Chicago: ALA, 1992.

———. Office of Library Personnel Resources, *Academic and Public Librarians: Data by Race, Ethnicity and Sex*, 1986, p. 7, 13.

ALISE (Association for Library and Information Science Educators). *Library and Information Science Education Statistical Report 1999*, Arlington, VA.: ALISE, 1999.

Beggs, Joyce, M. and Dorothy C. Doolittle. "Perceptions Now and Then of Occupational Sex Typing: A Replication of Shinar's 1975 Study." *Journal of Applied Social Psychology* 23 (1993): 1435–1453.

Birdsall, William F. "Librarianship, Professionalism and Social Change." *Library Journal* 107 (February 1, 1982): 223–226.

Boyce, Bert R. "The Death of Library Education." *American Libraries* (March 1994): 257–259.

Brand, Barbara B. "Pratt Institute Library School: The Perils of Professionalization." In *Reclaiming the American Library Past: Writing the Women In*. Edited by Suzanne Hildenbrand. Norwood, N.J.: Ablex, 1996, 251–278.

Bryan, Alice. *The Public Librarian*. New York: Columbia University, 1952.

Bushman, John. "Asking the Right Questions about Information Technology." *American Libraries* (December 1990): 1026–1030.

Butler, Pierce. "Librarianship as a Profession." *The Library Quarterly* 21 (October 1951): 235–247.

Campbell, Jerry D. "Choosing to Have a Future." *American Libraries* (June 1993): 560–566.

Campbell, Lucy B. "The Hampton Institute Library School." In *Handbook of Black Librarianship*. Edited by E.J. Josey and Ann Shockley Allen. Littleton, Colo.: Libraries Unlimited, 1977, 35–46.

CRISTAL-ED. Charting a New Direction in Education. [Online] Available at *http://www.si.umich.edu/crystaled/charting.html* (December 17, 1997).

———. Objectives of the CRISTAL-ED Project [Online]. Available at *http://www.si.umich.edu/cristaled/objectives.html* (December 17, 1997).

Davis, Donald G. Jr. "Curtis, Florence Rising." In *Dictionary of American Library Biography*, Edited by Bohdan S. Wynar. Littleton, Colo.: Libraries Unlimited, 1978, 108–109.

Debons, A. "The Information Professional: A Survey." In *The Information Profession*. Proceedings of a Conference Held in Melbourne, Australia (November 26–28, 1984). Edited by James Henri, and Roy Sanders. Melbourne: Centre for Library Studies, 12985.

Dewey, Melvil. "The Profession." *Library Journal* 114 (June 15, 1989): 5. Reprinted from *American Library Journal* 1 (1876).

*Dictionary of American Library Biography*. Edited by Bohdan S. Wynar. Littleton, Colo.: Libraries Unlimited, 1978.

Duffy, Joan R. "Images of Librarians and Librarianship: A Study." *Journal of Youth Services in Libraries* (summer 1990): 303–308.

Estabrook, Leigh. "Productivity, Profit, and Libraries." *Library Journal* 106 (July 1981): 1377–1380.

Fisher, David. P. "Is the Librarian a Distinct Personality Type?" *Journal of Librarianship* 20 (January 1988): 36–47.

Gambee, Budd L. "Fairchild, Mary Salome Cutler." In *Dictionary of American Library Biography*. Edited by Bohdan S. Wynar. Littleton, Colo.: Libraries Unlimited, 1978, 167–170.

Garrison, Dee. *The Apostles of Culture: The Public Librarian and American Society, 1876–1920*. New York: Free Press, 1979.

———. "The Tender Technicians: The Feminization of Public Librarianship." *Journal of Social History* 6 (winter 1972–1973): 131–156.

Grotzinger, Laurel A. "Kroeger, Alice Bertha." In *Dictionary of American Library Biography*. Edited by Bohdan S. Wynar. Littleton, Colo.: Libraries Unlimited, 1978, 295–298.

———. *The Power and the Dignity: Librarianship and Katharine Sharp*. New York: Scarecrow, 1966.

————. "Sharp, Katharine Lucinda." In *Dictionary of American Library Biography*. Edited by Bohdan S. Wynar. Littleton, Colo.: Libraries Unlimited, 1978, 470–473.

Harris, Roma M. *Librarianship: The Erosion of a Woman's Profession*. Norwood, N.J.: Ablex, 1992.

Hauptman, Robert, "Iconoclastic Education: The Library Science Degree." *Catholic Library World* 58 (May-June 1987): 252–253.

Heim, Kathleen and Leigh Estabrook. *Career Profiles and Sex Discrimination in the Library Profession*. Chicago: ALA, 1983.

Hildenbrand, Suzanne. "A Historical Perspective on Gender Issues in American Librarianship." *The Canadian Journal of Information Science* 17 (September 1992): 18–28.

————. "Women in Library History: From the Politics of Library History to the History of Library Politics." In *Reclaiming the American Library Past: Writing the Women In*. Edited by Suzanne Hildenbrand. Norwood, N.J.: Ablex, 1996, 1–23.

————. "'Women's Work' within Librarianship." *Library Journal* 114 (September 1, 1989): 153–155.

Holley, Edward G. "The Merwine Case and the MLS: Where Was ALA?" *American Libraries* 15 (May 1984): 327–330.

Irvine, Betty Jo. *Sex Segregation in Librarianship: Demographic and Career Patterns of Academic Library Administrators*. Westport, Conn: Greenwood, 1985.

Josey, E.J. "Minority Representation in Library and Information Science Programs." *The Bookmark* (fall 1989): 54–57.

Karlowich, Robert A. and Nasser Sharify. "Plummer, Mary Wright." In *Dictionary of American Library Biography*. Edited by Bohdan S. Wynar. Littleton, Colo.: Libraries Unlimited, 1978, 399–402.

Lynch, Beverly. P. "Education and Training of Librarians." In *Rethinking the Library In the Information Age*. Washington, D.C: U.S. GPO, 1989, 75–92.

Maack, Mary Niles. "Women in Library Education: Down the Up Staircase." *Library Trends* 34 (winter 1986): 401–431.

————. "Toward a New Model of the Information Professions: Embracing Empowerment." *Journal of Education for Library and Information Science* 38 (fall 1997): 283–302.

Main, Linda. "Research versus Practice: A 'No' Contest." *RQ* 30 (winter 1990): 226–228.

Mason, Richard O. "What Is an Information Professional?" *Journal of Education for Library and Information Science* 31 (fall 1990): 122–138

McCook, Kathleen de la Peña and Paula Geist. "Diversity Deferred: Where Are the Minority Librarians?" *Library Journal* (November 1, 1993): 35–38.

McPheeters, Annie L. *Library Service in Black and White: Some Personal Recollections, 1921–1980*. Metuchen, N.J.: Scarecrow, 1988.

Morrisey, Locke J. and Donald O Case. "There Goes My Image." The Perception of Male Librarians by Colleague, Student, and Self." *College and Research Libraries* (September 1988): 453–464.

Nielsen, Brian. "The Role of the Public Services Librarian: The New Revolution." In *Rethinking the Library in the Information Age*. Washington, D.C.: GPO, 1989, 179–200.

Paris, Marion. *Library School Closings: Four Case Studies.* Metuchen, N.J.: Scarecrow, 1988.

*Public Libraries in the United States of America: Their History, Condition, and Management: Special Report.* Washington D.C.: GPO, 1876.

Rayward, W. Boyd. "Library and Information Sciences: Disciplinary Differentiation, Competition, Convergence." In *The Study of Information: Disciplinary Messages.* Edited by Fritz Machlup and Una Mansfield. New York: Wiley, 1983, 343–363.

Reeves, William Joseph. *Librarians as Professionals.* Lexington, Mass.: Lexington Books, 1980.

Rice, James. "The Hidden Role of Librarians." *Library Journal* 114 (January 1989): 57–59.

Robbins-Carter, Jane and Charles A. Seavey. "The Master's Degree: Basic Preparation for Professional Practice." *Library Trends* 34 (spring 1986): 561–580.

Saracevic, Tefko. "Closing of Library Schools in North America: What Role Accreditation?" *Libri* 44 (November 1994): 190–200.

Scherdin, Mary Jane. "Vive la Difference: Exploring Librarian Personality Types Using the MBTI." In *Discovering Librarians.* Edited by Mary Jane Scherdin. Chicago: ACRL, 1994, 125–156.

Schuman, Patricia Glass. "The Image of Librarians: Substance or Shadow?" *The Journal of Academic Librarianship* 16 (1990): 86–89.

Sineath, Timothy W. ed. *Library and Information Science Education Statistical Report, 1995.* (Draft report). Raleigh, N.C.: ALISE, 1995.

Swisher, Robert, Rosemary Ruhig DuMont, and Calvin J. Boyer. "The Motivation to Manage: A Study of Academic Librarians and Library Science Students." *Library Trends* 34 (fall 1985): 219–234.

Vann, Sarah K. *Training for Librarianship before 1923.* Chicago: ALA, 1961.

Weibel, Kathleen and Kathleen M. Heim. *The Role of Women in Librarianship 1876–1976: The Entry, Advancement, and Struggle for Equalization in One Profession.* Phoenix: Oryx, 1979.

White, Carl M. *A Historical Introduction to Library Education: Problems and Progress to 1951.* New York: Scarecrow, 1976.

White, Herbert S. "The Future of Library and Information Science Education." *Journal of Education for Library and Information Science* 26 (winter 1986): 174–181.

Wiegand, Wayne A. *Irrepressible Reformer: A Biography of Melvil Dewey.* Chicago: ALA, 1996.

Williamson, Charles C. *Training for Library Service: A Report Prepared for the Carnegie Corporation of New York.* Boston: Updike, 1923.

Wilson, Patrick, "Bibliographical R&D." In *The Study of Information.* Edited by Fritz Machlup and Una Mansfield. New York: Wiley, 1983, 389–397.

Windsor, Justin. "A Word to Starters of Libraries." *American Library Journal* 1 (September 1876): 1–3.

Winter, Michael F. *The Culture and Control of Expertise: Toward a Sociological Understanding of Librarianship.* Westport, Conn: Greenwood, 1988.

# Selected Readings

The literature of library and information science is vast. The following list of readings is intended as a starting place for exploring this literature. The headings reflect the major chapters in the book.

*Ethical issues*
*Impact of technology*
*Information policy*
*Information policy and libraries*
*Information science*
*Intellectual organization of libraries*
*Librarianship*
*Libraries as organizations*
*Mission and values of libraries*

Additional assistance is provided by the list of selected periodicals, indexes, and encyclopedias in Appendix A.

## ETHICAL ISSUES

*Books*

Hauptman, Robert. *Ethical Challenges in Librarianship*. Phoenix: Oryx, 1988.
──────, ed. *Ethics and the Dissemination of Information*. Special Issue of *Library Trends* 40 (Fall 1991): 199–375.
Lancaster, F.W., ed. *Ethics and the Librarian: Proceedings of the Allerton Park Institute: Volume 31*. Urbana-Champaign, IL: Graduate School of Library and Information Science, University of Illinois, 1991.
Lindsey, Jonathan A. and Ann E. Prentice. *Professional Ethics and Librarians*. Phoenix: Oryx, 1985.
Mason, Richard O., Florence M. Mason, and Mary J. Culnan. *Ethics of Information Management*. Thousand Oaks, Calif.: Sage, 1995.
Mintz, Anne P., ed. *Information Ethics: Concerns for Librarianship and the Information Industry*. Jefferson, N.C.: McFarland, 1990.

*Articles*

American Library Association. "ALA Code of Ethics." *American Libraries* 26 (July/August 1995): 673.
"ASIS Professional Guidelines." *Bulletin of the American Society for Information Science* 20 (December/January 1994): 4.
Baker, Sharon L. "Needed: An Ethical Code for Library Administrators." *Journal of Library Administration* 16 (1992): 1–17.
Barnes, Robert F. "Some Thoughts on Professional Ethics Codes." *Bulletin of the American Society for Information Science* 12 (April/May 1986): 19–20.
Bierbaum, Esther Green. "Searching for the Human Good: Some Suggestions for a Code of Ethics for Technical Services." *Technical Services Quarterly* 11 (1994): 1–18.
Capurro, Rafael. "Moral Issues in Information Science." *Journal of Information Science* 11 (1985): 113–123.
Dowd, Robert. "I Want to Find Out How to Freebase Cocaine; or Yet Another Unobtrusive Test of Reference Performance." *The Reference Librarian* 25–26 (1989): 483–493.
Du Mont, Rosemary Ruhig. "Ethics in Librarianship: A Management Model." *Library Trends* 40 (fall 1991): 201–215.
Estabrook, Leigh. "The Library as a Socialist Institution in a Capitalist Environment." In *The Economics of Information*. Edited by Jana Varlys. Jefferson, N.C.: McFarland, 1982.
Finks, Lee W. "Librarianship Needs a New Code of Professional Ethics." *American Libraries* 22 (January 1991): 84–92.
──────. "What Do We Stand For? Values without Shame." *American Libraries* 20 (April 1989): 352–356.
Froehlich, Thomas J. "Ethical Considerations of Information Professionals." *Annual Review of Information Science and Technology (ARIST)* 27 (1992): 291–324.

————. "Ethical Considerations in Technology Transfer." *Library Trends* 40 (fall 1991): 275–302.

Goehner, Donna M. "Vendor-Library Relations: The Ethics of Working with Vendors." In *Understanding the Business of Library Acquisitions*, 137–151. Chicago: ALA, 1990.

Hauptman, Robert. "Professionalism or Culpability? An Experiment in Ethics." *Wilson Library Bulletin* 50 (April 1976): 626–627

————, ed. *Journal of Information Ethics*. Jefferson, N.C.: McFarland, 1991–.

Hendrickson, Kent. "Library Vendors: How Do They Use Us?" *Library Acquisitions: Practice and Theory* 13 (1989): 121–123.

Lennon, Donald R. "Ethical Issues in Archival Management." *North Carolina Libraries* 51 (spring 1993): 18–22.

Mintz, Anne P. *Information Ethics: Concerns for Librarianship and the Information Industry: Proceedings of the 27th Annual Symposium of the Graduate Alumni and Faculty of the Rutgers School of Communication, Information, and Library Studies.* April 14, 1989. Jefferson, N.C.: McFarland, 1989.

Rathbun, Susan R. "Ethics Issues in Reference Service: Overview and Analysis." *North Carolina Libraries* 51 (spring 1993): 11–14.

Rubin, Richard. "Ethical Issues in Library Personnel Management." *Journal of Library Administration* 14 (1991): 1–16.

————. "Moral Distancing and the Use of Information Technologies: The Seven Temptations." *Ethics in the Computer Age: Conference Proceedings*. Gatlinburg, Tenn., November 11–13, 1994. New York: ACM, 1994, 151–155.

Rubin, Richard E. and Thomas J. Froehlich. "Ethical Aspects of Library and Information Science." *Encyclopedia of Library and Information Science*. v. 58 (Supplement). New York: Marcel Dekker, 1996, 33–52.

Smith, Martha M., ed. *Information Ethics* (Special Issue), *North Carolina Libraries* 51 (spring 1993).

Vitell, Scott and Donald L. Davis. "Ethical Beliefs of MIS Professionals: The Frequency and Opportunity for Unethical Behavior," *Journal of Business Ethics* 9 (1990): 63–70.

## IMPACT OF TECHNOLOGY

*Books*

Birdsall, William F. *The Myth of the Electronic Library: Librarianship and Social Change in America*. Westport, Conn: Greenwood, 1994.

December, John, and Neil Randall. *The World Wide Web Unleashed 1996*. Indianapolis: Sams, 1995.

Grosch, Audre N. *Library Information Technology and Networks*. New York: Marcel Dekker, 1995.

Lancaster, F. W. *Toward Paperless Information Systems*. New York: Academic, 1978.

McClure, Charles R., William E. Moen, and Joe Ryan. *Libraries and the Internet/ NREN: Perspectives, Issues, and Challenges*. Westport, Conn.: Mecklermedia, 1994.

Saunders, Laverna M., ed. *The Virtual Library: Visions and Realities*. Westport, Conn.: Meckler, 1992.

Weizenbaum, Joseph. *Computer Power and Human Reason: From Judgment to Calculation*. San Francisco: W. H. Freeman, 1976.

*Articles*

Bartlett, Virginia. "Technostress and Librarians." *Library Administration and Management* 9 (fall 1995): 226–230.

Birdsall, William F. "Breaking the Myth of the Library as Place." In *The Myth of the Electronic Library: Librarianship and Social Change in America*. Westport, Conn: Greenwood, 1994, 7–29.

Brod, Craig. "How to Deal with 'Technostress.'" *Office Administration and Automation* 45 (August 1984): 28–47.

Bushman, John. "Asking the Right Questions about Information Technology." *American Libraries* 21 (December 1990): 1026–1030.

Champion, Sandra. "Technostress: Technology's Toll." *School Library Journal* 35 (November 1988): 48–51.

De Gennaro, Richard D. "Technology and Access in an Enterprise Society." *Library Journal* 114 (October 1, 1989): 40–43.

Dowlin, Kenneth E. "Distribution in an Electronic Environment, or Will There Be Libraries As We Know Them in the Internet World?" *Library Trends* 43 (winter 1995): 409–417.

Evans, John E. "Administering the Library Automation Process." In *Principles and Applications of Information Science for Library Professionals*. Edited by John N. Olsgaard. Chicago: ALA, 1989, 101–119.

Fine, Sara F. "Terminal Paralysis or Showdown at the Interface." In *Human Aspects of Library Automation: Helping Staff and Patrons Cope*. Edited by Debora Shaw. Urbana-Champaign, IL: Graduate School of Library and Information Science, 1985, 3–15.

Garrett, John R. "Digital Libraries: The Grand Challenges." *Educom Review* 28 (July/August 1993): 17–21.

Hahn, Trudi Bellardo. "Pioneers of the Online Age." *Information Processing and Management* 32 (January 1996): 33–48.

LaGuardia, Cheryl. "Virtual Dreams Give Way to Digital Reality." *Library Journal* 120 (October 1, 1995): 42–44.

Levy, David M. "Going Digital: A Look at Assumptions Underlying Digital Libraries." *Communications of the ACM* 38 (April 1995): 77–84.

Martinez, Michael E. "Access to Information Technologies among School-Age Children: Implications for a Democratic Society." *Journal of the American Society for Information Science* 45 (July 1994): 395–400.

Stieg, Margaret F. "Technology and the Concept of Reference or What Will Happen to the Milkman's Cow." *Library Journal* 115 (April 15, 1990): 45–49.

Weingarten, Fred W. "Superhighway Speed Limit Abolished: Information Policy Swerves." *American Libraries* 27 (January 1996): 16–17.

———. "Five Great Roles for Libraries and Librarians within the NII." *American Libraries* 27 (January 1996): 17.

Whitney, Gretchen. "Automation for the Nineties: A Review Article." *Library Quarterly* 64 (July 1994): 319–331.
Wiederhold, Gio. "Digital Libraries, Value, and Productivity." *Communications of the ACM* 38 (April 1995): 85–96.

## INFORMATION POLICY (GENERAL)

*Books*

Burger, Robert H. *Information Policy: A Framework for Evaluation and Policy Research.* Norwood, N.J.: Ablex, 1993.
Computer Professionals for Social Responsibility. *Serving the Community: A Public Interest Vision of the National Information Infrastructure.* Washington, D.C.: CPSR, October 1993.
Information Infrastructure Task Force. *The National Information Infrastructure: Agenda for Action.* Washington, D.C.: GPO, September 15, 1993.
————, Working Group on Intellectual Property Rights. *Intellectual Property and the National Information Infrastructure.* Washington, D.C.: Department of Commerce, September 1995.
Lynch, Clifford A. *Accessibility and Integrity of Networked Information Collections.* Washington D.C.: Office of Technology Assessment, 1993.
*Rethinking the Library in the Information Age.* Washington, D.C.: GPO, 1989.
Science Applications International Corporation. *Information Warfare: Legal, Regulatory, Policy and Organizational Considerations for Assurance.* Washington D.C.: Joint Staff, The Pentagon, 1995.
U.S. National Commission on Libraries and Information Science. *Libraries and the National Information Infrastructure: Proceedings of the 1994 Forum on Library and Information Services Policy.* Washington, D.C.: NCLIS, May 1994.

*Articles*

American Library Association. *Principles for the Development of the National Information Infrastructure.* Chicago: ALA, 1993.
Bearman, Toni Carbo. "National Information Infrastructure." In *Bowker Annual.* New York: R.R. Bowker, 1995, 65–69.
Bishop, Ann P. "The National Research and Education Network (NREN): Promise of a New Information Environment." Syracuse, N.Y.: ERIC Clearinghouse on Information Resources, November 1990.
Bortnick, Jane. "National and International Information Policy." *Journal of the American Society for Information Science* 36 (May 1985): 164–168.
Braman, Sandra. "Defining Information: An Approach for Policymakers." *Telecommunications Policy* (September 1989): 242.
Gomery, Douglas. "In Search of the Cybermarket." *The Wilson Quarterly* (summer 1994): 9–17.

McCain, Roger A. "Information as Property and as a Public Good: Perspectives from the Economic Theory of Property Rights." *Library Quarterly* 58 (1988): 265–282.

McClure, Charles R., John Carlo Bertot, and John C. Beachboard. "Enhancing the Role of Public Libraries in the National Information Infrastructure." *Public Libraries* 35 (July-August 1996): 232–238.

McClure, Charles R., Mary McKenna, William E. Moen, Joe Ryan. "Toward a Virtual Library: Internet and the National Research and Education Network." *Bowker Annual* 38th ed. New York: Bowker, 1993, 25–45.

McKenna, Mary. "Libraries and the Internet." Syracuse, N.Y.: ERIC Clearinghouse on Information and Technology, December 1994, 1–4.

Rothberg, Marc. "Privacy and the National Information Infrastructure." *Educom Review* 29 (March/April 1994): 50–51.

Shill, Harold B. "Privatization of Public Information: Its Impact on Libraries." *Library Administration and Management* 5 (spring 1991): 99–109.

Tennant, Roy. "Internet Basics." Syracuse, N.Y.: ERIC Clearinghouse on Information Resources, October 1992.

Tenner, Edward. "Learning from the Net." *The Wilson Quarterly* (summer 1994): 18–28.

Vagionos, Louis and Barry Lesser. "Information Policy Issues: Putting Library Policy in Context." In *Rethinking the Library in the Information Age*. Washington, D.C.: GPO, 1989, 9–42.

Ward, Maribeth. "Expanding Access to Information with Z39.50." *American Libraries* 25 (July/August 1994): 639–641.

Weingarten, Fred W. "The Next Generation Internet: Government Policy and the Future of the Net." *American Libraries* 28 (September 1997): 13–15.

———. "Technological Change and the Evolution of Information Policy." *American Libraries* 27 (December 1996): 45–47.

COPYRIGHT

Agha, Syed Salim. "Ethics and Copyright: A Developing Country Perspective." *IFLA Journal* 23 (1997): 251–257.

Bielefield, Arlene. *Libraries and Copyright Law*. New York: Neal-Schuman, 1993.

Bronmo, Ole. "Copyright Legislation, Fair Use and the Efficient Dissemination of Scientific Knowledge." *IFLA Journal* 23 (1997): 290–294.

Cornish, Graham P. "Electronic Copyright Management Systems: Dream, Nightmare or Reality?" *IFLA Journal* 23 (1997): 284–287.

English, Jane and Kirti Jacobs. "Royalties and Payments: Why Pay for Copyright? What Are Words Worth?" *IFLA Journal* 23 (1997): 270–274.

Gasaway, Laura N. and Sarah K. Wiant. *Libraries and Copyright: A Guide to Copyright Law in the 1990s*. Washington, D.C.: Special Libraries Association, 1994.

Giavarra, Emanualla. "European Copyright User Platform." *IFLA Journal* 23 (1997): 288–289.

Greene, Lisa H. and Steven J. Rizzi. "Database Protection Legislation: Views from the United States and WIPO." *Copyright World* (January 1997): 36–42.

Heller, James S. "The Impact of Recent Litigation on Interlibrary Loan and Document Delivery." *Law Library Journal* (spring 1996): 158–177.

———. "The Public Performance Right in Libraries: Is There Anything Fair About It?" *Law Library Journal* 84 (spring 1992): 315–340.

Jackson, Mary E. "Copyright: The Worrisome Element in Electronic Document Delivery." *Wilson Library Bulletin* 67 (December 1992): 81–82, 119–120.

Norman, Sandy. "Copyright and Fair Use in the Electronic Information Age." *IFLA Journal* 23 (1997): 295–298.

Parker, James. "PLR in a Copyright Context." *IFLA Journal* 23 (1997): 299–304.

Pearse, Richard. "Library Open-Distribution Systems and Copyright Infringement in Canada and the United States." *Law Library Journal* 86 (summer 1994): 399–443.

Sato, Seiji. "Libraries and Publishers in the Digital Environment." *IFLA Journal* 23 (1997): 263–265.

Tepper, Laurie C. "Copyright Law and Library Photocopying: An Historical Survey." *Law Library Journal* 84 (spring 1992): 341–363.

U.S. Congress. Office of Technology Assessment. *Copyright and Home Copying: Technology Challenges the Law*, OTA-CIT-422. Washington, D.C.: U.S. GPO, October 1989.

———. *Intellectual Property Rights in an Age of Electronics and Information*. OTA-CIT-302 Washington, D.C.: U.S. GPO, April 1986.

Valauskas, Edward J. "Copyright: Know Your Electronic Rights!" *Library Journal* 117 (August 1, 1992): 40–43.

Webster, Duane E. "Copyright, Libraries, and the Electronic Information Environment: Discussions and Developments in the United States." *IFLA Journal* 23 (1997): 280–283.

FEES

Bierman, Kenneth J. "How Will Libraries Pay for Electronic Information?" *Journal of Library Administration* 15 (1991): 67–84.

———. "Costs of Electronic Information." In *Encyclopedia of Library and Information Science*, Volume 54. New York: Marcel Dekker, 1994, 122–143.

Halliday, Jane. "Fee or Free: A New Perspective on the Economics of Information." *CLJ* 48 (October 1991): 327–333.

HEALTH INFORMATION

Center for Democracy and Technology. "CDT's Health Information Privacy Issues Page." Available [Online] at *http:/www.cdt.org/privacy/health* (March 5, 1997).

Donaldson, Molla S. and Kathleen N. Lohr. *Health Data in the Information Age: Use, Disclosure, and Privacy*. Washington, D.C.: National Academy Press, 1994.

U.S. Congress. Office of Technology Assessment. *Protecting Privacy in Computerized Medical Information*. Washington, D.C.: GPO, 1992.

NATIONAL SECURITY

Computer Scientists for Social Responsibility. "The Clipper Chip: Frequently Asked Questions (FAQ)." Available at *http://www.cpsr.org/do...ipper/clipper-faq.html* (September 7, 1997).

Molander, Robert C., Andrew S. Riddile, Peter A. Wilson. *Strategic Information Warfare: A New Face of War*. Available at *http://www.rand.org* (September 7, 1997).

Science Applications International Corporation (SAIC). *Information Warfare: Legal, Regulatory, Policy and Organizational Considerations for Assurance*. Washington, D.C: Joint Staff, The Pentagon, 1995.

U.S. Congress. Office of Technology Assessment. *Information Security and Privacy in Network Environments*. OTA-TCT-606. Washington, D.C.: GPO, September 1994.

## INFORMATION POLICY AND LIBRARIES

*Books*

McClure, Charles R., William E. Moen, Joe Ryan. *Libraries and the Internet/NREN*. Westport, Conn.: Mecklermedia, 1993.

Swan, John C. and Noel Peattie. *The Freedom to Lie: A Debate about Democracy*. Jefferson, N.C.: McFarland, 1989.

White House Conference on Library and Information Science. *Information 2000: Library and Information Services for the 21st Century*. Washington, D.C.: GPO, 1991.

*Articles*

ACCESS TO FEDERAL INFORMATION

Cornwall, Gary T. "The Dissemination of Federal Government Information: Prospects for the Immediate Future." *Journal of Government Information* 23 (1996): 299–306.

Inter-Association Working Group on Government Information Policy. "Summary of Activities, Principles, Goals, Priorities, and the Draft Legislative Proposal." Available [online] at *http://www.lib.berkeley.edu/GODORT/iawg_sum.html* (June 1997).

Kadec, Sarah. "Public Access to Government Electronic Information." *Bulletin of the American Society for Information Science* (October/November 1992): 22–24.

McConnell, Bruce W. "New Wine in Old Wineskins: U.S. Government Information in a Networked World." *Journal of Government Information* 23 (1996): 217–225.

Sherman, Andres M. "Statutory Reform of the U.S. GPO: A View from the GPO." *Journal of Government Information* 23 (1996): 265–279.

Shill, Harold B. "Privatization of Public Information: Its Impact on Libraries." *Library Administration and Management* 5 (spring 1991): 99–109.

William, Jane. "Recent Changes for Three Federal Library and Information Agencies: Lessons to the Field, Lessons from the Field, or Neither?" *The Bowker Annual 1997*. 42nd ed. New Providence: R.R. Bowker, 1997.

INTELLECTUAL FREEDOM

Abbott, Randy L. "Pressure Groups and Intellectual Freedom." *Public Library Quarterly* 10 (1990): 43–61.

American Library Association. ALA Public Information Office. "Coping with Challenges." *American Libraries* 27 (April 1996): 85–88.

———. Office of Intellectual Freedom. *Intellectual Freedom Manual*, 5th ed. Chicago: ALA, 1996.

Asheim, Lester. "Not Censorship but Selection." *Wilson Library Bulletin* 28 (September 1953): 63–67.

———. "Selection and Censorship: A Reappraisal." *Wilson Library Bulletin* 58 (November 1983): 180–184.

Broderick, Dorothy. "Censorship: A Family Affair?" *Top of the News* 35 (spring 1979): 223–232.

Hopkins, Dianne McAfee. "A Conceptual Model of Factors Influencing the Outcome of Challenges to Library Materials in Secondary School Settings." *Library Quarterly* 63 (January 1993): 40–72.

Morgan, Candace. "Fighting the War against Censorship: A National Perspective." *Library Journal* 120 (October 15, 1995): 36–38.

Schladweiler, Chris. "The Library Bill of Rights and Intellectual Freedom: A Selective Bibliography." *Library Trends* 45 (summer 1996): 97–125.

Serebnick, Judith. "A Review of Research Related to Censorship in Libraries." *Library Research* 1 (summer 1979): 95–118.

———. "Self-Censorship by Librarians: An Analysis of Checklist-Based Research." *Drexel Library Quarterly* 18 (winter 1982): 35–56.

Swan, John. "Untruth or Consequences." *Library Journal* 111 (July 1986): 44–52.

FEES

Coffman, Stephen. "Fee-Based Services and the Future of Libraries." *Journal of Library Administration* 20 (1995): 167–186.

Coffman, Steve and Helen Josephine. "Doing It for Money." *Library Journal* 116 (October 15, 1991): 32–36.

Young, Peter R. "Changing Information Access Economics: New Roles for Libraries and Librarians." *Information Technology and Libraries* 13 (June 1994): 103–114.

LAWS

Fuller, Peter F. "The Politics of LSCA during the Reagan and Bush Administrations: An Analysis." *Library Quarterly* 64 (July 1994): 294–318.

NATIONAL INFORMATION INFRASTRUCTURE

*ALAWON: ALA Washington Office Newsline: An Electronic Publication of the American Library Association Washington Office.* Chicago: ALA.
Flanders, Bruce. "NREN: The Big Issues Aren't Technical." *American Libraries* 22 (June 1991): 572–574.

PRESERVATION

Cloonan, Michele Valerie. "The Preservation of Knowledge." *Library Trends* 41 (spring 1993): 594–605.
Conway, Paul. "Digitizing Preservation." *Library Journal* 119 (February 1, 1994): 42–45.
Cox, Richard J. and Lynn W. Cox. "Selecting Information of Enduring Value for Preservation." In *Rethinking the Library in the Information Age*. Washington, D.C.: GPO, 9–42.
Lamolinara, Guy. "Metamorphosis of a National Treasure." *American Libraries* 27 (March 1996): 31–33.

## INFORMATION SCIENCE

*Books*

Allen, Bryce L. *Information Tasks: Toward a User-Centered Approach to Information Systems*. San Diego: Academic Press, 1996.
Aluri, Rao and Donald E. Riggs, eds. *Expert Systems in Libraries*. Norwood, N.J.: Ablex, 1990.
Baker, Sharon L. and F. Wilfred Lancaster. *The Measurement and Evaluation of Library Services*. Arlington, Va.: Information Resources, 1991.
Buckland, Michael K. *Information and Information Systems*. New York: Praeger, 1991.
Chen, Ching-Chih and Peter Hernon. *Information Seeking: Assessing and Anticipating User Needs*. New York: Neal-Schuman, 1982.
Debon, Anthony, Esther Horne, and Scott Cronenweth. *Information Science: An Integrated View*. Boston: G.K. Hall, 1988.
Flynn, Roger R. *An Introduction to Information Science*. New York: Marcel Dekker, 1987.
Machlup, Fritz and Una Mansfield, eds. *The Study of Information: Interdisciplinary Messages*. New York: Wiley, 1983.
Neill S.D. *Dilemmas in the Study of Information: Exploring the Boundaries of Information Science*. Westport, Conn.: Greenwood, 1992.

Ólsgaard, John N., ed. *Principles and Applications of Information Science for Library Professionals*. Chicago: ALA, 1989.

Taylor, Robert S. *Value-Added Processes in Information Systems*. Norwood, N.J.: Ablex, 1986.

Vickery, Brian and Alina Vickery. *Information Science in Theory and Practice*. Rev. ed. New York: Bowker-Saur, 1992.

## *Articles*

Allen, Bryce L. "Cognitive Research in Information Science: Implications for Design." In *Annual Review of Information Science and Technology (ARIST)* 26 (1991): 3–37.

Belkin, N. J. "Anomalous State of Knowledge for Information Retrieval." *Canadian Journal of Information Science* 5 (1980): 133–143.

Borko, H. "Information Science: What Is It?" *American Documentation* 19 (January 1968): 3–5.

Brittain, J.M. "What Are the Distinctive Characteristics of Information Science?" In *Theory and Application of Information Research: Proceedings of the Second International Research Forum on Information Science.*, August 3–6, 1977. London: Mansell, 1980, 34–47.

Buckland, Michael. "Documentation, Information Science, and Library Science in the U.S.A." *Information Processing & Management* 32 (January 1996): 63–76.

Bush, Vannevar. "As We May Think." *Atlantic Monthly* 176 (July 1945): 101–108.

Chatman, Elfreda A. "The Impoverished Life-World of Outsiders." *Journal of the American Society for Information Science* 47 (1996): 193–206.

Davies, Roy. "The Creation of New Knowledge by Information Retrieval and Classification." *Journal of Documentation* 45 (December 1989): 273–301.

Dervin, Brenda. "Useful Theory for Librarianship: Communication, Not Information." *Drexel Library Quarterly* 13 (July 1977): 16–32.

Dervin, Brenda and M. Nilan. "Information Needs and Uses." In *Annual Review of Information Science and Technology (ARIST)* 21 (1986): 3–33.

Dowlin, Kenneth E. "Special Reports: Access to Information," *Bowker Annual*. 32nd ed. New York: R.R. Bowker, 1987, 64–68.

Durrance, Joan C. "Information Needs: Old Song, New Tune." In *Rethinking the Library*. Washington, D.C.: GPO, 159–178.

Ellis, David. "The Dilemma of Measurement in Information Retrieval Research." *Journal of the American Society for Information Science* 47 (1996): 23–36.

———. "Paradigms in Information Retrieval Research." In *Encyclopedia of Library and Information Science*. Vol. 54. New York: Marcel Dekker, 1994, 275–291.

Harter, Stephen P. "Variations in Relevance Assessments and the Measurement of Retrieval Effectiveness." *Journal of the American Society for Information Science* 47 (1996): 37–49.

Herner, Saul. "Brief History of Information Science." *Journal of the American Society for Information Science* 35 (May 1984): 157–163.

Hewins, Elizabeth T. "Information Need and Use Studies." In *Annual Review of Information Science and Technology (ARIST)* 25 (1990): 145–172.

Ingwersen, Peter. "Information and Information Science." In *Encyclopedia of Library and Information Science*. Vol. 56. New York: Marcel Dekker, 1995, 137–174.

Jacoby, Jacob. "Perspectives on Information Overload." *Journal of Consumer Research* 10 (March 1984): 432–435.

Koenig, Michael E. "Information Services and Downstream Productivity." In *Annual Review of Information Science and Technology* 25 (1990): 55–86.

Krikelas, James. "Information-Seeking Behavior: Patterns and Concepts," *Drexel Library Quarterly* 19 (spring 1983): 5–20.

Kuhlthau, Carol C. "Inside the Search Process: Information Seeking from the User's Perspective." *Journal of the American Society for Information Science* 42 (June 1991) 361–371.

Mann, Thomas. "The Principle of Least Effort." In *Library Research Models: A Guide to Classification, Cataloging, and Computers*. New York: Oxford University, 1993, 91–101.

Miksa, Francis L. "Machlup's Categories of Knowledge as a Framework for Viewing Library and Information Science History." *Journal of Library History* 20 (spring 1985): 157–172.

Nardi, Bonnie A. and Vicki O'Day. "Intelligent Agents: What We Learned at the Library." *Libri* 46 (June 1996): 59–88.

Neill, S.D. "The Dilemma of Method for Information Research: Is Information Science a Science, Social Science, or Humanity? In *Dilemmas in the Study of Information: Exploring the Boundaries of Information Science*. Westport, Conn.: Greenwood, 1992, 139–158.

Oppenheim, Charles. "The Institute's New Criteria for Information Science." *Journal of Information Science* 4 (1982): 229–234.

Orna, Elizabeth, and Graham Stevens. "Information Design and Information Science: A New Alliance?" *Journal of Information Science* 17 (1991): 197–208.

Rayward, Boyd. "Library and Information Sciences." In *The Study of Information: Interdisciplinary Messages*. Edited by Fritz Machlup and Una Mansfield. New York: Wiley, 1983, 343–363.

Saracevic, T. "Relevance: A Review of and a Framework for the Thinking on the Notion in Information Science." *Journal of the American Society for Information Science* 26 (November/December 1975): 321–343.

Schrader, Alvin M. "In Search of a Definition of Library and Information Science." *Canadian Journal of Information Science* 9 (June 1984): 59–77.

Shapiro, Fred R. "Coinage of the Term *Information Science*." *Journal of the American Society for Information Science* 46 (1995): 384–385.

Shaw, Debora. "The Human-Computer Interface for Information Retrieval." *Annual Review of Information Science and Technology (ARIST)* 26 (1991): 155–195.

Shera, Jesse H. and Donald B. Cleveland. "History and Foundations of Information Science." In *Annual Review of Information Science and Technology* 12 (1977): 249–275.

Smith, Linda C. "Artificial Intelligence and Information Retrieval." In *Annual Review of Information Science and Technology (ARIST)* 22 (1987): 41–77.

————. "Citation Analysis." *Library Trends* 30 (summer 1981): 83–106.

Taylor, Robert S. "Value-Added Processes in Libraries." In *Value-Added Processes in Information Systems*. Norwood, N.J.: Ablex, 1986, 71–95.

Wallace, Danny P. "Bibliometrics and Citation Analysis." In *Principles and Applications of Information Science for Library Professionals*. Edited by John N. Olsgaard. Chicago: American Library Association, 1989, 10–26.

Wellisch, Hans. "From Information Science to Informatics: A Terminological Investigation." *Journal of Librarianship* 4 (July 1972): 157–187.

Yuexiao, Zhang. "Definitions and Sciences of Information." *Information Processing and Management* 24 (1988): 479–491.

## INTELLECTUAL ORGANIZATION OF LIBRARIES

*Books*

Berman, Sanford. *The Joy of Cataloging: Essays, Letters, Reviews, and Other Explosions*. Phoenix, Ariz.: Oryx, 1981.

————. *Prejudices and Antipathies: A Tract on the LC Subject Heads Concerning People*. Metuchen N.J.: Scarecrow, 1971.

Carpenter, Michael and Elaine Svenonius, eds. *Foundations of Cataloging: A Sourcebook*. Littleton, Colo.: Libraries Unlimited, 1985.

Chan, Lois Mai. *Cataloging and Classification: An Introduction*. New York: McGraw-Hill, 1994.

Chan, Lois Mai, Phyllis A. Richmond, and Elaine Svenonius, eds. *Theory of Subject Analysis: A Sourcebook*. Littleton, Colo.: Libraries Unlimited, 1985.

Foskett, A.C. *The Subject Approach to Information*. 5th ed. Hamden, Conn: Linnet, 1996.

Fugmann, Robert. *Subject Analysis and Indexing: Theoretical Foundation and Practical Advice*. Frankfurt: Indeks Verlag, 1993.

Lancaster, F. W. *Indexing and Abstracting in Theory and Practice*. Urbana, Ill.: Graduate School of Library and Information Science, University of Illinois, 1991.

————. *Vocabulary Control for Information Retrieval*. 2nd ed. Arlington, Va.: Information Resources, 1986.

Lubetzky, Seymour. *Principles of Cataloging: Final Report, Phase I: Descriptive Cataloging*. Los Angeles: Institute of Library Research, 1969.

Mann, Thomas. *Library Research Models*. New York: Oxford, 1993.

Pao, Miranda Lee. *Concepts of Information Retrieval*. Englewood, Colo.: Libraries Unlimited, 1989.

Ranganathan, S.R. *Elements of Library Classification*. 3rd ed. Bombay: Asia Publishing, 1962.

Rowley, Jennifer, E. *Organising Knowledge*. 2nd ed. Aldershot, Eng.: Gower, 1992.

Soergel, Dagobert. *Organizing Information: Principles of Data Base and Retrieval Systems*. Orlando: Academic Press, 1985.

Svenonius, Elaine, ed. *The Conceptual Foundations of Descriptive Cataloging*. San Diego: Academic Press, 1989.

Wilson, Patrick. *Two Kinds of Power: An Essay on Bibliographical Control*. Berkeley: University of California, 1968.

## Articles

Baker, Nicholson. "Discards." *New Yorker* 70 (April 4, 1994): 64–86.
Bates, Marcia. "Rigorous Systematic Bibliography." *RQ* 16 (fall 1976): 7–26.
Cromwell, Willy. "The Core Record: A New Bibliographic Standard." *LRTS* 38 (October 1994): 415–424.
Gaynor, Edward. "From MARC to Markup: SGML and Online Library Systems." *ALCTS Newletter* 7 (1996): Supplement pages A-D.
Henderson, Kathryn Luther. "'Treated with a Degree of Uniformity and Common Sense': Descriptive Cataloging in the United States—1876–1976." *Library Trends* 25 (July 1976): 227–271.
Mann, Thomas. "The Principle of Least Effort." In *Library Research Models*. New York: Oxford, 1993, 91–101.
Tillett Barbara B. "A Taxonomy of Bibliographic Relationships." *Library Resources and Technical Services* 35 (April 1991): 150–158.
Vellucci, Sherry L. "Herding Cats: Options for Organizing Electronic Resources." *Internet Reference Services Quarterly* 1 (1996): 9–30.
Ward, Maribeth. "Expanding Access to Information with Z39.50." *American Libraries* 25 (July/August 1994): 639–641.
Younger, Jennifer A. "Resources Description in the Digital Age." *Library Trends* 45 (winter 1997): 462–481.
Zeng, Marcia Lei. "Developing Control Mechanisms for Intellectual Access for Discipline-Based Virtual Libraries: A Study of Process." In *Annual Review of OCLC Research 1995*. Dublin, Ohio: OCLC, 1996, 61–64.

## LIBRARIANSHIP

### Books

Abbott, Andrew. *The System of Professions*. Chicago: University of Chicago, 1988.
American Library Association. Office of Library Personnel Resources. *Academic and Public Librarians: Data by Race, Ethnicity and Sex*, 1986, 7,13.
Baum, Christina D. *Feminist Thought in American Librarianship*. Jefferson, N.C.: McFarland, 1992.
Gorman, G.E. *The Education and Training of Information Professionals: Comparative and International Perspectives*. Metuchen, N.J.: Scarecrow, 1990.
Harris, Michael H. and Stan A. Hannah. *Into the Future: The Foundations of Library and Information Services in the Post-Industrial Era*. Norwood, N.J.: Ablex, 1993.
Harris, Roma M. *Librarianship: The Erosion of a Woman's Profession*. Norwood, N.J.: Ablex, 1992.
Hildenbrand, Suzanne, ed. *Reclaiming the American Library Past: Writing the Women In*. Norwood, N.J.: Ablex, 1996.

Josey, E.J. and Ann Allen Shockley. *Handbook of Black Librarianship*. Littleton, Colo.: Libraries Unlimited, 1977.

*Rethinking the Library*. Washington D.C.: U.S. Department of Education, 1989.

Scherdin, Mary Jane, ed. *Discovering Librarians*. Chicago: ALA, Association of College and Research Libraries, 1994.

Shera, J.H. *Sociological Foundations of Librarianship*. New York: Asia, 1970.

Vann, Sarah K. *Training for Librarianship before 1923*. Chicago: ALA, 1961.

Wiegand, Wayne A. *Irrepressible Reformer: A Biography of Melvil Dewey*. Chicago: ALA, 1996.

Winter, Michael F. *The Culture and Control of Expertise: Toward a Sociological Understanding of Librarianship*. Westport, Conn: Greenwood, 1988.

## *Articles*

### THE PROFESSION

Birdsall, William F. "Librarianship, Professionalism and Social Change." *Library Journal* 107 (February 1, 1982): 223–226.

Butler, Pierce. "Librarianship as a Profession." *The Library Quarterly* 21 (October 1951): 235–247.

Campbell, Jerry D. "Choosing to Have a Future." *American Libraries* 24 (June 1993): 560–566.

Davis, Donald G. Jr. "Education for Librarianship." *Library Trends* 25 (July 1976): 113–134.

Dewey, Melvil. "The Profession." *Library Journal* 114 (June 15, 1989): 5. Reprinted from *American Library Journal* 1 (1876).

Drake, David. "The 'A' Factor: Altruism and Career Satisfaction." *American Libraries* 24 (November 1993): 922–924.

DuMont, Rosemary Ruhig, Lois Buttlar, and William Caynon. "The Case for Multiculturalism." In *Multiculturalism in Libraries*. Westport Conn.: Greenwood, 1994, 1–21.

———. "The History of Multiculturalism in Libraries." In *Multiculturalism in Libraries*. Westport Conn.: Greenwood, 1994, 23–35.

Edwards, Ralph M. "The Management of Libraries and the Professional Functions of Librarians." *Library Quarterly* 45 (April 1975): 150–160.

Estabrook, Leigh. "The Growth of the Profession." *College and Research Libraries* 50 (May 1989): 287–296.

———. "Productivity, Profit and Libraries." *Library Journal* 106 (July 1981): 1377–1380.

Harris, Roma M. "Information Technology and the Deskilling of the Librarians." *Computers in Libraries* 12 (January 1992): 8–16.

Hildenbrand, Suzanne. "'Women's Work' within Librarianship." *Library Journal* 114 (September 1, 1989): 153–155.

Holley, Edward G. "Librarians, 1876–1976." *Library Trends* 25 (July 1976): 177–207.

Huber, Jeffrey T. "Library and Information Studies Education for the 21st Century Practitioner." *Journal of Library Administration* 20 (1995): 119–130.

Lancaster, F. Wilfred. "Whither Libraries? or, Wither Libraries." *College and Research Libraries* 50 (July 1989): 406–419.

Lynch, Beverly. P. "Education and Training of Librarians." In *Rethinking the Library in the Information Age*. Washington, D.C: GPO, 1989, 75–92.

Maack, Mary Niles. "Toward a New Model of the Information Professions: Embracing Empowerment." *Journal of Education for Library and Information Science* 38 (fall 1997): 283–302.

Malinconico, S. Michael. "Information's Brave New World." *Library Journal* 117 (May 1, 1992): 36–40.

Mason, Richard O. "What Is an Information Professional?" *Journal of Education for Library and Information Science* 31 (fall 1990): 122–138.

McCook, Kathleen de la Peña and Paula Geist. "Diversity Deferred: Where Are the Minority Librarians?" *Library Journal* 118 (November 1, 1993): 35–38.

Miksa, Francis L. "Melvil Dewey: The Professional Educator and His Heirs." *Library Trends* (winter 1986): 359–381.

Nelson, Anne. "How My Hometown Library Failed Me." *Library Journal* 115 (June 15, 1990): 82–85.

Nielson, Brian. "The Role of the Public Services Librarian: The New Revolution." In *Rethinking the Library in the Information Age*. Washington, D.C.: GPO, 1989, 179–200.

Passet, Joanne E. "Men in a Feminized Profession: The Male Librarian, 1887–1921." *Libraries and Culture* 28 (fall 1993): 385–402.

———. "'You Do Not Have to Pay Librarians': Women, Salaries, and Status in the Early 20th Century." In *Reclaiming the American Library Past: Writing the Women In*. Edited by Suzanne Hildenbrand. Norwood, N.J.: Ablex, 1996, 207–219.

Rice, James. "The Hidden Role of Librarians." *Library Journal* 114 (January 1989): 57–59.

Stern, Stephen. "Ethnic Libraries and Librarianship in the United States: Models and Prospects." In *Advances in Librarianship*, Volume 15. Edited by Irene P. Godden. San Diego: Academic Press, 1991, 77–102.

Warner, Alice Sizer. "Librarians as Money Makers: The Bottom Line." *American Libraries* 21 (November 1990): 946–948.

LIBRARY EDUCATION

Auld, Lawrence W.S. "Seven Imperatives for Library Education." *Library Journal* 115 (May 1, 1990): 55–59.

Boyce, Bert. "The Death of Library Education." *American Libraries* 25 (March 1994): 257–259.

Buckland, Michael. "Education for Librarianship in the Next Century." *Library Trends* 34 (spring 1986): 777–787.

Buttlar, Lois and Rosemary Du Mont. "Library and Information Science Competencies Revisited." *Journal of Education for Library and Information Science* 37 (winter 1996): 44–62

Buttlar, Lois and William Caynon. "Recruitment of Librarians into the Profession: The Minority Perspective." *Library and Information Science Research* 14 (1992): 259–280.

Dalrymple, Prudence W. "The State of the Schools." *American Libraries* 27 (January 1997): 31–34.

Davis, Donald G. Jr. "Education for Librarianship." In *American Library History: 1876–1976*. Vol. 25 of *Library Trends* (July 1976): 113–134.

Hauptman, Robert, "Iconoclastic Education: The Library Science Degree." *Catholic Library World* 58 (May/June 1987): 252–253.

Maack, Mary Niles. "Women in Library Education: Down the Up Staircase." *Library Trends* (winter 1986): 401–432.

Main, Linda, "Research versus Practice: A 'No' Contest." *Journal of Education for Library and Information Science* 30 (winter 1990): 226–228.

Marcum, Deanna B. "Transforming the Curriculum: Transforming the Profession." *American Libraries* 27 (January 1997): 35–38.

Paris, Marion. "Why Library Schools Fail." *Library Journal* 115 (October 1, 1990): 38–42.

Pemberton, J. Michael and Christine R. Nugent. "Emergent Field, Convergent Curriculum." *Journal of Education for Library and Information Science* 36 (spring 1995): 126–138.

Rayward, W. Boyd. "Library and Information Sciences: Disciplinary Differentiation, Competition, Convergence." In *The Study of Information: Disciplinary Messages*. Edited by Fritz Machlup and Una Mansfield. New York: Wiley, 1983. 343–363.

Robbins, Jane. "Yes, Virginia, You Can Require an Accredited Master's Degree for That Job." *Library Journal* 115 (February 1, 1990): 40–44.

Robbins-Carter, Jane and Charles A. Seavey. "The Master's Degree: Basic Preparation for Professional Practice." *Library Trends* 34 (spring 1986): 561–580.

Saracevic, Tefko. "Closing of Library Schools in North America: What Role Accreditation?" *Libri* 44 (November 1994). 190–200.

Schement, Jorge Reina. "A 21st-Century Strategy for Librarians." *Library Journal* 121 (May 1, 1996): 34–36.

White, Herbert S. "The Future of Library and Information Science Education." *Journal of Education for Library and Information Science* 26 (winter 1986): 174–181.

White, Herbert S. and Sarah L. Mort. "The Accredited Library Education Program as Preparation for Professional Library Work." *Library Quarterly* 60 (July 1990): 187–215.

Wiegand, Wayne A. "The Development of Librarianship in the United States." *Libraries and Culture* 24 (winter 1989): 99–109.

Wright, H. Curtis. "The Symbol and Its Referent: An Issue for Library Education." *Library Trends 34* (spring 1986): 729–775.

THE IMAGE OF LIBRARIANS

Agada, John. "Assertion and the Librarian Personality." In *Encyclopedia of Library and Information Science*. Volume 42. New York: Marcel Dekker, 1987, 128–143.

————. "Studies of the Personality of Librarians." *Drexel Library Quarterly* 20 (spring 1984): 24–45.

Carmichael, James V. Jr. "The Male Librarian and the Feminine Image: A Survey of Stereotype, Status, and Gender Perceptions." *Library and Information Science Research* 14 (October-December 1992): 411–446.

Duffy, Joan R. "Images of Librarians and Librarianship: A Study." *Journal of Youth Services in Librarianship* 3 (summer 1990): 303–308.

Durrance, Joan C. "Librarians: The Invisible Professionals." In *Bowker Annual*. 35th ed. 1990–1991, 92–99.

Fisher, David P. "Is the Librarian a Distinct Personality Type?" *Journal of Librarianship* 20 (January 1988): 36–47.

Lemkau, Jeanne Parr. "Men in Female-Dominated Professions: Distinguishing Personality and Background Features." *Journal of Vocational Behavior* 24 (February 1984): 110–122.

Morrisey, Locke J. and Donald O. Case. "'There Goes My Image.' The Perception of Male Librarians by Colleague, Student, and Self." *College and Research Libraries* 49 (September 1988): 453–464.

Schuman, Patricia Glass. "The Image of Librarians: Substance or Shadow?" *The Journal of Academic Librarianship* 16 (May 1990): 86–89.

## LIBRARIES AS ORGANIZATIONS

*Books*

American Association of School Librarians and Association for Educational Communications and Technology. *Information Power: Guidelines for School Library Media Programs.* Chicago: ALA, 1988.

Christianson, Elin B., David E. King, and Janet L. Ahrensfeld. *Special Libraries: A Guide for Management,* 3rd ed. Washington, D.C.: Special Libraries Association, 1991.

Gertzog, Alice and Edwin Beckerman. *Administration of the Public Library.* Metuchen, N.J.: Scarecrow, 1994.

Hamlin, Arthur T. *The University Library in the United States: Its Origins and Development.* Philadelphia: University of Pennsylvania, 1981.

Jones, Patrick. *Connecting Young Adults and Libraries.* 2nd ed. New York: Neal-Schuman, 1998.

Loertscher, David V. *Measures of Excellence for School Library Media Centers.* Englewood, Colo.: Libraries Unlimited, 1988.

Martell, Charles R. *The Client-Centered Academic Library: An Organizational Model.* Westport, Conn.: Greenwood, 1983.

Mount, Ellis. *Special Libraries and Information Centers: An Introductory Text,* 3rd ed. Washington, D.C.: Special Libraries Association, 1995.

Pungitore, Verna L. *Public Librarianship: An Issues-Oriented Approach.* New York: Greenwood, 1989.

Rubin, Richard E. *Human Resource Management in Libraries: Theory and Practice.* New York: Neal-Schuman, 1991.

Westin, Alan and Anne L. Finger, *Using the Public Library in the Computer Age: Present Patterns, Future Possibilities*. Chicago: ALA, 1991.

White, Herbert S. *Managing the Special Library*. White Plains, N.Y.: Knowledge Industry, 1984.

## Articles

Euster, Joanne R. "The New Hierarchy: Where's the Boss?" *Library Journal* 115 (May 1, 1990): 41–44.

Lynch, Beverly P. "Libraries as Bureaucracies." *Library Trends* 27 (winter 1978): 259–267.

Mathews, Virginia H., Judith G. Flum and Karen A. Whitney. "Kids Need Libraries: School and Public Libraries Preparing the Youth of Today for the World of Tomorrow." *School Library Journal* 36 (April 1990): 33–37.

Stahl, D. Gail. "The Virtual Library: Prospect and Promise, or Plus ça Change, Plus C'est la Même Chose." *Special Libraries* 84 (fall 1993): 202–205.

SPECIAL LIBRARIES

Arnold, Stephen. "Relationships of the Future: Vendors and Partners." *Special Libraries* 84 (fall 1993): 235–240.

Ojala, Marydee. "Core Competencies for Special Library Managers of the Future." *Special Libraries* 84 (fall 1993): 230–233.

Piggott, Sylvia E. A. "Why Corporate Librarians Must Reengineer the Library for the New Information Age." *Special Libraries* 86 (winter 1995): 11–20.

White, Herbert S. "The 'Quiet Revolution': A Profession at the Crossroads." *Special Libraries* 80 (winter 1989): 24–30.

SCHOOLS

Garland, Kathleen. "An Analysis of School Library Media Center Statistics Collected by State Agencies and Individual Library Media Specialists." *School Library Media Quarterly* 21 (winter 1993): 106–110.

Kuhlthau, Carol Collier, ed. *The Virtual School Library*. Englewood, Colo.: Libraries Unlimited, 1996.

Lance, Keith Curry, Lynda Welborn, and Christine Hamilton-Pennell. *The Impact of School Library Media Centers on Academic Achievement*. Castle Rock, Colo.: Hi Willow Research and Publishing, 1993.

Mathews, Virginia H. et al. "Kids Need Libraries: School and Public Libraries Preparing the Youth of Today for the World of Tomorrow." *School Library Media Quarterly* 18 (spring 1990): 167–172.

Rogers, JoAnn V. "School Library Media Center Statistics: A Progress Report." *Journal of Youth Services in Libraries* 9 (fall 1995): 69–76.

Zweizig, Douglas, L. "The Children's Services Story." *Public Libraries* 32 (January/February 1993): 26–28.

ACADEMIC LIBRARIES

Clayton, Howard. "The American College Library, 1800–1860." *Journal of Library History* 3 (April 1968): 120–137.
Hurt, Charlene S. "A Vision of the Library of the 21st Century." *Journal of Library Administration* 15 (1991): 7–19.
Jones, Plummer Alston Jr. "The History and Development of Libraries in American Higher Education." *College and Research Library News* 7 (July/August 1989): 561–564.
Neal, James G. "Academic Libraries: 2000 and Beyond." *Library Journal* 121 (July 1996): 74–76.
Smith, Eldred and Peggy Johnson. "How to Survive the Present While Preparing for the Future: A Research Library Strategy." *College and Research Libraries* (September 1993): 389–396.
Tenopir, Carol. "Electronic Reference in Academic Libraries in the 1990s." In *Annual Review of OCLC Research*. Dublin, Ohio: OCLC, 1995, 66–68.


PUBLIC LIBRARIES

Birdsall, William F. "Community, Individualism, and the American Public Library." *Library Journal* 110 (November 1, 1985): 21–24.
Coffman, Steve. "What If You Ran Your Library Like a Bookstore." *American Libraries* 29 (March 1998): 40–46.
D'Elia, George and Eleanor Jo Rodger. "Public Opinion about the Roles of the Public Library in the Community: The Results of a Recent Gallup Poll." *Public Libraries* (January/February 1994): 23–28.
Public Library Association. *Output Measures for Public Libraries*. 2nd ed. Chicago: ALA, 1987.
Ring, Daniel F. "Has the American Public Library Lost Its Purpose?" *Public Libraries* (July/August 1994): 191–196.
Scheppke, Jim. "The Governance of Public Libraries: Findings of the PLA Governance of Public Libraries Committee." *Public Libraries* (September/October 1991): 288–294.
Shearer, Kenneth. "Confusing What Is Most Wanted and What Is Most Used: A Crisis in Public Library Priorities Today." *Public Libraries* (July/August 1993): 193–197.
Summers, William F. "The Concept of the Indispensable Public Library." *Public Libraries* (July/August 1993): 212–215.
William, Patrick. "How Should the Public Library Respond to Public Demand?" *Library Journal* 115 (October 15, 1990): 54–56.

## MISSION AND VALUES OF LIBRARIES

*Books*

Benton Foundation. *Buildings, Books and Bytes: Libraries and Communities in the Digital Age.* Washington D.C.: Benton Foundation, 1996.

Ditzion, Sidney H. *Arsenals of a Democratic Culture.* Chicago: ALA, 1947.

Dunlap, Leslie W. *Readings in Library History.* New York: R. R. Bowker, 1972.

Eisenstein, Elizabeth L. *The Printing Press as an Agent of Change: Communications and Cultural Transformations in Early-Modern Europe.* Cambridge: Cambridge University, 1979.

Hamlin, Arthur T. *The University Library in the United States: Its Origins and Development.* Philadelphia: University of Pennsylvania, 1981.

Haro, Roberto P. *Developing Library and Information Services for Americans of Hispanic Origin.* Metuchen, N.J.: Scarecrow, 1981.

Hessel, Alfred. *A History of Libraries.* New Brunswick, N.J.: Scarecrow, 1955.

Jackson, Sidney, L. *Libraries and Librarianship in the West.* New York: McGraw-Hill, 1974.

Josey, E.J. ed. *The Black Librarian in America.* Metuchen, N.J.: Scarecrow, 1970.

———. *The Black Librarian in America Revisited.* Metuchen, N.J.: Scarecrow, 1994.

Kruzas, Anthony Thomas. *Business and Industrial Libraries in the United States, 1820–1940.* New York: Special Libraries Association, 1965

Ranganathan, S. R. *The Five Laws of Library Science.* New York: Asia, 1963. First published 1931.

Shera, Jesse. *Foundations of the Public Library.* Chicago: Shoe String, 1965.

Thompson, James Westfall. *Ancient Libraries.* Hamden, Conn.: Archon, 1962.

Winger, Howard W., ed. *American Library History 1876–1976.* Urbana-Champaign, Ill.: University of Illinois Graduate School of Library Science, 1975. Published as *Library Trends* 25 (July 1976).

*Articles*

Baker, Nicholson. "The Author vs. The Library." *New Yorker* (October 14, 1996): 50–61.

Blanke, Henry T. "Librarianship and Political Values: Neutrality or Commitment?" *Library Journal* 114 (July 1989): 39–43.

Broderick, Dorothy. "Net or Not, People Need Libraries." *American Libraries* 29 (January 1998): 62–64.

Clayton, Howard. "The American College Library." *Journal of Library History* 3 (April 1968): 120–137.

Cox, Richard. J. "Taking Sides on the Future of the Book." *American Libraries* 28 (February 1997): 52–55.

Cresswell, Stephen."The Last Days of Jim Crow in Southern Libraries." *Libraries and Culture* 31 (summer/fall 1996): 557–573.

Dain, Phyllis. "Ambivalence and Paradox: The Social Bonds of the Public Library." *Library Journal* 100 (February 1, 1975): 261–266.

Dowlin, Kenneth E. "Access to Information: A Human Right?" In *Bowker Annual*, 32nd ed. New York: R.R. Bowker, 1987, 64–68.

Estabrook, Leigh and Chris Horak. "Public vs. Professional Opinion on Libraries: The Great Divide?" *Library Journal* 117 (April 1, 1992): 52–55.

Garrison, Dee. "The Tender Technicians: The Feminization of Public Librarianship." *Journal of Social History* 6 (winter 1972–1973): 131–159.

Hanson, Eugene R. "College Libraries: The Colonial Period to the Twentieth Century." In *Advances in Library Administration and Organization*. Greenwich, Conn.: JAI, 1989, 171–199.

Harris, Michael. "The Purpose of the American Public Library." *Library Journal* 98 (September 15, 1973): 2509–2514.

Harris, Michael H. and Stanley Hannah. "Why Do We Study the History of Libraries?: A Meditation on the Perils of Ahistoricism in the Information Era." *LISR* 14 (April/June 1992): 123–130

Harwell, Richard and Roger Michener. "As Public as the Town Pump." *Library Journal* 99 (April 1, 1974): 959–963.

Jones, Plummer Alston Jr. "The History and Development of Libraries in American Higher Education." *College and Research Library News* (July/August 1989): 561–565.

Kaufman, Paula T. "Information Incompetence." *Library Journal* 117 (November 15, 1992): 37–39.

Neill, Sam D. "Why Books?" *Public Library Quarterly* 12 (1992): 19–28.

Nelson, Anne. "How My Hometown Library Failed Me." *Library Journal* 115 (June 15, 1990): 82–85.

Peters, Paul Evan. "Information Age Avatars." *Library Journal* 120 (March 15, 1995): 32–34.

Shearer, Kenneth. "Confusing What Is Most Wanted and What Is Most Used: The Crisis in Public Library Priorities Today." *Public Libraries* (July-August 1993): 193–197.

Summers, F. William. "The Concept of the Indispensable Public Library." *Public Libraries* (July/August 1993): 212–215.

Swan, John C. "Rehumanizing Information: An Alternative Future." *Library Journal* 115 (September 1, 1990): 178–182.

Tisdale, Sallie. "Silence, Please." *Harper's Magazine* (March 1997): 65–74.

Watson, Paula D. "Founding Mothers: The Contributions of Women's Organizations to Public Library Development in the United States." *Library Quarterly* 64 (1994): 233–269.

Zill, Nicholas and Marianne Winglee. "Literature Reading in the United States: Data from National Surveys and Their Policy Implications." *Book Research Quarterly* 5 (spring 1989): 24–58.

# Appendix A

# Association of Research Libraries Statement on Intellectual Property

INTELLECTUAL PROPERTY:
**AN ASSOCIATION OF RESEARCH LIBRARIES STATEMENT OF PRINCIPLES**

"The primary objective of copyright is not to reward the labour of authors, but [t]o promote the Progress of Science and useful Arts. To this end, copyright assures authors the right to their original expression, but encourages others to build freely upon the ideas and information conveyed by a work. This result is neither unfair nor unfortunate. It is the means by which copyright advances the progress of science and art."

—Justice Sandra Day O'Connor

AFFIRMING THE RIGHTS AND RESPONSIBILITIES OF THE RESEARCH LIBRARY COMMUNITY IN THE AREA OF COPYRIGHT

The genius of United States copyright law is that it balances the intellectual property rights of authors, publishers and copyright owners with society's need for the free exchange of ideas. Taken together, fair use and other public rights to utilize copyrighted works, as established in the Copyright Act of 1976, constitute indispensable legal doctrines for promoting the dissemination of knowledge, while ensuring authors, publishers and copyright owners protection of their creative works and economic investments. The preservation and continuation of these balanced rights in an electronic environment are essential to the free flow of information and to the development of an information infrastructure that serves the public interest.

The U.S. and Canada have adopted very different approaches to intellectual property and copyright issues. For example, the Canadian Copyright Act does not contain the special considerations for library and educational use found in the U.S. Copyright Act of 1976, nor does it place federal or provincial government works in the public domain. Because of these differences, this statement addresses these issues from the U.S. perspective.

Each year, millions of researchers, students, and members of the public benefit from access to library collections—access that is supported by fair use, the right of libraries to reproduce materials under certain circumstances, and other related provisions of the copyright law. These provisions are limitations on the rights of copyright owners. The loss of these provisions in the emerging information infrastructure would greatly harm scholarship, teaching, and the operations of a free society. Fair use, the library and other relevant provisions must be preserved so that copyright ownership does not become an absolute monopoly over the distribution of and access to copyrighted information. In an electronic environment, this could mean that information resources are accessible only to those who are able to pay. The public information systems that libraries have developed would be replaced by commercial information vendors. In the age of information, a diminished scope of public rights would lead to an increasingly polarized society of information haves and have-nots.

Librarians and educators have every reason to encourage full and good-faith copyright compliance. Technological advancement has made copyright infringement easier to accomplish, but no less illegal. Authors, publishers, copyright owners, and librarians are integral parts of the system of scholarly communication and publishers, authors, and copyright owners are the natural partners of education and research. The continuation of fair use, the library and other relevant provisions of the Copyright Act of 1976 applied in an electronic environment offer the prospect of better library services, better teaching, and better research, without impairing the market for copyrighted materials.

Although the emerging information infrastructure is raising awareness of technological changes that pose challenges to copyright systems, the potential impact of technology was anticipated by the passage of the Copyright Act of 1976. Congress expressly intended that the revised copyright law would apply to all types of media. With few exceptions, the protections and provisions of the copyright statute are as relevant and applicable to an electronic environment as they are to a print and broadcast environment.

The research library community believes that the development of an information infrastructure does not require a major revision of copyright law at this time. In general, the stakeholders affected by intellectual property law continue to be well served by the existing copyright statute. Just as was intended, the law's flexibility with regard to dissemination media fosters change and experimentation in educational and research communication. Some specific legislative changes may be needed to ensure that libraries are able to utilize the latest technology to provide continued and effective access to information and to preserve knowledge.

The Association of Research Libraries affirms the following intellectual property principles as they apply to librarians, teachers, researchers, and other information mediators and consumers. We join our national leaders in the determination to develop a policy framework for the emerging information infrastructure that strengthens the Constitutional purpose of copyright law to advance science and the useful arts.

## STATEMENT OF PRINCIPLES

*Principle 1: Copyright exists for the public good.*

The United States copyright law is founded on a Constitutional provision intended to "promote the progress of Science and Useful Arts." The fundamental purpose of copyright is to serve the public interest by encouraging the advancement of knowledge through a system of exclusive but limited rights for authors and copyright owners. Fair use and other public rights to utilize copyrighted works, specifically and intentionally included in the 1976 revision of the law, provide the essential balance between the rights of authors, publishers and copyright owners, and society's interest in the free exchange of ideas.

*Principle 2: Fair use, the library, and other relevant provisions of the Copyright Act of 1976 must be preserved in the development of the emerging information infrastructure.*

Fair use and other relevant provisions are the essential means by which teachers teach, students learn, and researchers advance knowledge. The Copyright Act of 1976 defines intellectual property principles in a way that is independent of the form of publication or distribution. These provisions apply to all formats and are essential to modern library and information services.

*Principle 3: As trustees of the rapidly growing record of human knowledge, libraries and archives must have full use of technology in order to preserve our heritage of scholarship and research.*

Digital works of enduring value need to be preserved just as printed works have long been preserved by research libraries. Archival responsibilities have traditionally been undertaken by libraries because publishers and database producers have generally preserved particular knowledge only as long as it has economic value in the marketplace. As with other formats, the preservation of electronic information will be the responsibility of libraries and they will continue to perform this important societal role.

The policy framework of the emerging information infrastructure must provide for the archiving of electronic materials by research libraries to maintain permanent collections and environments for public access. Accomplishing this goal will require strengthening the library provisions of the copyright law to allow preservation activities which use electronic or other appropriate technologies as they emerge.

*Principle 4: Licensing agreements should not be allowed to abrogate the fair use and library provisions authorized in the copyright statute.*

Licenses may define the rights and privileges of the contracting parties differently than those defined by the Copyright Act of 1976. But licenses and contracts should not negate fair use and the public right to utilize copyrighted works. The research library community recognizes that there will be a variety of payment methods for the purchase of copyrighted materials in electronic formats, just as there are differing contractual agreements for acquiring printed information. The research library community is committed to working with publishers and database producers to develop model agreements that deploy licenses that do not contract around fair use or other copyright provisions.

*Principle 5: Librarians and educators have an obligation to educate information users about their rights and responsibilities under intellectual property law.*

Institutions of learning must continue to employ policies and procedures that encourage copyright compliance. For example, the Copyright Act of 1976 required the posting of copyright notices on photocopy equipment. This practice should be updated to other technologies which permit the duplication of copyrighted works.

*Principle 6: Copyright should not be applied to U.S. government information.*

The Copyright Act of 1976 prohibits copyright of U.S. government works. Only under selected circumstances has Congress granted limited exceptions to this policy. The Copyright Act of 1976 is one of several laws that support a fundamental principle of democratic government—that the open exchange of public information is essential to the functioning of a free and open society. U.S. government information should remain in the public domain free of copyright or copyright-like restrictions.

*Principle 7: The information infrastructure must permit authors to be compensated for the success of their creative works, and copyright owners must have an opportunity for a fair return on their investment.*

The research library community affirms that the distribution of copyrighted information which exceeds fair use and the enumerated limitations of the law require the permission of and/or compensation to authors, publishers and copyright owners. The continuation of library provisions and fair use in an electronic environment has far greater potential to promote the sale of copyrighted materials than to substitute for purchase. There is every reason to believe that the increasing demand for and use of copyrighted works fostered by new information technologies will result in the equivalent or even greater compensation for authors, publishers and copyright owners. The information infrastructure however, must be based on an underlying ethos of abundance rather than scarcity. With such an approach, authors, copyright owners, and publishers will have a full range of new opportunities in an electronic information environment and libraries will be able to perform their roles as partners in promoting science and the useful arts.

Adopted by the ARL Membership
May 1994

Reprinted with permission, Association of Research Libraries

# Appendix B

# White House Conference on Library and Information Services Priority Recommendations

Recommendations earmarked for priority action by an early vote of the Conference delegates

## ADOPT OMNIBUS CHILDREN AND YOUTH LITERACY INITIATIVE

That the President and the Congress adopt a four-pronged initiative to invigorate library and information services for student learning and literacy through legislation which would consist of:

*School Library Services Title*, which would:

- Establish within the U.S. Department of Education an office responsible for providing leadership to school library media programs across the Nation.
- Create federal legislation to provide demonstration grants to schools for teachers and library media specialists to design resource-based instructional activities that provide opportunities for students to explore diverse ideas and multiple sources of information.
- Establish grants to provide information technology to school media centers, requiring categorical aid for school library media services and resources in any federal legislation which provides funds for educational purposes.

- Establish a federal incentive program for states to ensure adequate professional staffing in school library media centers. This would serve as a first step toward the goal for all schools to be fully staffed by professional school library media specialists and support personnel to provide, facilitate, and integrate instructional programs which impact student learning.

*Public Library Children's Services Title*, which would provide funding support for:

- Demonstration grants for services to children.
- Parent/family education projects for early childhood services involving early childhood support agencies.
- Working in partnership with day care centers and other early childhood providers to offer deposit collections and training in the use of library resources.

(Concurrently, funding for programs such as Head Start should be increased for early childhood education.)

*Public Library Young Adult Services Title*, which would provide funding support for:

- Demonstration grants for services to young adults.
- Youth-at-risk demonstration grants to provide outreach services, through partnership with community youth-serving agencies, for young adults on the verge of risk behavior, as well as those already in crisis.
- A national library-based "Kids Corps" program for young adults to offer significant salaried youth participation projects to build self esteem, develop skills, and expand the responsiveness and level of library and information services to teenagers.

*Partnership with Libraries for Youth Title*, which would provide funding support to:

- Develop partnership programs between school and public libraries to provide comprehensive library services to children and young adults.
- Establish and fund research agenda to document and evaluate how children and young adults develop abilities that make them information literate.
- Establish a nationwide resource-sharing network that includes school library media programs as equal partners with libraries and ensures that all youth have access to the Nation's library resources equal to that of other users.
- Encourage school and public library intergenerational demonstration

programs which provide meaningful services (e.g., tutoring, leisure activities, and sharing of books, ideas, hobbies) for latchkey children and young adolescents in collaboration with networks and private organizations, such as conducted by the American Association of Retired Persons (AARP).

- Create family literacy demonstration programs that involve school and public libraries and other family-serving agencies.
- Provide discretionary grants to library schools and schools of education for the collaborative development of graduate programs to educate librarians to serve children and young adults.
- Provide opportunities for potential authors who reflect our cultural diversity to develop abilities to write stories and create other communications media about diverse cultures for youth.
- Further, all legislation authorizing child care programs, drug prevention programs, and other youth-at-risk programs should include funds for appropriate books and library materials, to be selected in consultation with professional librarians.

## SHARE INFORMATION VIA NETWORK 'SUPERHIGHWAY'

That the Congress enact legislation creating and funding the National Research and Education Network (NREN) to serve as an information "superhighway," allowing educational institutions, including libraries, to capitalize on the advantages of technology for resource sharing and the creation and exchange of information. The network should be available in all libraries and other information repositories at every level. The governance structure for NREN should include representation from all interested constituencies, including technical, user, and information provider components, as well as government, education at all levels, and libraries.

## FUND LIBRARIES SUFFICIENTLY TO AID U.S. PRODUCTIVITY

That sufficient funds be provided to assure that libraries continue to acquire, preserve, and disseminate those information resources needed for education and research in order for the United States to increase its productivity and stay competitive in the world marketplace. Thus, a local, state, regional, tribal, and national commitment of financial resources for library services is an indispensable investment in the Nation's future. Government and library officials and representatives of the private sector must work together to raise sufficient funds to provide the necessary resources for the crucial contribution information services make to the national interest. The President and the Congress should fully support education and research by expanding and fully funding statutes related to information services, such as the Higher Education Act, Medical Library Assistance Act, Library Service and Construction Act (LSCA), College Library Technology Demonstration Grants, the National Research and Education Network (NREN), and other related statutes. Further, recommend amending Chapter II of the Education Consolidation and Improvement Act to allocate funds for networking school libraries.

## CREATE MODEL LIBRARY MARKETING PROGRAMS

That model programs be created to market libraries to their publics, emphasizing the library as a resource to meet educational, business, and personal needs. The models should promote all elements and components of the library community. The Congress also should appropriate funds to create the models for implementation on the local level.

## EMPHASIZE LITERACY INITIATIVES TO AID THE DISADVANTAGED

That literacy for all people must be an ongoing national priority. Because of the crisis in the disadvantaged rural and urban minority community, particular emphasis should be directed to African-American and other minority groups. Literacy initiatives should include the development of a national training model to aid libraries in establishing, implementing, and supporting literacy coalitions. To recognize the central role of libraries as providers of adult, youth, family, and workforce literacy services, the Congress should amend the National Literacy Act of 1991. Policy and funding approaches should include:

- Urging the Congress and state legislatures to appropriate funds for libraries to provide basic literacy and literacy enhancement programs and general information services in prisons.
- Developing national training models to aid libraries in implementing and supporting literacy programs, including development of new technologies and equipment to support literacy services.
- Supporting development, production, and dissemination of quality literacy materials.

- Reorienting Library Services and Construction Act (LSCA) Titles VI (Library Literacy) and VIII (Library Learning Center Programs) to state-based, rather than discretionary programs, to permit all LSCA literacy and family learning programs within a state to be effectively coordinated with other state and local literacy efforts, regardless of sponsorship.
- Guaranteeing access to literacy training at all levels for people with disabilities by offering instruction at accessible locations. Funding should be set aside to conduct literacy training programs in Braille and American Sign Language.

## ADOPT NATIONAL POLICIES FOR INFORMATION PRESERVATION

That the Congress adopt a national policy to ensure the preservation of our information resources. The assessment of preservation needs should be clearly articulated, with adequate funding provided for policy implementation. This policy must include:

- A broad-based program of preservation education and training essential to the long-term development of a multi-institutional preservation effort.
- A comprehensive policy for preserving information in non-paper media.
- The development and dissemination of new technologies, standards, and procedures in our libraries, archives, and historical organizations.
- Increased federal funding to support existing regional preservation centers and to create new centers in unserved regions of the country. Together, these resources will help to ensure that small libraries, archives, and historical organizations will have access to the information and services they need to preserve their collections.

## DEVELOP NETWORKING EQUITY FOR LOW-DENSITY AREAS

That networks connecting, small, rural, urban, and tribal libraries be developed and supported at the federal, state, and local levels to ensure basic library services to all end users. Equal opportunity to participate in our country's economic, political, and social life depends upon equal access to information. The federal government should provide additional funding, based on low-density populations, under the Library Services and Construction Act to address the networking needs of small and rural libraries. All rural and low-density population libraries should be provided with federal funds for a minimum of one access terminal on the National Research and Education Network.

## ENCOURAGE MULTICULTURAL, MULTILINGUAL PROGRAMS/STAFFS

That the President and the Congress enact legislation to authorize and fund a program which:

- Provides financial and technical assistance for library and information services for multicultural, multilingual populations.
- Creates a national database of multicultural, multilingual materials for use by libraries and information services, including research and demonstration projects for model library programs, serving our multicultural and multilingual populations.
- Reauthorizes the Higher Education Act and expands provisions to encourage the recruitment of people of multicultural, multilingual heritage, including those with disabilities, to the library and information services professions, and to support the training and retraining of library and information science professionals to serve the needs of multicultural, multilingual populations.

## AMEND COPYRIGHT STATUTES FOR NEW TECHNOLOGIES

That, at an early date, the Congress review and amend copyright legislation to accommodate the impact of new and emerging technologies to:

- Ensure that all library and information service users have access to all forms and formats of information and library materials.
- Provide the right to use information technology to explore and create information without infringing on the legitimate rights of authorship and ownership.
- Encourage networking and resource-sharing, while providing appropriate and manageable credit and compensation for authorship or ownership.
- Permit libraries and information services preferential fair-use status equivalent to that of educational institutions.

## ENSURE ACCESS TO GOVERNMENT INFORMATION RESOURCES

That the Congress amend the Freedom of Information Act to ensure access to all non-exempt information whether received by the federal government or created at public expense and regardless of physical form or characteristics. The Congress should create an advisory committee composed of library professionals, information industry representatives, and the general public to work with federal agencies to advise on the public's needs.

## ENACT NATIONAL INFORMATION POLICIES FOR DEMOCRACY

That the Congress enact national information policies which shall include, but are not limited to:

- Declaring libraries as educational agencies essential to free democratic societies.
- Assuring the freedom to read by affirming libraries' obligations to provide, without censorship, books and other materials with the widest diversity of viewpoint and expression.
- Protecting organizational and individual users from scrutiny over which library resources and databases they use.

## RECOGNIZE LIBRARIES AS PARTNERS IN LIFELONG EDUCATION

That the President and the Congress formally recognize all libraries as educational institutions for lifelong learning by specifically including libraries in all relevant legislation, regulations, and policy statements. This recognition will provide access to funding for adult learning and training, services to children, and efforts to eliminate illiteracy, while placing libraries in parallel partnership with the revolutionary *America 2000* education initiative. The Congress should fund a basic level of services and facilities for public libraries.

## DESIGNATE LIBRARIES AS EDUCATIONAL AGENCIES

That libraries be designated as educational agencies and that the President include members of the library community in implementing *America 2000*, appointing them to serve on relevant task forces and advisory groups. Further, that the Department of Education should designate a school library program officer to oversee research, planning, and adoption of the goals of *Information Power: Guidelines for School Library Media*

*Programs*. The Department of Education shall seek categorical funding for school library media programs.

## AN ADDENDUM

The following two proposals were included in early prioritizing of proposals for Conference floor discussion, but were not adopted in the final 95 Conference recommendations:

## ADD OFFICIAL IN DEPARTMENT OF EDUCATION

That the Department of Education include an Under Secretary of Education for Library and Information Services.

## ADOPT LAWS TO GUARANTEE ACCESS TO ALL WORKS

That the Congress and state legislatures adopt laws to guarantee that the Congress and the states recognize the right of the American public to access works of all authors, artists, scholars, politicians, and other public figures.

# Principles for the Development of the National Information Infrastructure (NII)

Representatives from fifteen national library and information associations met in September 1993 to discuss critical national policy issues dealing with the National Information Infrastructure (NII). The group reached a consensus on key principles and questions that must be used to guide the development of plans for the evolution of the NII in the areas of:

## FIRST AMENDMENT AND INTELLECTUAL FREEDOM

1) Access to the NII should be available and affordable to all regardless of age, religion, disability, sexual orientation, social and political views, national origin, economic status, location, information literacy, etc.
2) The NII service providers must guarantee the free flow of information protected by the First Amendment.
3) Individuals should have the right to choose what information to receive through the NII.

## PRIVACY

1) Privacy should be carefully protected and extended.
2) Comprehensive policies should be developed to ensure that the privacy of all people is protected.

3) Personal data collected to provide specific services should be limited to the minimum necessary.
4) Sharing data collected from individuals should only be permitted with their informed consent.
5) Individuals should have the right to inspect and correct data files about themselves.
6) Transaction data should remain confidential.

## INTELLECTUAL PROPERTY

1) Intellectual property rights and protection are independent of the form of publication or distribution.
2) The intellectual property system should ensure fair and equitable balance between rights of creators and other copyright owners and the needs of users.
3) Fair use and other exceptions to owner's rights in the copyright law should continue in the electronic environment.
4) Compensation systems must provide a fair and reasonable return to copyright owners.

## UBIQUITY

1) Libraries should preserve and enhance their traditional roles in providing public access to information regardless of format.
2) Network access costs for libraries, educational organizations, government entities and non-profit groups should be stable, predictable and location sensitive.
3) Resources must be allocated to provide basic public access in fostering the development of the information infrastructure.

## EQUITABLE ACCESS

1) The NII should support and encourage a diversity of information providers in order to guarantee an open, fair, and competitive marketplace, with a full range of viewpoints.
2) Diversity of access should be protected through use of nonproprietary protocols.
3) Access to basic network services should be affordable and available to all.
4) Basic network access should be made available independent of geographic location.
5) The NII should ensure private, government and nonprofit participation in governance of the network.

6) Electronic information should be appropriately documented, organized and archived through the cooperative endeavors of information service providers and libraries.

## INTEROPERABILITY

1) The design of the NII should facilitate two-way audio, video and data communication from anyone to anyone easily and effectively.
2) Interoperability standards should be encouraged and tied to incentives for the use of those standards in awards for Federal funding.
3) A transition period should provide compatibility between leading edge technology and trailing edge technology to allow users reasonable protection from precipitate change.
4) The Federal government should encourage interoperability standards and should tie incentives to the use of those standards.
5) Federal government information dissemination programs should adhere to interoperability standards.
6) Principles of interoperability should require directory and locator services, and non-proprietary search protocols, as well as a minimal set of data elements for the description of data bases.

Reprinted with Permission. American Library Association.

# Appendix D

# A Bill of Rights and Responsibilities for Electronic Learners

PREAMBLE

In order to protect the rights and recognize the responsibilities of individuals and institutions, we, the members of the educational community, propose this Bill of Rights and Responsibilities for the Electronic Community of Learners. These principles are based on a recognition that the electronic community is a complex subsystem of the educational community founded on the values espoused by that community. As new technology modifies the system and further empowers individuals, new values and responsibilities will change this culture. As technology assumes an integral role in education and lifelong learning, technological empowerment of individuals and organizations becomes a requirement and right for students, faculty, staff, and institutions, bringing with it new levels of responsibility that individuals and institutions have to themselves and to other members of the educational community.

ARTICLE I: INDIVIDUAL RIGHTS

The original Bill of Rights explicitly recognized that all individuals have certain fundamental rights as members of the national community. In the same way, the citizens of the electronic community of learners have fundamental rights that empower them.

*Section 1.*

A citizen's access to computing and information resources shall not be denied or removed without just cause.

*Section 2.*

The right to access includes the right to appropriate training and tools required to effect access.

*Section 3.*

All citizens shall have the right to be informed about personal information that is being and has been collected about them, and have the right to review and correct that information. Personal information about a citizen shall not be used for other than the express purpose of its collection without the explicit permission of that citizen.

*Section 4.*

The constitutional concept of freedom of speech applies to citizens of electronic communities.

*Section 5.*

All citizens of the electronic community of learners have ownership rights over their own intellectual works.

ARTICLE II: INDIVIDUAL RESPONSIBILITIES

Just as certain rights are given to each citizen of the electronic community of learners, each citizen is held accountable for his or her actions. The interplay of rights and responsibilities within each individual and within the community engenders the trust and intellectual freedom that form the heart of our society. This trust and freedom are grounded on each person's developing the skills necessary to be an active and contributing citizen of the electronic community. These skills include an awareness and knowledge about information technology and the uses of information and an understanding of the roles in the electronic community of learners.

*Section 1.*

It shall be each citizen's personal responsibility to actively pursue needed resources: to recognize when information is needed, and to be able to find, evaluate, and effectively use information.

*Section 2.*

It shall be each citizen's personal responsibility to recognize (attribute) and honor the intellectual property of others.

*Section 3.*

Since the electronic community of learners is based upon the integrity and authenticity of information, it shall be each citizen's personal responsibility to be aware of the potential for and possible effects of manipulating electronic information: to understand the fungible nature of electronic information; and to verify the integrity and authenticity, and assure the security of information that he or she compiles or uses.

*Section 4.*

Each citizen, as a member of the electronic community of learners, is responsible to all other citizens in that community: to respect and value the rights of privacy for all; to recognize and respect the diversity of the population and opinion in the community; to behave ethically; and to comply with legal restrictions regarding the use of information resources.

*Section 5.*

Each citizen, as a member of the electronic community of learners, is responsible to the community as a whole to understand what information technology resources are available, to recognize that the members of the community share them, and to refrain from acts that waste resources or prevent others from using them.

## ARTICLE III: RIGHTS OF EDUCATIONAL INSTITUTIONS

Educational institutions have legal standing similar to that of individuals. Our society depends upon educational institutions to educate our citizens and advance the development of knowledge. However, in order to survive, educational institutions must attract financial and human resources. Therefore, society must grant these institutions the rights to the electronic resources and information necessary to accomplish their goals.

*Section 1.*

The access of an educational institutions [sic] to computing and information resources shall not be denied or removed without just cause.

*Section 2.*

Educational institutions in the electronic community of learners have ownership rights over the intellectual works they create.

*Section 3.*

Each educational institution has the authority to allocate resources in accordance with its unique institutional mission.


## ARTICLE IV: INSTITUTIONAL RESPONSIBILITIES

Just as certain rights are assured to educational institutions in the electronic community of learners, so too each is held accountable for the appropriate exercise of those rights to foster the values of society and to carry out each institution's mission. This interplay of rights and responsibilities within the community fosters the creation and maintenance of an environment wherein trust and intellectual freedom are the foundation for individual and institutional growth and success.

*Section 1.*

The institutional members of the electronic community of learners have a responsibility to provide all members of their community with legally acquired computer resources (hardware, software, networks, data bases, etc.) in all instances where access to or use of the resources is an integral part of active participation in the electronic community of learners.

*Section 2.*

Institutions have a responsibility to develop, implement, and maintain security procedures to insure the integrity of individual and institutional files.

*Section 3.*

The institution shall treat electronically stored information as confidential. The institution shall treat all personal files as confidential, examining or disclosing the contents only when authorized by the owner of the information, approved by the appropriate institutional official, or required by local, state or federal law.

*Section 4.*

Institutions in the electronic community of learners shall train and support faculty, staff, and students to effectively use information technology. Training includes skills to use the resources, to be aware of the existence of data repositories and techniques for using them, and to understand the ethical and legal uses of the resources.

August 1993

Reprinted with permission. Frank Connolly, 1996. The Bill of Rights and Responsibilities for Electronic Learners is an American Association for Higher Education (AAHE) document developed as part of the Educational Uses of Information Technology project of EDUCOM.

# Appendix E

# Accredited Master's Programs in Library and Information Studies in the U.S. and Canada

**Alabama:**     University of Alabama. School of Library and Information Studies. Tuscaloosa, AL.

**Arizona:**     University of Arizona. School of Library Science. Tucson, AZ.

**California:**     San Jose State University. School of Library and Information Science. San Jose, CA.

University of California at Los Angeles. Graduate School of Education and Information Science. Los Angeles, CA.

**Connecticut:**     Southern Connecticut State University. School of Communications, Information and Library Science. New Haven, CT.

**Florida:**     Florida State University. School of Library and Information Studies. Tallahassee, FL.

University of South Florida. School of Library and Information Science. Tampa, FL.

**Georgia:** Clark Atlanta University. School of Library and Information Studies. Atlanta, GA.

**Hawaii:** University of Hawaii at Manoa. School of Library and Information Studies. Honolulu, HI.

**Illinois:** Dominican University. Graduate School of Library and Information Science. River Forest, IL.

University of Illinois. Graduate School of Library and Information Science. Champaign, IL.

**Indiana:** Indiana University. School of Library and Information Science, Bloomington, IN.

**Iowa:** University of Iowa. School of Library and Information Science. Iowa City, IA.

**Kansas:** Emporia State University. School of Library and Information Management. Emporia, KS.

**Kentucky:** University of Kentucky. School of Library and Information Science. Lexington, KY.

**Louisiana:** Louisiana State University. School of Library and Information Science. Baton Rouge, LA.

**Maryland:** University of Maryland. College of Library and Information Services. College Park, MD.

**Massachusetts:** Simmons College, Graduate School of Library and Information Science. Boston, MA.

**Michigan:** University of Michigan. School of Information and Library Studies. Ann Arbor, MI.

Wayne State University. Library and Information Science Program. Detroit, MI.

| | |
|---|---|
| **Mississippi:** | University of Southern Mississippi. School of Library and Information Science. Hattiesburg, MS. |
| **Missouri:** | University of Missouri. School of Library and Information Science. Columbia, MO. |
| **New Jersey:** | Rutgers University. School of Communication, Information, and Library Studies. New Brunswick, NJ. |
| **New York:** | Long Island University. Palmer School of Library and Information Science. Brookville, NY. |
| | Pratt Institute. School of Information and Library Science. Brooklyn, NY. |
| | Queens College. City University of New York. Graduate School of Library and Information Studies. Flushing, NY. |
| | Saint John's University. Division of Library and Information Science. Jamaica, NY. |
| | State University of New York at Albany. School of Information Science and Policy. Albany, NY. |
| | State University of New York at Buffalo. School of Information and Library Studies. Buffalo, NY. |
| | Syracuse University. School of Information Studies. Syracuse, NY. |
| **North Carolina:** | North Carolina Central University. School of Library and Information Sciences. Durham, NC. |
| | University of North Carolina. School of Information and Library Science. Chapel Hill, NC. |
| | University of North Carolina at Greensboro. Department of Library and Information Studies. Greensboro, NC. |
| **Ohio:** | Kent State University. School of Library and Information Science. Kent, OH. |

**Oklahoma:**          University of Oklahoma. School of Library and Information Studies. Norman, OK.

**Pennsylvania:**      Clarion University of Pennsylvania. Computer Information Science, and Library Science. Clarion, PA.

                       Drexel University. College of Information Science and Technology. Philadelphia, PA.

                       University of Pittsburgh, School of Library and Information Science. Pittsburgh, PA.

**Puerto Rico:**       University of Puerto Rico, Escuela Graduada de Bibliotecologia y Ciencia de la Informacion. San Juan, PR.

**Rhode Island:**      University of Rhode Island. Graduate School of Library and Information Studies. Kingston, RI.

**South Carolina:**    University of South Carolina. College of Library and Information Science. Columbia, SC.

**Tennessee:**         University of Tennessee. School of Information Sciences. Knoxville, TN.

**Texas:**             Texas Woman's University. School of Library and Information Studies. Denton, TX.

                       University of North Texas. School of Library and Information Science. Denton, TX.

                       University of Texas at Austin. Graduate School of Library and Information Science. Austin, TX.

**Washington:**        University of Washington. Graduate School of Library and Information Science. Seattle, WA.

**Washington, D.C.**   Catholic University, School of Library and Information Science. Washington, D.C.

**Wisconsin:**         University of Wisconsin—Madison. School of Library and Information Science. Madison, WI.

University of Wisconsin—Milwaukee. School of Library and Information Science. Milwaukee, WI.

**Canada:**

Dalhousie University. School of Library and Information Studies. Halifax, Nova Scotia, Canada.

McGill University. Graduate School of Library and Information Studies. Montreal, Quebec, Canada.

University of Alberta. Faculty of Library Science. Edmonton, Alberta, Canada.

University of British Columbia. School of Library, Archival, and Information Studies. Vancouver, BC, Canada.

University of Montreal, Ecole de Bib. et des Sciences, de l'Information. Montreal, Quebec, Canada.

University of Toronto. Faculty of Library and Information Science. Toronto, Ontario, Canada.

University of Western Ontario. School of Library and Information Science. London, Ontario, Canada.

# *Appendix F*

# Major Periodicals, Indexes, Encyclopedias, and Dictionaries in Library and Information Science

The following listing is a selective list of periodicals, indexes, encyclopedias, and dictionaries that relate directly to the field of library and information science. Emphasis is on U.S. publications. The periodicals are arranged in very general categories that are listed below, with many periodicals having overlapping scope. The categories selected are the following:

> **Academic Libraries**
> **Acquisitions, Selections, Collection Development**
> **Archives**
> **Audiovisual**
> **Automation/Information Technology**
> **Cataloging, Indexing, and Technical Services**
> **Children and Youth Services**
> **Documents**
> **History**
> **Information Science**
> **Interlibrary Loan**
> **International**
> **Libraries—General**
> **Library Education**

**Management**
**Preservation**
**Public Libraries**
**Reference Services**
**School Libraries**
**Special Libraries**
**State Publications**


## PERIODICALS


### Academic Libraries

*Choice*. Chicago: ACRL ALA.
*College & Research Libraries*. Chicago: ALA.
*College and Undergraduate Libraries*. Binghamton, N.Y.: Haworth.
*Journal of Academic Librarianship*. Greenwich, Conn.: JAI Press.
*Urban Academic Librarian*. New York: Library Association of the City University of New York.

### Acquisitions, Selections, Collection Development

*The Acquisitions Librarian*. Binghamton, N.Y.: Haworth.
*Collection Building*. Bradford, West Yorkshire, England: MCB University Press.
*Collection Management*. Binghamton, N.Y.: Haworth.
*Humanities Collections*. Binghamton, N.Y.: Haworth.
*Library Acquisitions: Practice and Theory*. Oxford, England: Elsevier Science.
*Popular Culture in Libraries*. Binghamton, N.Y.: Haworth.
*The Serials Librarian*. Binghamton, N.Y.: Haworth.

### Archives

*The American Archivist*. Chicago: Society of American Archivists.
*Archivist*. Ottawa, Ont.: National Archives of Canada.
*Library and Archival Security*. Binghamton, N.Y.: Haworth.

### Audiovisual

*Audiovisual Librarian*. Aberystwyth, Wales: Aslib, Association for Information Management.
*Video Librarian*. Brementon, Wash.: Video Librarian.

## Automation/Information technology

*CD-Rom Librarian.* Westport, Conn.: Meckler.
*CD-ROM Professional.* Wilton, Conn.: Online Inc.
*Computer and Information Systems Abstract Journal.* Bethesda, Md.: Cambridge
Scientific Abstracts.
*Computers in Libraries.* Medford N.J.: Learned Information Inc.
*Database: the Magazine of Electronic Database Reviews.* Wilton, Conn.: Online.
*The Electronic Library.* Medford, N.J.: Learned Information.
*Information Development.* West Sussex, England: Bowker-Saur.
*Information Services and Use.* Amsterdam: IOS Press.
*Information Technology and Libraries.* Chicago: Library and Information Technol-
ogy Association, ALA.
*Library Hi Tech.* Ann Arbor: Pierian Press.
*Library Hi Tech News.* Ann Arbor: Pierian Press.
*Library Software Review.* Thousand Oaks, Calif.: Sage Publications.
*Library Technology Reports.* Chicago: ALA.
*Microform Review.* West Sussex, England: Bowker-Saur.
*Online: the Magazine of Online Information Systems.* Wilton, Conn.: Online.
*Online and CD-ROM Review.* Medford, N.J.: Learned Information.
*Technicalities.* Lincoln, Nebr.: Media Periodicals.

## Cataloging, Indexing, and Technical Services

*Cataloging and Classification Quarterly.* Binghamton, N.Y.: Haworth
*Cataloging Service Bulletin.* Washington D.C.: Library of Congress.
*The Indexer: Journal of the Society of Indexers and of the Affiliated American, Austra-
lian and Canadian Societies.* London: Society of Indexers.
*Journal of Internet Cataloging.* Binghamton, N.Y.: Haworth.
*Knowledge Organization: An International Journal Devoted to Concept Theory, Classi-
fication, Indexing, and Knowledge Representation.* Frankfurt, Germany: Index
Verlag.
*Library Resources and Technical Services.* Chicago: ALA.
*Technical Services Quarterly.* Binghamton, N.Y.: Haworth.

## Children and Youth Services

*Book Links.* Chicago: ALA.
*Bulletin of the Center for Children's Books.* Chicago: University of Chicago.
*Emergency Librarian.* Vancouver, BC: Dyad Services.
*The Horn Book Magazine.* Boston: Horn Book.
*Journal of Youth Services in Libraries.* Chicago: Association for Library Service to
Children and Young Adult Library Services Association, ALA.
*VOYA: the Voice of Youth Advocates.* Latham, Md.: Scarecrow Press.

## Documents

*Documents to the People.* Chicago: ALA.
*Government Information Quarterly: An International Journal of Policies, Resources, Services and Practices.* Greenwich, Conn.: JAI Press.
*Journal of Government Information: An International Review of Policy, Issues and Resources.* Oxford, England: Elsevier Science. (Formerly entitled *Government Publications Review.* Pergamon.)

## History

*Libraries and Culture: A Journal of Library History.* Austin, Tex.: University of Texas Press.
*Library History.* London: Library History Group of the Library Association.

## Information Science

*Information Processing & Management: An International Journal.* Oxford, England: Elsevier Science.
*Journal of the American Society for Information Science.* Silver Spring, Md.: American Society of Information Science.
*Journal of Documentation.* London: Aslib, Association for Information Management
*Journal of Information Ethics.* Jefferson, N.C.: McFarland.
*Journal of Information Science.* West Sussex, England: Bowker-Saur.
*Journal of Librarianship and Information Science.* West Sussex, England: Bowker-Saur.

## Interlibrary Loan

*Interlending and Document Supply.* West Yorkshire: England: MCB University Press.
*Journal of Interlibrary Loan, Document Delivery & Information Supply.* Binghamton, N.Y.: Haworth.

## International/Publications Focusing on Other Countries

*Aslib Proceedings.* Medford, N.J.: Learned Information.
*Australian Library Journal.* Queen Victoria Terrace, Australia: Australian Library and Information Association.
*British Library Journal.* London: British Libraries.
*Canadian Journal of Information and Library Science.* Downsview, Ontario: Canadian Association for Information Science.
*Canadian Library Journal.* Ottawa, Ontario: Canadian Library Association. (Suspended)
*Focus on International and Comparative Librarianship.* Birmingham, England: International Group of the Library Association.

*IFLA Journal*. Munich, Germany: K.G. Saur.

*International Forum on Information and Documentation*. The Hague, Netherlands: International Federation for Documentation.

*The International Information and Library Review* (IILR). London, San Diego: Academic Press.

*International Review of Children's Literature and Librarianship*. London, England: Taylor Graham.

*Library Association Record*. London, England: Library Association.

*Libri: An International Library Review*. Copenhagen, Denmark: Munksgaard International.

## Libraries—General

*American Libraries*. Chicago: ALA.

*Booklist*. Chicago: ALA.

*Catholic Library World*. Allenpark, Mich.: Catholic Library Association.

*Herald of Library Science*. India: Endowment for Library and Information Science.

*Library & Information Science Research: An International Journal*. Norwood, N.J.: Ablex Publishing Company.

*Library Hotline*. New York: Cahners.

*Library Journal*. New York: Cahners.

*Library Quarterly*. Chicago: University of Chicago.

*Library Trends*. Urbana-Champaign, Ill.: University of Illinois Press.

*Research Strategies*. Ann Arbor: Mountainside.

*The Unabashed Librarian*. New York: Marvin H. Scilken.

*Wilson Library Bulletin*. New York: H.W. Wilson. (no longer being published)

## Library Education

*Education for Information: The International Review of Education and Training in Library and Information Science*. Amsterdam: North-Holland.

*Journal of Education for Library and Information Science*. Raleigh, N.C.: Association for Library and Information Science Education.

## Management

*The Bottom Line: Managing Library Finances*. Bradford, West Yorkshire, England: MCB University Press.

*Journal of Library Administration*. Binghamton, N.Y.: Haworth.

*Library Administration and Management*. Chicago: Library Administration and Management Association, ALA.

*Library Mosaics: The Magazine for Support Staff*. Culver City, Calif.: Yenor.

*Library Personnel News*. Chicago: Office for Library Personnel Resources, ALA.

*Preservation*

*Conservation Administration News.* Austin, Tex.: Graduate School of Library and Information Science.

*Public Libraries*

*Public Libraries.* Chicago: Public Library Association, ALA.
*Public Library Quarterly.* Binghamton. N.Y.: Haworth.
*REFORMA Newsletter.* Washington D.C.: National Association to Promote Library Services to the Spanish Speaking.

*Reference Services*

*Internet Reference Services Quarterly.* Binghamton, N.Y.: Haworth.
*The Reference Librarian.* Binghamton, N.Y.: Haworth.
*RSR: Reference Services Review.* Ann Arbor: Pieran.
*RQ.* Chicago: Reference and Users Services Association, ALA.

*School Libraries*

*The Book Report: The Journal for Junior and Senior High School Librarians.* Worthington, Ohio: Linworth.
*Library Talk: The Magazine for Elementary School Librarians.* Worthington, Ohio: Linworth.
*Multimedia Schools.* Wilton, Conn.: Online.
*The School Librarian's Workshop.* Library Learning Resources.
*School Library Journal: The Magazine of Children's, Young Adult, and School Librarians.* New York: Bowker.
*School Library Media Activities Monthly.* Baltimore: LMS Associates.
*School Library Media Quarterly.* Chicago: American Association of School Libraries, ALA.
*Technology Connection.* Worthington, Ohio: Linworth.

*Special Libraries*

*Art Documentation.* Tucson: Art Libraries Society of North America.
*Art Libraries Journal.* Bromsgrove, England: Art Libraries Society/UK and Ireland.
*Art Reference Services Quarterly.* Binghamton, N.Y.: Haworth.
*Asian Libraries.* Hong Kong: Library Marking Services.
*Behavioral and Social Sciences Librarian.* Binghamton, N.Y.: Haworth.
*Business Library Review.* Langhorne, Pa.: Business Library Review.
*Church and Synagogue Libraries.* Portland, Ore.: Church and Synagogue Libraries Association.
*INSPEL: International Journal of Special Libraries.* Munich: International Federation of Library Associations.

*Journal of Business and Finance Librarianship*. Binghamton, N.Y.: Haworth.
*Judaica Librarianship*. New York: Association of Jewish Libraries.
*Law Library Journal*. Chicago: American Association of Law Librarians.
*Legal Reference Services Quarterly*. Binghamton, N.Y.: Haworth.
*Medical Library Association. Bulletin*. Chicago: Medical Library Association.
*Medical Reference Services Quarterly*. Binghamton, N.Y.: Haworth.
*Music Library Association Notes*. Canton, Mass.: Music Library Association.
*Music Reference Services Quarterly*. Binghamton, N.Y.: Haworth.
*The One-Person Library*. New York: OPL Resources.
*Science and Technology Libraries*. Binghamton, N.Y.: Haworth.
*Special Libraries*. Washington: Special Libraries Association.

*State/Regional Publications*

*Georgia Librarian*. Young Harris, Ga.: Georgia Library Association.
*Illinois Libraries*. Springfield, Ill: Illinois State Libraries.
*North Carolina Libraries*. Raleigh, N.C.: North Carolina Library Association.
*New Jersey Libraries*. Trenton, N.J.: New Jersey Library Association.
*Ohio Media Spectrum*. Columbus, Ohio: Ohio Educational Library Media Association.
*PLA Bulletin*. Harrisburg, Pa.: Pennsylvania Library Association.
*Show-Me Libraries*. Jefferson City, Mo.: State Library.
*Southeastern Librarian*. Tucker, Ga.: Southeastern Library Association.

## DICTIONARIES

Hartsill, Young, ed. *The ALA Glossary of Library and Information Science*. Chicago: ALA, 1983.
Prytherch, Ray. *Harrod's Librarians' Glossary*. Sheffield, England: Gower, 1995.

## ENCYCLOPEDIAS

*Encyclopedia of Library and Information Science*. New York: Marcel Dekker.
*Encyclopedia of Library History*. New York: Garland, 1994.
*World Encyclopedia of Library and Information Science*. 3rd ed. Chicago: ALA, 1993.

## INDEXES

*Information Management Index*. Washington, D.C.: U.S. Army Corp of Engineers.
*Information Science Abstracts*. Philadelphia: Documentation Abstracts.
*Library Information Science Abstracts*. London: Library Association.
*Library Literature*. New York: H.W. Wilson.

# *Appendix G*

# Summary of Major Library and Information Science Associations and List of Additional Associations

## AMERICAN LIBRARY ASSOCIATION (ALA)

The American Library Association is the oldest and largest library association in the world. Founded in 1876, anyone, including organizations, who has an interest in libraries can join. A wide variety of types of libraries participate in ALA membership and activities. These include state, public, school, and academic libraries, as well as libraries in government, commerce, the arts, the armed services, hospitals, and prisons. The stated mission of the organization is "to provide leadership for the development, promotion, and improvement of library and information services and the profession of librarianship in order to enhance learning and ensure access to information for all (American Library Association. *ALA Handbook of Organization 1996–1997*. Chicago: ALA, 1996, p. 29). Current membership exceeds 56,000 from seventy countries.

ALA is an impressive bureaucracy with eighteen round tables, eleven divisions, fifty-nine chapters, twenty-three affiliated organizations, and a headquarters staff exceeding 270 employees. ALA is operated by an executive director and executive board (American Library Association. *ALA Handbook of Organization 1996–1997*. Chicago: ALA, 1996). There is also a large number of committees comprised primarily of ALA members that play a critical role in reflecting the professional and political interests of the association. Round tables focus on such areas as armed forces libraries, ethnic materials, and government documents. Among the divisions are those focusing on children's and adult services, public libraries, academic libraries. Committees include those for accreditation of programs of library and information studies, library outreach, and the status of women in librarianship. The primary political lobbying is effected by the Washington Office of the American Library Association, which monitors political legislation and other activities that could affect the well-being of libraries and attempts to influence legislation so that it conforms to the goals of the ALA.

The association authors many publications including books and journals focusing on a variety of aspects of the profession. These include *RQ*, a publication of the Reference and Users Services Association (RUSA), *Public Libraries*, a publication of the Public Library Association (PLA), *Library Administration and Management*, a publication of the Library Administration and Management Division (LAMA), *Journal of Youth Services in Libraries*, a publication of the Association for Library Service to Children (ALSC) and the Young Adult Library Services Association (YALSA), *College and Research Libraries*, a publication of the Association of College and Research Libraries (ACRL), and *American Libraries*, the official organ of the American Library Association. Such publications not only provide news and information on library activities, but also serve as sources for published research, analysis, and continuing education in professional practice. The association also holds two major conferences a year: the Midwinter Meeting, which is primarily devoted to committee activities, and the Annual Conference, where there are major program presentations.

The association has recently undergone a major re-assessment of its goals leading to the adoption of "Goal 2000". The goals established are as follows:

*By the year 2000*

It is envisioned that by the year 2000 ALA will have achieved the following:

1.  ALA will be accepted by the public as a voice and the source of support for the participation of people of all ages and circumstances in a free and open information society.
2.  ALA will be an active formal participant in various national arenas dis-

cussing and deciding aspects of the information society that affect libraries and their publics.

3.  ALA will have identified and will be in collaboration with other organizations and groups working for broader public participation in the development of information society issues.

4.  ALA will have created a vision statement for broad distribution defining its position and role within the emerging information environment.

5.  ALA will have an expanded Washington Office with greatly increased ability to learn about, analyze, share information about and shape important national information issues in addition to tracking traditional library issues.

6.  ALA will have completed a five-year thematic cycle that has framed the advancement of these issues and coordinated the support of all areas of the Association in preparation for the 21st century.

7.  ALA will have provided training and support to library professionals and members of the public to create an awareness of the variety of social and technical issues related to the information society and to provide the necessary background for promoting further dialogue at the local level.

8.  ALA will have reviewed and adjusted its internal operations as a means of assisting all divisions and units in carrying out the new focus as appropriate to their sphere.

9.  ALA will have redefined library information education and provided five years of training for professionals to update their skills for the new information age.

## AMERICAN SOCIETY FOR INFORMATION SCIENCE (ASIS)

The American Society for Information Science was originally known as the American Documentation Institute. It was founded in 1937 by the Science Service and the microfilm services of the Bibliofilm Service of the U.S. Department of Agriculture. The money to finance the institute originally came from a grant from the Chemical Foundations, and the purpose of the institute was to produce scientific bibliographies, develop microphotography devices, and generally to explore other mechanisms for improving the communication of recorded knowledge. Originally only institutional members were permitted, but in 1952 changes were made to the bylaws of the organization to permit individual membership. In 1968 the name was changed to the American Society for Information Science. Membership now exceeds 4,300 individual and 115 institutional members. There are twenty-six local groups, twenty-six student groups, and twenty-one special interest groups (SIGs) in such areas as behavioral and social sciences, classification research, and numeric databases.

Today, the focus of ASIS is on all aspects of the information transfer process, including organization, storage, retrieval, evaluation, and dissemination of information. Its membership includes librarians, information scientists, administrators, and social scientists, and all others interested in the information transfer process. The society also functions as an instrument of professional development through conferences, continuing education programs, professional development workshops, and publications. Among its major publications are *Journal of the American Society for Information Science* and *Annual Review of Information Science and Technology*. ASIS also publishes its conference proceedings and is cosponsor of *Information Science Abstracts*.

## ASSOCIATION OF RESEARCH LIBRARIES (ARL)

The Association of Research Libraries (ARL) was founded in December 1932 as a not-for-profit organization. It is governed by a board of directors, executive director, and a small headquarters staff. Unlike most other library organizations, membership is restricted to North American institutions; many of these are university libraries, although some are major public libraries, special libraries, and national libraries. There are approximately 120 members.

The mission of ARL is "to identify and influence forces affecting the future of research libraries in the process of scholarly communication" (*Gopher://arl/cni.org:70/00/arl/arl* [7/21/96]). Obviously, there is much focus on the problems of university libraries, and ARL provides an important forum through its conferences for the exchange of information on topics related to their survival. ARL programs are intended to "promote equitable access to, and effective use of recorded knowledge in support of teaching, research, scholarship, and community service" (*http://arl.cni.org/arl/arlfacts.html* [7/21/96]). Their concerns focus on a variety of issues including federal information policy, scientific and academic publishing, preservation, computer networking, international relations, research and development, and management. In 1970 ARL created the Offices of Management Services (OMS), which is intended to improve the management of human resources and collections of research and academic libraries. This office collects statistics, prepares reports, and provides training and staff development in a variety of areas of management. Among the major publications of ARL are the *ARL Annual Salary Survey*, and their annual *Academic Library Statistics*.

## INTERNATIONAL FEDERATION OF LIBRARY ASSOCIATIONS (IFLA)

The International Federation of Library Associations and Institutions was founded in 1927, primarily to create a place for the leading librarians of Europe and America to meet and discuss contemporary issues of mutual interest. Today its international scope is much broader with more than 1,200 members from 120 countries. It is headquartered in The Hague.

Among the stated objectives of IFLA are to promote international understanding, cooperation, discussion, research, and development in all fields of library and information service activity; to promote continuing education of library personnel; to serve as an organization through which librarianship can be represented in international matters; and to develop and maintain guidelines for different types of library activities such as compilation of statistics and preservation.

Many of the major American library associations are members, including ALA, the Association of Research Libraries (ARL), and the American Association of Law Libraries (AALL). IFLA is organized into eight divisions: General Research Libraries, Special Libraries, Libraries Serving the General Public, Bibliographic Control, Collections and Services, Management and Technology, Education and Research, and Regional Activities. These divisions contain thirty-one different sections and ten round tables.

IFLA has a variety of programs that represent the main interests of the association. These interests include programs to develop international standard bibliographic descriptions through its Universal Bibliographic Control and International MARC program. IFLA also has a program to encourage countries to supply their own publications by loan or photocopy to other requesting countries through the Universal Availability of Publications program. Other programs involve promoting preservation and conservation of library materials, promoting electronic transfer of data (Universal Data Flow and Telecommunication program), and promoting the improvement of library and information services in developing countries (Advancement of Librarianship in the Third World program.)

IFLA issues a variety of monographs, professional reports, newsletters, and periodicals including *Libri*, *IFLA Journal*, and the *IFLA Directory*.

## THE MEDICAL LIBRARY ASSOCIATION (MLA)

The Medical Library Association was founded in 1898 as the Association of Medical Librarians. It is the second oldest national library association in the United States and serves as the primary professional association for health sciences librarians in the U.S. and Canada. The purpose of the MLA is to promote medical and allied scientific libraries as well as to support the exchange of medical literature among its members. MLA also attempts to promote educational and professional growth among health sciences librarians and provides a considerable number of continuing education programs to meet this purpose.

There are more than 3,700 individual members, 1,300 institutional members, and a growing corporate membership. The association has regional chapters and special interest sections including those for cancer librarians, educational media and technologies, pharmacy, drug information, and veterinary medical libraries.

In contrast to most other forms of librarianship, medical librarians can be certified, and MLA adopted its first formal certification program in 1949. The credentialling criteria established by MLA in 1988 stressed educational qualifications and knowledge in core areas of medical information and different levels of professional development for recognition by MLA's Academy of Health Information Professionals (AHIP). The association also produces monographic and periodical publications including the *Bulletin of the Medical Library Association*, *MLA News*, and *Handbook of Medical Library Practice*.

## SPECIAL LIBRARIES ASSOCIATION (SLA)

The Special Libraries Association is a not-for-profit corporation founded in 1909 as a response to a growing number of special libraries. It is an international association of librarians who work in special libraries serving such areas as business, research, government, and universities. There are more than 14,000 members with a variety of regional chapters and special subject divisions. The formal objectives of SLA are to:

> provide an association of individuals and organizations having a professional, scientific or technical interest in library and information science, especially as these are applied in the recording, retrieval, and dissemination of knowledge and information in areas such as the physical, biological, technical and social sciences and the humanities; and to

promote and improve the communication, dissemination and use of such information and knowledge for the benefit of libraries or other educational organizations (Prytherch, Ray, comp. *Harrod's Librarians' Glossary of Terms Used in Librarianship, Documentation, and the Book Crafts.* 7th edition. Hants (Eng): Gower, 1990, p. 581.)

The association provides a variety of services including consulting services to organizations that want to create or expand their information services and conducting continuing education courses to advance the role of the professional librarian. An Information Resources Center, which houses topics on the development and management of special libraries, is operated by SLA.

SLA has become more politically active since the 1980s to deal with governmental policy areas that have direct effect on special libraries, such as copyright implementation and compliance, networking legislation, government information policies, and telecommunications. The association produces a major publication in the field, *Special Libraries*, devoted to the management and operation of special libraries.

## LIST OF ADDITIONAL LIBRARY ASSOCIATIONS OR CLOSELY-RELATED ORGANIZATIONS

*General*

Canadian Library Association
Council on Library Resources
Information Industry Association
National Information Standards Organization
National Librarians Association

*Archives/Bibliographical*

Bibliographical Society of America
Society of American Archivists

*Arts*

American Film and Video Association (formerly the Educational Film
    Library Association)
Art Libraries Society of North America

Music Library Association
Theatre Library Association

*Asian-American*

Asian/Pacific American Librarians Association
Chinese-American Library Association

*Government/Federal*

Association for Federal Information Resources Management
Chief Officers of State Library Agencies
Federal Library and Information Center Committee
National Association of Government Archives and Records Adminis-
    trators

*Law*

American Association of Law Libraries

*Library Education*

Association for Library and Information Science Education

*Religious*

American Theological Library Association
Association of Christian Librarians
Association of Jewish Libraries
Catholic Library Association
Church and Synagogue Library Association
Lutheran Church Library Association

*Science*

Association of Academic Health Sciences Library Directors

*Visual Images*

Association for Information and Image Management
Association of Visual Science Librarians

# Appendix H

# Overview of Librarianship from the *Occupational Outlook Handbook*

**LIBRARIANS**

*Nature of the Work*

Librarians assist people in finding information and using it effectively in their personal and professional lives. They must have knowledge of a wide variety of scholarly and public information sources, and follow trends related to publishing, computers, and the media to effectively oversee the selection and organization of library materials. Librarians manage staff and develop and direct information programs and systems for the public, to ensure information is being organized to meet the needs of users.

There are generally three aspects of library work—user services, technical services, and administrative services. Increasingly, distinctions between these services are blurred, and many librarian positions incorporate all three aspects of the work. Even librarians who specialize in one of these areas may perform other responsibilities. Librarians in user services, such as reference and children's librarians, work with the public to help them find the information they need. This may involve analyzing users' needs to determine what information is appropriate, and searching for, acquiring, and providing the information. Librarians in technical services, such as acquisitions and cataloguing, acquire and prepare materials for use and may not deal directly with the public. Librarians in administrative services oversee the management and planning of libraries, negotiate contracts for services, materials, and equipment, supervise library employees, perform public relations and fundraising duties, prepare budgets, and direct activities to ensure that everything functions properly.

In small libraries or information centers, librarians generally handle all aspects of the work. They read book reviews, publishers' announcements, and catalogues to keep up with current literature and other available resources, and select and purchase materials from publishers, wholesalers, and distributors. Librarians prepare new materials for use by classifying them by subject matter, and describe books and other library materials in a way that users can easily **find** them. They supervise assistants who prepare cards, computer records, or other access tools that direct users to resources. In large libraries, librarians may specialize in a single area, such as acquisitions, cataloguing, bibliography, reference, special collections, or administration. Teamwork is increasingly important to ensure quality service to the public.

Librarians also compile lists of books, periodicals, articles, and audiovisual materials on particular subjects, analyze collections, and recommend materials to be acquired. They may collect and organize books, pamphlets, manuscripts, and other materials in a specific field, such as rare books, genealogy, or music. In addition, they coordinate programs such as storytelling for children, and literacy skills and book talks for adults; publicize services; provide reference help; supervise staff; prepare budgets; write grants; and oversee other administrative matters.

Librarians may be classified according to the type of library in which they work—public libraries, school library media centers, academic libraries, and special libraries. They may work with specific groups, such as children, young adults, adults, or the disadvantaged. In school library media centers, librarians help teachers develop curricula, acquire materials for classroom instruction, and sometimes team teach.

Librarians may also work in information centers or libraries maintained by government agencies, corporations, law firms, advertising agencies, museums, professional associations, medical centers, hospitals, religious organizations, and research laboratories. They build and arrange the organization's information resources, usually limited to subjects of special interest to the organization. These special librarians can provide vital information services by preparing abstracts and indexes of current periodicals, organizing bibliographies, or analyzing background information and preparing reports on areas of particular interest. For instance, a special librarian working for a corporation may provide the sales department with information on competitors or new developments affecting their field.

Many libraries have access to remote databases, as well as maintaining their own computerized databases. The widespread use of automation in libraries makes database searching skills important to librarians. Librarians develop and index databases and act as trainers to help users develop searching skills to obtain the information they need. Some libraries are forming consortiums with other libraries through electronic mail (e-mail). This allows patrons to submit information requests to several libraries at once. Use of Internet and other world-wide computer systems is also expanding the amount of available reference information. Librarians must be increasingly aware of how to use these resources to locate information.

Libraries may employ automated systems librarians who plan and operate computer systems, and information science librarians who design information storage and retrieval systems and develop procedures for collecting, organizing, interpreting, and classifying information. These librarians may analyze and plan for future information needs. (See statement on computer scientists and systems analysts elsewhere in the *Handbook.*) The increasing use of automated information systems enables librarians to focus on administrative and budgeting responsibilities, grant writing, and specialized research requests, while delegating more technical and user services responsibilities to technicians. (See statement on library technicians elsewhere in the *Handbook.*)

Some librarians apply their information management and research skills to other arenas outside libraries—for example, database development, reference tool development, information systems, publishing, Internet coordination, marketing, and training of database users. Entrepreneurial librarians may start their own consulting practices. They act as free-lance librarians or information brokers and provide services to other libraries, businesses, or government agencies.

*Working Conditions*

Working conditions in user services are different from those in technical services. Assisting users in obtaining the information for their jobs or for recreational and other needs can be challenging and satisfying. Working with users under deadlines may be demanding and stressful. In technical services, selecting and ordering new materials can be stimulating and rewarding. However, librarians may spend a significant portion of time at their desks or in front of computer terminals. Extended work at video display terminals may cause eyestrain and headaches.

Nearly 1 out of 4 librarians works part time. Public and college librarians often work weekends and evenings and may have to work some holidays. School librarians generally have the same workday schedule as classroom teachers and similar vacation schedules. Special librarians may work normal business hours, but in fast-paced industries, such as advertising or legal services, may work longer hours during peak times.

## Employment

Librarians held about 148,000 jobs in 1994. Most were in school and academic libraries; others were in public libraries and special libraries. A small number of librarians worked for hospitals and religious organizations. Others worked for governments at all levels.

## Training, Other Qualifications, and Advancement

A master's degree in library science (M.L.S.) is necessary for librarian positions in most public, academic, and special libraries, and in some school libraries. In the Federal Government, an M.L.S. or the equivalent in education and experience is needed. Many colleges and universities offer M.L.S. programs, but many employers prefer graduates of the approximately 50 schools accredited by the American Library Association. Most M.L.S. programs require a bachelor's degree; any liberal arts major is appropriate.

Most programs take 1 year to complete; others take 2. A typical graduate program includes courses in the foundations of library and information science, including the history of books and printing, intellectual freedom and censorship, and the role of libraries and information in society. Other basic courses cover material selection and processing, the organization of information; reference tools and strategies; and user services. Courses are being adapted to educate librarians to use new resources brought about by advancing technology such as on-line reference systems and automated circulation systems. Course options can include resources for children or young adults; classification, cataloguing, indexing, and abstracting; library administration; and library automation.

The M.L.S. provides general, all-round preparation for library work, but some people specialize in a particular area such as reference, technical services, or children's services. A Ph.D. degree in library and information science is advantageous for a college teaching or top administrative position, particularly in a college or university library or in a large library system.

In special libraries, the M.L.S. is usually required. In addition, most special librarians supplement their education with knowledge of the subject specialization, or a master's, doctoral, or professional degree in the subject. Subject specializations include medicine, law, business, engineering, and the natural and social sciences. For example, a librarian working for a law firm may also be a licensed attorney, holding both library science and law degrees. In some jobs, knowledge of a foreign language is needed.

State certification requirements for public school librarians vary widely. Most States require that school librarians—often called library media specialists—be certified as teachers and have courses in library science. In some cases, the M.L.S., perhaps with a library media specialization, or a master's in education with a specialty in school library media or educational media is needed. Some States require certification of public librarians employed in municipal, county, or regional library systems.

Experienced librarians may advance to administrative positions, such as department head, library director, or chief information officer.

*Job Outlook*

Employment of librarians is expected to grow more slowly than the average for all occupations through the year 2005. However, the number of job openings resulting from the need to replace librarians who leave the occupation is expected to increase by 2005, as many workers reach retirement age. Willingness to relocate will greatly enhance job prospects.

Budgetary constraints will likely contribute to the slow growth in employment of librarians in school, public, and college and university libraries as libraries reduce staff to cut costs. Although fewer new positions have become available in recent years, the number of M.L.S. graduates has been increasing. Thus, more applicants are competing for fewer jobs.

The increasing use of computerized information storage and retrieval systems may also dampen the demand for librarians. For example, computerized systems make cataloguing easier, and this task can now be handled by other library staff. In addition, many libraries are equipped for users to access library computers directly from their homes or offices. These systems allow users to bypass librarians and conduct research on their own. However, librarians will be needed to manage staff, help users develop database searching techniques, address complicated reference requests, and define users' needs.

Opportunities will be best for librarians outside traditional settings. Nontraditional library settings include information brokers, private corporations, and consulting firms. Many companies are turning to librarians because of their excellent research and organizational skills, and knowledge of library automation systems. Librarians can review the vast amount of information that is available and analyze, evaluate, and organize it according to a company's specific needs. Librarians are also moving into organizations to set up information on the Internet. Librarians working in these settings are often classified as systems analysts, database specialists and trainers, managers, and researchers.

*Earnings*

Salaries of librarians vary by the individual's qualifications and the type, size, and location of the library.

According to a survey by the American Library Association, the average salary of children's librarians in academic and public libraries was $35,000 in 1995; reference/information librarians averaged $35,600; cataloguers and classifiers earned $36,300; and department heads earned $42,000. Library directors had an average salary of $58,200. Beginning librarians with a master's degree but no professional experience averaged $28,300 in 1995.

According to the Educational Research Service, experienced librarians in public schools averaged about $40,400 during the 1994–95 school year.

According to the Special Libraries Association, 1994 salaries for special librarians with 2 years or less of library experience averaged $31,000, and those with 3 to 5 years of experience averaged $35,200. Salaries for special librarians with primarily administrative responsibilities averaged $54,600.

Salaries for medical librarians with 1 year or less experience averaged $25,300 in 1994, according to the Medical Library Association. The average salary for all medical librarians was $38,000.

The average annual salary for all librarians in the Federal Government in nonsupervisory, supervisory, and managerial positions was $48,200 in 1995.

## Related Occupations

Librarians play an important role in the transfer of knowledge and ideas by providing people with access to the information they need and want. Jobs requiring similar analytical, organizational, and communicative skills include archivists, information scientists, museum curators, publishers' representatives, research analysts, information brokers, and records managers. The management aspect of a librarian's work is similar to the work of managers in a variety of business and government settings. School librarians have many duties similar to those of school teachers.

## Sources of Additional Information

*Information on librarianship, including a listing of accredited education programs and information on scholarships or loans, is available from*
American Library Association, Office for Library Personnel Resources. 50 East Huron St., Chicago, IL 60611.

*For information on a career as a special librarian, write to*
Special Libraries Association, 1700 18th St. NW., Washington, DC 20009.

*Material about a career in information science is available from*
American Society for Information Science, 8720 Georgia Ave., Suite 501, Silver Spring, MD 20910.

*Information on graduate schools of library and information science can be obtained from*
Association for Library and Information Science Education, 4101 Lake Boone Trail, Suite 201, Raleigh, NC 27607.

*Information on schools receiving federal financial assistance for library training is available from*
Office of Educational Research and Improvement, Library Programs, Library Development Staff, U.S. Department of Education, 555 New Jersey Ave. NW., Room 402, Washington, DC 20208–5571.

*For information on a career as a law librarian, as well as a list of ALA-accredited schools offering programs in law librarianship and scholarship information, contact*
American Association of Law Libraries, 53 West Jackson Blvd., Suite 940, Chicago, IL 60604.

*For information on employment opportunities as a health sciences librarian, a list of ALA-accredited schools offering programs in health sciences librarianship and scholarship information, and credentialing information, contact*
Medical Library Association, 6 N. Michigan Ave., Suite 300, Chicago, IL 60602.

*Those interested in a position as a librarian in the federal service should write to*
Office of Personnel Management, 1900 E St. NW., Washington, DC 20415.

*Information concerning requirements and application procedures for positions in the Library of Congress may be obtained directly from*
Personnel Office, Library of Congress, 101 Independence Ave. SE., Washington, DC 20540.

State library agencies can furnish information on scholarships available through their offices, requirements for certification, and general information about career prospects in the State. Several of these agencies maintain job hotlines which report openings for librarians.

State departments of education can furnish information on certification requirements and job opportunities for school librarians.

Many library science schools offer career placement services to their alumni and current students. Some will allow non-affiliated students and jobseekers to use their services.

**Source**: *Occupational Outlook Handbook, 1996–97 Edition*. Washington, D.C.: Department of Labor, Bureau of Labor Statistics, February 1996 (Bulletin 2470), pp. 148–150.

# *Appendix I*

# Selected Library and Information Science Listservs and Discussion Groups

There are many LISTSERVs and discussion groups that deal with library and information science. They can often be identified by examining the home pages of various library and information science organizations.

| | |
|---|---|
| AALLNET | American Association of Law Librarians (AALL) |
| ACRL-FRM | Association of College and Research Library Forum (ALA) |
| ALAOIF | Office of Intellectual Freedom (ALA) |
| ALASC-L | Student chapters of ALA |
| ALA-WON | ALA Washington Office Newsline |
| ALAWORLD | International Relations Round Table (ALA) |
| ALSC-L | Association for Library Service to Children (ALA) |
| ARCHIVES | Society of American Archivists |
| ARL-EJOURNAL | Association of Research Libraries (Discussion of management of electronic journals. |

| | |
|---|---|
| ARL-ERESERVE | Association of Research Libraries (Discussion of the management of electronic reserves) |
| ARLIS-L | Art Library Societies |
| ASIS-L | American Society for Information Science (ASIS) |
| ELMSS | American Association of Library Media Specialist (ALA) |
| EURSLA-1 | SLA International Relations Committee (SLA) |
| INFOLIT | National Forum on Information Literacy (ALA) |
| JESSE | Association for Library and Information Science Education |
| LITA-L | Library and Information Technology (ALA) |
| MARS-L | RUSA Machine Assisted Reference Section (ALA) |
| MEDLIB-L | Medical Library Association (MLA) |
| MLA-L | Music Library Association |
| PUBLIB | Public library issues |
| PUBYAC | Youth services issues |
| SLAGR | SLA Governmental Relations (SLA) |
| SLMS21ST | School Library Media Specialist in the 21st Century (ALA) |
| YALSA-L | Young Adult Library Services Association (ALA) |

# Index

# Richard Rubin

Richard Rubin is Associate Professor at the School of Library and Information Science at Kent State University, Kent, Ohio. He has taught Foundations courses for nearly 10 years. He received his A.B. in Philosophy from Oberlin College, his M.L.S. from Kent State University, and his Ph.D. from the School of Library and Information Science at the University of Illinois. He has spoken and presented workshops throughout the United States primarily on aspects of human resource management including hiring, performance evaluation, discipline and termination, worker motivation, and ethics in the workplace.

Dr. Rubin is the author of numerous publications including two books, *Human Resource Management in Libraries: Theory and Practice* (Neal-Schuman, 1991) and *Hiring Library Employees* (Neal-Schuman, 1994). His articles have appeared in a variety of journals including *Library Quarterly* and *Library and Information Science Research*, and he co-authored (with Thomas Froehlich) the article on ethics in library and information science for the *Encyclopedia of Library and Information Science*.